# WORLDS
*in*
WORDS

# WORLDS
## *in*
# WORDS

• • •

*Essays in the History of Words*

**BRIAN CHARLES BURKE**

*Philadelphia • 2021*

Copyright © 2021 by Brian Charles Burke
All rights reserved

No part of this book may be used or reproduced in any manner whatsoever without written permission, except in the case of brief quotations embodied in critical articles and reviews.

ISBN:  978-1-7369414-0-9 paperback
       978-1-7369414-1-6 hardcover

For information, contact briancharlesburke@verizon.net

*For though the origin of most of our words is forgotten, each word was at first a stroke of genius, and obtained currency because for the moment it symbolized the world to the first speaker and to the hearer. The etymologist finds the deadest word to have been once a brilliant picture. Language is fossil poetry.*

Ralph Waldo Emerson

# CONTENTS

• • • •

*Introduction*     1

## Words

*Good Words*

1. Word     9
2. Crackin' Good Chatter     12
3. Word as Name and Fame     15
4. The Fateful and the Banal     19
5. Fussy People     22

*Bad Words*

6. Inditing Indicting     25
7. Criticism     28
8. Badmouthing     32
9. Bad Feeling     35

*Rhetoric for Better or Worse*

10. Short and Sweet     38
11. Articulating the Flow     41

## The Four Elements and the Elemental

12. Earth     47
13. Man and Woman     50
14. Life     53
15. Air     56
16. Breath     59
17. Soul     62
18. Fire     65
19. Flame     68
20. Fiery Feelings     73
21. Water     76
22. Affluent Water     79
23. Clouds     83
24. Precipitating Water     86

| | |
|---|---|
| 25. Stormy Precipitation | 89 |
| 26. "My Cup Runneth Over" | 93 |
| 27. To Eat | 96 |
| 28. Earthy Roots | 99 |
| 29. European Names for American Plants | 103 |
| 30. Bread | 106 |
| 31. The Importance of Things | 109 |
| 32. Drink Drank Drunk | 110 |
| 33. Trees and True Love | 114 |
| 34. Trees, Bark and Book | 118 |
| 35. Wild | 122 |

## Time

| | |
|---|---|
| 36. Morn and Even / Morning and Evening | 131 |
| 37. Directions on the Compass | 133 |
| 38. Time | 136 |
| 39. Night and Day / Day and Night | 140 |
| 40. Hours, Minutes and Seconds | 142 |
| 41. Days of the Week | 146 |
| 42. The Months | 149 |

## Five Senses and Their Organs between Sense and Nonsense

| | |
|---|---|
| 43. Sense and the Sensational | 155 |
| 44. Eye | 157 |
| 45. Sight and Insight | 160 |
| 46. Imaginative Sight | 162 |
| 47. Ear and 'Earing | 167 |
| 48. Nose and Smell | 170 |
| 49. Hand | 173 |
| 50. Touch | 177 |
| 51. Tongue and Taste | 181 |
| 52. Nonsense | 184 |

## Kin, Kindness and Character

| | |
|---|---|
| 53. Birth in Three Steps: Conception, Bearing and Birth | 191 |
| 54. Ken within Kin | 193 |
| 55. Kindness and Benevolence | 197 |
| 56. Gentility and Civility | 201 |
| 57. Generosity and Charity | 204 |

| | | |
|---|---|---|
| 58. | *How* Should I Know? or How Should *I* Know? | 208 |
| 59. | Faith and Credit | 212 |
| 60. | Simple States and Complex Standing | 215 |
| 61. | The Complex Cast of Characters | 218 |
| 62. | Headstrong Stubbornness | 220 |

## Family

| | | |
|---|---|---|
| 63. | Chaste and Unchaste | 227 |
| 64. | Caste Defiled | 230 |
| 65. | Marriage | 232 |
| 66. | The Marriage Ceremony | 235 |
| 67. | Fathers and Patrons | 237 |
| 68. | Father and Mother and the Fatherland/Motherland | 240 |
| 69. | Son and Daughter | 242 |
| 70. | Brother and Sister | 244 |

## Man and His Physical Frame

| | | |
|---|---|---|
| 71. | Body | 251 |
| 72. | Clothing | 253 |
| 73. | Heart | 257 |
| 74. | Friday's Child | 260 |
| 75. | Head | 263 |
| 76. | Headgear | 266 |
| 77. | Mind | 268 |
| 78. | Out of One's Mind | 271 |
| 79. | Angry Mind | 275 |
| 80. | Mood, Humor and Temper | 279 |
| 81. | Maniacs and Muses | 282 |
| 82. | Bravery | 284 |
| 83. | The Virtue of Goodness | 287 |

## Physical, Psychological and Social Good

| | | |
|---|---|---|
| 84. | Holistic Health | 293 |
| 85. | Sound Sanity and Sanitation | 296 |
| 86. | Happiness | 299 |
| 87. | Holidays | 304 |
| 88. | Parties | 307 |
| 89. | Work | 311 |
| 90. | Hard Work | 314 |
| 91. | Leisure | 317 |

| | | |
|---|---|---|
| 92. | Play, Game, and Sport | 319 |
| 93. | 'Let's Have Some Fun' | 322 |
| 94. | Joyful Fair-Going Cheer | 325 |

## Psychological and Social Evil

| | | |
|---|---|---|
| 95. | Evil | 331 |
| 96. | Crime and Sin | 334 |
| 97. | Stealing with Stealth | 337 |
| 98. | The Complexity of Duplicity | 340 |
| 99. | Tricks | 343 |
| 100. | Cheap Tricks | 346 |
| 101. | Tricky Talking | 350 |
| 102. | The Persuasive Spiel | 353 |
| 103. | Sophisticated Sleaze | 357 |
| 104. | Guilty Feelings | 360 |
| 105. | Breaking the Law | 363 |
| 106. | Erring from the Straight and Narrow | 366 |
| 107. | The Straight and Narrow | 369 |
| 108. | War and Peace | 372 |
| 109. | Pride | 376 |

## Social Frameworks

| | | |
|---|---|---|
| 110. | Protection Bringing Danger / Danger Bringing Fear | 383 |
| 111. | Humble Abodes and Manorial Mansions | 385 |
| 112. | The Resting Place | 388 |
| 113. | Domineering in the Domicile | 391 |
| 114. | The Hill and the Plain | 393 |
| 115. | Menials in the Noble's Domain | 395 |
| 116. | Master and Majesty | 398 |
| 117. | Authors and Authority | 402 |
| 118. | Sedate Authority | 405 |
| 119. | Royal Realms and Regular Rules | 408 |

## *E Pluribus Unum*—Unity from Plurality

| | | |
|---|---|---|
| 120. | Dignity | 413 |
| 121. | God | 416 |
| 122. | One-Two-Three, I-You-He | 418 |

**Notes** 423

# WORLDS
*in*
# WORDS

# INTRODUCTION
• • • •

When I started to teach Latin, Greek, and English at Germantown Academy, Toby Wagner, a friend of the school, told me about the first ancient Greek word that he had learned as a boy. The classic romance of this one word had inspired him to get my help so that he could learn more. His first Greek word came from a famous episode in the history of Greece after its golden age. On a long trek home from an unsuccessful campaign against the Persians, the Greek army of the Ten Thousand enthusiastically shouted *thalassa, thalassa,* from Mount Theches, when they had their first glimpse of the Black Sea. Sighting this sea, they had an assurance of a route to the Mediterranean Sea and their homes in Greece.

In the hope of sharing his interest in words, Toby had given a copy of the *Oxford English Dictionary* (*OED*) to Germantown Academy. He put a bookplate in its thirteen volumes expressing the hope that they might do "yeoman service" for the students of the school. Toby and I could have explored English derivatives of *thalassa* in volume 11 and the degree to which ancient Athens' aspiration to thalassocracy, rule by sea power, brought her golden age to its end. He would have enjoyed bringing new understanding to the word that he had learned fifty years before.

Thinking about that phrase on the bookplate, I realize that Toby had confidence in the down-to-earth "service" that the *OED* might do for an education. Without a claim to gentility in English society, a yeoman knows his rights, but gets down to hard work. In the course of our work, Toby was surprised that I had gotten to the age of 24 without learning how this monument of English lexicography might serve my own education. He wasted no time in making me aware of the opportunity; and I wasted no time in seizing it. I soon had a copy in my classroom; and my students learned that the initials *OED* opened a treasure house for the study of language. They saw me poring so often over its volumes that one felt sure that I had read all thirteen of them! He did not realize that I am a slow reader.

I realized that the *OED* could forge an essential link in a classical education. In college, I had focused on appreciating classical Greek and Latin prose and poetry, but I gradually realized that this appreciation would take me and my students only halfway toward the goal of being accomplished students of language. I could not foresee their eventual voca-

• 1

tions or avocations, but I did know that they would all speak and write the mother tongue and that their study of Latin and Greek would lay an invaluable foundation—but only a foundation—for their understanding. The *OED*, completing the etymological histories of many English words that started in ancient Greek and Latin, would round out the education that I hoped they were acquiring.

Talking about words in class, I traced their meaning evolving as they passed from Latin and Greek into Romance, Germanic or Slavic languages. In this appreciation, we could trace the changing meanings of words from literal to metaphoric use and *vice versa*. A word first used by Vergil in antiquity, by the bard of *Beowulf* in 900, or by Chaucer in 1400, has told different stories in succeeding centuries. Every word and every man have their own stories to tell. In fact, these stories trace their lives with the words, by which they have lived. I started to listen to words telling the story of their lives. In the essays of this book I bring together words of related meanings and let them tell their life stories.

Following the lead of English words, I have written these essays to add to my students' knowledge of language. With a very good memory for these details, they would not find the subjects of these essays surprising. Each one starts with some of my *obiter dicta*, "things said by the way," about words and their lessons, as we were translating Latin or Greek or reading English. Each essay elaborates—more than my students may have expected—these side comments that I made for many years. On any day in class in 1970, for example, I might have told them that I would be back in few days with more details about a particular word. By now, in 2020—quite a bit later!—I am bringing new understanding to the words that we talked about as long ago as fifty years or more. With greater maturity, how much more able are we both to understand and to appreciate! In this sense, each essay puts a capstone on the study of language that my students and I have shared.

Building skill in language takes time. God has given us a duty to be kind and moral, and He has given us language so that we may pick the right words for the job. When a teacher writes W.C., word choice, in the margin of a student's essay, he may also be suggesting that living a good life involves choosing the right word to define it. My students should excuse me for taking my time in getting back to them, because choosing the right word takes a lifetime.

Of course, my students have both motivated and inspired my work. I would never have written these essays without them. They reflect the next step after the conversations about words in class and out. This next step remains so rooted in my reflections about language that I consider it my autobiography, polished up after many years. Fifty years after my conversations with Toby Wagner, two friends studying Russian motivated me to complete the project and expand it into the PIE, Proto-Indo-European, roots of Russian. God bless them all!

Focusing on specific words and their cognates, the essays engage in punning word play that may cause some confusion. The most basic form of humor, puns juxtapose two meanings of a word without expanding them in narratives. Juxtaposing one use of a word in 1600 with another in 1900 challenges readers to untie the knot of its two meanings. If they assume that one word has one meaning, puns confuse them, because they display different facets of a word's history. Words, like people, evolve. By analogy, someone who knew the readers at age fifteen might be confused by what he finds fifty years later.

By means of words, language defines the world and recreates it. Whatever our world may be, words expand or contract it. For a few years, I taught Latin to elementary school children on Saturday morning. One of the students in the class told me that he had learned the meaning of the word altruism that week. He understood sharing instinctively, but a new word gave him a chance to define and refine his understanding, character, and actions.

To follow this defining and redefining, each essay in this book starts with simple truths—for example, it is nice to be nice—and elaborates the ramifications of its etymology. Following words creating their worlds, it examines fundamental verbal images and their constellations of meaning so basic that we take them for granted. From simplicity to complexity, I point out the many-layered stories that arise from simple words. These evolutions teach us about them and ourselves.

In following paths of meaning, an essay unfolds their moral implications in punning resonances. Take the word moral: do Americans have moral mores or moralistic morality? Taken together, words resonate in moral questions. We can take some pleasure in following this simplicity woven into complexity. Plato and his friends felt a similar pleasure in the *Symposium*, at which their teacher helped them to weave an understanding of love from the concrete to the abstract.

Let's get down to some concrete practicality before the abstraction.

After each essay, I list words as though the cast of characters of the story that I have told, including Greek, Romance, Germanic, and Slavic branches of the Proto-Indo-European (PIE) word family. You may wish to consult this list before, during or after you read the essay, since the one clarifies the other. As players in my etymological dramas, some PIE roots, like those of sight, knowledge and birth, have such foundational importance that they become major players, which you will see more than once. These family trees of the words set up constellations of meaning for the essay. The date in parentheses marks the first year in which the word appeared in English according to the *OED*. Sometimes two dates follow a word to mark its change in meaning or its use as noun or verb.

"Where do you get your information?", someone has asked, after I have read her an essay. "I quote the dictionary," my reply, "the same one to which I sent my students, as we were reading a text in class." Let me be specific to credit the *OED* as my source. English quotations from *OED* describe the character and life of a word. The stories about words in this book cover a wide spectrum of experience, but each essay starts with quotations culled from the *OED*. So that my stories may flow unencumbered, I rarely mention this source, but the reader can assume it. To supplement the *OED*, I sometimes quote a Latin or Greek author for the classical meaning of a word or an English author, especially Beowulf, Chaucer or Shakespeare, for its later history.

The world of words is concrete. A student learning them recreates creation in so many concrete details that he may think that language has no other content. Even in these small details, he has the opportunity to see slices of an alternative, linguistic reality, with which he may compare his own. These essays bring together such opportunities in the seemingly endless concreteness of words. They also challenge him to reach beyond the inevitably narrow frame of his native tongue, as he has learned it.

Most readers have probably had the opportunity to reach beyond their native tongue by studying a foreign language in school or by speaking it at home. If he has studied an Indo-European language—Latin or a language derived from Roman roots, that is, a Romance language (Italian, French, Spanish, Portuguese or Romanian); German or a language, like English, derived from Germanic roots; and Russian or a language derived from Slavic roots—he may hear echoes of his knowledge in the lists of words after the essays. The essays harmonize and elaborate the words in the lists, and the continuity of foreign languages in English. If he has not studied an Indo-European language, the essays create a world new to him explicitly but one that he has always known implicitly. He knows his mother tongue; but, like some waif separated from his larger family, he has only a faint recollection of its members. The lists and the essays, introducing him to his family of languages, allow him to communicate with these ancestors, whose insights will fulfill his understanding.

Even if the reader has become acquainted with one member of the Romance, Germanic or Slavic families, his relations may not look alike.

For example, one list and its essay focus on the Proto-Indo-European (PIE) root for the English word head, and include the Romance contribution derived from the Latin word *caput*. Both head and *caput* belong to the same PIE family, even though they do not look alike. In English, the words chief and head are both synonyms and cognates, derived from the same root; but head comes into English from a Germanic root, and chief, from a Romance root.

Even within Romance, words sometimes come from different directions: in the passage from Latin and French to English, they may appear as doublets. Take legal and loyal as examples: they both come from the Latin root *lex legis*, law, but legal, directly from the Latin adjective *legalis*; and loyal, from *loi*, the French form of the Latin word. Loyal (1531) and legal (1500) describe a binding relationship, one personal, the other formal. *Loi* less obviously owes its origin to the Latin *legem*, because it has dropped the 'g,' the internal consonant of the Latin word. As another example, Latin *aqua*—cf. aquatic—also dropped its internal consonant 'q' to become *eau*, water, in French. Aquatic resembles *aqua*, but *eau* does not.

Even though the lists and essays explain these relationships between words of the same families, a previous acquaintance with languages can prepare the reader to recognize his relatives. Seeing words organized into constellations of meaning helps him to understand their history. Words, coming into English as *emigrés*, so to speak, bring with them foreign accents that introduce new shades of meaning. Germanic head and Romance chief are synonyms, but the Romance *emigré* brings with him romance from a foreign land that his native relative does not have.

Language and literature share the same root and grow into the same plant. Each list and its essay introduce characters that emerge from these linguistic layers in worlds of potential stories. Like the Greek word for sea, *thalassa*, words tell good stories on their own; in company, they tell better ones. In the following essays, I elaborate their moral complexities. They grow naturally from their constellations of meaning into others; and together, they unite into a world. Between these worlds, the final three essays takes up the question that arises from a man's decision to adhere either to unity or to duality. Before the final essay concludes with One-Two-Three, their words may remind you of many stories that you have read and lives that you have led. Words may also recall old worlds, in which you have lived, and lead you to new worlds, which you may love.

# Words
····

# Good Words

## 1. Word

>**The word** was in the beginning with God.
>**A word** to a wise man is sufficient.

These two statements represent God and the multitude of men's words in His creation. God created men by **The Word** and gave them an opportunity to say as many **a word** as they might wish. A book about men's words should plunge right into their deep sea; but, to begin, let's start with eleven essays about **a word**, then dive down into the depths, and postpone **The Word**, the Creator, for a final word in the penultimate essay. As we begin, my word!—so many words teach wisdom to the wise! A few words at first can explain their importance for better in the first five essays or for worse in the next four.

Now mark my words! Take care of pennies, and dollars take care of themselves—take care of words, and concepts take shape by themselves. With such care, The Word, the great creative concept, will put together all these shapes in the end.

Let's start back near the beginning of English: around A.D. 800, what did Beowulf say about words? He valued his words connecting with his works (*worda ond worka*)—he did not talk without acting. This Lord of the Seamen, therefore, respected both in keeping a sworn word (line 1100) and in promising action (*gylpworda*). His sword spoke for his words. Because he was as good as his word, people took him at his word. From his word-hoard (*wordhord*), they poured forth, gently, wisely, properly and weightily (*wíde hæfde*). Lord Beowulf made his words work.

Beowulf spoke words; five hundred years later, Chaucer wrote them. In the *Prologue* to *Canterbury Tales*, on the other hand, he professed his duty as a storyteller to "rehearse as ever he can" his characters' words as they spoke them: *Whoso shal telle a tale after a man, / He moot reherce as ny as evere he kan / Everich a word* (731–733). He concludes his pledge by quoting Plato on the word as "cousin" to the deed: *The wordes moote be cosyn to the dede*. Beowulf fought to make his deeds true to his words; Chaucer wrote to make them true to his characters.

Storytellers respect their hero's words. Because he is true, he stands true to them. Think how much we value them in particular. When we ask

"What's the word?" (1000), we don't intend to shoot the breeze. It serves as a household word (1375) for specific, important statement. We bring word (971) about news. We give the word (1000) in command. We put in a good word (1205) for a friend; and we take him at his word (1535), when he gives us the last word (1587). We weigh his words, word for word, because they have weight.

We respect words and we report them verbatim (1481), word for word. Latin *verbum* shares its PIE root with German *Wort* and English word, but it has not survived as commonly in Romance languages, in which parable, as Jesus' word in teaching, gave the word for word in Romance. In French, a man speaks his *parole*, his word of honor (1814). English, parol (1377) and word were once synonyms. On parole, a man has gained release from prison by giving his word to return.

Latin *verbum* did survive in two academic English words. In grammar, verb describes the most important word in the sentence, so important that even alone it makes a sentence: Stop! Look! Listen! In literature, a proverb says a word for the wise. Too many verbs, no matter how weighty, and too many proverbs, no matter how wise, make men verbose. Benjamin Disraeli called William Gladstone "a sophisticated rhetorician, inebriated with the exuberance of his own verbosity." Consider Beowulf and Gladstone as bywords in their day. Gladstone might have considered Beowulf a primitive, less educated, version of himself, but would the monster slayer have considered himself much improved by the grand old man of Parliament? Both had verve (1697); but, on either side of the 1000 years separating them, each one appreciated it differently. In any language—and in any age—words have power.

Neither the Roman's *verbum*, nor Jesus' parable has given French its word for word. Although classical authors scorned early, colloquial Latin *muttum*, word, cognate with mutter and perhaps with myth, mystery and myopia, it survived as *mot*, word, in French. A motto (1589) explains pictures with a word. From widely different sources, the synonyms, byword, proverb and motto indicate a wide world of pithy words that say a lot. When you put a few of them together, they can say a lot that is good. *Verbum sapienti sat est*, a word for a wise man is sufficient.

Great and bold carpenters of words, logodaedali, long for logocracy, the rule of words. Their voices cry in the wilderness. All of us, at the least, should hope that alogical logophobes will not drain words of their blood and abandon their desiccated shells in the wilderness. In all this palaver, logic finds a way. Beowulf, the fighter, and Chaucer, the writer, lived by their words. *The wordes moote be cosyn to the dede.* Plato's motto gives a word to live by. Amen!

## Words

In this list of words, the date in parentheses marks the first year of a word's use in English, according to the OED (*Oxford English Dictionary*). English or Romance derivatives are indented beneath the word, from which they are derived. When two cognate English words, like 'word' and 'verb,' come from a Germanic and a Romance root, this list makes a distinction between the Germanic English 'word' and the Romance English 'verb.'

One PIE (Proto-Indo-European) root gives German, English, Latin and French their words for word. It also gives Greek and Russian their words for the speech of rhetoricians and physicians.

### Four families of the PIE root *uer*, to speak

1. German: *Wort*
   Germanic English: word (*Beowulf*[1]), byword (1050)
2. Latin: *verbum*, word. *Verbum sapienti sat est*. A word for a wise man is enough.
   French: *verbe*, verb; *verve*, liveliness in the use of words
   Romance English: verb (1388), proverb (1374), verbose (1672)
3. Greek: *rhetor*, a speaker
   English: rhetoric, the art of speaking
4. Russian:
   врач (vrach), physician or shaman, 'speaking' words of power
   врать (vrat), to lie (not all "words of power" being true)

### Two PIE roots give Romance and Greek words for word

1. **PIE root *guel*, to throw**
   Latin: *parabola* (Greek *para* + *bola*, throwing alongside), comparison, parable
   French: *parole*, word; Spanish: *palabra*; Portuguese: *palavra*
   English: parable (1325), parole (1616), parlor (1225), palaver (from Portuguese)
2. **PIE root *leg*, to pick, choose, read or speak**
   Greek: *logos*, word, logic
   English:
   logic (1362), logical (1500)
   logodaedalus (1611), "a great and bold carpenter of words" (Ben Jonson), after Daedalus, builder of the labyrinth and the wings to escape from it
   logorrhea, verbal diarrhea, often pathologically incoherent

### Hebrew: *Amen*, truly, the last word confirming all previous words

## 2. Crackin' Good Chatter

Beowulf and Chaucer lived by their words, but sometimes words live on their own. How can we disparage them for their babbling or chattering; since we also made these sounds in infancy, and we have evolved with them into adulthood? Our primordial ancestors, birds and rodents—and, of course, our beloved companions, felines and canines—have never gotten beyond them. As moral beings, we may hope to make our words cousins to our deeds, but we consistently communicate with as much sound as sense. Speech can't be all that it's cracked up to be, and the human animal started and is still expressing himself in sounds ranging from howls to hums. Onomatopoeia, "making the name," describes words with sounds that make sense.

To speak, in origin, meant to crackle, much like babble, chatter, groan and grumble that more obviously imitate sounds of the human voice. To crack (1450), originally referring to brisk chatter, but, no longer in common use, has survived in isolated phrases: cracking a joke implies a guffaw at the punch line, which may punctuate its wit with a wisecrack. Cracking also boasts: before a race, a farmer cracked up (1844) his horse, so that it became the crack mount of the day, until the event might prove that his nag was not all that it was cracked it up to be. As a cracker (1509) he came naturally to boasting—probably the origin of Americans' loud and boastful Georgia crackers, popularly said to have been named for cracking corn. Boasting described a loud noise (1300) before it meant praising oneself (1340)—showoffs love to make noise. Even without boasting, crackin' good talk that puts some heart into it can get a little raucous.

A god and an animal, one high and the other low in the scale of creation, do not communicate in human language—except in miraculous circumstances—but both do somehow communicate. Raucous and rumor trace their origins to the PIE root *reu* or *re/ra/ru*, representing an animal's bellowing or a god's thunder: Rudra, "the Roarer," courses through heaven as the Vedic god of storms; and an animal in rut bellows with lust. Latin *rumor*, with the same meaning as the English word, murmurs indistinctly. When Ovid describes *rumor*, he defines it by the distance rumble of surf or thunder.[2] At such distance, rumor-bearers rarely bring the truth and rumor-mongers do not care in what shape they pass it on: "Rumor is a pipe blown by surmises, jealousies, conjectures" (*2 Henry IV*). Rumor in human voices sounds thinly duplicitous.

Rumor descended from thunder, but it does not instill fear. Grim and grumble (1586), also descended from thunder, have instilled terror. Pogrom—Russian translated from Yiddish—organized massacre, means reverberating thunder. Grumbling has always made sounds of discontent: "Wise men affirm it is the English way, / Never to grumble till they come to pay," Daniel Defoe quipped in 1701. The English even named such a noisy malcontent a grumbletonian (1690). By analogy, a murmuronian approaches a grumbletonian, but with muted thunder: Latin *murmur* also expresses subdued resentment, its first meaning in English (1381). Atavistically true to their animal nature, men howl when they feel anger or annoyance.

Small creatures make sharp, high pitched noises, like a whine, originally, a shrill cry of pain (1275): "Whip him," Mark Antony thunders, "... till <he> whine aloud for mercy" (*Antony and Cleopatra*). By the sixteenth century (1530), whiners complained feebly. The common man—always the little guy—whines in his most unheroic moments, that is, most of his life. The PIE word family to which whine belongs includes sibilant words like whistle. Whist!(1382), for example, demanded silence earlier than 'Shush!'. Whist (1680), the card game, required silence and "spread a universal opium over the whole nation," Horace Walpole observed in 1742.

Linguist Joseph Shipley has suggested that the Sibyl was named onomatopoetically after the sacred snake, whose sibilance she siffled. A snake, as the great tempter in the Garden of Eden, hissed out his subtle inducements to Eve. Only this once in Biblical history does a snake speak. We have no indication of what he sounded like, although Milton suggests conspiring sibilance when he calls him a "spirited sly snake."

English has a word for insinuatingly evil sibilance with a witty cover. Persiflage, light banter, emphasizes by its root, smoothly shrewd sibilance, siffling its sneers. Lord Chesterfield first used it in reference to "ministerial shrugs and persiflage." In moral and evangelical tracts, especially against the slave trade, Hannah More pictured it as sneering humor: "The cold compound of irony, irreligion, selfishness, and sneer, which make up what the French so well express by the term *persiflage*" (1799). In this cool climate, Voltaire, the French master of persiflage, offended the British: "If persiflage be the great thing," observed Carlyle, "there was never such a *persifleur*.... of all Frenchmen the most French. He is properly their god—such god as they are fit for." Brits, by the contrast of their own accent, can mock Gallic sibilance: 'Zi French, zo zlippery!'

Throughout history, many onomatopoeic roots—like grumble and rumble, hiss and whistle, creak and crow—have run a gamut of sounds with sense. To express emotions, a man does not usually need strong words for fulminating thunderously like storm clouds, murmuring deeply like the sea or whining shrilly like the wind. Common chatter wings him back to his avian ancestors' twitter. Birds chattered (1225) before he did; they also twittered (1374), clucked (1481) and cooed (1670). With a contented cluck, he singsongs their primal sagacity after he has twittered like a chit-chatting chatterbox.

## Words

Some words make sounds that make sense. It seems just in the sound of things that whips crack, but fires crackle; hinges creak, but frogs croak; crackers crack, but papers crinkle. The resemblance can never be perfect: for example, both whips and crackers crack, even though we know the difference between the sound of cured cowhide and crisply baked dough. The following PIE roots have had such lively sounds that Romance, Germanic and Slavic languages have made sense of them.

An entry of a Latin verb gives its first two principal parts—*e.g.* the Latin verb 'to crack,' *crepo*, I crack, and *crepare*, to crack.

1. **PIE root *gerh*, to resound, cry out hoarsely**
    Latin:
    *crepo crepare/crepito*, to crack, creak, rattle, rustle, jingle, tinkle or fart
    *corvus* and *gruis*, crow and crane
        English:
            to crepitate, to crackle (in lungs or joints) or fart
            decrepit, creaking with age
    German:
    *krachen*, to crack and *Kräcker*, cracker; *Krähe*, crow; and *Kranich*, crane
        English: to crack and cracker; crow and crane
            Russian: крекер (kreker), borrowed from English cracker
    Russian: журавль (zhurvl), crane
2. **PIE root *reu*, the sound of wind**
    Latin:
    *rugio rugire*, to roar, bellow
    *rugo rugare*, to belch; *ructo ructare*, to vomit
        English:
            eructation, erumpent gas blasting from the mouth or the earth
            rut, bellowing of an animal in lust
    Russian: рыгать (rygat), to belch

3. Related to PIE *reu: re/ra/ru*, **roaring and thunder**
   Latin: *rumor*, murmur, rumor, voice of the people
      English: rumor (1374); raucous and riot
   Germanic English: to rumble
   Russian: реветь (revet'), to roar
4. **PIE root *ghrem*, thunder, wrath**
   English: to grumble and grimace; grim
   Russian: гром (grom), thunder
5. **PIE root *kwey/kueis*, a hissing sound**
   English: to whine and whisper; whistle and whisk
   Russian: свист (svist), whistle
6. **PIE root *suei*, to hiss**
   Latin: *sibilo sibilare*, to hiss
      French: *siffler*, to whistle, hiss; and *persiflage*
   Russian: шипеть (shipet), to hiss

# 3. Word as Name and Fame

### Name and Naming

In the beginning, after God created animals, Adam took over by naming them (*Genesis* 2.19). More essentially and to the point, God also participated when He named Abram according to his place in His plan. After He established a covenant with Abram, "Exalted Father," He renamed him Abraham, "Father of the Multitude;" because, He said, "Thou shalt be a father of many nations" (*Genesis* 17.4). God and His name are synonymous. When prophets chastise men breaking this covenant, they speak in the name of the Lord, with His power. When people sing praise to His name, they sing it to him (*Psalm* 18.49).

The Bible values names, because they place people in their covenant with God. Hebrew *shem* and Greek *onoma*, both meaning name, appear over 1000 times in its books. Without the seal of divine covenant in Biblical culture, secular naming characterizes an essential human activity. Names had such importance for the ancient Greek that he invented writing to record them.[3] God creates—man recreates. Hebraic or Hellenic, man's ancient parents handed down naming as a legacy.

Our parents carried on this ancestral legacy when they named us. Procreating a person culminates in creating his name. He makes that name more or less worthy by the way he lives his life. Names create worlds ever new, but not necessarily ever better. In a man's recreation of creation, he brings his name to consequential, inevitable fame. In the end, we all make ourselves, that is, our names, good, bad or midway between.

The PIE root *kleu* includes both proclaiming fame and hearing it. Ancient Greek culture reached beyond the immortality of procreation, which Socrates in the *Symposium* dismisses as unremarkable, to the immortality of fame, *kleos*, that Homer memorializes in his narrative of Achilles. Clio, the Muse of history, proclaimed it; and some men, like Heracles, carried it about in their names. Sophocles' "wisdom" made him famous; Pericles' fame got "around." Fame—Greeks claimed it, proclaimed it, and praised it.

History illustrates the transience and vagaries of name and fame. Slavs claimed fame by taking слава (slava), fame, as their name. Since ancient Rome often made slaves of Slavs around the Black Sea, a backwater of its empire, Latin derived slave from Slav. Their name proclaimed fame, but conquest enslaved it. The nineteenth century pronouncing these blond, blue-eyed Caucasian slaves the Aryan master race sharpened the edge of this irony. In the whims of history, how can name, Latin *nomen* be an omen of fate? Parents' naming a child Abraham celebrate divine choice, without necessarily anticipating it.

One character from medieval epic and one from Shakespearian romance show their names faming or defaming. Before Beowulf introduces himself, simply to the point—*Béowulf is mín nama* (line 343)—fame has preceded him: *Béowulf wæs bréme—blaéd wíde sprang*— "Beowulf was famed—renown sprang wide" (line 19). In their roots, *bréme* and *blaéd*, famed and renown, make a stir. Cognate with English brim that first represented crashing surf rolling up the shore, *bréme* represents the buzz of fame. In Romance, fame, cognate with fable and affable, refers to the buzz of people speaking. From a cognate Greek root, aphasia refers to an inability to speak. Russian известность (izvestnost), fame, refers to what they see. Fame evolves from what people say, see, and also hear. What people saw or heard of Beowulf's conduct and what they said as a consequence confirmed his word as cousin to his deed.

Shakespeare's *All's Well That Ends Well* brings a name down to earth by pointing out its potential emptiness in the life of the protagonist, Helen. She laments that her parents have not satisfactorily honored her, because they did not give her a family name as noble as that of Bertram, the man whom she hopes to marry: "I am from humble, he from honored name." Children recreate the name that their parents have given them by making it their own, but Helen wishes to propagate a noble branch onto her family tree: ". . . my low and humble name to propagate / With any branch or image of thy state." Her king wisely advises her to rise above mere names. She has, he emphasizes, all that is worthy of the "name of life": "Youth, beauty, wisdom, courage, all / That happiness and prime, can happy call." He also advises Bertram, who objects to Helen's ignoble name, that "good alone is good without a name." The King has the right idea: since we do not all profit from divine covenant or human aristocracy in name and fame, we should first seek to be called good, and leave the rest to fate. We waste life blood in pursuing ephemeral names.

To continue and conclude with Shakespeare's regal advice: a name begins a life, but only a life earns it. A name's conclusion tells its fame. "I am become a name," Tennyson's Ulysses concludes, "For always roaming with a hungry heart / Much have I seen and known; cities of men / And manners, climates councils, governments, / . . . I am part of all that I have met." Our names conclude our lives, because they have included them. With whatever name Ulysses has passed through life, "I am part," he claims, "of all that I have met."

## Words

From its PIE root, English name also means fame. A number of other roots bring fame together with name.

The lists in this book give the nominative and genitive of Latin nouns—e.g. *flos floris*, flower—because Romance and English derivatives come from the genitive stem, as in English floral.

### Four families of the PIE root *onomen*, name

1. Greek: *onoma*, name, fame; *onomai*, I blame, call names
    English: onomastics, the study of names
2. Latin: *nomen nominis*, name. *Nomen est omen.*—Name is omen.
    Italian: *nome*, name, reputation; Spanish: *nombre*
    Latinate English: nominal
    French: *nom*, name
      Romance English: noun
3. German: *Name*, name; *Nomen*, noun
    English: name (825)
4. Russian: имя (imya), name

### Three families of the PIE root *kleu*, to proclaim

1. Greek: *kleiein*, to proclaim, make famous
    Clio, the muse of history, proclaiming fame

-cles / -kles, suffix in Hera<u>cles</u>, fame of Hera; Peri<u>cles</u>, fame around (*cf.* the suffix peri- in peri-meter, measurement around)
2. Polish: *slow*, word
   Russian:
   слово (slovo), word
   слава (slava), fame; Slavs' name, literally, their fame
       (-slav appended to names, Yugo-slavia, Czecho-slovakia)
   много-словный (mnogo-slovnyy), of many words, verbose
3. Medieval Latin: *sclavus*, slave
   Italian: *schiavo*; French: *esclave*, slave; Spanish: *esclavo*
   German: *Sklave*

## PIE root *beh*, to speak

Greek: *aphasia*, inability to speak
Latin: *fama*, fame
   Italian and Spanish: *fama*
   English: fame, fable, and affable

## PIE root *ueid/vid*, to see

Latin: *video videre* and *visus*, to see
Russian: весть (vest), message, news; известность (izvestnost'), fame

## PIE root *ker*, army

German: *Ruhm*, fame; *rufen*, to shout

## PIE root *brem*, to make a noise

Greek: *bremein*, to roar like the ocean
Grimm's law: 'f' and 'b' interchange (*cf.* Latin *frater* and English brother).
Latin: *fremo fremare*, to grumble, complain
   Italian: *fremere*, to shake, tremble
English:
   breme (*Beowulf*), renowned; 1300, tempestuous
   brim (1205), seashore; (1562), topmost rim

## PIE root *bleh*, to bloom

Latin: *flos floris*, bloom
German: *blat*, blossom, blowing, prosperity
English: *blaed*, blast, prosperity

# 4. The Fateful and the Banal

Man recreates creation by naming names which retain power by looking back to their origin. In formal speech, when our ancestors had no intention of shooting the breeze, they looked to the divine for boundaries. All told, fateful or banal, fatuous or ineffable—or both at the same time—words tell the tale of our lives.

In English, telling and saying originally described careful speech. Saying aspires to meaning. A red light means something, even when it says nothing—it means Stop!, unless you see it in the red light district. Stop right there!—let's get back to saying grace or the rosary. A saying or an old saw specifically quotes literature. In saying, we also see, because the two verbs have the same origin: a saga, therefore, both says and sees. Derived from the Old English root *talian*, to reckon or enumerate, to tell tells specific tales. A bank teller (1382) takes care because he tells (888) the total of transactions. A fortune teller tells a good lifeline from a bad one before telling her curious quester what to do, because her advice may have a telling effect on his life. She can say much and tell little, but if she tells his fortune, she also sees his future as a seer.

In Latin, to speak, *fari*, poetic and archaic, has its personification in *Fas*, whom Ausonius, in the fourth century A.D., called "the first of the gods, which for the Greeks is Themis," goddess of Justice: *prima deum Fas quae Themis est Graiis*. Roman priests spoke her divine word, *fas*, which they identified as the right and proper thing to do. *Fatum*, fate, her word, though spoken, represents unspeakable, ineffable, mystery. From a Greek parallel and cognate, *prophemi*, I speak forth—'f' in Latin changing to 'ph' in Greek—prophets speak God's prophecy, the Greek cognate of the Latinate fate. God's word, far from being ineffable or even fateful, was also practical. In the daily business of ancient Rome, Roman priests set the *fasti*, the days spoken of, that is, allowed for business, on the calendar.

Priests reserved *dies nefasti* for the gods. A nefarious man does the unspeakable in violating these boundaries, committing *nefas*, an iniquitous deed and an abomination to men. Speaking the unspeakable, nefarious men confessed before those who had made a profession of faith. The Romans were careful to avoid *nefas*, when they cautiously addressed their prayers to a god: *Si fas est*, "if it is God's will." In the same spirit, Thomas Cranmer introduced the Lord's Prayer, "we are bold to say...."

In Celtic realms, fairy referred to lesser—in size, in power, and in importance—spiritual powers as likely to plague a peasant—wounding his cattle with fairy-arrows or pinching his pregnant wife with fairy-nips—as to awe him by "twinkling fairy-dances in light and shade." In sophisticated literature, tales about them, mere fairy-tales, serve only to amuse. Titania, for example, the fairy queen in Shakespeare's *Midsummer Night's Dream*, commands her entourage to do a circle dance and sing their song: "Come now a roundel and a fairy song." Traditionally, in their diminutive size, fairies had childlike beauty, described by the adjective fay; but not all fairies are fay. Thomas Malory named the most famous one, Morgan le Fay, a protean enchantress in his Arthurian romance, *Le Morte d'Arthur*.

The power of speech, holy in fame, fable, and fatality, so essentially defines humanity that the infant is one not speaking, *infans*. Since even the goddess *Fatua* might speak in language that sounded as fatuous as that of a babbling babe, *homo fans*, speaking man, also does not always speak to tell the truth. (One verb in Latin, *hariolari*, means both to prophesy and to talk nonsense.) A fable, a story of hearsay, gives rise to the fabulous; and fame flies on the swift wings of what others say: "that second life in others' breath." If not famous or fabulous in the mouths of others, we can at least be affable, easy to talk to, on our own, in confabulation, by which word we humorously define and dignify our chatter.

Confabulation can make the banal sound fancy. Like fatuous, banal, in origin, described business. Ban represented a Germanic cognate of the Roman *fasti*, but in its original meaning, not business but a call to arms. In war-torn Europe, bans became so frequent that banal meant commonplace. Banal though the bans may have been, they could not be carelessly abandoned. Many men were banished to suffer the fate of bandits, because they did not respond to them. Making their humble boon to their liege lord, they might in return have received his generous boon of freedom.

Multifarious—-farious, from *fari*!—speech has aspired to God's truth and man's laws. Skeptics may dismiss these aspirations as so many roundels in fabled fairy rings. Our ancestors also realized that bans might end up banal and fates only fatuous. Whether a fatuous banality of men or a fateful boon of the gods, we can never banish speech from our lives. How sad the fate of the skeptic! Just because he can never profess the ineffable, should he profess—or really, confess—only the affable?

## Words

Let's look a little more at the PIE root *beh*, to speak. From its Romance and Germanic branches, English derives words for speech in law and religion. Ban attests to the Germanic interest in law, and fate to the Romance interest in religion. When we speak, our words can reach beyond us. The list gives a perfect participle of a verb (*confessus/professus*), when it is important in the formation of an English derivative like confession or profession.

### PIE root *beh*, to speak

Greek: *prophemi*, I speak out (*cf.* a prophet "speaking out" for a god)
Latin:
> *for fari*, to speak; *fatum*, fate—what has been spoken by God
> *fas*, God's saying (What He speaks, He wills.); *Fatua*, Roman goddess
> *infans infantis*, literally, not speaking; infant
> *dies fasti*, "days spoken for" in the calendar; *nefas*, unspeakable
> *confiteor confiteri confessus*, to make a full statement—of past action
> *profiteor profiteri professus*, to make a public statement—of future action
>> Italian: *fato*; Spanish: *fado* and its doublet *hado*
>> The English derivatives from Latin *fari* span five centuries:
>> Thirteenth Century
>>> profession (1225)
>>
>> Fourteenth Century
>>> fame (1300), what people say; fable (1300), a story of what people say
>>> fairy (1300), enchantment; and its diminutive creature, a fay (1393)
>>> fate (1374); to confess (1386)
>>
>> Fifteenth Century
>>> confabulation (1450); ineffable (1450), not to be spoken of (e-)
>>
>> Sixteenth Century
>>> fabulous (1546) and multifarious (1593)
>>
>> Seventeenth Century
>>> nefarious (1604) and fatuous (1633)

German: *verbannen*, to ban (Grimm's law: 'f' of *fari* and 'b' of ban interchange.)
> English:
>> ban (1000), call to arms
>> boon (1175), request; or (1460), gift, two sides of one coin
>>> (*cf.* Latin *munus*, in munificent and remuneration)
>>
>> banished (1375), bandit (1593), banal (1753)

### PIE root *seku*, to remark

Greek: Thespis, literally, divinely uttered; god of drama
> English:
>> to see (888); seer, one who sees the future
>> an old saw (950), to say (971), saying (1303), and saga (1709)

**PIE root *del*, to trick, recount**
Old English: *talian*, to reckon, enumerate
    English: to tell (888)

## 5. Fussy People

In the beginning of all the fuss, *logos* meant word. Its verb form, *lego*, can mean either I speak or I read—flip sides of the same record, because the ancients spoke what they read. Greek and Latin have each chosen a different meaning for *lego*: it means I speak or I gather in Greek; and it means I read in Latin. These two classical roots have given English a few choice words. Originally, a teacher read his lecture, a derivative of *lego*. Since he read it, he certainly hoped that it would be legible. Speaking a *logos* with careful thought, he used logic; but herein lie perennial problems, because a man does not always use it. The meaning of the Latin verb *lego* can explain this problem: in addition to meaning I read, it also means I pick or I choose. Before we speak or read words, we naturally pick and choose them, but since we do not always pick or choose logically, we do not always speak or read logically. Picky (1867) and choosey (1862) people, often too fussy for their own good, pick away at logic to the detriment of its creative, ancestral *Logos*.

Before we get to these fussy people, let's at least start with some logical picking and choosing. From Greek, English has derived eclecticism that anthologized the best of ancient philosophies—putting the best of Platonism together with Stoicism or Epicureanism. Since it sees something good in each one of these philosophies, someone has called it "the higher virtue which binds men to endeavor to pursue an eclectic course" (1865). Milton used elective, the Latinate doublet of eclectic, to describe virtue as unconstrained free will. Don't we all love freedom of choice—the great luxury, but the great bane—of the modern world!?

The Greek and Latin heritage of the PIE root *leg* starts us on a path to fussy, but picky and choosey's derivation from picking and choosing suggests that no word in English originally meant fussy. Eclecticism makes an appreciative, rational choice; and selective or elective only suggests a fussy one. Fastidious (1440), full of pride or disdainful, comes the closest to a fussy origin. Although fastidious can mean disdainful in "proud youth—fastidious of the lower world" and fussy in "a fastidious age of false refinement," the "proud youth" could feel at home in "false refinement." Only a fine line separates disdainful from fussy, since both are pretty sniffy.

Let's follow some derivatives from fine (1300), since their distinctions have evolved from fine to fussy, and even to logic that is not fine. Finical (1592), finicking (1661), and especially finicky (1825) with its -y, resemble picky and choosey in putting crotchety twists on their roots. As derivatives from fine, they denote "affectedly fastidious" speech, manners or dress, which fine could connote after the end of the sixteenth century: "He's only a working-man . . . He hasn't got your fine ways" (1885). Although fine, unlike fastidious, can only mean fussy by connotation; finicky or finical, like picky and choosey, denoted this meaning exclusively: "a pretty, little, delicate, ladylike, finical gentleman" (1829).

Squeamish (1450) and mincing (1390) have lent themselves to fussy characters. Of unknown origin, squeamish (1450) first meant "easily affected with nausea." Since a squeamish stomach is picky about food, squeamish, by 1581, naturally came to mean generally picky. Mincing does not as easily lend itself to fussing as does squeamish. From Latin *minutiare*, to make minute, mincing first chopped up small pieces, as in chopping meat to mincemeat. By 1530, one could affectedly mince one's speech, gait or expression. Speaking directly in honesty, we do not mince our words; but walking carefully on ice, we do mince our steps. We mince a smile by making it affectedly brief. When Pope refers to "finical style which consists of the most curious, affected, mincing metaphors" (1727), he makes finical synonymous with mincing. Mincing and finical/finicky refer to affectations; squeamish, to gut feelings.

In fine and finally (!), let's complement our fine logic with fussy (1831). It originated from fuss (1701), which recreates its sputter—"echoic of the sound of something sputtering or bubbling." Fussy folk fidget over trifles. Fussiness does not imply fastidious disdain, squeamish guts or finicky, mincing affectation. General Winfield Scott's soldiers, for example, called him "Old Fuss and Feathers," because he fussed over military decorum. Perhaps he got his training from his mother, who fussed over him as a child.

Particular (1386) has its own particular history and pre-paration. In origin, particular emphasizes part of an individual. Each one has his own particular likes and dislikes. Some individuals, however, are more particular than others. We have a luxury in being particular about our own particulars: "People," on the other hand, "who have to work for their living, must not be too particular" (1879). Particular people have personal preferences. Pernickety (1808), perhaps a playful version of particular, adds particular fastidiousness to particular; and persnickety (1905) gives a snicker to pernickety particularity. American tourists, for example, may make persnickety comments about foreigners' pernickety disdain.

If we are fastidious about fussiness, we can find consolation in realizing that both we and fussy characters enjoy a freedom particular to the modern world. Fussy dates proliferate after 1800: pernickety (1808), particular (1814), fussy (1831), choosey (1862), picky (1867) and persnickety (1905). The man persnickety about particular people forgets what diversity is all about.

## Words

We should choose words carefully, because fussy people are waiting to catch us when we don't. Understandably, fussy vocabulary often frets more than it reflects. Words for rational choice have more forthright roots than words for fussing, which sputters more than it utters.

**PIE root *leg*, to pick; but picking out words in reading or in speaking**

Greek: *logos*, word; and *lego*, I say or I gather
    English:
        logic (1362), rational use of words
        eclectic (1683), gathered from various sources
        anthology, literally, picking flowers (*cf.* anthomania)
Latin: *lego legere*, to pick, choose, read
    English:
        to elect and elective (1530); to select and selective
        lecture, a reading; and legible, readable

**PIE root *wer*, high, swelling**

Latin and English: *verrusa*, wart
    English: varicose, swollen
Old Church Slavonic: врьхъ (vrixu), top, peak
Russian:
    веред (véred), abcess, pain, doublet of вред (vred)
    при-вередливый (pri-vered-livyy), picky, literally, too sensitive
        to pain

**PIE root *suei*, as in swap, sweep, sway and swift**

Russian:
    совать (sovat), to butt in
    суета (sujeta), fuss, vanity; суетливый (suyetlivyy), fussy

# Bad Words

## 6. Inditing Indicting

From the PIE root *deik*, to point out, English derives the Greek paradigm and the Latinate digit. The index digit points out a paradigm, and a paradigm points out an example. Without a little discretion, I use my digit to point out a friend as a paradigm of virtues. More common than these two extraordinary derivatives, the group of words derived from Latin *dicere* represent formal, precise speech. Dictionaries like the *OED* and *Black's Law Dictionary* record the precise and proper diction of these roots in law, literature and religion. With these resources, we can anticipate the predicament of predicting their predication as better or worse, and we can preach modestly about their conditions.

Before considering formal precision, let's look at a few words derived from the Latin verb *loqui* of the PIE root *tolku* representing conversational speech. Words in the *loquor* family indicate that some men often speak with an idle or a troublesome tongue. Loquacious people ramble on with chatty, garrulous motormouths. Together, they speak in the colloquial, just the sort of speech English teachers tell us to avoid, as they themselves avoid it when they speak in colloquies at their colloquia. Don't sink to the colloquial at a colloquium! Colloquially or formally, in slander, they speak obloquiously. Malevolent obloquy gets them into trouble, but they can tactfully talk their way around it by circumlocution.

On the other hand, people speaking fluently and forcefully take their adjective eloquent from the *loquor* family because the word for oratorical speech in the *dicere* family took another meaning in the word edict. Eloquent speakers have mastered elocution, the art of proper delivery, pronunciation and gesture in oratory. Eloquent elocution can slip into grandiloquence or magniloquence, just pompous hot air.

About formal speech, let's start with crucial predications in the survival of a nation: in time of war, when the ancient Romans saw that their state was in grave danger, they entrusted it to a dictator. Acting according to the exigencies of the crisis, the dictator dictated, that is, spoke what was to be written down as law. When the common citizen dictates, he intends his words to be put on paper, but not on law books. The dictator dictated edicts. The Romans trusted him, because he had dedicated himself to their good. In his dedication, he stated complete allegiance. When the danger passed, the dictator abdicated dictatorship. After he had rid the state of danger from without, he might have become so addicted to power that he created more lasting danger from within; but dedication overcame addiction.

In time of peace, conditions of legal agreement constitute things "said together," to which the parties adhere when contracts draw them together. The spelling of the word condition erroneously changes its root *condicion* by replacing the 'c' with a 't'. More than five hundred years after its first use, conditions referred to present situations—the ravages of war, for example, leave the poor in wretched conditions.

Violating dictates of dictators or conditions of contracts, a man can be brought to book and indicted; that is, a legal charge may be recorded against him. In a court of law, a witness—Latin *index*—indicates what he knows of the indictment; and the judge, literally, a man saying law, speaks the truth by his verdict, literally, truth spoken. Even in well meant jurisdiction, if a judge has made a mistaken judgement beforehand, the defendant may suffer judicial prejudice and the consequent odium of public malediction. Suffering this prejudice with stoic heroism, he can hope that a poet with the proper diction may indite a ditty in his honor. Indicting the charge against him and inditing its defense have different purposes but the same pronunciation. When the inditement of innocence prevails over the indictment of crime, even after death, his spirit at least, vindicating itself and receiving posthumous benediction, can utter a happy valediction from above.

In either inculpating indictment or exculpating inditement, words may attempt veridical precision, but there is always someone, in either case, who would deny them a happy valediction. My inditement of indictment may provoke obloquy making either an indictment of indictment, that is, an attack on lawyers indicting; or an indictment of inditement, an attack on poets inditing vindications of the men indicted.

In either case of a lawyer's indictment or of a poet's inditement, my ditty's dicta may vindicate prejudice that all speech is loquacious folly, an idiotic soliloquy, full of grandiloquently magniloquent eloquence, signifying nothing. This vindication may turn to vindictive revenge: "The first thing we do, let's kill all the lawyers"—and all the poets too, who also confuse us by playing with words. As the first duty in predicting this predicament, we should preach the modest predication of good lexicography: we are better with words than without them, but never the best.

## Words

PIE roots for speech introduce the possibility of preachers preaching and damning, or judges indicting and condemning. Not preachers or judges, but with these same roots, addicts can prejudice and avenge. What a predicament we have in predicting whether men use these roots for better or worse! We praise the better, but no one of us can entirely avoid the worse.

Two PIE word roots represent speech, one formal, the other conversational.

1. **PIE root *deik*, to point out**
   Latin:
   *dico dicere*, to say; *dictum*, a thing said
   *dico dicare*, to proclaim; *dicto dictare*, to proclaim often
   *digitus*, finger pointing out; *index indicis*, a man pointing out
   *iu-dex iudicis*, man saying the law (*ius iuris*), judge
   *iu-dicium*, saying the law, judgement

   The English derivatives from Latin *dicere* span five centuries:
   The Thirteenth Century
   to preach (1225), doublet of predict (*cf.* French *prédire* and *prêcher*)
   to indict (1270), to proclaim in writing, charge with a crime
   jurisdiction (1276), saying of law; prejudice (1290), saying law beforehand
   edict (1297), proclamation; verdict (1297), the truth (ver-) said
   to judge (1290), to say the law; (1303), noun
   The Fourteenth Century
   ditty (1300), that which has been said
   condition (1315 and 1856), speaking together
   to indite (1340, pronounced the same as indict), to proclaim in writing
   to avenge (1375) and to revenge (1375), doublets of vindicate
   predicament (1380), a situation or difficulty proclaimed beforehand
   judicial (1382), relating to saying law; dictator (1387), man proclaiming
   index (1398), the index finger; (1578), a table of contents
   The Fifteenth Century
   benediction (1432), speaking well; paradigm (1483), pointed out alongside
   The Sixteenth Century
   dictionary (1526), a book of speech (*cf.* diction [1542], speaking)

to dedicate (1530), to commit completely (de-) by proclaiming
to vindicate (1533), to proclaim the power (vin-) of truth
to abdicate (1541), to proclaim a resignation
to predict (1546), to speak of beforehand (*cf.* its doublet, to preach [1225])
to predicate (1552), to proclaim beforehand (Quadruplets preach, predict predicament, and predicate all speak beforehand.)
to addict (1560), to proclaim devotion to; to dictate (1592), to proclaim

The Seventeenth Century

valediction (1614), saying farewell; to indicate (1651), to proclaim
dictum (1697) and its Italian doublet, ditto (1625), that which has been said

2. **PIE root *tolku*, talk**

Latin: *loquor loqui* and *locutus*, to speak, talk
English:
obloquy (1460), speaking against (ob-)
elocution (1509), speaking out (e-)
circumlocution (1510), speaking around (circum-)
colloquy (1563), speaking together; its Latin doublet, colloquium (1609)
grandiloquence (1589), speaking grandly; soliloquy (1604), speaking alone
magniloquence (1623), speaking magnificently
loquacious (1667), full of speaking
colloquial (1751), characteristic of speaking together

# 7. Criticism

Although we are better with words than without them, we often make a bad use of them by making others feel worse than we are. Better to pride ourselves on the words with which we criticize ourselves than on words with which we criticize others. In court, words condemn and censure men's faults by the power of the law. Outside court, even when we vituperate human faults, we can also deprecate bad behavior and demonstrate good alternatives. Critical language sharpens its offense, but it's critical that criticism be as good as its effort to make bad characters good.

Some of the earliest words for criticism have come from ancient Roman courts of law. To damn and its intensive to condemn, derived from the PIE root *da-*, to divide, refer to the fine that divided a man from his money. By 1325, when damn passed from man's sentence to God's, condemn took up the judicial (1340), and left damn to hellish eternity or the eternally hellish. "Out damned spot!," laments Lady Macbeth, in realizing that guilt for her murder, damning her to both of the two sentences, cannot be washed away in this life or in the next. She damns the spot, because it damns her;—not the spot, but she suffers damnation. With what torture does this human soul witness her guilt; and with what tortuous and torturous delusion does she bear witness!

With the Latin verb *censere*, to express an opinion, a Roman magistrate passed judgment on citizens' morals and their taxes. A censorious (1536) censor (1592) both censures (1380) and takes a census (1613) for taxes. The Church first took censure as its province in both fearing and promulgating "the infallible censure of God;" and then it passed on some of this infallibility to the state (1470) that judged, according to Swift's sardonic humor, the loss of Gulliver's eyes "too easy a censure." Finally, by the end of the sixteenth century, indignant moralists took up censure, when they wrote tracts as the vehicles of their censorious pontification. In any one of these three areas—holy church, sovereign state or moralizing laymen—indignation can cloud moral vision: "Those who are most indulgent to their own, are most censorious of others' sins" (1646).

Roman law and morality have also given English some other early words for criticism. In origin, to reprove (1325), to rate (1386), to reproach (1489), to vituperate (1542), and to objurgate (1616) had some moral sense. Latin *probus*, excellent, describes healthy crops and, metaphorically, healthy characters. *Probare*, approving, proves what is excellent. Its antonym, *reprobare*, disapproving, gives English reprove and reprobate, the man reproved. Reproving, therefore, rebukes in a moral framework—the reprobate, reproved for departing from probity, proves worthy by returning to it. Although to rate may trace its origin to Latin *reputare*, to think back, its modern meaning does not reflect its thoughtful origin: "Queen Elizabeth rated the great nobles as if they were schoolboys" (1874).

Both reproaching (1489) and vituperating (1542) bring a reprobate to account. Vituperating gathers (*parare*) vices (*vitium*), just as reproaching brings a person back (*re-*), near to his fault. (Latin *prope*, near, became the -proach of both ap-proach and re-proach.) Reproached, he approaches his fault. Vituperation reproaches with strong, even abusive language. Although objurgating, by its Latin root, *ob-iurem-agere*, prosecutes (*agere*) law (*iurem*) against (*ob*) a malefactor, an objurgatory (1576) tone rebukes as sharply as vituperation. In and, especially, out of court, morality can fight its battles with the language of Billingsgate. Vituperation started its life moral, but it has ended it as gratuitous insult: An employer, for example, may remark that his employees have submitted a seriously flawed report and add, vituperatively, that they must be a bunch of idiots.

In the seventeenth century, words of constructive criticism fostered morality: castigating (1607), remonstrating (1627), deprecating (1628), abominating (1644) and reprimanding (1681) seek moral goals. To castigate—a triplet of chastise (1325) and chasten (1526)—drives (-igate) a person to chaste (cast-) behavior by severe criticism. We need drive to get others to chaste goals! Remonstration demonstrates a mistake: people, for example, remonstrate to their friend the evils of smoking. Deprecating prays earnestly against an evil—having remonstrated the evils of her smoking, they deprecate her indulgence. If she continues, they reprimand her by demanding that the habit be repressed (Latin *reprimandus*, to be repressed). In a severe reprimand, they abominate her smoking as unnatural, a shameful abomination (1325). To abominate avoids (ab-) evil omen (-ominate). Though strong in reprimanding or castigating, they remain moral in opposing evil and urging good. The seventeenth century had also mustered ebullient, effusive and exuberant to describe a man overflowing with goodwill. The effusive seventeenth century also overflowed in demonstrating goodwill when it remonstrated.

These strong words of moral rebuke just go to show that there is no easy path in castigating evil. Saint Augustine, for example, assiduously avoided demeaning vilification, but he pulled no punches in remonstrating and abominating the evils that damn the human soul. Goodwill can also have the drive to make castigation kind.

**Words**

Just as a prefix can turn the PIE root *deik* to ediction or addiction, any word or action may imply criticism, but a few PIE roots, in particular, can make judgments: dividing, spreading, assessing, thinking, outstanding, driving, fitting, gathering or praying.

1. **PIE root *da*, to divide**
   Latin: *damno damnare*, to damn or condemn, declare guilty
      English: to damn (1300) and to condemn (1300)
2. **PIE root *kla*, to spread out**
   English: laden, weighed down
   Russian:
      класть (klast), to put
      проклинать (proclinat), to damn, curse

3. **PIE root *kens*, to assess**
   Latin: *censeo censere*, to express an opinion
      English:
         censure (1380), censor (1592), censorious (1536), census (1613)
      Russian: цензура (tsenzura), censure
4. **Two verbs using the PIE root *per*, first, outstanding**
   1. Latin:
      *probus (pro*, forth + *-bus*, growing), well grown, excellent
      *probo probare*—changing 'b' to 'v'—to approve
      *reprobare*, to disapprove
         English: to reprove (1325); reprobate (1545), the man reproved
   2. Latin: *vitupero vituperare*, to vituperate (*parare*, to gather+*vitium*, vice)
         English: to vituperate (1542)
5. **PIE root *dhab*, to fashion, fit**
   Latin: *faber*, craftsman
      Latinate English: fabric and to fabricate
   Germanic English:
      daft, fitting; then, gentle or meek; finally, stupid
      deft—doublet of daft—deft hands make things fit
   Russian:
      добрый (dobryy), good, kind; Dubrovnik, Dobro-Venedik, good Venice
      одобрять (odobryat), to approve
   As an example of 'f' changing to 'd,' the PIE root *dhe*, to set, has given to Romance English the word fact and to Germanic English the word deed.
6. **PIE root *peue*, to cut, prune, think**
   Latin: *reputare*, to think back
      English: to rate (1386), to impute blame, to scold
7. **Two verbs using the PIE root *ag*, to drive**
   1. Latin: *castigo castigare*, to castigate (*castus+agere*, to drive to chastity)
         English: to castigate (1607)
   2. Latin: *objurgo objurgare*, to objurgate (*ob+iurem+agere*, to drive law against)
         English: to objurgate (1616) and objurgatory (1576)
8. **PIE root *prec*, prayer**
   Latin: *precor precari*, to pray
      English: to deprecate (1628), to pray earnestly against

9. **PIE root *tre*, three**
   Latin: *testis*, witness, a third party
     English: to protest
     Russian: протестовать (protestovat), to protest

# 8. Badmouthing

In courts, judges censure judiciously and condemn judicially. Outside courts, gossips malign judgmentally. Maligning without moral purpose— or using it, instead of serving it— they speak evil invidiously and maliciously. These inveterate reprobates cultivate a perverse joy in disparaging or vilifying; and more fiercely, in chiding or scolding. If justice is served, they end up before a real judge, answering to laws against their malice, at least when it rants in public and, especially, in print. Justice, however, may only have validity in law and lexicography. Like the cruel heads of the Hydra, malice always increases by the slur of its spawn.

Malicious gossips belittle personal worth. They takes a man's colors down a peg or two, when they disparage (1292) or defame (1303). Just as disgrace takes away grace and dishonor takes away honor, defamation takes away fame, often wrongfully: malicious tongues, for example, defame a lady's good name. In Russian, зло-словить speaks an evil word (zlo+slovo, evil word). Social defamation disparaged. At first, disparaging married a man beneath the rank of his peers (Latin *par*, equal)—hypergamy, on the other hand, married him above it. Later (1386), it lowered him in esteem; and, finally (1536), it belittled him. We make this idea vivid when we speak of a put-down or a slight.

Vilifying (1450) and depreciating (1646) also lower personal worth. Vilifying by cheap-shots makes a man look and feel cheap: "Wealth and pride make the man of humble rank sensible of his inferiority and vilify his condition" (1790). Depreciating puts him down by putting his price down—his personal stock, so to speak, depreciates. Mockery adds a bit of spice to vilification and depreciation: raillery (1653), on the other hand, usually means good humored banter. Caviling (Latin *cavilla*, jest) makes frivolous objections.

Maligning cares so little about truth that it lies when it slanders (1340) and traduces (1586) with obloquy (1460) and calumny (1564). Obloquy, though derived from the Latin *ob*, against and *loqui*, to speak, first described abusively evil speech. Slander (1290), a doublet of scandal, scandalizes a man by malicious lies. Calumny, a doublet of challenge and a cognate of cavil, accuses falsely. Hamlet, for example, bids

Ophelia his bitter adieu: "Be thou as chaste as ice, as pure as snow, thou shalt not escape calumny." A traducer, by words, and a traitor, by deeds, betray good faith. Malice practices three skills: lies, mockery, and provocation.

Violence by words goes subtly hand in hand with violent wounds. Words also wound. The history of chiding (1000) brings the two together. Occurring uniquely in English, it engaged first in angry brawls. Only later did it content itself with angry words (1175). Chiding, however, could still threaten violence: in *A Midsummer Night's Dream*, Helena alludes to its violence when she bewails Demetrius' bullying: "But he hath chid me hence, and threat'ned me / To strike me, spurn me, nay, to kill me too."

Railing seemed more verbally than physically violent. Its Latin root *ragire*, to neigh, suggests incoherent chiding: a man rails and rages to satisfy his ill humor. Some may remain impervious to it as just so much loud noise. Shylock expresses confidence that his bond for a pound of flesh has weight no matter how strident the protests: "Till thou canst rail the seal from off my bond, / Thou but offend'st thy lungs to speak so loud." Almost as violent, scold (noun, 1200; verb, 1377) had a literary origin: skald in Old Norse was a satiric poet. (Libel, also, a "little book" of lies, arose as literature.) A scold, usually a woman of abusive speech, so commonly plagued a community that Blackstone (1769) records *communis rixatrix*, the common scold, as the legal term for this public nuisance. Perish the thought of a mother as nothing but a scold, but she does scold her children when their misbehavior tries her patience.

A chiding scold badmouths shamelessly and in-your-face. Even more physical than scolding and chiding, to affront (1315) first slapped the face (Latin *ad*, to+*frontis*, face) or even assaulted: the scold, with unblushing effrontery (1715), puts her victim to shame by public affront (1598). Upbraiding suggests an affront by throwing (-braid) up a charge against someone. Without murderous intent, affront and its brother effrontery deal openly and in-your-face: "I express my resentment by the superficial effrontery of my brows" (1720). Brows on the exterior demonstrate feelings from the interior. Because mean words wound by mean looks, browbeating (1582) describes angry looks complementing words. In Russian, ругать (rugat), to abuse, originated in a wolfish snarl. Snarly abuse inflicts wounds cooly or derisively.

Scolds make no serious effort: "The man who acts the least," Alexander Pope observed, "upbraids the most" (1715). In their hearts, they may realize that their lies don't deserve it. Cheap shots, put-downs and in-your-face brow-beatings also do not require much moral effort: "To spread suspicion, to invent calumny, to propagate scandal," Samuel Johnson observed, "requires neither labor nor courage" (1751). If scolds understood the discriminating definitions of their art, they could recognize vilifying, depreciation, disparaging, railing and affront as its fine points; but why should they bother? Meanness by any slur would be as bad.

## Words

Badmouthing makes things bad by cheap shots, lies, snarls, whatever can be in-your-face demeaning.

### PIE root *melo*, bad

Latin:
*malus*, bad, evil
*malignus*, evil in nature, the suffix *-gnus* referring to birth
    English: malign (verb, 1426; adjective, 1430)

### PIE root *per*, value

Latin: *pretium*, price
    English: to appreciate (1769) and to depreciate (1646)

### PIE root *kleu*, to proclaim; and *ghwel*, to deceive

Greek: Clio, the muse of history, proclaiming fame
Russian:
    слово (slovo), word; слава (slava), fame
    зло-словить (зло-слово, zlo+slovo, evil word), to defame

### PIE root *ker*, to cry out; and *krsnos*, black

English: crow, identified both by its color and its sound
Russian:
    черный (chernyy), black; Chernobyl, city named for its "black grass"
    чернить (chernit'), to blacken, slander

### PIE root *regnati*, to open the mouth

Latin: *ringor*, I snarl
    English: rictus, opening of the jaws, gape
Russian: ругать (rugat), to swear, abuse

### No certain PIE root

Latin: *vilis*, cheap
    English: to revile (1303), to vilify (1450)

# 9. Bad Feeling

Ill humor frets with sour looks. Sourpusses may content themselves with looking sour, as they fret; but old crabs vent their spleen acrimoniously. With whatever acumen sourpusses or sour mouths make their edge acrid, they turn life's sweet fruit sour when ill humor makes them sore, just as French wine (*vin*) turns sour to vinegar.

Fretting chews a sharp edge, but not quite as literally as it used to. Back when Beowulf was battling the sons of Cain, the monster Grendel fretted, that is, he devoured, Beowulf's hearth-companions; and then the funeral pyre fretted what was left of them. Many years later, worries, rather than monsters or fire, were doing the chewing. By the beginning of the thirteenth century, they were fretting a man's heart to death; and, by the end of the century, a man was fretting his heart with worries: "So many curiosities drive one crazy," Hawthorne mused in his notebook, "and fret one's heart to death." Worry worts have also fumed as much as they have fretted, because a smoking fire gnaws away more subtly than a blazing one. Since we have forgotten the image of fretting's mordant bite, we can sharpen its corrosive edge by saying that worry gnaws away at our hearts.

Fretting makes men sore. First, Grendel's fretting made one of Beowulf's hearth companions sore for his evening's rest (*sum sáre angeald / aefenraeste*) and then his survivors felt sore at the death of their dear one (*sare æfter swæsne*). Like fretting, sore describes physical and mental pain; its cognate synonyms, sorry and sorrow, describe only mental pain: Grendel's carnage caused "the greatest heart-sorrow" (*hygesorga mæst*). Much later, when Macbeth shudders at the sight of his bloody hands, he calls it "a sorry sight," because it causes him an agony of guilt. Like the double edge of our contemporary understanding of sorry as regret for oneself or compassion for others, sore also moves between the physical and the mental— "Malice and hatred are very fretting and vexatious and apt to make our mind sore and uneasy" (1694). A sore point (1690) or a sore subject (1803) transfers personal pain to its impersonal cause. For Beowulf, also, sore things cause sorrow (*He ða mid þære sorhge, þe him sio sar belamp*). In slang, sore meaning angry still expresses the touchiness of a sore wound. Both fretful and sore people suffer emotional upset as a wound. Cut to the quick, they feel sore and fret over the injury.

Bitterness (971) bites with mental or physical pain, wounding with an intense animosity that pains more actively than sore. A sore subject, for example, causes bitter resentment. When, in addition, the milk of human kindness turns sour (1000), perversity makes men sour when goodness goes bad. Peevish, a likely doublet of perverse, describes a person perversely sour, and "childishly fretful." The sore subject that provokes a man's bitter resentment brings him in his peevish old age to a sour outlook on life.

Crabbed (1330) and cross (1523) express annoyance rather than animosity or bitter resentment. In origin, crabbed people fought like the clinging crustacean. Later (1375), a crabbed man, often a crabby (1550) old man, felt out of humor. As a boy, I called old ladies crabby when they did not put up with the hubbub of my playmates. Cross first meant crosswise and, much later (1639), crossed out of good humor. Cross, however, describes only a temporary condition. My mother, for example lamented that my thoughtless play made her cross. Crabbed describes a man inveterately cross. Luckily, I only had to deal with an occasionally cross parent and crabby neighbors.

Even lower in their degree of resentment, crank, cranky, and crook, from the PIE root for twist, describe twisted personality. What do cranks and crooks have in common? Crooks (1886) twist justice to fill their pockets, and cranks twist ideas to fill their egos. What do a bishop's crook and a crotchet needle have in common? They both end in a twist. Crotchety (1825) people with their crotchets, twists of personality, may be cranky and maybe even crabby. If you cross crotchety cranks or crooks, just cross their path and they will make you bear their cross.

Classical roots—*acer*, sharp and *asper*, rough—describe bitterness formally. Acrid feelings, turning to acrimony, speak acrimoniously. Acrid describes bitter, sour personality. Tempers sour first: "Their acrid temper turns, as soon as stirred," Cowper observes, "The milk of their good purpose all to curd" (1781). Acrid temper, consequently, turns acrimonious in disputes. Oliver Goldsmith coined cantankerous (1772) to describe an acrimonious personality. Rancorous, cankerous, cantankerous cranks plunge into acrimony with mulish delight.

Asperity (1664) describes roughness without bitterness. An impartial judge speaks with the asperity of the law without acerbity of heart. When a rough situation is drawn out (ex-), a person becomes ex-asperated (1534); when its bitterness is drawn out, his pain becomes exacerbated (1660). We feel exasperated when we see misery exacerbated.

So sadly, but so strongly, have sore and sorrow, crabby, cranky, bitter and cross been woven into human frailty's plaits an' pleats that these native words want no help from the learned. The same may be said about bitter old crabs as the last essay said about in-your-face scolds: if they understood the discriminating definitions of their art, they could recognize fret and crotchet, acrid and acrimony as its fine points, but their fretting makes them too busy to bother. Why should they exacerbate their black lily by discriminating between acrimony and asperity? This exasperating challenge to refine their word choice would just make them crabbier than ever. What a sorry plight for human sight!

## Words

Gnawed, sharpened, soured, twisted or struck, good feelings turn bad.

### PIE root *ed*, to eat (see the essay, "To Eat," for an elaboration of this root)

Latin: *edo edere* and *esus*, to eat
German: *fressen*, to devour—*Essen und Fressen*, to eat and to eat ravenously
    English: to fret (*Beowulf*)

### PIE root *ak*, sharp, sour

1. Latin:
    *acer acris* (genitive), sharp
      English: acrimony (1542), acrimonious (1775), acrid (1781)
    *acuo acuere*, to sharpen
      English: acumen (1531)
    *acidus*, acid; *vinum acetum*, sharp wine
      French: *vin aigre*, English vinegar
2. Greek: *oxos*, sharp, vinegar
    English: oxy-moron, sharp dullness
    Russian:
      уксус (uksus), vinegar ("sharp wine")
      острый (ostryy), sharp; Mr. Ostry / Mr. Sharp

### PIE root *guher*, warm, hot

English: furnace
Russian: горький (gor'kiy), bitter, unhappy

### PIE root *ger*, twist

Latin: *crux crucis*, cross
English: cross (1523), crank (1000), crook (1290), and cranky (1821)

### PIE root *tewk*, to strike

Latin: *tundo tundere* and *tusus*, to strike
    English: contusion and obtuse
Russian: Под-тачивать (pod-tachivat), to fret

# Rhetoric for Better or Worse

## 10. Short and Sweet

Even if we think that we are professing God's word or the court's jurisdiction, let's praise the virtue of making it short and sweet. Everyone—a wise man saying old saws or a storyteller telling tales, a poet inditing ditties or a judge indicting criminals, a sinner confessing sins or a believer professing belief—can profit from Polonius' aphorism: "brevity is the soul of wit." He realized that ancient aphorisms expressed the wisdom that characterizes wit. In fact, a few decades before Polonius' aphorism in 1603, the Latinate terminology for witty brevity had entered English. Good or bad, better or worse though our time on this terrestrial globe may be, let's seize the day by enjoying a brief of this wit. First, we'll make short-shrift of the nastily short, and then cut to the chase with the enjoyably brief.

Anglo-Saxon short (888) entered English long before Shakespeare's Polonius recommended Romance brevity (1509). In polite society, short-tempered folk demonstrate it as they cut annoyances short. From an Indo-European root, *ker*, to cut, short describes something cut short like shirts or skirts. 'Make it short!' demands brevity, even if it cuts meaning. Making a long story short, in short, cuts the palaver. When Gray in his *Elegy*, refers to "the short and simple annals of the poor," he means implicitly that they would have been longer, if a cruel fate had not cut them short. We are short with people whom we dislike. "I will be bitter with him," says Phoebe of a young man whom she dislikes, "and passing short" (*As You Like It*). Her short is not sweet, but bitter.

In modern English, we could translate "passing short" as "very curt." Curt (1630), entered English almost eight hundred years after its cognate, short. Curtailment is also at the root of curt which first described speech of dry, fragmented monosyllables and, by the nineteenth century, lack of courtesy. Curt, beyond short, but just a little short of gruff, describes abrupt dismissal.

People—especially country folk—suspect highfalutin verbosity. Like Calvin Coolidge from Vermont, the inhabitants of ancient Laconia had such a reputation for short shrift that laconic (1589) describes their speech. They studied to be brief: after the Laconians in Sparta received an enemy's boast that if he entered Sparta he would destroy it, they replied "If." Stripping statement of its polite padding, laconic brevity may seem impolite or, at best, brusque; but the Spartans picked the right conditional conjunction for an enemy!

Kurt fellows who cut it short could make their laconic statements more worthy of polite and enjoyably brief adjectives. As a noun, Romance brief first described the epitome of court documents in the Roman Empire. A lawyer takes a brief when he accepts a case and carries it in his brief case. The adjective brief, though a synonym of short, has retained its dignity and manners: we can speak briefly without being curt by cutting it short.

Having made short-shrift of Anglo-Saxon short and sweet, let's pass on to a classical threesome—concise, succinct and terse—that describe brevity in rhetoric. By *concisus*, cut up, Cicero refers to the stylistic brevity of Cato whose archaic brevity Cicero's prolixity eclipsed. No one could accuse Cicero of cutting it short! Entering English with this Ciceronian bias, concise (1590) at first referred to excessive brevity, but found a home in concise expressions of philosophical syllogisms or business letters. Classical pedigree has rescued concise from the surly end of short or curt, but not entirely from obscurity: "The concise style expresses not enough but leaves something to be understood" (1636).

*Succinctus*, describing a man with his robe "girt up" for a fast walk, also described a girt-up style, when it had come back into favor after Cicero. In English, succinct (1432) referred to style five years (1585) before concise. Not bearing the stigma of Cicero's bias against brevity of expression, succinct describes a verbal equivalent of the traveller who has consolidated his baggage, put on his walking shoes and readied himself for a long haul. We cut an account to make it concise; we compress it to make it succinct: a merchant's letter is concise and to the point; an author's narrative, succinct and clear.

The third and highest word of praise for the art of brevity, *tersus*, wiped clean or polished, draws its image from a *dies tersus*, a bright and sunny day, wiped clean of its clouds. In a style that is *tersus*, wiped as clean as polished and elegant marble, Horace put together such memorable phrases as *simplex munditiis*, "simple in elegance" and *Carpe diem*, "Seize the day!" Terse (1601), therefore, refers to polish and concise elegance.

A pithy (1529) narrative gets down to the core of meaning—picture the essential core of life in the pith of a tree or the meat of a nut. If this pith has weight, it is compendious (1388).

In sum, life is too short to be curt, but not so long that it should curtail our admiration for brevity. Curt or brief, take care not to become obscure—*Brevis esse laboro, obscurus fio*, Horace observes, "I labor to be brief, I become obscure." Get to the heart, polish it up and weigh it out in terse, pithy, compendious gems.

## Words

Whether we are working for good or evil, cutting our subject in many pieces or binding those pieces into one or weighing them all together clarifies meaning. The art of rhetoric provides the means for this clarity, although it has gained such a bad reputation that deceit instead of transparency may now seem to be its goal.

### PIE root, *ker / sker* to cut

1. Romance
   Latin: *curtus*, maimed, short
   Italian and Spanish: *corto*; French: *court*, have been cut
   German: *kurz*; English: curt (1630)
2. Germanic
   English: short (888)
3. Slavic
   Russian: краткий (kratkiy), brief, concise

### PIE root *braghu*, short

Latin: *brevis*, short
   Italian and Spanish: *breve*; French: *bref*
   English: brief, as noun (1292), as adjective (1325)

### PIE root *kenk*, to bind, clasp

Latin:
   *cingo cingere*, to tie, to gird
   *succinctus*, with robe "girt up" and ready for swift movement
      Italian: *succinto*; Spanish: *sucinto*
      French and English: succinct

### PIE root *sek*, to cut

Latin: *concido concidere* and *concisus*, cut up
   English: concise (1590)

### PIE root *terh*, to rub

Latin: *tergo tergere* and *tersus*, to wipe clean, polish
   English: detergent; terse (1601)
Russian: тереть (teret'), to rub, polish

### PIE root *pen*, to draw, stretch

Latin: *compendo compendere*, to weigh together
   English: compendious (1388)

## 11. Articulating the Flow

Brevity is the soul of wit, but a wit should know its limits. *Praecipitandus est liber spiritus*—when "the free spirit must be set in headlong motion," words flow, before we can tell their number. As stories evolve, storytellers elaborate; as truth evolves, philosophers explicate; and passionately poetic souls effuse beyond limits. "I'm sensible redundancy is wrong," Byron laments, "but could not for the muse of me put less in't." Much less sensible, a tedious wind bag puts more in't: his wit knows too much to keep silent and too little to be brief. Tediously diffusing for an ego or passionately effusing for a muse—how easily can we tell the difference?—either one can have the good sense to control words in their flow.

Prolix and diffuse describe prose that overflows. The prolix overflows in minute, usually tedious, detail. Prolixity describes lengthy, detailed narrative. Literary critics deprecate it: "Conscious dullness has little right to be prolix" (1758), Dr. Johnson pronounced. The diffuse, flowing off in a flood and drowning in details, inundates the succinct. Dif-fused shares its root and meaning with con-fused: language can be so diffused, observed one author in 1535, "that it may not be understood." Emma in Jane Austen's novel suggests a gender distinction for the diffuse, when she identifies a proposal of marriage written by a man, but rewritten by a woman, as "too strong and concise, not diffuse enough for a woman." A man, even a scatterbrain, she speculates, may, from the depths of his manhood, summon strength to be concise.

Dr. Johnson would deprecate the prolix or the diffuse; but with some drops of honey, he might praise it as mellifluous. Mellifluous wisdom approaches Horace's ideal of joining "the useful with the sweet," *utile dulci*, the honey on the cup of wisdom. Mellifluous prose can make the prolix or the diffuse enjoyable, but we can enjoy Alexander Pope's poetry as concisely mellifluous: "Ye gentle gales, beneath my body blow, / And softly lay me on the waves below!" How mellifluously do his phrases flow!

Poets admire Alexander Pope's felicitous poetry. Whether or not they make a happy choice of just the right word on their own, they can hope to enjoy good luck in their search. Felicity (1386) describes luck helping art to find the right word, "a happy faculty in the art of speech." It derives its root from Latin *felix* that first described fertile fruit. With a felicity of expression, Pope laetified his words, making them, metaphorically, fruitful and happy.

In the age of Shakespeare, other words described prolixity—fluent, redundant, voluble, glib and facile. Fluent first described a flowing style. Fluent speakers have passed the stage of halting articulation. We appreciate mother nature's redundant blessings redounding to our good, but redundant words overflow artlessly. Voluble and glib (1602) also describe artless, endless flow. Voluble words just roll along. Voluble sophistry or evil should be subject to control, and even kind-hearted goodness needs it: "Her tongue, so voluble and kind," Prior describes thoughtless talk, "It always runs before her mind" (1720). The glib—Dutch *glibberen*, to slide—are too slippery for their own good: "I want that glib and oily art / To speak and purpose not," Cordelia protests to King Lear. Glib talkers, with too little consideration or too much craft, appear facile, which, in 1590, first described the affable and debonair. Fluent words flow, redundant ones overflow, the voluble keep on flowing, the facile flow easily and the glib slide by.

With the good luck to find just the right words, we hope to express them in articulate concinnity (1531). We articulate words when we speak more coherently than grumbling or groaning, but we can only claim to be articulate when we speak artfully and succinctly. Art as articulation joins limbs in a graceful body. Concinnity (1531), as an ancient grammarian defined it—*concinnare est apte componere*, "to harmonize is to compose aptly"—describes gracefully balanced articulation.

Prolixity flows off diffusely; but rhetoric, which many suspect as tedious or bombastic, can rescue it from flowing tediously or piling up bombastically. By its course, it schools prolix words as they roll off in theirs—its words, felicitously chosen, and fluently facile, mellifluous in wisdom and harmonious in concinnity.

## Words

Five PIE roots for liquid, water, rolling and pouring describe flowing words naturally overflowing.

1. **PIE root *leiku*, to flow away**
   Latin: *liqueo liquere* and *lixus*, to be liquid, to flow; *prolixus*, flowing forth
   English: prolix (1432) and prolixity (1374)
2. **PIE root *ghewd*, to pour**
   Latin: *fundo fundere* and *fusus*, to pour; *diffusus*, poured in different directions
   English: diffuse (1400)
3. **PIE root *aue*, water**
   Latin: *unda*, wave; *undo undare*, to rise in waves
   English: redundant (1604)

4. **PIE root *velu*, to roll**
   Latin: *volvo volvere* and *volutus*, to roll; *volubilis*, rolling
   English:
   voluble (1588)
   Volvo, "I roll," a car company that first made ballbearings
5. **PIE root *beu*, flowing**
   Latin: *fluo fluere*, to flow; and *mel mellis*, honey
   English: fluent (1589); mellifluous (1432)

## Two PIE roots describe art and articulation

1. **PIE root *ar*, to join**
   Latin: *ars artis*, joining, art; *artus*, joint
   English: articulate (1586) and to articulate (1616)
2. **PIE root *kelh*, to turn**
   Greek: *colon*, limb
   English: colon, punctuation mark (:), separating a limb in the sentence
   tricolon, a sentence with three limbs
   Russian: члено-раздельный (chleno-razdel'-nyy), articulate, literally, section of limb; член (chlen), limb + раздел (razdel), section, from рассекать (rassekat), to cut

# The Four Elements and the Elemental

. . . .

# 12. Earth

In Sonnet 146, Shakespeare laments his wasteful self-importance. To emphasize the limitation which this waste imposes, he addresses himself as "poor soul, the center of my sinful earth." His earth encompasses the limited territory of his "poor soul." It is as small as his ego makes it. Earth is large, but each man's individual earth is small. Shakespeare's meditative use of this word points to its wide range of meaning. Along with air, fire and water, earth is elemental, but man expends so much of himself on this element that he makes much of the expense.

In the beginning, "the Lord God formed man of the dust of the ground and breathed into his nostrils the breath of life" (*Genesis* 2.7). By a word play in Hebrew, untranslatable in English, man, *adam*, is synonymous with *adamah*, earth. By another, Latin *homo*, man, is synonymous with *humus*, earth. Both the Hebrew and the Latin etymologies bring man down to the earth, which has given him birth. Human mortality stands in contrast to divine immortality.

With more dignity, the Hebraic "son of man" designates man in contrast to God. As God looks down from heaven on sons of men, He wonders what they could mean to him: "What is man, that thou art mindful of him?" the Psalmist asks, "and the son of man, that thou visitest him?" (*Psalm* 8.4). God, the Psalmist continues, has made man "a little lower than the angels, and hast crowned him with glory and honour." Birth gives humanity its substance and sets its limit, but God has crowned this lowly beginning with enough glory that a "son of man" can disparage a lowly birth. Man can call another man a *terrae filius,* son of the earth, with parentage so undistinguished that he may as well claim earth as mother. Few men join Emily Dickinson in enjoying the thought that they are nobodies—"I'm Nobody. Who are you? / Are you—Nobody—too?"

Earth has given man his substance, which it reclaims at death: "In the sweat of thy face shalt thou eat bread, till thou return unto the ground; for out of it wast thou taken: for dust thou art, and unto dust shalt thou return" (*Genesis* 3.19). After death, man has traditionally been put in the ground, inhumed or interred, in a shroud or a coffin, the latter a civilized version of his fate proclaimed in *Genesis*.

Before it has received him back into its bosom, earth gives man a living by the "sweat" of his brow. The earth that nurtures plants English calls by its Latin name, humus. The OED defines it best: "the dark-brown or black substance resulting from the slow decomposition of organic matter on or near the surface of the earth, which, with the products of decomposition of various rocks, forms the soil in which plants grow." No wonder man is said to come from, and return to, the earth, since he shares the fate of all "organic matter."

Earth-bound, man stands opposite divinity; he also stands on *terra firma*, dry land opposite water. Cognate with the adjective torrid, *terra* designates land dried by the sun. Land, not earth, best fits its meaning. Territory reflects the meaning of its Latin root, because it parcels out earth within boundaries. Terraces also set boundaries for land graded on a hillside. To describe the whole world, the Romans expanded it in the phrase *orbis terrarum*, orb of lands. Very much in the middle of their orb of lands, Mediterranean, "in the middle of land," modifies the noun in the phrase *Mare Mediterraneum*, "sea in the middle of land." Many lands of the Roman Empire bounded the Mediterranean.

Subterranean characterizes *terra* in its other English derivatives. The "son of earth" should feel a kinship with terriers. He came from earth and they dig in it to scare up rabbits, so that he may serve them up in savory stews. What more basic earthenware might he use to serve these stews than terra cotta, baked earth, tureens?

Six hundred years after the first appearance of earth, its adjective earthy brought things down to earth. Raw onions, for example, have an earthy taste which they lose when cooked. As cognates, raw and crude describe uncooked vegetable matter or flesh in nature. Raw tastes do not usually appeal to cultivated palates. Applied to humanity, earthy describes man in nature, unrefined and uncultured. "Sons of the earth" should enjoy earthy manners, activities and tastes, since they are raw, so to speak, without preparation. Cultivated dining calls raw vegetables crudités, but cultivated manners call raw language crude.

Adam received his matter and his name from earth; but, from God, he breathed in proud spirits that rise above it. Once above it, he disdains a *terrae filius* for a common birth. Also above it, he measures it out for his own territory, distinct from others'. Back on it and from it, his earth-bound life gains a living by the sweat of his face, but his aspiring pride disparages this living as earthy. After he has wrested more from the earth in life than he received at birth, he returns to it in death. Man's "poor soul," Shakespeare's sonnet concludes, with "so short a lease" on his own "sinful earth," feeds "on Death, that feeds on men."

## Words

*Homo sapiens* aspires to heaven, but earthy nature keeps him down to earth. It humbles him from birth and inhumes him after death. He lives on its territories and off its humus. It is as large or as small as his world makes it.

### PIE root *ghdhem*, earth, in three families

1. Greek: *chthon*, earth; *chamai*, on the earth
    English:
        chthonic, of the earth, as in chthonic deities
        autochthonous, of the earth itself
        chameleon, a lion on the earth; camomile, apple on the earth
2. Latin:
    *humus*, earth; *humilis*, low, close to the earth, humble
    *homo*, man, as a creature of the earth, a plausible cognate of *humus*
        English:
            humus (1796), planting soil
            to inhume and exhume; posthumous, humble, humility
        Russian: гу́мус (gúmus), humus
3. Slavic
    Polish: *ziemia*
    Russian:
        земля (zemlya), earth, land; заминдар (zamindar), landholder
        змея (zmeya), snake (creature of the earth)
        земля-ника (zemlyanika), strawberries, earth-berries, found on the
            ground (*cf.* German *Erdbeere*)
        Мать Земля (mat zemlya), Mother Earth, Russian folk divinity

### PIE root *trast*, to dry up

Latin: *terra*, dry land, earth; *orbis terrarum*, the earth (the orb of lands)
    French: *terre*, earth; Spanish: *tierra*; Italian: *terra*
    English:
        to inter (1303), to bury
        terrestrial (1432) and territory (1432)
        terrier (1440), a dog burrowing in the earth
        terrae filius (1590), son of earth
        tureen (1706), earthenware; terra cotta (1722), "cooked earth"
    Russian: территория (territorija), territory

### PIE root *er*, earth

Dutch: *aardvark*, literally, earth pig
English: earth (950); earthy (1555)

## 13. Man and Woman

When Carl Linnaeus named man *Homo sapiens* in 1758, he marked him as distinctly wise. Linguists also trace this distinction back to an etymology when they link man as cognate with mind. One PIE linguist has questioned—perhaps facetiously—the wisdom of both links, made "presumably," he observes, "under the illusion that man is a cognitive creature." Man, made in God's image according to *Genesis*, can claim to have more wisdom than apes, but many a modern moralist may question how much good this has done him when she observes his preference in language to distinguish man more than woman. We can feel embarrassment when we realize that our words preserve fossils of such archaic belief.

In spite of *Homo sapiens*' claim to cognition in the Enlightenment, God gave him a humble origin. After God named him Adam, linking him to the earth, from which he was formed, He gave him authority to name his fellow creatures on earth. God's name for Adam encompasses both male and female: "Male and female created he them; and blessed them, and called their name Adam" (*Genesis* 5.2). Other words for man similarly bring him to her epicene center.

Man's first name in English alluded to humanity without a distinction in gender. In A.D. 825, man referred to both man and woman: "The Lord put but one pair of men in paradise" (1597), a biblical scholar wrote in reference to our first parents. In Hebrew, Adam means man as mankind generically; but, specifically, *ish*, man, and *isshah*, woman, allow the play on the two words in the description of woman's creation from Adam's rib: "She shall be called woman (*isshah*), because she was taken out of man (*ish*)." Jerome by translating *ish* and *isshah*, as *vir* and *virago* in the *Vulgate*, Luther by translating them as *Mann* and *Männin* in the *Lutherbibel*, and King James's team by "man" and "woman"—all three translations—recreate the Hebrew word play. After man referring to both, woman from man offers the alternative.

Like Hebrew, Greek and Latin have the advantage of separate words for mankind and man, but their English derivatives have taken very different paths. Greek *anthropos* refers to man as mankind. Philanthropic, true to its root, describes a man loving and benefitting mankind. Greek *aner/andros* refers to a man distinct from a woman. Philandering takes an odd path from its Greek root. It describes a man's loving women with frivolous intentions. Philanthropy is a virtue; philandering may be not an unquestioned vice, but it does mankind little good.

Latin *vir* refers to a man distinct from a woman. Virility describes his physical power. Virtue, originally describing his moral power, has gone through many transformations. Cicero tells a story about humanity as the complement and corrective to virility: Caius Marius, a stoic old Roman endured pain like a man (*vir*), but he remained sensible enough as a man (*homo*) not to seek it out. Man's humanity balances his virtue and virility with humane understanding.

Like Adam and *anthropos*, Latin *homo* also refers to man as mankind: *Homo sapiens* describes mankind. In English, humane describes a kind and benevolent humanity, but the parallel with the Greek derivatives stops there. Virtue and virility distinguish between virile manliness and virtuous humanity. The Greek derivatives balance philanthropists with philanderers; the Latin balance of virility with virtue opens a broader field.

Although Alexander Pope reminds us that "the proper study of mankind is man" (1732), English still lacks a neat distinction between the generic and specific use of man. It suffers from this lack. (French has made up for this lack by deriving from *homme* the pronoun *on*, meaning we, you, someone or they.) We may realize that man refers to both men and women in the word mankind, but pronouns like anyone and someone as generic alternatives to man still put us in a dilemma: anyone can realize that they still give him a problem. Man, what a drag it is to feel pangs of guilt when the chicks accuse us of misogyny because we refer—without a second thought—to a man strutting his stuff!

We see the depth of verbal androcracy in English having a word for a man's misogynism early in the seventeenth century, but not, until late in the nineteenth, for a woman's misandrism, a word not included in the first edition of the OED. Discovering such words or discovering that they have been ignored is like walking through a museum filled with instruments of torture: how could people have lived—and talked—like that? By Jove, it's enough to make us all misanthropes or should I say misandrists!

Let's hope for better words in better worlds. In English, pronouns like yo or they/them, replacing he/she/it, balance the scale between male and female persons, just as French *on* makes us all equal. The ancient Greeks' concept of beauty as epicene shows a middle ground. Their statues combine the best of a handsome male and a beautiful female. When a man finds this balance, they—*pace* schoolmarms, not 'he' or 'she,'—can feel that they belong. When a man grows from this center, they approach the angels.

## Words

Etymologies take us back to basics: by their roots, women bear life and nourish it; and men rise from the earth, virtuous and strong.

**Four PIE roots for man**

1. **PIE root *mon*, man; from PIE root *men*, mind: Man has mind.**
   German: *Mann*
   English: man (825), male or female; (1000), male
      to man (1122), to supply a force for defense
      woman (893), literally wife-man, a female. Wife may refer to a veil, as Latin *nupta*, the woman veiled for nuptials.
      mankind (1300)
   Russian: муж (muzh), husband

2. **PIE root *nert*, man**
   Greek:
   *aner andros*, man; *andreia*, courage
      Greek English:
         to philander; Andrew and Andrea are courageous
         androcracy, rule of men (*cf.* democracy, plutocracy)
   *anthropos*, man
      Greek English: philanthropic (1789), misanthropic (1762)

3. **PIE root *ghdhem*, of the earth**
   Latin: *homo*, man; *homo sapiens*, wise man (nomenclature of Carl Linnaeus)
   Italian: *uomo*
   French:
      *homme*
      *on* (derived from *homme*), we, you, one, someone, or they
   Spanish: *hombre*
   English: humanity (1386), kindness and benevolence; humane (1500)

4. **PIE root *uiro*, man**
   Latin: *vir*, man; *virtus*, the quality of a man, virtue
      (*cf.* Greek *andreia*; Russian мужество)
   Italian: *virtù*; French: *vertu*; Spanish: *virtud*
   English:
      virtue (1225), quality of a man; virile (1490), manly
      virago (1000), used by Jerome in *Genesis* 5.2

**Two PIE roots for woman**

1. **PIE root *guen* related to *gen*, bearing life**
   Greek: *gyne*, woman
      Greek English:
         gynaecocracy (1612), gynarchy (1577), misogynist (1620)
         androgynous (1651), both male and female, epicene

Russian: жена (zhena), wife (see the essay on marriage for words from this root)
Germanic English: quean (archaic) and queen, woman
2. **PIE *dhel*, to suckle**
Latin: *femina*, woman
Italian: *femmina*; French: *femme*

# 14. Life

## Life Made Lively

No man's life fills the earth; because, no matter how lively, it cannot attain the variety of mankind's. Contrasting the two Greek nouns for life may start to demonstrate its potential: *bios*, life as in biology, and *zoe*, life as in zoology, distinguish between animal and human life. A lion, the king of beasts, can never write his zoography—in fact, zoography can not exist—but the lowliest peasant in the kingdoms of men can write his biography. Man's proud spirit makes something of life, celebrating and enhancing it, as a lion can not, but expressing this enhancement in language stretches and strains the noun life and its compounds. When man tries to put some life into it, he finds a tradition of language to describe his accomplishment. Let's get lively and see how vivacious it can make us.

Some may say that life just is; but only God, the great I AM, is. Vital describes the constant change in the process that is human life: the vital spirit moves respiration and circulation in organs that the Romans called *vitalia*, the vitals, the heart and lungs energizing life. With advancing age, vital spirits diminish until they no longer have the power to sustain life. Vitality gives youth its special energy. It represents that spirit of natural man that can make much of life.

Beyond the spirit of his natural self, man also comes to know the spiritual. As soon as the noun life first came to life in English, it inherited a Judaeo-Christian distinction similar to that between *zoe* and *bios*: corporal and spiritual life. In traditional language, animal spirits and the spiritual soul animate the body. In his spiritual soul, man reaches out. To sustain life, for example, a spider lives off flies; as a man can, so to speak, live off men. Uniquely, man can also live off the land by his industry to reach out to men and benefit mankind. He sustains spiritual life by living up to ideals and living down mistakes. Romance has contributed a few lively words that define his reaching out and up.

The synonyms, Romance vivacity, and English liveliness, entered the language within a couple of generations of each other. Liveliness can describe age living into its tenth decade or youth exuding wit, imagination and style. Vivacity, the continental import, refers to all that liveliness implies, but it has enjoyed greater popularity. Liveliness pales beside vivacity's verve. With old-fashioned Italian or French panache, it shines as the concomitant of beauty and grace in women. Vivacity set the stage for the even greater panache of vivacious two hundred years later.

Writers describing liveliness or vivacity have chosen the Romance verb to vivify more than the English verb to enliven. Extraordinarily, Romance vivifying predates the native Germanic enlivening by almost a century. An artist enlivens his painting with color. A preacher so enlivens his sermons with wit that he enlivens the believer with spiritual knowledge. To vivify makes nature shine a little brighter: "The bright autumnal sunshine was vivifying the many-tinted trees of the Bois de Boulogne." It even brings moral topics to life: "Human beings can not dispense with some vivifying element in their religion."

Germanic lively, on the other hand, predating Romance vivid by six hundred years, gained a firm place before its Romance synonym made its appearance. Vivid made up for its late arrival by a grand sweep: "Sweet sounds awaken latent harmonies within us, and these produce a vivid idea of the beautiful (1806). Literati sought out vivid to hyperbolize their profusion: "Every page teems with vivid thought and glowing fancy." Artists embraced it: "The love of vivid colors seems to increase as we descend south." Lively has stayed up north where it belongs: "A description gives us more lively ideas than the sight of things themselves." When it looked south, it did so objectively: "The French like all lively folks are extreme in everything." Or it looks even more objectively at those who seem to have gone south: "Men of lively imaginations are not often known for solidity of judgement." Germanic folk conjure up vivid pictures of people who get too lively.

Man's life can reach only so far. His spirit can rise on the wings of the morning, and descend to the depths of the sea, to paraphrase the Psalmist, but greater thoughts, like grains of sand, outnumber and overwhelm his own. Vivacious, in its "reachings and graspings," reaches far—often too far—beyond lively and vivid. It has described man's soul seemingly without man: "that nimble quick vivacious orb, all ear all eye, with rays round shining bright" (H. More, *Song of the Soul*, 1647). Vivacious students, teachers soberly admonish and prescribe, should demonstrate that they have learned specifics. "Vivaciously surly" French soldiers and "vivaciously charming" (1816) French women suggest that vivacity can overreach humanity in persistence and manner. Look alive! should motivate vital spirits to live a life that is lively but also livable.

## Words

Life and its lively compounds in English make the most of their PIE root *leip*. They are complemented in English by Romance derivatives from the PIE root *guei*. Together, these derivatives create Romance and Germanic pairs like alive and vivid, enliven and vivify, liveliness and vivacity.

One PIE root gives the Germanic language family words about life and living:

### PIE root *leip*, to anoint, stick, continue, remain, live

Latin: *adipum*, animal fat
    English: adipose, of body tissue used for fat
German: *Leben*, to live and life; *Leib*, originally, life; body
    English:
        to live (825), alive (1000), life (900), lively (1000)
        livelihood (1000), liveliness (1398), to enliven (1633), livable (1664)

### Five families of the PIE root *guei*, life

Greek *bios*; *cf.* parallel in Latin *vita*.
1. Greek: *bios*, <u>extensive</u> life (of humans)
    English: biology, biography and amphibious
    Russian: биография (biografija), biography; биология (biologiya), biology
2. Latin: *vivo vivere* and *victus*,[4] to live; *vita*, life; *vivus*, alive; *vivax vivacis*, lively
    Italian: *vivere*, *vita*, *vivo* and *vivace*; to live, life, alive, vivacious
    French: *vivre*, *vie*, *vivant* and *vivace*
    Spanish: *vivir*, *vida*, *vivo* and *vivaz*
    English:
        vital (1386), vitality (1592), vivacity (1432),
        vivacious (1645), vivid (1638), to vivify (1548)
Greek *zoe* has a parallel in Russian жизнь (zhizn').
3. Greek: *zoe*, <u>intensive</u> life (of animals)—only humans write biographies.
    English: zoology and zoo
    Russian: зоология (zoologiya), zoology
4. Russian:
    жить (zhit'), to live
    живѣте (živěte), Live!, representing ж (zhe), letter of Cyrillic alphabet
    жизнь (zhizn'), life; жилище (ziliste), dwelling

5. German: *keck*, bold, sassy
   English: quick, meaning alive, surviving in three phrases:
   1. "the quick and the dead"
   2. to cut to the quick (the living flesh),
   3. the quick flesh beneath fingernails

# 15. Air

Of the four elements, air is everywhere but nowhere, invisible but ubiquitous. The OED says as much in a fuller definition: "transparent, invisible, inodorous, tasteless gaseous substance which envelopes the earth, and is breathed by all land animals." This far, the definition itself seems transparent, but it goes on to becloud the air by contrasting airy myth with modern mechanism: "one of the four 'elements' of the ancients, but now known to be a mechanical mixture of oxygen and nitrogen." "But" opens a Pandora's box, from which miasmic "mechanical mixture" escapes. Its miasmic mixture puts air somewhere *but nowhere* anyone wants to be.

Quality of life takes starts with quality of air. In the industrial world, we can not be sure of breathing the fresh morning air that filled the lungs of our Edenic ancestors. With no certainty of its quality, we qualify air by the adjective ambient (1596). Ambient, by its root, describes anything that goes around: in Roman antiquity ambitious men literally 'went around' the Forum soliciting votes. It also describes anything that surrounds: from the ambient misery of poverty, people run into the ambient arms of charity. Since its first use, ambient has described sky, clouds, winds, and planets. Food critics use its noun form ambience to describe the atmosphere of restaurants. The air around us should be the same wherever we go; but because it is not, ambient air has come to describe air in open air at a particular time and in a particular place.

Ambient air surrounds us in a particular sphere, so to speak, of our activity; air surrounds and envelops our terrestrial sphere. Atmosphere—"the mass of aeriform fluid surrounding the earth"—forms a sphere surrounding our sphere. In origin, it served to represent the air (atmo-) sphere that astronomers observed around planets. Greek atmo-sphere means air-globe or air-ambient in Latinate English.

Just as ambient air carries particulates, usually polluted ones, atmosphere carries "all manner of exhalations," literal or metaphorical. In heat and humidity, for example, urban atmosphere can be stifling. On the other hand, John Stuart Mill has celebrated the atmosphere of freedom: "Genius can only breathe freely in the atmosphere of freedom." In this liberating atmosphere, we might happily endure the stifling heat of a city.

After *aer*, Latin used the word *aura* to represent breeze or atmospheric influences such as light or heat. In English, it describes the distinctive but intangible exhalation of a person's character, an individual's atmosphere or ambient air. Character, effusing its aura, envelops a person, as atmosphere envelops a planet. Embracing spiritual values, sentimental Victorians spoke of being "wrapped in the aura of ineffable love" (1859).

Even though air first appears as "transparent" and "invisible," the real and ideal stuff of mankind so pervades it that air can be, so to speak, palpable. It describes that certain something in a man's distinctive appearance or style. His hat, for example, on a tilt, gives him a jaunty air. Like its synonym aura, it aspires, like the dandy taking on airs. How often do his dreams make much of airy nothing! Without the hard work that makes aspirations real, goodness for many people dissipates into so much airy nothing.

Some people consider air itself just so much airy nothing, no more than "the free space above our heads, in which birds fly and clouds float." Natural science, however, dignifies terms relating to this aeriform fluid by giving them the Latin form *aer*: aeronauts piloting aeroplanes know aerodynamics. Aerophobia does not dismay their aery hearts, although aeromancy may instruct them. By practicing that mantic art, a moistened finger in the wind divines where it blows and what it bodes. An aerialist, before funambulating across Niagara Falls, practices it to his benefit.

We can not live without air, but we can not live with it when it blows up a storm. Wind shares its root with weather. In summer, it bestows God's air-conditioning; in winter, it wields the Devil's pitchfork. Under that diabolical sting, we take a winter walk to catch a breath of fresh air only to find that the cold wind so takes our breath away that we scarcely catch a breath at all. Weather is all about wind.

Air melds so much in the air of life and consciousness that we have turned it to many purposes. When Spring is in the air, we catch a breath of fresh air, humming a happy air as we go. Living in air, ambient air, and atmospheres, we also create our own. We breathe it literally and exude it metaphorically. Shakespeare's Prospero disparages it:

> These our actors, as I foretold you, were all spirits, and
> Are melted into air, into thin air.
> . . . We are such stuff
> As dreams are made on, and our little life
> Is rounded with a sleep (*The Tempest*).

But, out of thin air, dreams persistently take shape: the poet's pen, another Shakespearean character observes, gives to "airy nothing a local habitation and a name." With the motto, *Dum spiro spero*, "While I breathe, I hope," we make thin air thick with life.

## Words

German *Luft* gave English lyft, its first word for air. The word air itself first entered English as a relatively late import from Latin. The history of air aspires to both the Germanic lofty and the Romance airy.

### PIE root *aue, ue, ven*, wind, vapor

1. Sanskrit: *mahatma*, great (mah-) spirit (-atma), Mahatma Gandhi, "great spirit"
2. Latin: *aer*—borrowed from the Greek—air
   Italian: *aria*, air and song (*cf.* Russian ария [arija])
   French: *air*
   English:
      aerobic, relating to the body's use of air; aeroplane (1869)
      air (1300), airy (1398); air, a light and sprightly tune
3. Latin: *aura*, air, breeze, atmospheric influences such as light or heat
   French: *orage*, storm
   English: aura (1732), a subtle exhalation from any substance
   Russian: аура (aura), aura
4. Greek: *aetmos*, vapor
   English: atmosphere (1638)
   Russian: атмосфера (atmosfera), *cf.* воздух (vozdux), air

### PIE root *uendh*, to turn, wind, wander; and *ve*, to blow

1. Latin: *ventus*, wind
   Italian: *vento*; French: *vent*; Spanish: *viento*
   English: vent, to ventilate
2. German: *Wind*
   English:
      wind; wend (past tense, went)
      window, the wind's eye; weather, the way the wind blows
3. Russian: ветер (veter), wind, breeze

### PIE root *aidh*, to burn

Latin: *aether*—borrowed from Greek—upper, purer, air, ether
   English: ethereal (1513), impalpable, refined and delicate
Russian: эфирный (efírnyj), ethereal

PIE root *ghed*, to unite, be suitable
English: to gather and good
Russian: год (god), year, time; по-года (pa-goda), weather

# 16. Breath

In its first meaning, breath emitted a fragrance like the breath of fresh air that John Milton welcomed as "gentle breaths from rivers pure." Eventually, the odor also emanated as an exhalation of human respiration, like the rabble's "stinking breath" that the noble Casca scorns. Breath is complicated enough that it deserves more than one word to describe it. Inhalation, exhalation, and respiration elaborate the three steps of breathing. Let's take a deep breath and hope for inspiration in our aspiration to elaborate spiration.

Respiration brings together both inhaling and exhaling. When we wish to purify the air that we inhale and exhale, we wear a mask called a respirator. Another pair of verbs, inspire and expire, have also meant the same thing as inhale and exhale. William Harvey (1578–1657) observed that the lungs "inspire and expire the air," with difficulty, in the foul atmosphere of the city, but easily, in the pure air of the country. Inspiration and expiration have coordinated in respiration, but they have followed divergent paths of meaning.

Long before it entered English, inspiration had aspired to a high calling. In Vergil's *Aeneid*, before "faithful Aeneas" (*pius Aeneas*) dares to enter the underworld, he consults the Sibyl in whom Apollo, the Delian prophet (*Delius vates*), "inspires a great mind and spirit" (*magnam cui mentem animumque Delius inspirat vates*). More than three hundred years later, Jerome, in his Latin translation of the Bible, the Vulgate, translated *Genesis* 2.7—"The Lord God breathed into his nostrils the breath of life"—*inspiravit in faciem eius spiraculum vitæ*, "he inspired the breath of life into his countenance." He represented "breath of life" as *spiraculum vitae*, more commonly understood as *spiritum vitae*. Milton uses the phrase "breath of life" as synonymous with "the spirit of man." Like inspiration, spirit also aspired to spiritual heights.

Jerome used inspiration in his Biblical translation even where it did not seem to belong. He translated the apostle Peter's reference to the "holy men of God" being "moved by the Holy Spirit" as their "having being inspired by the Holy Spirit" (*Spiritu Sancto inspirati*). The reference in the Greek text to their "being carried" (*pheromenoi*) Jerome translates as "having been inspired." People have long respected inspiration, even when they did not know where it came from: "The noblest souls of whatever creed have insisted on the necessity of an inspiration," Matthew Arnold observed in 1865, "a living emotion to make moral action perfect." To whatever source they might have ascribed it—pagans, to Delian Apollo; Jews and Christians, to Yahweh; and skeptics, to some power above their understanding—all men have respected inspiration as a gift.

Two more compounds complement the spirit of inspiration. A soul, once inspired, then aspires and also perspires up the steep and stoney path toward heavenly beatitude or some goal, usually one high and holy. (Perversely, a criminal mind may aspire to perfect the art of robbing banks.) Inspiration, aspiration, perspiration—the engine of the human spirit arises from respiration, simple breathing, an automatic function of human physiology. Physiological mechanism and creative genius encompass the poles of human life.

Just as God has "breathed into" Adam's nostrils "the breath of life," life passes away from the body with the final expiration of breath. Dryden's Homer describes the death of Hector at the hands of Achilles as a departure of the "laboring breath" from the "load of clay" that, just moments before, had been "the manly body":

> Hector ceased. The Fates suppress'd his laboring breath,
> And his eyes stiffen'd at the hand of death;
> To the dark realm the spirit wings its way,
> (The manly body left a load of clay,)
> And plaintive glides along the dreary coast,
> A naked, wandering, melancholy ghost!

The breath, *spiritus* in Latin and *pneuma* in Greek, "wings its way" out of the body. Homer shares with Thomas Hobbes a skepticism about the destination of the spirit: "God only knows," Hobbes lamented, "what becomes of a man's spirit when he expires." With his last breath, Hector expires his soul, "a naked, wandering, melancholy ghost." Some breath of life enters man by inspiration and leaves him—God knows where—with the final expiration. Whatever the destination, expiring words in the final breath have always weighed heavy in the scale of life. The devoted soul, with his last words, repeats the name of his beloved.

The dusky origin of Russian душа (dusha), spirit, confirms the image of the spirit shrouded in mist. душа is also related to the Russian verb to breathe, дохнуть (doxnut), and the noun, вдох (vdox), breath. Since it seems unlikely for breath and breathing to be associated with fog, their origins must have been shrouded in the mists of time. In the evolution of the English spirit and its compounds, air came first and then it was inhaled. Smoke and dusk have put the origin of душа in the fog.

Breath breathes a world both physical and spiritual. When "the Lord God breathed into his nostrils the breath of life," Adam respired, then aspired. Breathing never got him into trouble. Aspiring certainly did. He aspired and then with Eve he conspired to their ruin. Their conspiracy dissipated the God-inspired breath of life and it expired souls in this dissipation.

## Words

Five PIE roots describe breath. Steam and smoke share roots with it. Since respiration incorporates spirit, Slavic and Romance share soul with breath.

1. **PIE root *speis*, to breathe**
    Latin: *spiro spirare*, to breathe; and *spiritus*, breath
       Italian: *respirare* and *espirito*
       French: *respirer* and *esprit*
       Spanish: *respirar* and *espiritu*
       English:
          spirit (1250), inspiration (1303); to inspire (1382), to breathe life into
          to conspire (1382), to breathe together for a bad purpose
          to respire (1425), to expire (1400), to aspire (1460), to perspire (1646)
2. **PIE root *bhret*, exhalation from heat, steam**
    English:
       breath (893) odor; (1340), warm air exhaled from the lungs
       to breathe (1300)
3. **PIE root *henslare*, to breathe**
    Latin: *halo halare*, to breathe
       English:
          to inhale (1725), to breathe in
          to exhale (1400), to evaporate; (1589), to breathe out
4. **PIE root *hehtmen*, to breathe**
    German: *atmen*, to breathe
5. **PIE root *dheu*, smoke, dust**
    1. Greek: *thumos*, spirit, soul, anger, thyme (an incense); *thuma*, sacrifice
    2. Latin: *tus, turis*, incense; *fumus*, smoke
       French: *fumée*; Italian: *fume*; Spanish: *humo*

English:
>thyme, an herb used as incense; thurifer, bearing incense fume; dusk, misty twilight

3. Germanic and Slavic
   German: *dunst,* fog
   English: deer, a breathing animal
   Polish: *dusza,* spirit, soul
   Russian:
   >дух (dux), spirit, ghost; and дохнуть (doxnut), to breathe
   >дым (duim), smoke; вдох (vdox), breath
   >Compounded, these words provide others for sanity or insanity, *etc.*

# 17. Soul

## The Ghost of an Idea about Soul

The incorporeal eludes concrete understanding, but theologians boldly seek to know the unknowable; and poets boldly seek to materialize the immaterial. In its words for soul, language gives both poets and theologians a start. To put some flesh on the bones of this abstraction, it has drawn from the three mercurial elements: air, fire, and water. Two powerful embodiments, fire and water—sun, blazing from its empyrean, and sea, surging from its depths—have represented the *anima mundi.* Air, evocative because it is ethereal, has provided more inspiration. With this inspiration, Germanic words from time immemorial, along with those from ancient philosophy in the Greek or Latin Bible, have represented the soul.

Soul (825), first in *Beowulf,* has been associated with two images. In one, it rises as a cognate from the sea that has brought creation to life, to which early man returned heroic souls on fiery barques after death. In another, soul is born of the quick moving wind. Appropriately, it has a shadowy etymology. Whatever its origin, soul represents the soulful (1863) seat of emotions and man's divine spark. Soul searching, we may seek it in ourselves, but there is not a soul alive who can not at least understand its images.

Like soul, *anima* represents soul in the world or in the individual. Masculine *animus,* intellect, and feminine *anima,* soul, two animating (1398) forces, resemble Yin and Yang. A fragment of the Roman playwright Accius explains the difference: *Sapimus animo, fruimur anima; sine animo anima est debilis*—"We have wisdom in the *animus,* we have delight in the *anima*; without *animus*, *anima* is weak." In other words, *animus* has use, *anima* gives joy; but joy lacks substance without use.

Eastern divinities have names from the *animus/anima* root: Asura in Hindu, Ahura in Persian. In the lowliest creation, however, an animal (1398) has an *anima*. Deer, a Germanic parallel to animal, takes its origin from the Indo-European root for smoke and breath that looks like smoke in cold air. King Lear (3.4) refers to 'deer' as any animal: "mice and rats and such small deer." German *tier*, the cognate of deer, also means animal. Divinity consists either wholly or partly of *anima* and she—*anima* is of feminine gender—shares it with creatures of her creation.

Of dark, Germanic parentage, ghost takes root in fright. "Come from the grave," it represents a restless spirit of the dead in its earliest and latest meaning. Tormented ghosts, however, can include missions of mercy in their restless wandering. Marley's ghost "doomed to wander through the world," haunts Ebenezer Scrooge, after, it laments, "my spirit never roved beyond the narrow limits of our money-changing hole." In life, Marley did not know that "any Christian spirit working kindly in its little sphere, whatever it may be, will find its mortal life too short" for doing good. Dickens' *A Christmas Carol* pairs ghosts with spirits in reforming Scrooge into a sprightly spirit keeping Christmas well, "if any man alive possessed the knowledge."

When Seneca called Jove *animus ac spiritus mundi*, "animus and spiritus of the world," he used both roots for divinity. Since the time of this pagan, Romance and English have chosen one and then the other. *Anima* survived in Romance as a word for soul; *spiritus*, with the authority of the Vulgate, replaced the *animus/anima* root in some words of English and Romance.

Like Dickens, we may also choose between spirit and ghost. In English, spirit (1250) first represented the animating, vital principle, then a supernatural being (1300) and, finally, a soul (1375). Ghost, the Germanic translation of Romance 'spirit,' translated Holy Spirit in the Vulgate as Holy Ghost (900). Holy Spirit has greater age and authority in the classical tradition; but Holy Ghost has greater age and authenticity in English, and sounds, to some folk, at least, more spiritual, or should we say, more ghostly. Take your pick.

The Vulgate has also inspired other usage. When God breathed a soul, literally, a spirit, into the nostrils of man, the word in the Vulgate is *inspiravit*. Air represents soul as "the breath of life": "And the Lord God breathed into his nostrils the breath of life; and man became a living soul" (*Genesis* 2.7). Inspiration (1303) first meant "breathing in" the spirit of God and, much later (1651), "breathing in" an exalted impulse. By air, God inspires a spirit at birth and man expires, breathes out, this spirit or gives up the ghost, at death (*cf.* the King James translation of *Matthew* 27.50).

Pneuma, straight from Plato's Academy and the Greek Bible, represents the divine and human soul that the English ghost and the Latinate spirit have translated. Pneuma has the most ancient spiritual authority, but it exists in English only as a term of theology. Psyche, a little lower than the angels as an abstraction and the main character in the story of Cupid and Psyche, represents the soul of man, or, to be specific, of woman. Both pneuma and psyche arose from Greek philosophy and entered English as its offspring. The two words distinguish between the higher and lower soul that the one Latin word *anima* represents.

Whatever names we give them—soul, spirit, ghost, *anima*, pneuma or psyche—they all go where the wind wills: "The wind (*pneuma / spiritus*) breathes (*pnei / spirat*) where it wills;[5] you hear the sound of it, but you do not know where it comes from, or where it is going. So with everyone who is born from spirit" (*John* 3.8). Man, locked in corporeal reality, aspires to incorporeal spirit; but he has only the ghost of an idea about it, even though his language has embodied it in words.

## Words

Seven PIE roots represent soul in three geographic families.

### I. Germanic and Slavic

1. **German:** *seel / see*, sea
   English: sea; soul (825), the seat of emotions and man's godly spark
2. **PIE root *gheidz*, to frighten, be angry**
   German: *geist*, spirit
   English: ghost (800), an equivalent of spirit; ghastly (1305), like a ghost
3. **PIE root *dheu*, smoke, dust**
   Greek: *thumos*, soul
   German: *dunst*, fog
   Polish: *dusza*, spirit, soul
   Russian:
       дух (dux), spirit, ghost; дохнуть (doxnut), to breathe
       душа (dusha), spirit, soul
   English: deer, a breathing animal
   German: *tier*, animal, cognate of deer

### II. Romance and Greek

4. **PIE root *ane*, breath**
   Latin, *anima*, breath

Italian: *anima*; French: *âme*; Spanish: *alma*
English: animal (1398) has an *anima*
Greek: *anema*, wind
English: anemometer measures wind
5. **PIE root *speis*, to breathe**
Latin: *spiritus*
Italian: *spirito*; French: *esprit*; Spanish: *espiritu*
English:
spirit (1250), vital principle; (1300), angel; (1375), soul
sprightly (1596), sprites (1300)

### III. Greek

6. **PIE root *pneu*, to breathe**
Greek: *pnein*, to breathe; *pneuma*, soul of God
English: pneuma (1884) and pneumonia
7. **PIE root *bhes*, to breathe**
Greek: *psychein*, to breathe; *psyche*, soul of man
English: psyche (1647) and psychology (1693)

# 18. Fire

Just as we may see air as ancient and elemental, we may also see fire as "one of the four elements of the ancients;" and we could also add a 'but' to distinguish the place of this element in antiquity in contrast to its place in modernity. The ancients did not attribute fire, like its kindred elements, earth, air, and water, to the sphere of men in the world, but to the sphere of gods in heaven. In their geocentric cosmos, the earth reigned at the center. Circumambient air surrounded the earth; and circumambient fire surrounded the circumambient air surrounding the earth. In other words, a circle of air within an atmosphere of fire surrounded the earth and separated the world of men from that of gods.

From fire, Sir Walter Raleigh wrote, God created heaven: "It pleased God first of all to create empyrean heaven" (*The History of the World*, 1614). *Em-pyreos* designates creation "in fire." By fire, God first created the empyrean realm of divinity. Indo-European culture attributed fire to divinity. In Latin, *ignis* descended from Agni, a Hindu deity of fire.

Man possesses within himself a spark of celestial fire, a divine seed. In his story of creation, Ovid recounts the father of Prometheus creating man from "seeds" that are "kindred" to heaven: "He retained from the lofty ether the seeds of kindred heaven" (*ab alt (o) aethere cognati // retinebat semina caeli*). The ether (*aethere*), derived from the Greek verb *aithein*, to burn, associates fire with divinity "from the lofty ether." Since the gods kept fire as their special virtue, Prometheus completed his father's work by stealing it from immortals to benefit mortals.

The Hebrew creation myth portrayed God creating light (Hebrew *or*) and not fire (Hebrew *esh*). Fire characterizes creation in Ovid and Raleigh's pagan myths. Its divinity, separate from men, but planted within them as a seed for good or ill, gives a clue to our concept of the word.

In the Judaeo-Christian tradition, fire on earth emanates from God's power: "Is not my word like fire?," Yahweh said to the prophet Jeremiah (*Jeremiah* 23.29). His word sets the prophet's ablaze. At Pentecost, The Holy Spirit descended upon the disciples in wind and fire: "And suddenly there came a sound from heaven as of a rushing mighty wind, and it filled all the house where they were sitting. And there appeared unto them cloven tongues like as of fire, and it sat upon each of them" (*Acts* 2.2–3). After the Spirit had breathed over the house, tongues of fire "appeared" to the disciples. Similarly, but not as dramatically, humans strike sparks from the fire of genius or of love within them. "I am glad that my weak words," says Cassius in Shakespeare's *Julius Caesar*, "have struck but thus much show of fire from Brutus." Brutus, "the noblest Roman of them all," possesses the nobility within, from which Cassius strikes fire.

Paganism made ethereal fire divine—Christianity made it demonic. Any man, by himself and unaided by theology, can also turn his divine fire within to evil. Both by Christian reversal of pagan values and by human perversity, fire has represented as much evil as good—and maybe more. When evil talk was destroying Christian community, the Apostle James lamented the fire of *gehenna* in the "world of iniquity." The tongue, he proclaims, bears the fire of hell: "And the tongue is a fire, a world of iniquity . . . the fire of hell" (*James* 3.6).

Shakespeare's characters meld pagan with Christian imagery. Macbeth, with a bow before the divinity of stars, contrasts their ethereal "fires" with his infernal "desires": "Stars, hide your fires, / Let not the light see my black and deep desires." Since infernal fire burns black, he contrasts the celestial empyrean with his own inferno. In its lambent passage through centuries and cultures, fire has burned both bright with goodness and black with evil.

Taking root from evil or good seed, fire has bloomed with the "fearful symmetry" that inspired William Blake:

Tyger Tyger, burning bright,
In the forests of the night;
What immortal hand or eye,
Could frame thy fearful symmetry?

In what distant deeps or skies.
Burnt the fire of thine eyes?
On what wings dare he aspire?
What the hand, dare seize the fire?

Who, like Prometheus, would "dare seize the fire"?—from what depths or heights—perhaps from "deeps" or from "skies" on "wings"? Similarly, Phlegethon, the ancient river of fire, circled the earth like a wind, before it entered the depths like a river. Whoever the creator and whatever the source, the heartless Tyger lives in the same world with the gentle Lamb:

When the stars threw down their spears
And water'd heaven with their tears:
Did he smile his work to see?
Did he who made the Lamb make thee?

Contemplating this shocking incongruity of the Creator making Lambs and Tygers, Blake changes "could frame" of the final question—"What immortal hand or eye, / Could frame thy fearful symmetry?"— to "dare frame." Blake, the Promethean poet, also dares to measure one extreme of the "fearful symmetry" with the other.

Elemental fire, by its enigma of good with evil, inspires my own question:

Fire, Fire, burning bright,
By your seeds of love and fright,
Whence grow these roots for good or ill,
That make men marvel still?

## Words

Fire is both obvious and enigmatic.
In Latin, it descends from divinity.
In Romance, it is the focus of the home.
In Russian, it is a party around that focus.

### PIE root *Agni*, a Hindu and Vedic deity in the sun and lightning.

Sanskrit: *agni*
Latin: *ignis*, fire
    English: to ignite (1666), ignition (1612)
Russian: огонь (agon), fire.

### PIE root *fyr*, fire

German: *Feuer*
    English: fire (825)

Greek: *pur/pyr*, fire
> Grimm's law: 'f' and 'b' interchange, as in Latin *pater*/English *f*ather.
> English:
>> pyre, a fire, mostly in reference to a funeral pyre
>> em-pyrean, heavenly, sublime; of pure fire, the seat of God
>
> Russian: пир (pir), feast, literally, a fire around which the feast is held

**No PIE root**

Latin: *focus*, fireplace, hearth, center of house, home, family; in Kepler's
> Latin, point of convergence (1604)

Romance languages took *focus* and not *ignis* as their word for fire:
French: *feu*
> English:
>> curfew, *coeverfu*, literally "cover fire," an evening bell
>>> ordering hearths banked to prevent conflagrations
>>
>> foyer, center room containing the hearth; fuel

Spanish: *fuego*; Italian: *fuoco*
Portuguese: *Fogo de Chão*, fire on earth, barbecue of Brazilian gauchos
English: center of activity (1796)
Russian: фокус (fokus), focus. топка (topka), hearth (PIE *tep*, warm)

## 19. Flame

We inhabit earth, drink water, and breathe air, but even these elements frighten us by their violence—earth quakes, water floods, and air blows up a storm. Fire blazes—rages far beyond them. It has served us since culture began—candle and hearth date from A.D. 700—but we have always regarded it with caution and fear. In language, naturally, fire also requires such care that more PIE roots describe it than any of the three other elements. As though in a caldron, it seethes with the complex blaze beneath it.

Consider the classic pair, fire and water. We appreciate water as beloved and familiar, even though it does sometimes rise up and act up; fire, less familiar, more remote and exotic, frightens us in itself, no matter how much we control it. Modern technology has controlled it. A household of the nineteenth century used fire in cooking, heating and lighting with less control and more danger. Long before Edith Piaf lit her torch about love, a newspaper reporting "the same old story," did not write about love, but about flames bursting from oil lamps. We take pleasure in seeing children playing with water; but, no matter how much we may control it, we take fright at even the thought of their playing with fire. By contrast, we know that the fires of love will teach them good lessons without necessarily killing them. Jove should feel some coldly vindictive pleasure when he sees fire out of control. See what happens, he gloats, when Prometheus steals my fire and hands it over to mortals' incompetence!

The ancients saw two manifestations of Jove's thunderbolt that Prometheus stole: *fulgor* shines, *fulmen* sets on fire. Translating these two Latin words by their English derivatives, effulgence flashes, fulmination strikes fire. Similarly, some PIE roots for fire refer to its heating, shimmering, shining or glowing; others, literally, to its burning. Fire, with intense simplicity but sparkling complexity, seethes with metaphor.

Of all the images for fire, flame takes the most protean shapes. It first occurred in the phrase 'flame of fire,' because fire exhales it as a breath, an afflatus—afflatus shares its root with flame. As an afflatus, it can chill, cool, warm or heat. A beautiful jewel radiates a pure flame or the moon, a silver one. Flame can exist as subtle, kindling heat, sustaining life, or as love and ambition, inspiring it. With its tongues or spires breathing out and inflamed, it conflates when compassion inflames a noble heart or hatred inflames a wicked one. Metaphor aside, literal fire confounds all this musing, as it reduces the houses of the noble, and the wicked alike, to ashes.

Flames only describe one facet of a blaze. Kindling, blazing, and smoldering, fire in its spectrum, both blanches and blackens. Kindling foments, blazing shines, and smoldering smokes. Kindle, cognate with candle and kin, alludes to the taper generating fire or the generating itself. With wet kindling, fire smolders without blazing, but once ablaze in flames, it bursts forth in blazing blasts. Having blazed out, it smolders, expiring in smoke. Compare our pleasure in sitting by a fireside with that of sitting by a fountain. Fire blazes out in a drama with a beginning, middle and end; water, soothes by its consistent, rhythmic purling.

Fire's lambent licking and bathing the surface of its combustibles fascinates us with a beauty that surpasses the purling of water. It's colors encompass the poles of the spectrum, white to black. Flavescent, fire burns yellow; blazing full, it burns white hot; having blazed itself out, it burns its smoldering ash black. Art imitates fiery form and color. Flamboyant coloring, like that of a flamingo, represents this wavy radiance.

Fire blazes most cruelly—but effectively—in war. In the earliest years of the Middle Ages, the Byzantines carefully guarded their formula for Greek fire, an incendiary bomb, especially effective as "sea fire" or "wet fire" in naval battles. Like napalm, "wet fire" broke from poetic oxymoron to real destruction. As a lethal weapon incinerating ships of the Arabs, it preserved the Byzantine empire.

70 • WORLDS IN WORDS

More generally throughout history, an incendiary or a firebrand, aflame with ardent conviction, inflames other men's minds or their property, if they dare to disagree with him. Arsonist described him as willfully and maliciously setting fires four hundred years before incendiary. Since an incendiary tosses an incendiary bomb, the two usually associate in war; the arsonist does his worst in time of peace. Incendiary bombs in World War II exploded the destruction of Greek fire.

Fiery words surprise us. We expect most words to have a literal meaning before figurative ones, but some words for fire contradict this expectation. To burn, for example, meant to feel passionate anger or love (825) long before it meant to be on fire (1000). Ardent also meant burningly eager or passionate (1374) before it meant ablaze (1440). These words entered English as metaphors. On the other hand, cremation, in Latin and in English, always referred to incinerating the dead. Fire fuels our imaginations as much as our hearths.

## Words

Be careful! Once burned, twice warned! Not just twice, but by eleven PIE roots. What aspect of fire sparks your imagination—black or blank, glowing or seething, blazing or smoking, flame or flamboyant, brand or brandish?

1. **PIE root *as*, to be dry, burn, glow**
   Latin: *ardeo ardere* and *arsus*, to be on fire; *aridus*, arid
     English:
       ardent, (1374), burningly eager or passionate; (1440), on fire
       arson (1275), setting fires maliciously; azalea, growing in arid soil
2. **PIE root *aidh*, to surge, seethe, burn**
   Latin: *aedes* and *aedificium*, a building with a hearth
     English: edifice, to edify; estuary, inland channel of seething water
3. **PIE root *atr*, fire**
   Latin: *ater*, black (with smoke); *atrium*, the room black with smoke
     English:
       atrabilious, melancholy; literally, of black bile
       atrocity, a deed of frightfully dark cruelty
4. **PIE root *kau*, to burn**
   English:
     caustic (1555), burning; (1771), sarcastic
     holocaust (1250), an offering that burns the whole sacrifice

5. **PIE root** *eus*, **to burn**
   Latin:
      *uro urere* and *ustus*, to burn
      *comburo comburere* and *combustus*, to burn completely
      *bustum*, funeral monument
        English: combustion (1477); bust, statue of upper body on a tomb
   French: *brûler*, to burn (perhaps derived from Latin)
   English: to brew (893), to broil (1375)
6. **PIE root** *ker*, **to burn**
   Latin: *cremo cremare*, to burn dead bodies; *carbo carbonis*, charcoal, burnt wood
      English: cremation (1623), to cremate (1874), ceramic (1850)
   German: *Herd*, floor where fire is made, fireplace
      English: hearth (700)
   Russian: курить (kurit'), to smoke, burn
7. **PIE root** *kand*, **to glow, be white**
   Latin: *incendo incendere* and *incensus*, to burn; *candidus*, bright, shining
   English:
      candle (700); incense (1290), a gum fragrant when burned
      to incense (1494), to anger; (1531), to incite
      candid (1630), white; (1633), free from malice
      incendiary (1611), relating to arson; (1614), a man setting fires
      sandalwood, wood burned as incense
8. **PIE root** *guher*, **heat**
   Latin: *calidus*, hot
      Spanish: *calido*; Italian: *caldo*; French: *chaud*
        English: caldron (1300), large kettle
   Latin: *furnus*; *fornax fornacis*,
      English: furnace (1225)
   Greek: *thermos*, heat
      English: thermos, thermometer
   Russian: гореть (gorit), to burn; горячий (goryachiy), hot
   горн (gorn), fireplace; горючее (geruchje), fuel
9. **PIE root** *bhel*, **to shine, blaze, burn, shimmer**
   Greek: *phlox*, flame; *phlegein*, to burn
   Latin:
      *fulgeo fulgere*, to shine; *fulmen fulminis*, lighting setting on fire, thunderbolt
      (*Fulgor splendet; fulmen incendit.—Fulgor* shines; *fulmen* sets on fire.)

*flagro flagrare*, to burn; *in flagrante delicto*, in the flagrant crime, in the act
English:
to fulminate, (1450), to publish condemnation; (1610), thunder
flagrant, (1513), blazing; (1515), passionate; (1706), notorious
conflagration (1555); effulgent (1738), radiant
flavescent (1853), turning pale yellow

*blancus*, white
French: *blanc*, white; Spanish: *blanco*; Italian: *bianca*
English:
to blaze (1225), to burn with a bright flame
to blanch (1400); (1605), to make white with fear
blank (1325); blanket (1300), blank white cloth for bed covering
black (890) Fire, first white, in the end, makes everything black.
German: *Birke*, birch
Russian:
белый (bielyj), white; береза (bereza), birch, the white tree
блистать (blistat), to shine

*flamma*, flame
Italian: *fiamma*, flame; *fenicottero*, flaming
French: *flamme*, flame; *flamant*, flamingo
Spanish: *llama, flamenco*
English:
flame (1340), portion of ignited vapor, spire or tongue-like (1374), bright beam from a heavenly body
flamingo (1565)
flamboyant (1832), *cf. flambé*, wavy in form, gorgeous in color
Russian: пламя (plamy), flame (*vide* Grimm's law); фламинго (flamingo)

10. **PIE root *bhereu*, to bubble, stir, boil**
Latin: *ferveo fervere*, to burn, be hot, seethe
English:
to burn (825), to feel passionate anger or love; (1000), to be on fire
brand (950), piece of wood on the fire; (1000), fire, torch or sword
to breed (1000), to cherish, keep warm; and brood
fry (1290), to cook food in fat; breath (1340), warm air from the lungs
to brandish (1325), to threaten; (1340), to flourish a sword
brimstone, sulphur in a solid state, hellfire
fervent (1400), ardent or burning; (1465), raging

11. **PIE root *smeugh*, smoke**
English: smoke, to smolder, smell

## 20. Fiery Feelings

Fire so fuels our imagination that it provides a metaphor for our fiery feelings. Before our fuming bursts into flame or even blows up, our moral restraint can control and direct it—God can feel wrath and an indignant man can feel incensed. Without restraint or direction, fury sets a man ablaze, changing him for the worse, and reducing him to elemental chaos.

The root of mad (725), the oldest English word for anger, hints at frightening volatility. Mutation, a cognate of mad, points to its origin in change. Madness changes men in frightening ways. It first referred to ruinous imprudence, as Shakespeare's "mad humor of love." By 1000, mad as insane and by 1300, beside oneself with anger, eventually also referred to nature in chaos: "Mad winds that howling go from east to west" (1836). Today, mad can mean angry as a colloquialism, but it bubbles from the same caldron of its origin.

*Rage*, the French form of Latin *rabies*, passed into English as rage (1300). In English, rabies (1611) describes rabid dogs. In French, *rage* preserves the double edge of *rabies*, as both rabies and rage. Like mad, rage refers to all sorts of frenzy: storms rage, as do headaches. Even fashion can be all the rage. Three hundred years after its first appearance (1615), rabid described the fury of man, disease or nature: "All the rabid flight of winds that ruin ships are bred in night" (Chapmen's *Odyssey*).

Mad, rage, and rabid blaze through a broad range of meaning. On the other hand, the adjective enraged (1398), and its verb to enrage (1513), a much later entry into English, have referred to great anger since the eighteenth century. They first described a man enraged by thirst, famine or even by poetic frenzy. We now understand the adjective as describing anger that possesses the body: "A man may intensely hate another," wrote Charles Darwin in his book, *The Expression of the Emotions in Man and Animals*, "but until his bodily frame is affected, he cannot be said to be enraged" (1872). Enraged describes anger more intense and specific than mad.

Outrage (1303) sounds like rage, but the two have no connection in their roots and only a little connection in meaning. From the Latin *ultra*, beyond, and *ultraticum*, a thing beyond, outrage goes "beyond" the bounds of right conduct. In French, for example, *outré* means both eccentric and outraged. We feel outraged when we suffer an outrage, whether or not we feel rage.

Just as rage and mad have originated in natural or feral ferocity, and in the passions of man, some words for anger actually originate in natural elements. The word family including fury (1374), furious (1374), and furor

(1477), all cognate with fume (1400), originate in incense-induced Bacchic frenzy. In their first use, they also referred to raging emotions in men, ferocity in beasts or chaos in the elements. Furor, like rabies, a learned borrowing of a Latin word into English, may be more formal: for example, the press in a furor over the fury of the mob. Like mad and rage, however, furor and its derivatives slash a wide and tumultuous swathe.

Literary in origin, to incense (1435) starts a fire, as when sins incense the wrath of God. Like furor, it could refer to the fire of passion: the holy fire of love incenses a lover. By the end of the fifteenth century, a man could be incensed with anger—in modern use, indignant. For example, the outrage of judicial malfeasance so incenses the journalist that he chastises it by the indignation of his pen. Unlike the other words for furious anger, to incense and furor exercise control and direct indignation to moral ends.

In His divine plan, God's wrath speaks in fire. The Lord "goes forth like fire," says the prophet Jeremiah. "For behold, He will come in fire and His chariots like the whirlwind, to render His anger with fury, and His rebuke with flames of fire" (*Isaiah* 66.15). With an animism now considered simplistic, Julius Caesar thought that the Germans worshipped fire ("Vulcan") as a god: "they place in the number of the gods those alone, whom they see, the Sun and Vulcan" (*Deorum numero, eos solos ducunt, quos cernunt, Solem et Vulcanum* [*Bellum Gallicum* 6.21]). From the Germanic roots of English, Wednesday commemorates the God Wotan/Odin whose fury, *wode*, was divine. Judaism or paganism does not make fire a divinity, but uses it to punish blasphemy.

Like God, Jove hurls righteous and well aimed lightening bolts. Similar to God's wrath coming in fire, Jove's bolt from the blue, *fulmen*, gave English the verb 'to fulminate.' Fulmination issues formal condemnation. Martin Luther, in his *Ninety-Five Theses*, hopes that Pope Leo "intends to fulminate those who, through the pretext of indulgences, machinate a fraud of holy charity and truth" (*Fulminare intendit eos, qui per veniarum pretextum in fraudem sancte charitatis et veritatis machinantur*). When the Pope, *ex cathedra*, fulminates in Papal Bulls, like Jove or Jehovah, he strikes down blaspheming idolaters. Human indignation can only aspire to this righteousness and at least to coruscation before its fulmination.

In addition to bursting into flame or fulminating, anger can explode violently: "The Emperor began to rage; he ground his teeth and fast blew" (1350)—"blew" his top in the middle of the fourteenth century, by his own powers, we assume. Much later, in the age of steam, blowing one's stack like a steam-driven locomotive could describe explosive anger. If an angry man did not let off some steam, he might also blow a gasket.

Modern technology supplies new images of explosive power. After World War II, for example, a man on a bathing beach had to watch out for bikinis, especially when WACs, wacky for khaki, were wearing them. He could have known what happened to Bikini, after which they had been named. In his stupefaction, however, did he distinguish between the beauty and the madness detonating the bombshells? Beauty detonates madness and or is it the other way round? Love's "mad humor" blurs distinctions between the two. A few years later, in the age of ballistic missiles, an angry man, who did not cool his jets, blasted into orbit by his own propulsion.

When angry men see only red, their bloody fire burns so furiously that they lose control. No wonder gods fulminate in righteous indignation, which men only imitate. As though in the fury of conflagrations or whirlwinds, rage can plunge to outrage. Storm-tossed, men may at least batten down the hatches and ride through the gale; but, engulfed in a fire storm, they have no hope.

## Words

Roots for anger progress from changing, smoking, glowing or shining to burning. Seizing, possessing or frightening also describe anger. Generally, an angry man is set on fire and possessed.

### PIE root *mei*, to change

Latin: *muto mutare*, to change
    English: mutation
English:
    mad (725)
    maim (1475); its doublet mayhem (1472), a wound removing a limb

### PIE root *dheu*, smoke, dust

Latin: *fumo fumare*, to smoke; *furor*, furor (1477)
    English: fury (1374), madness from the inhalation of smoke at sacrifices
    Russian: фурия (furia), Fury, virago

### PIE root *rabh*, to take, seize

Latin:
    *rabio rabere*, to be mad, rave
    *rabies*, madness in men or in rabid dogs
        French: *rage*, rage or rabies; Italian: *rabbia*; Spanish: *rabia*
        English: rabies (1661) and its doublet rage (1300); rabid (1611)

### PIE root *vat*, to inspire

Latin: *vates*, prophet, looking for omens from the Vatican Hill in Rome
 English: vatic, relating to a seer
German:
 *wut*, fury; *Wüt*, one filled with divine frenzy; and *wütend*, furious
 Wotan, a god raging in battle, the eponymous god of Wednesday
English: wood (725)—nothing to do with trees—insane

### PIE root *bhoyh*, to frighten

Latin: *foedus*, filthy
 Italian: *fedo*, filthy; Spanish: *feo*, ugly
Russian: бешенство (beshenstvo), madness, rage, rabies

## 21. Water

Science has called earth geo-sphere, air atmo-sphere, and water hydro-sphere. The geosphere lays the foundation either as *terra firma* or ocean floor. The hydrosphere completely covers 70% of the geosphere, and it partially covers the 30% on which man lives. Man should consider himself lucky to have his 30%, and especially lucky that the hydrosphere does not entirely stop at the seashore but permeates land in subtle interconnections. Without it, *terra firma* might wither to *terra deserta*. With their symbiotic interconnections, these three spheres nurture life.

 The hydrosphere, though not perfectly spherical in its proportion of 70% to 30%, is perfectly interconnected. Obviously, it includes the ocean; and, subtly, enveloping the geosphere from aquifers, ground-water, rivers, ponds, and creeks, it weaves its way back to the ocean. It springs from the earth, rises up as clouds, and falls down as rain, as it all flows down to the sea. Water resembles fire in its subtlety and plasticity.

 By these interconnections, terra firma takes a watery veil in Mother Nature's archetypal marriage. Fostering birth and growth, water represents the seed; and earth, the womb. In another elemental marriage—one a little more beneath the surface—fire supplies seminal heat and water, fetal fluid, as female in this union as it is male in the other. In Latin, *aqua* and *terra* are both feminine gender—*ignis*, masculine. Whatever its gender or garments, water supplies to Mother Nature the stock for her stew and the yeast for her loaf. Nothing animal or vegetable comes to birth without it.

 Man has always differentiated the natures of water's subtly faceted omnipresence. Most basically, he could drink fresh-water and not sea-water. The sea inspired fear. Its god, Neptune, shook the earth with his trident and rolled tidal waves over its surface. His sea-maidens were a slippery lot, lovely things without souls, not to be trusted. Fresh-water, on the other hand, man had in such short supply that he revered it as *aqua sacra* and celebrated it as *aqua casta*. Sacred, it symbolized God's justice: "Let judgment run down as waters," proclaimed the Prophet Amos, "and righteousness as a mighty stream" (*Amos* 5.24). Chaste, it symbolized a man's pure life: the pious man "shall be like a tree planted by the rivers of water that bringeth forth his fruit in his season; his leaf also shall not wither; and whatsoever he doeth shall prosper" (*Psalms* 1.3). Water also runs as life-giving currents through metaphor and poetry.

Not just symbolizing human purity flowing from divine justice, water embodied divinity. Rivers rising from springs, wells tapping aquifers, each one had its divinity, celebrated in its shrine. Their sacred waters in ritual washing of hands—the ancient Greeks called it χέρνιψ (chernips), from χείρ (cheir), hand, and νίπτω (nipto), I wash—purified human activity. Washing hands before and after a meal had as much meaning for religion as it had for hygiene. In *Revelation* also, "a pure river of water of life, clear as crystal" flows from the throne of God (22.1).

"Drink deep," Alexander Pope, recommends, from the springs of inspiration, because "a little learning is a dangerous thing." And yet, inspiring springs are where you find them: Hebrew, eye, ahyin, also means spring, because beautiful eyes sparkle like a "soft, limpid, turquoise blue." In the geosphere, humble springs may suffice, but classic inspiration flows from the Pierian Spring: *sic flumine largo / plenus Pierio defundes pectore verba*, "thus full in a generous flood, you shall pour forth words from your Pierian heart." The Roman poet Horace, finding his inspiration in the humble Bandusian spring (*O fons Bandusiae*) near his farm, calls its water "more radiant than crystal" (*splendidior vitro*). Hymning this humble presence of divinity, Horace concludes with a boast wrapped in an idyllic scene:

> *Fies nobilium tu quoque fontium*
> *me dicente cavis imposit (am) ilicem*
> *saxis, unde loquaces*
> *lymphae desiliunt tuae.*

> You shall become, you also, one of noble fonts,
> With me singing of the oak placed over hollow,
> Stones, whence, loquaciously,
> Your waters leap down.

The poet will immortalize the Bandusian font. He call her waters *lymphae*, referring to them as divine. Latin synonyms *nympha* and *lympha* both refer to a water deity.

Like mermaids, their oceanic sisters, fresh water-nymphs could also make mortals suffer, when they appeared to them in human form. If an unlucky man looked at a water-nymph, her sight drove him mad or, more precisely, lymphatic (1656). These spirits from classical lore, like the little people of the Celts, could bring harm to mortals. Wisely propitiating them as they rose from the earth for the benefit of the upper world, men built shrines at their springs. Ancient shrines to water spirits evoke the pagan past, but a spring house on a farm on its own offers a special place for rest beside cool and "loquaciously" purling water.

Not all liquids are *aqua casta*, *aqua pura* or quintessential *aqua vitae*, water of life. In *Revelation*, it flows from the throne of God. Anticipating the joys of heaven, men dignified the alcoholic liquor that they distilled from barley malt with the title *aqua vitae*, the water of life—a monkish joke that winks jovially at the anticipation of joys in heaven tapped from an oaken barrel on earth. The Gaelic translation, *usquebaugh*, entered English as whiskey.

To mix or not to mix? should not have to be the question, but scarcity makes it so. Water often mixed with liquor in stock phrases like wine-and-water, rum-and-water or whiskey-and-water. *Merum* in Latin and mere (1545) in English first described pure, undiluted wine. Wine or whiskey, so diluted that it had hardly a suggestion of alcohol, was facetiously called *mera aqua*, pure water or water-bewitched. "Bewitched" seems hyperbolic, but imagine the disappointment of a man, hoping to drink whiskey mixed with a little water, finding water mixed with very little whiskey—so little that the water seems pure. Mere whiskey, pure joy—mere water, purely outrageous and provoking redundancy. How could this happen?—what more soulless power might ruin water of life from heaven than a witch from the other place?

Water as a name for even alcoholic beverage should cause no surprise. In its flowing and mixing, water plunges us into deep seas and pools of experience. Life comes from it, and man has praised it as divine. No wonder that Jesus spoke of salvation, as he sat by Jacob's well. Salvation in this world and metaphor for the next, water nurtures man though life to death and back to life.

## Words

We take water for granted, because it seems inexhaustible.
We can also spend money like water, as though there is no tomorrow.
Fire is the power of air; but water, the power of earth.

PIE root *akua*, water

Latin: *aqua*, water; *aqua vitae*, water of life,
    French:
        *eau*—*aqua* without the 'q'
        *eau de vie*; Gaelic: *usquebaugh*; English: whiskey
    Italian: *acqua*; Spanish: *agua*
    English: aquatic

PIE root *waed, wod, ud*

Greek: *hydor*, water
    English: hydration, hydrosphere; hydrogen, begetting water
German: *Wasser*, water; *Kirschwasser*, literally, cherry water; cherry brandy
    English: water (897)
Russian:
    вóда (voda), water
    вóдка (votka), vodka, alcoholic liquor distilled from wheat, rye, corn or potatoes (*cf. aqua vitae*, water of life)
    ведро (vedro), bucket; good weather in Old Church Slavonic

## 22. Affluent Water

The pre-Socratic philosopher Heraclitus described life in flux: *Panta rhei*, "All things flow." As an example, he observed that the same man can not put his hand in the same river twice, because both the man and the river are always changing. In the flow, man has drawn sustenance from the river and traveled on it to do business. Both are in flux, but the river nurtures men by its flow. Its streams bring water to life and its confluences influence men's geographical and moral explorations that transcend transience.

    Men have always lived by water and moved with its currents. Long before locomotion and automotion made river boats superfluous for inland travel and trade, water had given currency to civilization and its gold. Take the Delaware Bay as an example: in the early sixteenth century, explorers sailed from the ocean up the bay to its tributaries. As they sailed upstream, they found coves or inlets, in which they tied up their boats. Because a creek made a crook in the stream, they called these coves creeks in providing natural docks. When William Penn arrived in Philadelphia in the late seventeenth century, he tied up his boat in Dock Creek off the Delaware River; and the people of his city lived close to its banks until the nineteenth century. Some creeks might flow from long tributaries, but they retained the name of their first use. The Wissahickon Creek, a tributary of the Schuylkill, would not be called a creek in England. Off the boat in creeks, settlers traced streams to springs. They wanted to settle on land having a spring or a stream with an affluence of pure water. Voyages of exploration and settlement, from the dark deep of the ocean to the sparkling spring of the meadow, poured forth an affluence of prosperity that made the explorers and settlers affluent.

Sailing upstream, Europeans brought their civilization to America; and Americans, settled and flourishing, shipped their products downstream to Europe. Down every channel—springs, brooks, and streams influent into rivers—the Delaware River and the mighty inundation of its bay, American products flowed back to Europe. Farmers and merchants of the Delaware Valley facilitated the effluence. Canals made navigation safe at points on the Schuylkill, where the river channel was dangerous. They led to Philadelphia at the confluence of the Delaware River with the Schuylkill, selected as the best location for trade. Until the advent of railroads, imports flowed upstream and exports downstream almost as fluently as the currents. Long before its use for travel and trade, water just kept rolling along; and it still rolls along, long after canal barges have stopped passing through the locks. In the meantime, men have evolved, both with its nurture and without it.

William Penn described the site of Philadelphia as "high and dry, yet replenished with running streams" (*A Further Account*, 1685). Francis Pastorius, the leader of his German community, "almost" reached hyperbole: "Fresh streams and springs are almost without number." Especially as the spiritual father of Pennsylvania, Penn knew that he worked in vain to manage aquatic springs of his City of Brotherly Love if he could not trust its moral ones: "Pride, avarice, and luxury," he had named as the lusts, "from whence all other mischiefs daily flow, as streams from their proper fountains" (1669, *No Cross, No Crown*). With mischievous streams increasing, "the rich hold fast and press to be richer, and covet more," he observed, "which dries up the little streams of profit from smaller folks." When he was lamenting about lustful streams sixteen years before he boasted about the "running" ones, he could not have anticipated that his "Holy Experiment" would teach the world about the confluence of morality with prosperity.

To represent currents, literal and moral, Penn chose stream, a word of native hue. From its first use, it described both streams of wealth and of the water on which wealth was carried, upstream or downstream. Stream originates the flow, "forming a river, rivulet or brook." It refers to a current in a larger body of water, as the Gulf Stream in the Atlantic Ocean. Streams of water from springs join with other streams to make rivers and bays. When Cowper praised the blessing of well-watered land, he could have been describing the Delaware Valley: "Streams never flow in vain; where streams abound, How laughs the land with various plenty crown'd!" (1782). Entering English four hundred years later, river, imbued with Romance coloring, did not evoke the sweet and silver native streams.

Entering English even later, Romance compounds like abundant and abound first described flowing water, but they lost the literal sense which the Germanic word stream and the Romance word river have retained. William Penn, alluding to Christians of the apostolic age as models of brotherhood, praised their simplicity that he hoped might also abound in his "Holy Experiment": "What simplicity, what spirituality, what holy love and communion, did in that blessed age abound among them!" "Forsaking the cities, they lived solitarily in fields and gardens," as he hoped Quakers might live in their City of Brotherly Love, which he called a "Green Country Town." "To godliness," he urged that his fellow Quakers, add "brotherly-kindness; and to brotherly-kindness, charity; for if these things be in you and abound . . . , you shall be neither barren nor unfruitful: for so an entrance shall be ministered unto you abundantly, into the everlasting kingdom." "Neither barren nor unfruitful," brotherly Quakers, by 'abounding' in fruits of the spirit, have an entrance into God's kingdom ministered "abundantly." Their harvest abounds from the good earth more than from its fonts of justice.

Isaac Watts' hymn, "O God our help in ages past," echoes Heraclitus' image of transience:

> Time, like an ever-rolling stream,
>     Bears all its sons away;
> They fly forgotten, as a dream
>     Dies at the opening day,

Only God, Watts concludes, can guide man's transient life while it "shall last." Citizens in a city of brotherly love contradict this impermanence by growing together, Francis Pastorius boasted, "as trees planted by streams of water" and bearing "fruits of peace." In this affluence of brotherly love, their children reach a confluence with a new age.

## Words

Six roots describe flowing water: four for streams, and one each for wave and channel.

1. **PIE root (s)reu, to flow**
    - A. German: *Strom*, stream
        English: stream, literal (875) and figurative (900)
        Russian:
            струя (struya), stream
            остров (ostrov), island, surrounded by streams
    - B. Latin: *rivus*, river, river bank
        French: *rivière*; Spanish: *rio*
        English: river (1297), rivulet (1587)
    - C. Polish: *rzeka*, river
        Russian: река (reka), river; ручей (ruchey), brook, creek

2. **PIE root *ap*, water as a living force**

Hindi: Punjab, *panj*, five + *ab*, water (*cf.* punch made with five ingredients)
Greek: *pentapotamia*, land of five rivers.
Latin (Celtic borrowing): *amnis*—water personified and divinized—river
    English: Avon, Aberdeen—place names from the Celtic lands
English: julep (1400), from Arabic *julab* (*gul*, rose and *ab*, water)

3. **PIE root *bhleu*, to flow**

Latin:
    *flu fluere*, to flow; *fluctus*, wave
    *flumen*, river; *fluvius*, flowing, a river
        Italian: *fiume*; French: *fleuve*
        English:
            influence, (1374), flowing in; (1439), exercising power
            fluvial (1398), cognate with pluvial (*vide* Grimm's law)
            confluence (1538), flowing together.
            *Koblentz*, confluence of Moselle and Rhine (Latin *confluentes*)
            affluent, (1413), overflowing in good fortune; (1769), wealthy
            effluent (1603), flowing out

4. **PIE root *tek*, to run, flow or to beget**

Latin: *texo texere* and *textus*, to weave
    English: textile
Russian: по-ток (po-tok), stream, brook

5. **PIE root *waed, wod, ud*, water, wave**

Latin: *unda*, wave
    Italian: *onda*, wave; French: *onde*; Spanish: *ola*, wave

English:
> to undulate (1664), to flow like a wave,
> abundant (1366), flowing out, abounding, wealthy
> to abound (1382), to have in full, overflowing measure
> redundant (1604), flowing back, repeating
> to redound, to swell (1382), to return as honor or disgrace (1474)

Russian: волна (volna), wave

### 6. PIE root *kann*, reed, hemp

Greek: *kanon*, rod, rule
> Latin: *canna*, reed; *cannabis*, genus of hemp
> Italian: *cannoli*, little tubes filled with ricotta cheese
> Spanish: *canasta*, a card game played with cards from a canister
> English:
>> canon (of Scripture), canonical; cane, can and canister; canvas
>> canal (1449), water pipe; (1538), channel for inland navigation
>> (channel and canal are doublets)

## 23. Clouds

Children love to look up to the sky and imagine clouds as ships, mountains, castles or whatever vaporous nuances they may conceive. To the hymnist, clouds flow as "fountains of goodness and love." PIE words for clouds also reflect this imaginative effort. The Latin root for cloud describes it as misty; the English, as solid, and the Russian, as just trailing along.

In English, cloud is a doublet of clod. In 1300, it first referred to watery vapor in the air. Much earlier, back in 893, clod was doing its job as a hill or a mass of rock. Only later did it get its hands dirty as a handful of earth. It took a while before it vaporized into the heavens.

Science also took its time in distinguishing between the shapes of clouds. In 1803, Luke Howard adapted a number of Latin words for that purpose: "It may be allowable to introduce a methodical nomenclature applicable . . . to the Modifications of Cloud." He went on to call a cloud piling up a cumulus, spreading out a stratus or curling up a cirrus (Latin, *cirrus*, curl). What imagination! He looked up to the sky and imagined that he saw beautifully curling locks.

Latin has given English three roots for cloud, perhaps because all their vapor kept changing shape. *Nubes*, cloud, refers to a misty covering. Nebula was originally a cataract in the eye (1661) and later a cloud of stars (1727). The adjective nebulous at first described cloudy weather (1387), then, in astronomy, a cloudy star (1679), and much later, a cloudy issue (1831), as in Carlyle's mention of "nebulous disquisitions on religion." What should more be appropriately airy that complements to a woman's beauty? A snowy and fleecy woman's scarf is a nubia: "Emerging... in my nubia and snowy wrap" (*Confessions of a Frivolous Girl*, 1881). The female form could shine in "the nimbus of petticoat" (1854). Nebula, nebulous and nubia all refer to foggy conditions. In whatever vaporous form, the Russian облако (oblako) alludes to their slow movement as they trail along and draggle through the sky.

The Germanic root *nibel* emphasizes their dark side. The Nibelungen, for example, a supernatural race of dwarfs, dwell in the underworld (*nibel*) and guard a hoard of gold and a magic ring. Nimbus, reflecting both dark and light, first referred to the splendor of deity (1616): the manhood of John the Baptist was "lost in the nimbus of celestial glory" (1874), but later it described a storm cloud.

Nuance, derived from the French, takes a middle ground between foggy mist and darkness. Just as we see shades of light in a cloud formation, nuance refers to a shade of meaning, a slight difference. Nuance gives us a nuance in our understanding of clouds.

Clouds are nebulous, changing in shade from dark to light and in shape from mountains to curls. With children looking up to the sky, we may also wonder at the imagination of their names.

## Words

Clouds accumulate air in dark, swelling and misty piles like feathers and curls. Five PIE roots describe them:
English derives cloud from clump and piles;
Romance, from mist;
Slavic, from darkness, feathers and draggling.

### 1. PIE root *gel*, to ball up, clump

English: clod (893) and cloud (1300)

### 2. PIE root *ku*, to swell

Latin: *cumulus*, pile
English: cumulus, rounded mass of cloud with a horizontal base
Russian: куча (kucha), pile

## 3. PIE root *nebos*, cloud

Latin:
> *nubes nubis*, cloud, mist; *nebula*, mist, vapor, cloud
> *nimbus*, raincloud, halo
>> French: *nuage,* cloud
>> Russian:
>>> нюанс (nyuans), nuance
>>> нимб (nimb), nimbus

English: nebulous, nimbus; Nibelungen, children of the mist; nuance
German: *nebel,* mist
Russian: небо (nebe), heaven

## 4. PIE root *teme*, dark, obscure

Latin: *tenebrae*, darkness; *temeritas*, blind chance
> English:
>> temulant, clouded with drink
>> temerity, acting rashly on blind chance

Russian: темнота (temnota), darkness; тень (ten), shadow, shade, ghost

## 5. PIE root *pet*, rush, fly

Greek: *pteron*, wing, feather
> English: ptero-dactyl, wing finger

Russian:
> перо (pero), feather, pen
> перистое облако (peristoye oblako), feathery cloud

German: *Feder,* feather—Grimm's law: 'f' and 'p' interchange.
> English:
>> feather—cognate with Latin *penna*. A pen is a quill.
>> fern, a feathery plant

## PIE root *velkti*, to drag

Polish: *oblok*, cloud
Russian:
> волочить (volchit) and влачить (vlachit), to draw, drag, draggle, trail
> облако (oblako), cloud, which trails along in the sky
> облачаться (oblachat'sya), to robe

## No known PIE root

Greek: *halos*, threshing floor, disk of the sun or moon
English: halo, circle of light surrounding the sun or moon

Russian:
>  гало (galo), halo
>  ('h' to 'g' in гýмус [gúmus]/humus; Peterhof and Петергóф)

**No known PIE root**

Latin: *cirrus*, curl, tendril, fringe
>  English and French: cirrus, a curly cloud; Spanish: *cirro*, cirrus

## 24. Precipitating Water

Atmosphere, sphere of *atmos*, vaporous air in Greek, envelopes earth, encircling the geo-sphere with its own atmo-sphere. Its vapor, condensing in clouds, precipitates in mist, rain, snow or hail. Our world flows with life because of this symbiotic balance of atmosphere ever-flowing between geosphere and hydrosphere. In the seventeenth century, the scientific term atmosphere (1638) offered a more accurate word for Jupiter, literally, "father of the sky," to whom ancient lore—which many observant ancients did not consider valid—attributed the precipitation of vapor. By that time, only the quaintly learned might describe a rainy day with a line from an ancient poet, "the whole place is soaked from pluvial Jove," *pluvio de Jove cuncta madent*. The Jove/Juppiter that we usually see in marble or bronze holds a lightning bolt, but the ancient Romans hoped that he might blast their enemies with that ban, but on them shower his blessing in rain. Understandably, they weighed the balance in their favor. The etymologies of words precipitating from Romance, Germanic and Slavic roots have preserved some of the classic pluvial tradition.

Let's start with light vapor. Mist so transiently folds and unfolds in borders between liquid and solid, dawn and high noon, ignorance and enlightenment that its use as metaphor (888) predating its moist substantiality (1000) should not surprise us. Sunshine piercing through mist-shrouded mountains, and their mists folding away to green, have always appealed to men as metaphors for gradual enlightenment: their faith shining through mists of despondency and gloom. Words representing mist demonstrate a few of its facets: English and French brume, from Latin *bruma*, a contraction of *dies brevissima*, the "briefest," darkest day of the year, point to its chill darkness in the winter solstice; Italian *nebbia*, Portuguese *névoa*, and German *Nebel*, its "nebulous" nature; French *brouillard*, its "brewing" vapor; and Russian туман (tuman), its "smoke." Mist mixes a brew of dark cloud, moisture and chill. Mizzle, a cognate of mist, approximates its cloudy, vaporous nature. As mists enfold, mizzles drizzle.

Rain (825), heavier than mizzle or drizzle, precipitates with "sensible velocity." Rain has weight. As a word, also, older than mist (1000), mizzle (1483) or drizzle (1543), it had a literal meaning centuries before its metaphorical one in Chaucer's "salt tears" trickling down "as rain." (Mist's metaphorical meaning, on the other hand, predated its literal one.) Rain also has weight that creatures could feel and then announce in creation long before lexicographers could pronounce it in dictionaries. English preserves the Romance root for rain in the plover that, time out of mind, announced the barometric change when atmosphere precipitated to hydrosphere. Rilke celebrates this avian rain-herald, German *regenpfeiffer*, rain-piper, in his poem "Before Summer-Rain" (*Vor dem Sommeregen*): the rain-piper, "alone and strong," with "loneliness and zeal," resembles Saint Jerome in the wilderness, whose voice "the downpour will answer."[6]

The plover listens to the sky god. Job, like Jerome, also listened to God, whom he praised for His wonders in giving rain on the earth and in sending water on the fields (*Job* 5.8–10). God sometimes withheld rain that nurtured men and, instead, sent lightning that destroyed them. The Norse god Thor and his Graeco-Roman equivalent, Jove, both gave their names to the fifth day of the week, Thursday or *Jeudi*, which the Germans named *Donnerstag*, Thunder's Day. Thor and Jupiter, the thunderers, also destroyed as well as nurtured.

Is rain good or bad? Russian sees it both ways. In a turnabout of a good sky-god sending rain, Russians call rain a bad sky, дождь (dozhd). Like the Germans with their *Donnerstag*, Russian in дождь (dozhd) has associated rain with an evil. On the other hand, Russian also looks to the wet, iridescent side of weather: ведро (vedro), both good weather and bucket, derived from the PIE root *wed*, wet, describes it in terms of water. Its word for rainbow, радуга (raduga), with its root in gladness, points, to the "bow of promise," the sign of God's covenant with man after the rains that destroyed all life. At the root of an alternative word for rainbow, рай-дуга (rayduga), рай (ray), paradise, promises a pot of gold at the end of the rainbow. Sky gods can be tricky, and no one can count on them to be like jovial *Jupiter Serenus* all the time.

We all enjoy good weather, but we accept bad weather, because it fits nature's balance. In the other direction, nature's god in heaven causes his sun to rise on both the good and the bad. The English noun god, by its etymology, does not relate to good; but good, by its etymology, does relate to год (god), which means year in Russian. 'God'(год) fits with weather, по-года (pa-goda), which pleases, угодить (ugodit), by balancing good with bad. The sky god, similarly, does not always do man good, when he balances the scale by doing the year good in the symbiosis of atmosphere with hydrosphere. Bad weather happens to good people, because good weather can not always do them good.

## Words

### Words for precipitation rise from three PIE roots

1. **PIE root *pleuk*, flowing, floating**
   A. Latin: *aqua pluvia*, rain water (flowing water)
      Italian: *piove*, it rains; *pioggia*, rain
      French: *il pluit* and *pluie*; Spanish: *llueve* and *lluvia*
         Romance English: plover (1312), bird associated with rain
         Latinate English: pluvial (1656)
      Latin:
      *arcus pluvius*, an arc of rain
      *Iris*, goddess of rainbows. Iridescent glass has rainbow colors.
         French: *arc en ciel*; Spanish: *arco iris*
         Italian: *arco baleno*, an arc as big as a whale
   B. Greek: *pleo*, I float, sail
      Latin: *pluit*, it rains; Russian: плыть (plyt), to float, sail, swim
   C. Grimm's law: 'p' and 'f' interchange: *pater*/father, *pyre*/fire, *pluvial*/*fluvial*.
      German: *fliessen*, to flow; English: to flow, float
2. **PIE root *reg*, wet as rain**
   Latin: *rigo rigare*, to wet
      English: to irrigate
   German: *Regen*, to rain; *Regenbogen*, rain (*regen*-) bow (-*bogen*)
   English: to rain (825) and rainbow (1000)
3. **PIE root *eu* or *dus* + *dyu*, good or bad + sky**
   Greek: *eudia*—*eu*, good + *dia*, sky—good weather
   Czech and Polish: *déšť* and *deszcz*
   Russian: дождь (dozhd), rain—*dys*, bad (*cf.* dysfunction) and *div*, sky

### Russian rainbow, радуга (raduga)/рай-дуга (rayduga) has three possible roots

1. **PIE root *rad*, ray**
   English: radius, a ray of light; radiant, radiator, radio—Rainbows radiate rays.
   Russian: радуга (raduga); радио (radio)
2. **Greek: *eros*, love**
   Russian: рад (rad), glad
3. **PIE root *rehs*, wealth**

Latin: *res*, thing, good thing, goods, wealth
Russian: рай (ray), paradise; рай-дуга (rayduga), rainbow

### Two PIE roots provide words for thunder

1. **PIE root *gromo*, to thunder, rage**
   Russian: гром (grom), thunder
2. **PIE root *stenh*, to thunder**
   Latin: *tonitrum*, thunder; *attonitus*, thunderstruck
   English: astonished, thunderstruck
   Russian: стенáть (stenat), to moan, groan

### Finally, one PIE root holds a key to the suitability of seasons

**PIE root *ghed*, to unite, be suitable**
English: good meaning suitable—Everything is good for something.
Russian:
   год (god), year, time; погода (pagoda), weather
   угодить (ugodit), to please, oblige, hit a target

# 25. Stormy Precipitation

If we picture precipitation as no more than vapor in precipitously headlong flight, we disregard its complex temperament. To get down to Germanic roots, let's start with storms stirring up their tempers, because stir and storm are cognates. How stormily do they stir up their tempers! Like Aeolus, the king of the winds, tearing up their "hollow mountain" in Vergil's *Aeneid*, we can stir up a couple of paragraphs—just as he did—with a few of their stormy blasts. To wrap up a couple more Germanic roots, wind and weather are also cognates. To bring these words together: weather stirs up winds that blow up storms. Long after Vergil in the Classical Age described Aeolus' duty to "soften and temper" the winds, Goethe in the Romantic Age described Faust's duty to loosen them in *Sturm und Drang*.

In the Romance word family, storms stir things up with a few more twists. Latin *aura*, air, on its own, stirs up to wind, and blows up to storm, *orage* in French. Romance words sometimes grow from a single root of their Roman mother, but storms' tossing about with so many twisters account for the variety of words that describe them. Only French, for example, uses *orage* for a storm. Other Romance languages define it differently. Before the time of a tempest, an Italian or a Frenchman may say *Il tempo è magnifico* or *Le temps fait beau*—literally, "the time is beautiful"—in describing beautiful weather. From the same root as *tempo* or *temps*, Italian *tempesta* or French *tempête*, in the timely tempering of weather, have tempestuously lost their temper. Never trust 'time' to keep its good temper!

The temper of time easily turns bad. On the isle of Malta, *maltempata* calls the time of tempest bad. With greater originality, Romanian and Albanian *furtunë* refers to the bad fortune that blows no good. With an eye to its tortuous power, Spanish *tormenta* refers to tormenting winds that English, with the same root, blows up to tornado. So many different ways of naming pandaemonium! We hope for times to remain in good temper, but when they blow up tempestuously, they stir up bad fortune in turbulent winds that twist sky together with land and sea.

Add another layer to this complexity in the words that English sailors have brought home from around the world: monsoon from India, typhoon from Greece, hurricane from the West Indies, tornado from Spain, squall from Norway, mistral from France, and tsunami from Japan. What savage souvenirs! Blowing up a storm inspires so much fear and wreaks so much havoc that people around the world have special words to describe it. In the *Aeneid*, after Aeolus has loosed the winds to do their worst, Neptune steps in with higher authority, and asks them indignantly: "So now, winds, do you dare to mix earth with sky, without me giving the nod? . . ."[7] Neptune, the Earth Shaker, did not allow wind and weather to shake things up too much. Let's also put the top back on the Aeolian mountain.

Even without *Pandaemonium Aeolianum* bursting its brazen dungeon, winter precipitation in its various forms make a mess. Snow turns to sleet, and hail to ice, or back to popcorn snow. Let's slosh (1844) through the PIE family of snow (825), and the cognate pair of sleet (1300) and slush (1641). The root for snow shows a remarkable uniformity in Germanic, Romance and Slavic branches of the Indo-European family, but its compounds with rain get slushy. German snow, *Schnee*, with *Schnee-regen*, snow-rain, and Russian дождь со снегом (dozhd' so snegom), rain with snow, represent the simplest union that makes sleet. Italian *neve* adds a suffix *-ischio*, snowish; Spanish *agua-nieve* mixes water-snow; and French serves up a snowmelt with *neige fondue*. Everything has some purpose. Who knows?—in water ice, we can see fond fun due for children. In contrast to these compounds, the English word sleet stands remarkably on its own, with slush, only coming three hundred years later to represent the mess that warm earth melts.

Sleet makes a mess—hail threatens harm with its bullets hailing down from heaven. Rain, stirred up in storm clouds, congeals as hail. *Grando*, its Latin root, had a popular etymology, "congealed drops of water, greater that usual" (*guttae aquae concretae solito grandiores*), that suggests a derivation from the same root as that of grand. A Russian word for sleet, крупа (krupa), suggests a gritty nature like that of hail. In English, hail, actually drawn from a root for peeble, describes sleet with girth, but English speakers soon felt the necessity of redundantly adding stone to confirm its image as hailstone (1000). Midway between snow and hail, *graupel*, soft hail, has taken the popular name popcorn snow.

Having precipitated in all these consistencies to earth, water congeals to solid ice in frigid winter weather. The Romance root *gel* describes it as glacially glossy, like the French *crème glacée*, prosaically called ice cream or, since noun should not modify nouns, iced cream, when men use the rugged power of ice to congeal peaches or berries with cream. The root, *(s)lab*, describes it as glossy for slipping and sliding, terrorizing the lame on crutches, but delighting the lithe on skates.

Glacial and icy often describe the *froideur* that freezes human warmth. Frigid rigidity in nature awaits the melting thaw of Spring, but men do not wisely melt in season. In nature, to observe Russian roots, the year (год, [god]) fits with weather (по-года [pa-goda]), because it pleases, угодить (ugodit), by balancing good with bad. If only human tempers might find a similar balance by an assurance of seasonal warmth!

## Words

**Four PIE roots represent storms that stir up and fly about, or pour down and break**

1. PIE root *stur*, to stir, rotate
   Latin: *turbo turbare*
      English: turbulence
   German: *Sturme*, storm; English: storm (825)
   Russian: шторм (storm), storm
2. PIE root *bew/dheu*, to smoke, fly about
   English: fume and fury
   Russian: буря (burya), storm—Burka, as surname, means storm.
3. PIE root *kehl*, to split, cleave, break
   Latin: *procella*, storm, gale (*cf. clava*, club; *clades*, destruction; *gladius*, sword)
   Russian: колоть (kolot), to split, cleave, break
4. PIE root *lehi/leib*, to pour
   Latin: *libo libare*, to taste, sprinkle, spill
      English: libation, pouring a drink offering
   Russian: лить (lit'), to pour; and ливень (liven), downpour

### Four PIE roots represent snow, sleet, and hail

1. **PIE root *sneiguh*, snow**
   Latin: *nix nivis*
      Italian: *neve*, snow; and *nevischio*, sleet
      French: *neige*; and *neige fondue*, snow melt
      Spanish: *nieve*; and *aguanieve*
      English: from Spanish, *Sierra Nevada*, snowy sawtooth (mountain)
      German: *Schnee*, snow; and *Schneeregen*, sleet
      English: snow (825, noun; 1300, verb)
   Russian:
      снег (sneg), snow
      дождь со снегом (dozhd' so snegom), sleet (rain with snow)
2. **PIE root *grew*, to fall, cognate with Germanic gross and great**
   Latin: *grando grandinis*
      Italian: *grandine*; Spanish: *granizo*; French: *grêle*
   Russian: град (grat)
3. **PIE root *kaghlo*, round pebble**
   German: *Hagel*; English: hail (825)
4. **PIE root *kroupeh*, grainy, gritty**
   English: *graupel*, soft hail, popcorn snow
   Russian: крупа (krupa), grits, groats or sleet

### Three PIE roots represent ice

1. **PIE root *ieg*, ice, frost**
   German: *Eis*; English: ice (*Beowulf*)
   Russian: иней (ínej), frost
2. **PIE root *gel*, bright, shiny, smooth; to freeze**
   Latin: *glacies*
      French: *glace*; Italian: *ghiaccio*; Spanish: *hielo*
      English:
         glacial—frozen
         glide, glib—smooth
         gloss, glaze, glad, glee—bright
3. **PIE root *(s)lab*, slip**
   English:
      slip, slump
      slum—Slums have slipped to slump
      (*cf.* a ghetto, which has always been intended to be what it is).
   Czech: *led*; Polish: *lod*; Russian: лед (led), ice

## 26. "My Cup Runneth Over"

Humans exist as elemental creatures consisting of earth, air, fire and water. Consistently, ancient medicine considered that their wellbeing depended on their holding these elements in balance. Human character, it theorized, flowed from fluids called humors, which could be either good or bad. It counted four of them and associated them with the four elements, likening blood to air, black bile to earth, yellow bile to fire, and phlegm to water. As humors effused more or less, they made men sanguine, choleric, atrabilious or phlegmatic. With proper temper and temperature, blood balanced with phlegm, as air with water; and yellow bile, with black bile, as fire with earth.

Balance is all. Out of balance, man's temper could rise or sink with tragic consequences. In Shakespeare's *Othello*, for example, Desdemona, mistakenly assumes that her husband Othello's arid nurture in tropical clime has dried up his jealous nature: "I think the sun where he was born, drew all such humors from him." This naiveté about her husband's ill humors sets her up as their pathetic victim. His excess ancient medicine would label as choler or atrabilious exuberance.

Exuberantly atrabilious, Othello murders Desdemona. The atrabilious man's darksome nature commits atrocities, but good humor bubbles over in sanguine men. Life-blood—Romance *sangue*, *sang* and *sangre*—makes them sanguine: "Blood is the most kindly humor, answering to the love of God" (1380). God's love spreads out 'largely' in sanguine men: "The sanguine man of blood hath hardiness, wrought to be loving, large of his dispense" (1430). Christian humanists, particularly those in the seventeenth century, have given us words that should make us sanguine about the potential of goodness in human nature.

Boiling, bubbling and pouring describe this effusion. At first, ebullient referred to boiling water (1599) and later (1620) to evilly boiling humors. Finally, by the end of the seventeenth century, ebullience bubbled over with goodness: "the fountain of life ought to be ebullient in every regenerate Christian" (1664). We greet each other ebulliently and have recreated the same image, without the heat, when we speak of bubbly personalities, now more quixotic than thoughtful.

Coined in the middle of the seventeenth century, effervescent (1651) first referred to boiling liquid and much later (1800) to ebullient personality: "an effervescence of the sublimer affections." Effervescence bubbles more than ebullience: in *Uncle Tom's Cabin*, Harriet Beecher Stowe describes "juveniles effervescing in all those modes of gambol and mischief." Alluding to similar heat, we refer to those who are fervent (1400), later fervid (1656), or ardent (1387) in expressing love.

Without heat, exuberant (1513) refers to the fountain of life overflowing. Exuberant from the Latin *uber*, breast as a noun or fruitful as an adjective, first described crops exuberant in prolific luxuriance. Just as ebullient, exuberant described overflowing joy in the middle of the seventeenth century: "exuberant goodness as may justly ravish us to an amazement" (1648). Richard Steele later spoke of "exuberant love to mankind" (1711).

Also in the middle of the seventeenth century, effusive (1662) described goodwill pouring out: "effusive charity and humanity" (1662). In his sermon, *The Duty and Reward of Bounty to the Poor* (1671), Isaac Barrow described "plentiful and promiscuous effusion of good": "He that sows does not regard one particular spot, but throws all about so much as his hand can hold, so far as the strength of his arm doth carry. It is likewise called *watering*, which also seems to import a plentiful and promiscuous effusion of good, dropping in showers upon dry and parched places." Broadcasting seeds of goodness over the poor like heaven pouring rain over dry earth, charitable men recreate the profusion of God's creation.

Some skeptics can not allow themselves to profess such effusion of the "Gushing School" (1864). They would suggest considering its waste in a cognate antonym of effusion: futile (1612) describes people pouring out words as unreliably as leaky ships. Effusion does not necessarily flow profoundly, when its prolixity pours out its words in logorrhea. Protect us, Lord, from "the bubblings of our own vain hearts" (1655). Christian humanists in the last half of the seventeenth century, however, saw no futility in the good humors of the Holy Spirit. They rallied ebullient, effusive and exuberant to describe a man overflowing with goodwill. This humanity in the seventeenth, the most effusive of centuries, was contradicting the dry and stern morality of the Puritans.

With God's macrocosm overflowing into the human microcosm, the Bible naturally sees righteousness coursing like "an ever-flowing stream" (*Amos* 5.24). Good humors flow out in affluent exuberance of good will. Prefixes like e- and ex- may anticipate excess, but this extraordinary goodwill exults in elation. When our cup runneth over, let caring share.

## Words

Water and fire nurture life. Water overflows; with fire, it boils over. Words describing goodwill pouring out suggest that the human microcosm reflects water flowing and overflowing, and fire warming and burning in the macrocosm. Blood, coursing through our veins, nurtures the sanguine humor that pulses goodwill through our lives in exuberant streams. Three PIE roots describe pouring out; and five, heating and bubbling. By contrast, Russian expresses the effusive by the PIE root *peth*, to spread.

## Pouring Out

1. **PIE root *ugh* or *ud*, wet**
   Latin: *humeo humere*, to be wet; and *humidus*, wet
     English: humor (1340) and humid (1549)
   *Cf.* PIE root *ster*, to erect
     English: structure
     Russian: настроение (nastroyeniye), mood
2. **PIE root *gheu*, to pour**
   Latin: *fundo fundere* and *fusus*, to pour
     Spanish: *efusivo*
     English: effusive (1662) and futile (1612)
3. **PIE root *eudh*, udder**
   Latin: *uber ubris* (noun), breast, richness; (adjective), rich, fruitful, prolific
     Italian: *esuberante*; Spanish: *exuberante*
     French and English: *exubérant* and exuberant (1513)
   German: *Euter*, udder
   English: udder (1000), rich source of nourishment for young animals
   Russian: вымя (vymya), udder

## Heating and Bubbling

1. **PIE root *as*, to be dry, burn, glow**
   Latin: *ardeo ardere* and *arsus*, to be on fire
     English: ardent (1374), burningly eager or passionate; (1440), on fire
2. **PIE root *bhereu*, to bubble, stir, boil**
   German: *brennen*, to burn
   English: to burn, (825), to feel passionate anger or love; (1000), to be on fire
3. Latin: *ferveo fervere*, to burn, seethe, be hot; *fervesco fervescere*, to become hot
   English:
     fervent (1400), ardent or burning; (1465), raging
     effervescent (1651)
4. **PIE root *bew/dheu*, to smoke, blow, inflate**
   Latin: *bullio bullire*, to boil

Italian: *bollente*
English: ebullient (1599)
5. **PIE root *kuep*, to boil**
Latin: *cupio cupere*, to desire
English:
to covet
Cupid, the god of desire
Russian: кипучий (kipuchiy), ebullient
*Cf.* PIE root *peth*, to spread—a petal spreads out
Latin:
*pando pandere*, to spread
*pateo patere*, to lie open
French: *expansif*; Italian: *espansivo*
English: expansive and patent
Russian: экспансивный (ekspansivnyy), effusive

## 27. To Eat

After we breathe, we sustain life by ingesting food. Social and psychological complexities complicate the relative simplicity of eating. Complexities also fold into complicity, since eating both fostered Adam and Eve's innocence and ruined it when they ate all round the limits that God had set. As we deal with such involved fare, we should not bite off more than we can chew. Let's put a few words on our plate. By ruminating on their concrete histories, we can digest a few simple explanations for abstract complexities.

To take a basic root, Latin *edere* and *esse*, to eat, tells a characteristic story about the way we live and speak. It was so simple that its forms resembled those of the Latin verb *sum esse*, to be. *Est* in Latin meant both "he is" and "he eats." This simplification in form led to complication in meaning. Since we use the verb 'to be' more than the verb 'to eat,' *est* eventually meant only "he is," and *edit* meant "he eats." This alternative form resolved one complication but created another, since *edit* also meant "he produces" or "he edits." The language needed a good edit, and popular usage supplied it in time; since no trace of the simple verb *edere* survived into Romance. This verb had to put on a little weight to survive. In language, putting on weight usually means compounding with prefixes. In this case, *edere* compounded with *com-* to become *comedere*, to eat completely. After dropping the consonant 'd,' Spaniards took it up as their verb, *comer*. *Comamos*, let's eat, warms the Hispanic soul.

Italians and the French were not satisfied with the Spaniards' intensification by compounding. They thought that eating deserved a more colorful verb. English has lively ways of describing eating: chow down, gobble up, pig out. Latin also devised a vivid colloquialism to describe it. On the comic stage, the character *manducus*, the chomper, had a large mouth and a hooked nose. His cloddish vivacity and hoggish edacity found its home in the verb *manducare*, to chomp. Chomping replaced eating in Italian and French. Italian grandmothers sing out *Mangia! Mangia!*, Eat!, Eat!—twice, just for emphasis, as their families dig in.

The evolution of the Romance verbs *mangiare*, *manger*, and *comer* tells a story about our complicated relationship to eating. Thoreau has advised, "Simplify, simplify;" but humanity replies, "Complicate, complicate." The simple Latin verb to eat only survived in Spanish by becoming a bit obese to make eating complete. In Italian and French, it did not survive at all. These languages replaced it with a more vivid verb that turned eating into chomping. Our natural self-indulgence does not allow eating to be simple; and our natural ego loves to make full, almost hyperbolical, statements. At the least, we have made eating vivid and full. The least, however, is hardly enough.

Since most slices of humanity want much more than the least, something as simple as eating becomes so complicated that we may be led astray into either gluttonous compulsion or starving repulsion. We label these extremes with an objective term, eating disorders. In some way, we all fall out of order. German *Essen*, to eat, has its extreme, *Fressen*, to eat up, guzzle. The one describes humans; the other, animals, or humans eating like animals. English, to fret, to gnaw at, has the same root. We often fret about our diet. Germans describe the excess of their gourmandizing in the phrase *Essen und Fressen*. Most people love to push the limits.

Animal appetite also serves to describe human excess. Words describing wolfish gullets need no intensification to represent voracity. In a free translation of Juvenal's tirade against sybaritic excess (*Satires* 11), William Congreve pairs gluttony and want, by which he means destitution:

Well may they fear some miserable end,
Whom gluttony and want, at once attend,
Whose large voracious throats have swallowed all (1693).

Congreve translates Juvenal's *gula*, from which we derive gullet and gulosity, as gluttony. In the inveterate proclivity of excess, spendthrifts spend more than they have to consume more than they can eat. They end 'miserably' in hopeless and helpless destitution.

Excessive egotism and self-indulgence slip down the slopes that Juvenal and William Congreve's moral indignation denounces. Wolfish voracity comes naturally to wolves. Let's ruminate on one more root as a clue to this excess: in addition to *edere*, to eat, compounding to *com-edere*, to eat completely, it also compounds to *ob-edere obesus*, to eat all round. The word root compounds to make the adjective form 'obese,' but—thankfully!—not quite so automatically to make the human form obese. Only eating all round, *all the time*, can do that. Thoreau is at least half right: simplicity should sometimes straighten out complexity. It might save us from a stew of complicity like the one that expelled our first parents from the Garden.

## Words

All animals need to eat, but human animals make it order or chaos. Words for eating tend toward an excess that makes men either animals or epicures.

### PIE root *ed*, to eat

Latin: *edo edere / esse,* and *esus*, to eat. *Esse*, to be and to eat
    English: edible
Latin: *com-edere*—intensive—to eat completely
    Spanish: *comer*, to eat
    English: comestible
Latin: *obedere obesus*, to eat all round
    Italian and Spanish: *obeso*, obese
    English: obesity (1611), obese (1651), the result of eating all round
German: *Essen*
English: to eat (825)
Russian: есть (yest'), to eat; еда (yeda), meal; обед (obed), main meal

### PIE roots *per*, thoroughly, compounded with *ed*, to eat

German: *fressen*, to eat up, guzzle
English: to fret, to gnaw at; fretting, gnawing worry

### PIE root *menth*, to chew

Latin: *manduco manducare*, to chomp
    Italian: *mangiare*; French: *manger*
    English: manger, a feed trough for animals

### PIE root *pa*, to feed

Latin: *pasco pascere* and *pastus*, to feed, pasture
Russian:
    пастбищ (pastbishch), to pasture
    пастись (pastis'), to feed, graze; пища (pishcha), pabulum, food

**PIE root *gwora*, food**

Latin: *vorare*, to devour
    English: to devour (1315), carnivorous (1646), omnivorous (1656), voracious (1698)
Russian: жрать (zhrat'), to devour; обжора (obzhora), glutton

**PIE root *gel*, throat**

Latin: *gluttio gluttire*, to swallow, gulp down; *gula*, gullet, gluttony
Russian: глотка (glotka), throat; глотать (glotat'), to swallow, gulp down
English: glutton (1225) and gluttony (1225), gullet (1382), gulosity (1500)

# 28. Earthy Roots

When I tell some people that I set all our roots at great store, they respond by saying that they set most store by potatoes. I get right down to the good earth of their store and dig up my favorites. I like potatoes too, but I particularly favor onions—every dish that I prepare starts with them. Let's get down to these two edible roots that nourish us. No treatment of earth is complete without its bounty. What can be more wonderfully, edibly, earthy? Just to make a beginning, potatoes and onions top the list. They end up by combining deliciously in the same pot, but they start out by telling very different stories about their times and cultures.

    Chaucer's Summoner is a low and lecherous fellow, but at least he eats a healthy diet: "Well loved he garleek, oynons, and eek lekes." If good moral folk scorn such good food, as just another part of his low life, they miss the best of earthy nourishment. In lofty morality, they can rate themselves at the top of creation. At the bottom, they can scorn as low vegetative life men like the Summoner without the animation of mind or morality; but getting down to their roots—etymological and edible—they get their vigor from veggies that put them on the top. Our mothers had the right idea. Remember their refrain at the dinner table: 'Eat your vegetables!'

    Of the same root as tumor and tumid, tuberous vegetables swell in their tubers. Tubers also swell with nourishment: "a rootstock, some portion of which is thickened by the deposition of nourishing material." The plant stores this "nourishing material" for its survival, until men dig it up for theirs. Linnaeus chose Latin *tuber* to describe the potato (1555), which, itself, a word of Haitian origin, has survived in Spanish and Italian *patata*, and in English potato.

    Beyond Spanish, Italian and English, this original word potato has gained only limited currency in the languages of the world. It had a legitimate claim to be the first and, therefore, the correct name, but, as a strange and foreign-sounding word, it painted no picture that might appeal to the imagination. In the sixteenth century, the popularity and novelty of this new delicacy from the Americas inspired a name that associated it with the earth: Peter Martyr in *De orbe Novo* (1516), described the potato as "of the color of earth," *terrei coloris*; and José de Acosta in his *Historia Moral y Natural de las Indias* (1590), compared its clumps to earthy lumps: *son a modo de turmas de tierra*, "they are in the manner of lumps of earth." Potatoes' earthy appearance appealed to the imagination: the Latin phrase *terrae tuber*, tuber of the earth, became German *Kartoffel*, Russian картофель (kartofel'), Romanian *cartof*, and Armenian կարտոֆիլ (kartofil). A spud, a spade-like tool, with three short, sturdy prongs, that dug them up, also named them.

Also following the earthy association of *terrae tuber*, Germans called the potato *Erdapfel*, earth apple, which at first also described melons and cucumbers. The Polish called it *ziemniak* (*cf.* Russian, земля [zem-lya], earth), simply, "from the earth." Supplying a noun derived from *terrae tuber*, French called it *pomme de terre*, fruit of the earth, and *pommes frites*, French fries. These names attest to the potato's earthy origin and appearance as its identifying feature. (By the similarity of the truffle to this *terrae tuber*, the phrase also became Italian *tartuffo*, truffle, a special treasure dug up from the earth.)

Getting down to earth has a down side. By its association with lumpy shapes and misshapen shanty behavior, we use their image to disparage the couch potato's humbling bumbling as small potatoes. Potatoes and couch potatoes do not impress by their beauty of form: as a nickname, spud alludes to a stumpy, dumpy shape. At times, we may have belittled these gifts from the earth; but with all humanity and at all times, we love our spuds. Back in the day, the rustic, nicknamed Spud, dug them up with his thick three-prong spud, roasted them and hawked them in the market.

The onion claimed as much ancient fame around the Mediterranean as the potato, arriving much later from the Americas, has claimed modern fame around the world. In their own places, both are ancient. Like the Haitian potato, Romance *cepa* has no certain etymology, because it is just what it has always been since time began. Roman "rustics," according to the ancient author Columella, "call a *cepa* an *unionem*"—*Cepam vocant ūniōnem rustici*—from which English derived onion.

We enjoy vivid names: Europeans named a potato for its earthy origin and appearance; and Roman farmers called a *cepa* an *unionem*, onion, to highlight its union of many layers in one—*e pluribus unum*. Onion, as a doublet of union, focuses on the layering of its tuber—"close concentric coats"—in contrast to garlic. Chive is also derived from *cepa*, but it now describes the leaves and not the tuber of its plant.

Because they have different names, onions and scallions or shallots may seem to describe different vegetables. Actually, they are the same vegetable, derived from the same name—after, in the case of scallions or shallots, they have been incorporated into a noun phrase. This etymology follows a common process in language: the adjective from a phrase describing one type of ancient onion, *cepa Ascalonia*, an onion imported from Ashkelon, a port in Israel, became the name of scallions and shallots, which are young and tender spring onions. In a similar process of choosing the adjective of a noun phrase to represent its noun, English peach is derived from the adjective of the Latin phrase *persicum pomum*, an apple imported from Persia; and quince is derived from the adjective of the Latin phrase *cotoneum pomum*, an apple imported from Kydonia, modern Khania, a port in Crete. Peaches have their names because they come from Persia; quinces, from Khania; and shallot or scallions, from Ashkelon. These fruits and vegetable are eponymous in deriving names from their places of origin. We often use adjectives to represent nouns. In a market, we can ask for a Yukon Gold or an Idaho, without adding potato to the adjectives.

Take your pick: roasted spuds or creamy Delmonico's, onion rings or *Soupe à l'oignon*—potatoes and onions can find a home in every kitchen and please every palate. Their etymological histories that reflect the highs and lows of history do not hinder their melding perfectly in the pot. The American melting pot cooks up best on the stove. When onions flavor fried potatoes or chives perk up a baked potato, no one tastes the burden of history.

## Words

### PIE root *weg*, to be strong

Latin: *vegeo vegere*, to be alive, to give force; *vigor*, force
English: vegetable (1400), of plant growth; (1746), plant in a garden

### PIE root *teue*, to swell

Latin: *tuber*, swelling, tumor
    English: tuber
    *Cf.* Russian: клубень (kluben'), tuber, cognate with globe and glome; and, Greek bulb, first referring to an onion

Latin: *terrae tuber*, tuber of the earth
>Italian: *Tartuffo*, truffle; a religious hypocrite in Molière's comedy
>English: truffle (1591), edible fungus
>German: *Kartoffel*, potato; Russian: картофель (kartofel'), potato

## Of uncertain origin

Latin:
*cepa*, onion, which Isidore of Seville associates with *caput*, head:
*Cepa vocatur quia non aliud est nisi caput.*
"It is call a *cepa*, because it is nothing other than a head."
>Italian: *cipolla*; Spanish: *cebolla*; French: *ciboule*, spring onion, scallion
>German: *Zwiebel*
>English: chive

Latin: *cepa Ascalonia*, onion of Ashkalon, seaport in Israel
>English: scallion and shallot, derived from *Ascalonia*

## PIE root *oino*, one

Latin: *unio unionis*, union or onion
>French: *oignon*, onion
>English: onion (1356) and union (1432)

## PIE root *lewg*, to bend

English: leek
Russian: лук (luk), onion
>PIE root *ghaiso*, spear and *lewg*
>English:
>Edgar, Roger, Gertrude, Gerald, names incorporating gar/ger, spear
>gore—with his *gar*, a bull *gores* a matador with much *gore*—a spear, its piercing action and the bloody result in one root
>>(*cf.* spud, a spade, the spuds it digs up; and Spuds or Spuddy, the man digging up, roasting, and selling them)
>
>garlic (gar-lic), literally, spear-leek (*cf.* garfish, spearfish), in reference to the cloves as spears or horns

## PIE root *gheim*, winter

Sanskrit: Himalaya, abode of snow; and Latin: *hiems*, winter
Greek: *cheimon*, winter; *chimera*, a monster born of winter storms
Russian: зима (zima), winter

## 29. European Names for American Plants

In fourteen hundred and ninety-two, Columbus sailed to buy nothing new. He sailed to buy the same old spices by a new route—very old, indeed ancient, spices by a very new, indeed, revolutionarily new, route. He was sailing West by what he hoped was a direct root to India, to which his countrymen had already been sailing, by a very indirect root, East. India, at the time, described all of East Asia. His successors eventually called the islands that he discovered the West Indies, in contrast to the East Indies. But he, not expecting to find anything between Spain and India, labeled indigenous peoples in his path simply as Indians. Finding a fit for the new and unfamiliar in a world of the old and familiar tests men's discernment.

Sometimes, things do not really fit. Indian, as a name for Native Americans, screams colonialism ignoring their ethnicity and cultural identity that multiculturalism respects. Colonies, never founded for the good of mankind, use—and abuse—the unknown in service to the known. In a similarly colonial example of known identity appropriating the unknown, the name of the Roman province Asia of the Orient, now called Turkey, was extended east through the entire continent to the Pacific Ocean. Continuity, by the comfortable old ways of knowing, gives an impression, at least, of standing on solid ground.

Although we use the names sweet corn and peppers without hesitation, we might also feel uncomfortable about their imprecise fit. When Columbus came to America, he and other Europeans were accustomed to their old food and not ready for the new; in fact, they had been commissioned to find these old products, not new ones. Understandably, they fit a new food into the category in which they had been commissioned to trade.

One of these products, the berry of *Piper Nigrum*, black pepper, Mediterranean and Germanic people knew by its Latin name long before they might have named it by a Romance or Germanic derivative. Heading west to acquire *Piper* from India, Spaniards found *Capsica*, the fruit of the potato family, and they called it *pimiento*, the masculine of *pimienta*, black pepper, because some spicier members of the *Capsica* family, like cayenne pepper, tasted as hot as the Indian pepper for which they were searching. Englishmen and Russians call both products pepper and use adjectives to make a distinction. In Latin, *capsica*, box, refers to the boxlike shape of the fruit. From *capsica*, English also derives chest and the cash it holds.

Native names for peppers do survive in chili and cayenne. The native name for the red-hot varieties of these peppers, *chilli*, spelled with a single 'l' in English, derived from a Nahuatl word meaning sharp that describes its taste. The Tupi language of Brazil has contributed Cayenne, the name of an island where this pepper is grown.

Englishmen also applied their own generic word, corn, meaning grain, to designate the berry of *Piper Nigrum* as a peppercorn. They also applied this word, which they used to describe wheat, rye or barley, to the grain that American Indians called maize. Latin *cornu* means horn, kernel or grain, cognates of the same family as *cornu*. Indian corn passes muster for the British meaning of its name, because it does have kernels. *Cornu* pours out words in a cornucopia!

Indian corn, as a staple of American diet, has taken many forms and names. Hasty pudding, flavored with ginger or maple syrup, started as a British pottage made with wheat flour; but its version with maize became so American that Yankee Doodle used it in his metaphor: "Father and I went down to camp, / Along with Captain Gooding, / And there we saw the men and boys / As thick as hasty pudding." If not stirred, corn meal does become lumpy and "thick."

Loose corn kernels and beans cooked in bear fat, Narraganset Indians called succotash. Equivalent in its nutritive value to the beans and rice that nourishes people around the world, succotash has brought many Americans through lean times. As mush, corn meal dishes usually characterize the south and the Southwest. From corn meal, the colonists made hominy, an Algonquian word, also known as grits. Farther south, Mexican bake tortillas, a flatbread made of corn meal.

As an exception to the known appropriating the unknown, the last syllable of the Narraganset Indian word *askuta-squash*, squash, has described foods from the Latin *cucurbita* family, the root of gourd. These gourds, not fitting into any convenient European category, won squash as their own special name (*squash* in Italian, French and Spanish; *quetschen* in German, and сквош (skvosh) in Russian). Ironically, the best known of these, pumpkin, takes its origin from a Latinate root (*pepo peponis*, melon).

When we sit down to an American Thanksgiving dinner, we enjoy vegetables like succotash, winter squash and pumpkin pie, which proudly declare American independence. With multi-colored flint corn, small pumpkins and colorful gourds pouring from a cornucopia as decor, Thanksgiving both looks and tastes American.

Our understandings mixed with our misunderstandings about varieties of Indians, peppers and corn are good evidence that the same word applied to different things causes confusion. Since America has always accumulated layer upon layer of cultural import, this misunderstanding is understandably American. The same confusion may also arise from different words applied to the same thing. On the other side of the ocean, imagine the curiosity of an eighteenth century British corn factor in the Corn Exchange when he first heard of corn in hominy, tortillas, and succotash, and his surprise when he tasted them in a taco.

## Words

### PIE root *pippa*, pepper

Latin: *piper*, pepper
    Italian:
        *pepe nero*, black pepper; *peperoncino di Cayenna*, cayenne pepper
        *pepe verde*, green pepper; *peperone* or *peperoncino*, red pepper
    French:
        *poivre noir*, black pepper; *poivre de Cayenne*
        *poivron vert* or *rouge*; pepper, green or red
    English: pepper (1000), peppercorn (1000)
Russian:
    черный перец (chernyy perets), black pepper
    кайенский перец (kayyenskiy perets), cayenne pepper
    зеленый перец (zelenyy perets), green pepper
    красный перец (krasnyy perets), red pepper

### PIE root *peik* / *peig*, to cut, mark, adorn

Latin: *pingere*, to paint; *pigmentum*, plant juice, from which pigments are derived
    Spanish:
        *pimienta negra*, black pepper; *pimienta de cayena*
        *pimiento verde* or *rojo*, pepper, green or red; *pimento*, allspice
        French: *piment rouge*, from Spanish, cayenne pepper
        English:
            pimento, red sweet pepper stuffed in an olive
            pint, a bottle "painted" to mark content; pinto, painted horse

### PIE root *ger*, to ripen, grow old

1. Greek: *geron*, old man
    English: gerontology
2. Latin: *granum*, grain
    Italian: *grano*, wheat
    English: grain

3. Latin: *cornu*, horn; *cornucopiae*, horn of plenty
   English: corn (700), the fruit of various plants; cornucopia, horn of plenty
4. Russian: зреть (zret), to ripen; зерно (zirno), grain

PIE root *kap*, to take, grasp

Latin: *capsica*, chest; *cornu*, horn

Of no certain root

Spanish: borrowed from Taino, *mais*, maize
   Italian and French: *mais*, corn
   English: maize; Russian: маис, maize
Russian: кукуруза (kukuruza)—*cf.* Latin *cucurbita*, maize
   German: *Kukuruz*, maize, borrowed from the Slavic

# 30. Bread

Corn—Asian, European or American—sustains human life. Ground, mixed with water and dried in the sun, it starts to resemble what the English language calls bread. The origins of words for it have focused on its shape as loaf, its preparation and its value as food in the pantry. Its story tells of food that sustains human life. It also reaches beyond itself to the domestic and social scene associated with this sustenance and to the mystery of life itself.

Sustenance sustains life with bare essentials. Since a staff sustains a man, the Hebrew prophet Ezekiel called bread the staff of life: "Son of man, behold, I will break the staff of bread in Jerusalem: and they shall eat bread by weight, and with care; and they shall drink water by measure, and with astonishment (*Ezekiel* 4.16). Ezekiel speaks of bread and water sustaining life. In combination with a dairy product—bread with milk or bread with cheese—it sustains it better.

Loaf, a very old word, first represented bread in English. It referred to the shape rising in the oven—"the undivided article as shaped and baked." "Shaped" gives a clue to its meaning: meatloaf, sugarloaf, and bread loaf have the same shape, but not the same material. Compounds of loaf point to the foundations of domesticity. Lady compounds la-, loaf, with -dy, to knead. From the -dy root, English also derives the word dough. A lady, therefore, kneaded the loaf of dough. The lord, the loaf-ward, guarded it. The lord and lady eventually left the kitchen, but they gained their status from kneading and guarding the loaf.

Latin *panis*, the Romance root for bread, focuses on its use as nourishment. Derived from *pascere*, to feed, *panis* represents food in general. In Hebrew, analogously, *lacham*, to eat, is cognate with *lechem*, bread or food. *Pater*, father, fulfills his duty as breadwinner by putting it on the table. Who can call himself a father, unless he fulfills this duty? "Or what man is there of you, whom if his son ask bread," Jesus asked, "will he give him a stone?" (*Matthew* 7.9).

The *paterfamilias* feeds his flock, as well as his family. As pastor, shepherd, he pastures his flock. By stocking his family's pantry with *pane* and pasta, he provides for their repast, which has become a literary word for a rich and plentiful meal. Soup, by contrast, derived from Latin *suppa*, bread sopped in milk, provides bare subsistence, the sop that lords throw to their subjects. Abraham Lincoln considered it good enough for his supper. Some beloved recipes preserve and ritualize this combination by specially shaped crackers in oyster stew, croutons in tomato soup and a French croûte—crust without the 's'—topped with cheese in *soupe à l'oignon*.

The Germanic words from this root—father, feed, food, and fodder—represent the same associations of their Romance cognates. The father feeds food to his family and fodder to his flock; just as the *pater* feeds *panis* to his family and pasture to his flock.

When family and friends gather round the table to eat bread compounds of the *panis* root focuses on this social life in general. In company, com-panions join the repast. Companion, a mess-mate with whom we share (com-) bread, has the same friendly and social reference of bread. Man's companionable nature defines him, as much as his wisdom, play or craft. To be alone contradicts his nature; but to be always in company may not best fulfill it. "Companions I have enough," observed Alexander Pope, "friends few." Companionship gets down to basics. In old age, a man's companion, his nurse, sees that he eats something better than bread and water.

Beyond the reference of *panis* to food, and loaf to shape, and their compounds to domesticity and sociability, English bread reaches in its implication to the nature of conviviality. We so readily associate a meal with breaking bread that bread has been derived from the Indo-European root to break. As old a word as loaf, bread is that which we break with companions at meals, at which we eat our "daily bread" (*Matthew* 6.11), as the Lord's Prayer has called it. By their breaking bread with Jesus, the disciples were able to identify him after his resurrection: "And they told what things were done in the way, and how he was know of them in breaking of bread" (*Luke* 24.35). Continuing this tradition, the early Christian community considered its fellowship to consist in the breaking of bread: "And they continued steadfastly in the apostles' doctrine and fellowship, and in breaking of bread, and in prayers" (*Acts* 2.42). These meals, beyond mere companionship, require that the company thank God for the bread before breaking it.

Bread also reaches to a mystery as a metaphor for life. Since daily bread sustains life in good company or bad, we may eat the "bread of sorrows" (*Psalm* 127.2), and "of tears" (*Psalm* 80.5) or "of wickedness" (*Proverbs* 4.17) and "of deceit" (*Proverbs* 20.17). When we eat the bread of idleness, we get what we do not deserve. As a literal reality, it should not constitute the whole of human life: "Man shall not live by bread alone," Jesus chided the Devil, "but by every word that proceedeth out of the mouth of God" (*Matthew* 4.4). And yet, as an abstraction, it does represent spiritual reality: "I am the bread of life; he that cometh to me shall never hunger" (*John* 6.35).

Bread represents the earned and the unearned, fulness and lack, spirit and flesh. By translating the Greek phrase, *artos epiousios*, by the Lain *panis supersubstantialis*, in the Vulgate, Jerome has suggested that "daily bread" gives substance surpassing substance.

## Words

Words for bread are derived from three roots:

1. **PIE root *bhreu*, to boil, ferment, brew; or, with less confidence, *bhreg*, to break**
   German: *Brot*, bread; and English: bread (950)
2. **Proto-Germanic root *khlaibuz*, bread**
   English:
       loaf (950), from Old English *hlaf*,
       lady (825), from OE *hlæfdize* - hlaf+dize - loaf+knead
       lord (950), from OE *hlaford* - hlaf+weard - loaf+guard
   Russian: хлеб (kleb), bread; кладовая (kladovaya), pantry
3. **PIE root *pa*, to feed**
   Latin: *pasco pascere* and *pastus*, to feed; *panis*, bread; *pastor*, and *pater*
       Italian: *pane*; French: *pain*; Spanish: *pan*
   English:
       pasture (1300), grass eaten by cattle; (1330), place where cattle eat grass
       com-pany (1250), com-panion (1297), and pantry (1300)
       pabulum (1733), food for plants or animals of lower orders

## 31. The Importance of Things

'Thing' does not do any-thing to help a writer reach his goal of being specific, but 'thing' and its Latin parallel, *causa*, at first very specifically meant some-thing. Our Anglo-Saxon and Italic ancestors placed these two nouns in a process of law. In both cases, their force in this specificity laid a foundation for their general reference to things.

Old English thing, a word first recorded in AD. 685, referred to a meeting at a fixed time or to a court of justice. For example, lawgivers and judges met in the Tyn-wold of the Isle of Man, in the Stor-ting of Norway and in the hus-tings of London. From the court, thing came also to refer to a man's case in court, which he would have considered a very important thing. In 1600, a man asking how things were going broached important matters, not trivialities.

Latin *causa* also referred to a legal case. In English, originally, ac-cusing calls a man to the case, ex-cusing calls him out of it; re-cusing, a judge calls himself back from it. In grammar, the ac-cusative accuses, that is, calls forth, a noun as the object of a verb. Before accusing, excusing or recusing, a legal case must claim *justa causa*, just cause. In other words, a court should only hear a case that is just; but the public does not think that every court always pronounces a verdict that is just. In French, when they consider a court's verdict unjust, they make it a *cause célèbre*, and debate it publicly. In the case of both *justa causa* and *cause célèbre*, cause refers specifically to a legal case, which citizens consider a cause for concern

Cause turned from the *cause célèbre* itself to its motivation, its cause, as we commonly understand the word. Cause also goes hand in hand with effect. In medicine, *causa* came to refer to causes of disease. Physicians look for them, especially for causes of death. Causes became so generally important that they supplied the root of be-cause, the causative conjunction, literally, "by cause." Theology has also used cause for its purposes, when it defined God as the *causa causans*, the "cause causing" creation. *Causa* in law and philosophy give a poignancy to the Mafia's indigenous name, *Cosa Nostra*, our cause. In its most general application, charitable causes deserve support and contributions.

The original Latin word for thing, *res*, as in real estate, also meant legal case, but it eventually meant so many other things that it lost its force. It survives in the phrase that begins an office memo, *in re* or simply *re*, "in the matter of." Since *causa* meant something specific and carried weight, Romance languages chose it as their word for thing: *cosa* in Italian and Spanish and *chose* in French. This choice of a legal term may appear surprising, but it does not stand alone. Romance also made a surprising choice of the root for its words for word: Latin and Greek *parabola*, parable, the word for Gospel teaching gave Italian *parola*, French *parole*, and Spanish *palabra*. Law and religion also exercised their *auctoritas* in choosing these basic words. A legal case rated as an important thing; and a parable, as an important word.

Things are trite because they have been true. Law so preserved ancient society that its word for legal process became common among all its peoples. When they asked how things were going, they had just cause to expect a specific answer. The thing about words is such that we should never dismiss them as nothing, especially when young ladies put on their best things.

**Words**

**No known PIE root**

Latin:
> *causa*, legal case, cause of an effect
> *causā* (ablative), for the sake of; *honoris causā*, for the sake of honor
> *causa causans*, the causing cause, a theological term for God
>> Italian and Spanish: *cosa*; Italian: *Cosa Nostra*; French: *chose*
>> English: cause (1315)
> *excusare* (*ex causā*), to call a man from a legal case, to excuse (1225)
> *accusare* (*ad causam*), to call a man to a legal case, to accuse (1297)
> *recusare*, to recuse (1387)

**PIE root *deh*, deed**

Russian: дело (dela), thing, case

**No known PIE root**

German: *Ding*, thing

**PIE root *wek*, to speak**

Russian: вещь (veshch), thing

# 32. Drink Drank Drunk

After an unsuccessful term in Congress, with his future in politics showing little promise, Abraham Lincoln considered going on the lecture circuit. His lecture on inventions started with man's first decent clothing in the Garden of Eden. As an appreciative and imaginative reader of the Bible, he saw humorous potential in the text. Personally, he joked that he, like our first parent, only drank Adam's ale. Since neither he nor Adam actually drank ale, Adam and Abe drank water. Lincoln's humorous and decorously Biblical profession of sobriety takes him back to the Garden of Eden. Only by going that far back could he be sure of finding unimpeachably sober company!

Lincoln's joke, playing on the perennial association of drinking with inebriation, challenges us to think about drink as something other than alcoholic; and it succeeds because we do not expect the challenge. The association is so deeply woven into language that the etymology of inebriation itself takes it back to prehistory. From a very ancient verb to drink, inebriation has staggered into English, sodden to its core with only the redemptive hope of inebriation by the joys of heaven. Its antonym, sober, literally, separate from ebriate, proves inebriation the rule and sobriety the exception. 'Twas ever thus, it seems—drinking up means inebriation. Since the time Adam was expelled from the Garden, his ale has not counted for much. The most prolific PIE root, *poi*, first meaning to swallow, gave Greek, Romance and Slavic words that come into English as bibulous and potable. Two of their derivations indicate opposite poles of the nature of a beverage. Poison, the older word, obviously, poisons; but a potion may work for either good or for bad, usually for good. In *Romeo and Juliet*, the sleeping potion proved all too good in sinking Juliet in a death-like sleep. Potable—this one word, at least—always points to sobriety: God bless the potable water that sustains human life, because not all water is potable. Only Edenic nature made this adjective superfluous.

One derivative of Latin *bibere* always means an alcoholic beverage: beer and beverage are cognates. In Russian, the striking similarity of the two words—Пить пиво! (Pit pivo), "Drink beer!"—identifies beer as the prototypal drink. In German *biergartens*, *gemütlichkeit* creates it own innocent, postlapsarian Garden.

English drink brings us close to a drunken, postlapsarian expulsion from the Garden. Ben Jonson's "Drink to me only with thine eyes" strikes us as an extraordinary metaphor because we expect drink from a cup and not from eyes. And don't we "look for wine" in the cup, as Jonson admits? The OED confirms this expectation, because its first example of the use of drink in 1000 puts beer in the cup.

If we drink and we drank, we are, in grammatical sequence, drunk, or, in the older sequence, drunken. In any sequence, at least after the Garden, drink and drunk have always gone together. Noah in his tent "drank of wine, and was drunken" (*Genesis* 9.21). What might Abraham Lincoln's wit have done with the consequence of this sequence?

The meaning of drink in English at first seems inflexibly inebriate. Cognate with draw, drinking draws liquid from its source. Draught is both a cognate and a synonym of drink. It resembles the Spanish verb *tomar*, to take or drink. In English, when we take a drink, we redundantly take a draw or a draught. The root of drink in draw widens the scope of drink. We may also, for example, drink in the beauty of a scene. When tobacco became popular in Europe, people said that they were drinking it. "The most divine tobacco," said Ben Jonson, "that I ever drunk." Rethink the meaning of the verb to smoke: if a smoker literally smoked tobacco, he would watch it go up in smoke. He can not smoke, as we understand the word, without inhaling, that is, drawing, drinking, the smoke into his breath and lungs. Words have complex personalities. Current usage may close the meaning of drink to the intake of liquids, but its root opens it to wider meaning.

By their similar roots, we can obviously identify drink with drunk, and beverage with beer, but we can less obviously explain this identity. Social historians have explained early Americans' extraordinarily high rate of alcoholic consumption by the scarcity of potable water. Could this problem of the polluted industrial world have been the same in prehistory, which must have enjoyed some degree of Edenic natural resource? For the source of this perennial association we can look to the nature of human appetite and aspiration. Our first parents drank water; but when their progeny found that they could use it in fermentation, they dignified it with the name *aqua vitae, eau de vie*, the water of life, in the hope that it could work for the good of life.

## Words

Must drinking lead to drunkenness?
Its three PIE roots indicate that tendency.
They lead to bibulous, ebriate, and drunk.
Only the Garden of Eden witnessed strict sobriety.

### 1. PIE root *hegw*, to drink

Latin: *ebrius*, drunk; *sobrius (se + ebrius*, apart from drink), not drunk
    Italian: *ubriaco*; French: *ivre*; Spanish: *ebrio*
       English: ebriate, inebriate, inebriation

2. **PIE root *poi*, to drink; originally, to swallow**
   A. Greek: *pinein*, to drink
      English: sym-posium (drinking together)
      Russian:
         пит (pit), to drink
         пиво (pivo), beer
         пьяный (p'yanyy), drunk
         питать (pitat), to feed
         вос-питать (vos-pitat), to rear up (вос), educate
         вос-питанный (vos-pitannyj), well-bred
   B. Latin: *potare*, to drink
      English:
         potable (1572)
         poison (1230) and potion (1350): Poisons harm, potions heal.
      Latin: *bibere*, to drink—In Romance, 'p' of *potare* changes to 'b' of *bibere*
         English: bibulous, imbibe, bib
      PIE roots for beer and drink are the same:
         Italian:
            *bere*, to drink (*io bevo*, I drink)
            *birra*, beer
         French:
            *boire*, to drink (*je bois*, I drink)
            *bière*, beer
         Spanish: *beber*, to drink (*yo bebo*, I drink)
         English: beverage
         French: *Bois de la bière!*, Drink beer!
         Russian: пить пиво! (pit pivo), Drink beer!

Since Greek beta ('b') came to represent 'v,' B in Russian sounds like 'v.' Betacism, interchange of b and v, characterizes Latin passing to Spanish. In Spanish, the similarity in sound of Latin *vivere*, to live, and *bibere*, to drink, inspired a witticism quoted by Don Quixote:

*Beati Hispani quibus vivere est bibere.*
Blessed are Hispanics for whom to live is to drink.

3. **PIE root *dhragh*, to draw, to drag**

English:
   to draw
   dray, a dray horse draws a cart

> to drink (1000), drawing liquid from a cup; drink (noun, 888)
> drunken (1050), drunk (1340), inebriate
> draft/draught, a draft of beer, drawn from a keg;
>> a draft of air, drawn, from a window, through a room.
>> We take a drink drawn from a cup and a draft drawn from a keg.
>> *Cf.* Spanish: *tomar* (Latin *autumare*, to affirm), to take, drink, as a parallel to English to drink, meaning to draw.

Russian:
> дёргать (dergət), to pull
> дрожки (droski), carriage, drawn by horses
> дорога (doroga), a road drawn through an area
> тракт and дорога, of the same PIE root, describe a road resembling English track. Tracks leave tracks for others to follow.

## 33. Trees and True Love

Helen, wife of the Greek king Menelaus, caught the eye of the young shepherd Paris, and made him one of history's most famous philanderers. Her infidelity, and especially, his stealing her away from Greece to Troy launched the ships that started the war. Before this famous desertion, Paris had first deserted his wife, Oenone. The Roman poet Ovid imagines her letter to Paris, lamenting his infidelity, but taking comfort in the beeches that "incised by you, preserve my names":

> **Inci/sae** ser/vant // a /te mea /nomina /**fagi**
> Et legor/ Oeno/ne/ **falce** no/tata **tu/a**;
> Et quan/tum trun/ci, // tan/tum mea /nomina /crescunt.
> Crescit (e) et / **in títu/los/** surgite / recta **meos**.[8]

Hyperbole characterizes love poetry: 'On how many beech trees, shall I declare my love for Oenone?', Paris must have asked himself. 'On more than one,' he must have answered; because her names, "incised" on beech trees, grow as much as their trunks. "Rise up straight," she exhorts the letters of her names, "as my titles." When they grow, the inscribed pledges of love magnify her rectitude (*cf. recta*).

Though men be false, trees are true. Ancient poets and lovers celebrated a sympathy between man and nature that reflects human morality, especially sentimentality. In prehistory, the Indo-European cognates tree and true sent down deep roots for lovers' making trees witness their truth and their troth. These roots had gotten down to enduring trust, long before Oenone lamented its betrayal. Druids, originally *dru-wid*, the oak-witted, understood more than dendrology.

Beeches, with smooth bark—beech and book have the same root—record our loves; but oaks corroborate them. In Russian, здрав-ствуй! (zdrastvuj), Hello! puts some timber in its greeting by a command, "Be sturdy like an oak!" In English, true meant faithful long before it meant consistent with fact. It ennobled the phrase true love. True heart and 'good man and true' illustrate the root uses of the word. Truman, true man, made it a name. A true man acted loyally in love long before he testified truthfully in court. Truth and true, as strong and firm oaks, live in the hearts of brave men and in the heart of true love.

Troth, good faith, shares its origin with truth. 'Upon my troth' or 'in troth' assure the truth of a man's words. Plighting one's troth, pledging one's truth, betroths: Juliet's father "betrothed and would have married her perforce" to another man after her marriage to Romeo. Truth so naturally confirmed wedlock that betrothal promised marriage. Parents so rarely betroth their daughters that the word has become archaic.

Truth and true love end stories happily, but they often start stories that end tragically. When we trust a man true in his troth, our trust, by its root, makes something firm: "Oh Lord, my God, thou art my trustful stay" (1589). With the same origin, both 'I trow' and 'I trust' take a risk. When King Lear's fool advises him to "learn more than thou trowest," he assumes that since Lear should not trust all that he learns, he should do more learning than trusting. Doublets, trusty and trustee, the first now used in folksy colloquialism and the other in the dignity of law, serve as helpers. True love, with the help of a trusty, appoints trysts for lovers, as places and times to meet that may be trusted, now understood, in ironic turnabout, as illicit and not to be trusted. Trust puts down firm roots; but when distrust uproots them, trustees settle the estate.

Facing betrayal and death, firmness may grow hard rather than strong. Latin *durus*, hard, gives English dure and its doublet dour, hardy or stern. Robert Burns chose it to describe the cruel North Wind: "Biting Boreas, fell and dour" (1794). Like the dour north wind, dour men endure by becoming obdurate, hardened against the opposition, more stubborn than obstinate in standing against it.

Focusing on health, robust derives its strength from Latin *robur*, oak. We should all hope to enjoy robust frames—"Thy frame, robust and hardy, feels indeed the piercing cold, but feels it unimpaired" (1784)—and robust minds: "They exhibit a robust sense, a mind stored indeed with classical erudition" (1836). If robust does not sound strong enough, we may beef it up with two more syllables in robustious. Hamlet chooses this hefty word to describe actors furious in their passions: "Oh, it offends me to the soul to hear a robustious periwig-pated fellow tear a passion to tatters, to very rags." Even more robust, rambunctious puts some vinegar into robustious.

Passion or good health makes our complexion glow red. *Robur* shares the same root with *ruber*, red, as in ruby red, because it often refers to the red oak, *Quercus rubra*. Ruddy complements robust by its reference to cheeks naturally suffused with a fresh, healthy redness, as in ruddy good health. Russian красный (krasnyj) means both red and beautiful. Rum in rumbustious ignites a ruddy glow of boisterous bluster.

Faith matters as much in the market place as in the religious meeting.
Confidence matters as much as knowing.
True men inspire trust because they are rooted, steadfast and firm.
Metaphor and abstraction have no place in this robust reality of trust.

## Words

Trees have such truth that the two words share the same etymology. Oaks, with deep roots in human consciousness, also have three PIE roots. The roots of trees describe their nature as robust, healthy, enduring, and true.

### 1. PIE roots *dru* and *doru*, wood; hence, solid and lasting

Latin: *durus*, hard, harsh, rough, hardy, tough
    English: to endure (1325); dour (1375), its doublet dure (1375);
        obdurate (1540)
Greek: *drus*, tree or oak
    Classical English:
        dryad, tree nymph
        druid, Celtic priest, knowing (-[w]id) the oak (dru)
    Germanic English:
        true (800), as solid as a tree; (1205), conforming with fact
        tree (825), to trow (888), and trust (1225)
        truth (893), fidelity; (1362), factual; its doublet troth (1175)
        trusty (1225) and its doublet trustee (1646)
        to betroth (1303), and tryst (1375)
Russian: дерево (derevo), tree, wood; дуб (dub), oak

### PIE root *dru*, tree, and PIE root *esu / eu*, well, good

    Greek: *eu*, well
    English: eulogy, euphemism, euphoria
    Russian:
        здрав-ый (zdravyy), sensible, reasonable
        здоровый (zdorovyy), healthy (doublet of здрав-ый), sturdy as an
            oak

здрав-ствовать (zdra-stveveti), to be well, prosper
здрав-ствуй! (zdrastvuj), hello!; literally, "Be sturdy like an oak!"

Without reference to trees, the PIE root *kailo* gives English its word for health:

**PIE root *kailo* / *quailu*, unharmed, whole, well**
    German: *Heil!*
    English:
        Hail!, Be thou hail!—Hail and farewell!
        Hale—hale and hardy—the same root as heal and health
        Wassail!—a toast—Be hail!(*ves*, Be![*cf.* was] + *heil*, healthy)
        *Cf.* Latin: *Ave*, Hail!; literally, Be well; *Ave, Maria*, Hail, Mary!

## 2. PIE root *reudho*, red—the only color with a PIE root

Latin: *robur roboris*, oak, strength—associated with the red oak
    Italian: *rovere*, oak; Spanish: *roble*, oak
    English:
        ruddy (1100), healthy redness of ruddy good health
        robustious (1548), robust (1549) and rumbustious (1778)
        to corroborate (1533)

In Russian, another PIE root celebrates the beauty of the color red:

**PIE root *gher*, to scrape, smear, tinge**
    Greek: *chromos*, color
    English:
        chrome, a metal of a brilliant color
        mono-chrome, of a single color
    Russian:
        красный (krasnyj), red, beautiful (OCS, *rudru*, red)
        красивый (krasivi), beautiful, handsome, fine
        Краásная плоóщадь (Krasnaya Ploshchad), Red Square

## 3. PIE root *perkus* / *prkweu*, holm oak, an evergreen

Latin: *quercus*, oak—'p' assimilated to 'k' (Greek *pente* and Latin *quinque*)
    Italian: *quercia*; Spanish: *Albu-querque*, white (alba-) oak (-*querque*)

Since pines replaced oaks in European forests, their names share the same root:

    German: *Fichte*, pine tree
    Russian: пихта (pixta), fir (Grimm's law: 'f' interchanges with 'p')

## 34. Trees, Bark and Book

### Our Deepest Roots

Tapping the deepest roots of language takes us up and out into the backcountry of time and place, to places like Oenone's beech grove. Out there, trees reach so far back in history that they make even ancient Indo-European roots seem recent. Take, for example, the Latin name of the holm oak, *ilex*, so ancient that it predates Indo-European. In other words, *ilex* predates prehistory. Out in the country, we may hesitate to venture into wild woods; let's jump right in and take tree spirits for our guides, as we enter these sacred groves in the life of mankind.

Trees take us back to prehistory, but mostly with eloquent silence, leaving behind just a few clues to their stories. In the most ancient of days, for example, the flexible wood of the yew supplied bows and arrows and the poison that made the arrows lethal. The Scythians passed their word *taxos*, yew, on to the Greeks, who passed it on to the English, who have taken the yew as their own. Shot across Eurasia, it wrote its history in blood. One of the oldest trees in the world, a yew in a churchyard in Llangernyw, North Wales, dates back 4,000 years to the Bronze Age. It has a special place in graveyards:

> Of all the trees in England,
> Oak, elder, elm and thorn,
> The yew alone brings lamps of peace
> For them that lie forlorn (Walter de la Mare, *Trees*).

For the background of books, let's look back one more time to Oenone's grove with its books of beech. Trees have always supplied a surface for writing, at first, for runes. German, *Buche*, beech and *Buch*, book, represent the similarity between beech trees and the books that they make. Beech trees provide one source, but only one, for paper. Latin *līber*, from which Romance languages derive their words for book, means tree bark. Its PIE root, *leup*, strip off, indicates the first step in primitive papermaking. Bark grew on trees, it seems, just for the purpose of being stripped off. Similarly, Russian вяз (vyaz), elm, supplied bark used to bind, вязать (vyazat), which also described binding duties, о-бязанности (obyazannosti).

Beech makes book; but papyrus makes paper for the book. The Phoenicians exported papyrus from their port of Byblos in Lebanon. Papyrus, unlike most paper, is made from the pith, and not from the bark—the inside, not the outside—of its plant. Papyrus also makes a book, because of its doublet *biblion*, book in Greek. English library and French *bibliothèque* contain the Greek and Latin words for book. Russian derives книга (kniga), book, from a tree trunk, but its word for paper refers to material of higher quality: бумага (bumaga) refers to cotton, used in making paper from rag.

After the stories about bows, beeches, and books, no tree represents cultural history as much as the olive, which the people around the Mediterranean basin have venerated. Flourishing in dry climate, olives have fed so many people—and so many lamps—that it represents ancient economy. Athena's gift to Athenians, it grew on the Acropolis and in the Grove of Academe. The symbol of Israel—"The Lord called you a thriving olive tree, / with fruit beautiful in form" (*Jeremiah* 11.16-17)—it supplied the fragrant wood for the doors of the Temple. The Apostle Paul compared his disciples to shoots of the wild olive, grafted onto the cultivated tree of Judaism: "Thou, being a wild olive tree, wert grafted in among them, and with them partakest of the root and fatness of the olive tree" (*Romans* 11.17).

Olive branches symbolize peace. When a dove brought an olive leaf to Noah in the Arc, he knew that the flood had subsided. Virgil in the *Aeneid* pictures Aeneas extending an olive branch to bring peace:

> Tum pater / Aene/as // **pup/pi** sic / fatur ab/ **alta**
> **pacife/rae**que ma/nu // ra/mum prae/tendit **o/livae**.[9]

On the Great Seal of the United States, the American eagle extends a branch (*ramum*) of the peace-bearing olive (*paciferae . . . olivae*) in its right talon.

More common—also, of course, more useful—than Oenone's beech grove or Druids' oak grove, the olive grove has its own name, olivet. The most famous, the Mount of Olives in Jerusalem, had the Garden of Gethsemane at its base. Gethsemane means "olive press" in Aramaic. The fruit from these groves has been so important that its oil has given us the generic word for oil; and red-olent to remind us of its fragrance. Spanish incorporated the Hebrew word for olive, *zayit*, in its phrase *aceite di oliva*, literally, olive of olive—so important that they had to say it twice! Portuguese selected *azeite* as olive oil. Olive oil is the oil of oils. Virgin olive oil, so called because it is organic in its manufacture, feeds humans. Lampante virgin olive oil feeds lamps, most significantly a menorah during Hanukkah.

Tree words ramify as broadly as they root deeply. What does an acorn have in common with the wild olive? Their names both share a similar root, which indicates an origin and purpose in the backcountry. *Ager* in

Latin referred to a uncultivated field out in the country. The culture of this field is agri-culture; studying its laws, agronomy. It supplied the root to both acorn and the wild olive *agri-elaios*. Acorn meant the fruit of the field, as it also specifically designated the nut of the oak. Christians, as Paul likened them to shoots of the wild olive, came from the backcountry of Judaism.

When men gather in cities from the country, town fathers plant trees from the country in cities. Trees light "lamps of peace" that bring all men closer to their better angels. They need no academic timber to construct their sociology, because in their history we hear echoes of a universal language.

## Words

The names of some trees go so far back that their origins remain unknown. Man has named the uses that he makes of them. Among these uses, it is no surprise that books and paper trace their origin to trees; also no surprise that some of these words describe the process of stripping the bark. Words like acorn and *taxus*, yew in Greek, surprise us by suggesting other uses.

### The Roots of Three Ancient Tree Words

1. Acorn
    PIE root *ag*, to lead
    Latin: *ager*, a field to which cattle are led to pasture
        English:
            agri-culture, culture of a field
            acre, at first, open land, not necessarily measured
            acorn (1000), fruit of the field; mast, food for swine
    PIE root *gwel*, acorn
    Latin: *glans*, acorn; Medical Latin, apex of penis or extremity of clitoris
        Italian: *ghianda*, acorn; French: *gland*
    Russian: желудь (zhelud), acorn
2. Yew
    PIE root *iwa*, berry, grape
    Latin: *uva*, bunch of grapes
        French: *if*, yew
    No known PIE root
        Greek:
            *toxon*, bow, arrow, poison, a word from Scythia
            *Taxus*, yew

Italian: *tasso*, yew; Spanish: *tejo*; Romanian: *tisa*
Polish: *cis*; Russian: тис (tis), yew
3. Olive
Aegean root, probably Cretan, *elaia*, olive
Greek: *agri-elaios*, of the field (wild) olive; *kalli-élaios*, beautiful (cultivated) olive
Latin:
*oliva*, olive—fruit, tree or branch; *oleum*, olive oil
*olere*, to smell, derived from odor, but made to resemble *oleum*, oil
Italian and Spanish: *oliva*; French and German: *olive*
French: *huile*, oil
English:
olive (1200), tree; (1398), fruit of the tree
olivet (1382), olive grove (*cf. arbor-etum* parallel to *oliv-etum*)
oil, olive oil (1175); (1398), any one of various oils
petroleum, oil found between rocks; redolent
Russian: олива (oliva)
Different roots for olive oil:
Spanish: *aceite* (Hebrew *záyit*, olive) *di oliva*, literally, olive of olive
Portuguese: *azeite*, olive oil
Russian: оливковое масло (olivkovoye maslo), olive oil
Romanian: *ulei de masline*, olive oil, literally, oil of oil

## Four Roots for Tree, Bark, and Branch

1. **No known PIE root**
   Latin: *arbor*, tree
   French: *arbre*; Spanish: *arbol*; Italian: *albero*
2. **PIE root *bheu*, be, grow**
   German: *Baum*, tree
   English:
   beam, tree (Old English), rafter
   boom, a long pole—Lowering it knocks a man overboard.
3. **PIE root *sker*, to cut, separate**
   Latin: *cortex*, bark of a tree; and *corium*, hide, leather
   French: *ecorce*, bark; *cuir*, leather; Spanish: *corteza*, bark; *cuero*, leather
   English: cork; and to excoriate, to flay
   Polish: *kora*; Russian: кора (kora), bark; корка (korka), crust, scab, peel
4. **No known PIE root**
   Russian:
   вяз (vyaz), elm

вязать (vyazat), to tie up, bind—elm bark, used for binding
о-бязать (vyazat), to bind, oblige
о-бязанности (obyazannosti), duties

**The Origin of Words for Book in Greek, Romance, German, and Slavic**

1. Greek: *biblion*, book; literally, pith of papyrus, named after Byblos, Phoenician port from which Greeks exported papyrus.
    English: Bible, The Book
    French: *bibliothèque*, library; Spanish and Italian: *biblioteca*
    Russian: библиотека (biblioteka)
2. Romance: PIE root *leup*, to strip off, bark
    Latin: *lībrum*, inner bark of a tree; *līber*, book
    French: *livre*, book; and *librairie*, bookstore
    Spanish and Italian: *libro*, book; and *libreria*, book store
    English: library
3. PIE root *bhago*, beech tree
    German:
    *Buche*, beech tree
    *Buch*, book—runes written on beechwood tablets or the tree itself
        Old English: *boc*, book; Russian: бук (buk), beech
    Latin: *fagus, fagea*
    Italian: *faggio*; Spanish: *haya*
4. Slavic:
    German: *kennan*, to know (*cf.* the English phrase 'beyond my ken') or, more probably, Proto-Slavic root for the trunk of a tree.
    Polish: *księga*, book
    Russian:
    книга (kniga), book
    книжный магазин (kninij magazin), bookstore
    *Cf.* Latin: *bombyx*, silk worm
        English: bombast, cotton padding, high-flown language
        Russian: бумага (bumaga), paper

# 35. Wild

Wild, primevally and autochthonously Germanic, describes anything in a state of nature—wild olives, wild flowers and wild oats, for example, or wild geese and wild boar. Men venture into the wild to hunt its fauna or to gather its flora, but they usually return to their welcoming hearths when the sun sets. Wilderness bewilders most of them, because their nature is not wild. Animals, by their nature, run wild in wilderness; in civilization, men running wild suffer a sad fate after sowing wild oats without gathering.

Although wild thrives outside cultivation, man, in Shakespeare's poetry, enters a "wild wood" to be "converted" from the wickedness of "the world" by an "an old religious man":

> And to the skirts of this wild wood he came,
> Where, meeting with an old religious man,
> After some question with him, was converted
> Both from his enterprise and from the world (*As You Like It*).

Man might seek solitude as a hermit in the wild wood; but his hermit's habitation as a place for converting city folk provides an humane exception that proves the wild rule of abandon.

Far from the imaginative transformation in Shakespeare's "wild wood," wilderness requires quite a hike from home. Transylvania, by its name, "across the forest," *terra ultra silvam*, defines itself as beyond the cultivated forests of Europe. Far from urbanity, it represents the wild behavior that city folk have always feared. By this fear, Bram Stoker's story about Dracula captivates readers. He calls Transylvania "one of the wildest and least known portions of Europe, . . . so wild and rocky, as though it were the end of the world," in which "every known superstition in the world is gathered," with wild roses and garlic growing in profusion. Transylvanians—people "brave, and strong, and simple" but "very, very superstitious"—Bram Stoker's emphasis—represent "simple" nature that has grown within a "very, very" defined culture.

In this cultural definition, "superstitious" Transylvanians arose from mankind's wild history. Remote from civilization, these medieval countryfolk had a culture that mixed paganism with Christianity, before they were finally evangelized. Since they lived in *pagi*, rural districts of Roman administration, they were called *pagani*. (Men living far out on the heath were called heathens.) Pagans preserved the customs of paganism: "Is there fate amongst us still, sent down from the pagan world of old, that such things must be?", laments Dr. Van Helsing, the arch-enemy of Dracula. He defines "such things" as "powers of devils" sent down from paganism. Thus it happened that a division of Roman provincial administration has warped into a synonym of primitive blood lust.

Wild, naturally, describes the oldest flora and fauna, and the most remote from human culture; and pagans, culturally, the oldest humanity in the wild and also the most remote from human culture. From wild and pagan, other degrees of civilization have evolved. Farmers in fields, rustics in rural villages, and foresters in forests—each one a greater distance than the other from civilization, to whom city folk have given names indicative of either amusement or scorn.

Farmers in villages lived short hike from the city. Neither urban nor urbane, their unrefined rusticity simply offended city folk. As a general term for a person in the countryside, the rustic, whom the sentimental tourist in *Dracula* admires as "brave, and strong, and simple," Count Dracula cold-bloodedly dismisses as "a coward and a fool." The clownish or unrefined rustic became a character in drama. Nicholas Udall's *Ralph Roister Doister* (1553), the first English comedy, introduced him as the roister. Roistering swaggers with uncouth behavior, a perennial source of scornful amusement to the sophisticated. His name could have been Reuben, nicknamed rube or Richard, nicknamed hick. Comedy, however, did not represent the uncouth rustic as much as melodrama which portrayed villains first living in villas, farmhouses. The villainy of villains is no longer synonymous with villages.

*Bauer* in German and *Boer* in Dutch, both meaning farmer, have given English its word boor. A neighbor was a nigh boor, a near farmer. In New York, the Bowery referred to a farm in Dutch. Boors have caused greater offense than rustics by their rude and insensitive behavior. They could be miscreants in religion, as well as in conduct. By contrast, Russian крестьянский (krest'yanskiy), peasant, literally means a Christian. With similar reasoning, French *cretin*, idiot, literally Christian, with benevolent condescension, dignifies the mentally deficient with being children of God.

After farms, forests stand beyond rusticity and urbanity. Derived from the phrase *silva forestis*, woods outside, the adjective *forestis*, 'outside,' has remained to bear the meaning of its noun *silva*. Originally, forests stood, literally, outside, but not so far outside that civilization did not govern them. Country also stood "alongside" (*contra*, against or opposite) the city, but not as remote as wilderness. Foresters made sure that no one poached on this open land belonging to the king. Poach might refer to poking into things not one's own or filling a poke with flora and fauna not one's own.

The villa produced villainy that is now not confined to any particular place; and the rustic, roistering that is now confined to books. The sylvan scene has surpassed both in supplying a word to describe wild behavior. Savage, six hundred years after wild, describes men acting like wild animals. It first referred to the flora and fauna of the forest and and gave names to its human inhabitants like Sylvester, Siivia, and Silas. Thereafter, it referred to the wild behavior of humans in the forest, sometimes intrepid, but more often cruel, as its modern meaning indicates. Since mankind should know better, men acting like wild animals cruelly contradict their nature. In *Dracula*, for example, a man cursed by the blood lust of vampires contemplates murder with "savage delight." Savage with its bloody claw lusts after wickedness that wild can not comprehend.

Traveling from the wilds to forests and farms takes us through time and social evolution. Words describing these stages reflect equal degrees of urban sophistication and pretense. Lacking humanity as savages, morality as villains, civility as roisters, sensitivity as boors, and religion as pagans, men living outside urban enclaves have caused amusement, disdain or disgust. Looking from outside in, rustics could have observed and named all these qualities among urbanites, who have named them, looking from the inside out.

In the beginning, there was nature, wild;
but, soon enough, nature, humanized,
and the humanizing set boundaries between itself and wild,
naming its characteristics with human pretense that was not so humane.

## Words

### PIE root *uelt*, open field

German: *wald*, forest
    English:
        wild (725), in a state of nature; (1300), uncivilized
        wilderness (1200), uncultivated land; (1340), where one is lost
        wild wood (1122)
        to bewilder (1684), to confuse; (1685), to lose in pathless places

### PIE root *beu*, to swell, flower

Latin:
    *Fauna*—woodland goddess, introduced as a term for animals by
        Linnaeus (1707–1778) to complement Flora, goddess of flowers
    *follis*, bellows, windbag
        Latinate English: follicle, little bag
        Romance English: fool, a head as empty as a bellows, an airhead
Germanic English: poke, bag

### PIE root *dhur*, outside

Latin: *foris*, outside; *forum*, outside area for meeting; *silva forestis*, woods
    outside
    French: *hors d'oeuvre*, literally, outside of the work; food outside dinner

English:
>forest (1300), unfenced land with trees and pasture
>forester (1298), king's official in charge of the forest
>foreign (1297), outside; (1447), of another nation

## Putative PIE root *hyle*, wood

Latin: *silva*, woods
>English:
>>sylvan (1582), of the forest; Silas and Silvia,
>>Sylvester (1657), a spirit of the woods
>
>Italian: *selvaggio*, and Spanish: *salvaje*
>French: *sauvage*, wild, savage
>English: savage (1300), in a state of nature; (1330), intrepid; (1606), cruel

Russian: Трансільванія, Transylvania

## PIE root *pag*, to join, make firm

Latin:
>*pango pangere* and *pactus*, to join, make firm, agree
>*pax pacis*, peace; and *pactum*, pact, a thing made firm
>*pagus*, country district <u>joined</u> to others
>*paganus*, pagan, inhabitant of *pagus*
>*pagina*, page, sheet of papyrus <u>joined</u> in a roll
>>Italian:
>>>*patto*, pact; and *pace*, peace
>>>*paese*, country; and *paesano*, peasant; *pagano*, pagan
>>
>>French:
>>>*pacte*, pact; and *paix*, peace
>>>*pays*, country; *paysage*, countryside; and *paysan*, peasant
>>>*paien*, pagan

Russian: паз (paz), groove, slot, joint
>*Cf.* Russian: крестьянский (krest'yanskiy), peasant; literally, Christian

## PIE root *sel*, abode

Latin: *solum*, ground, bottom
>French: *entresole*, between the ground floor and the first), balcony
>English: sole, bottom of the foot

Russian: село (selo), village, field; сельский (selskiy), rustic

## PIE root *reuos*, open field

Latin: *rus ruris*, country

English:
>rustic (1440), of the country; (1585), lacking in good breeding
>roister (1551), a swaggering, riotous fellow

## PIE root *dinghu*, tongue

Latin: *lingua*, tongue
Russian:
>язык (yazyk), tongue
>язычник (yazychnik), pagan; *cf.* gentile, referring to linguistic diversity

# Time
. . . .

# 36. Morn and Even / Morning and Evening

## Morn Morning and Even Evening

> The lark he rises early,
>   And the ploughman goes away
> Before it's morning fairly
>   At the guessing break of day;
> The fields lie in the dawning,
>   And the valley's hid in gold,
> At the pleasant time of morning
>   When the shepherd goes to fold.
>
> John Clare (1793–1864)

John Clare's "dawning" sets man in nature's light, rising or setting every morning and evening. At these "guessing" times of day, dark becomes light; and light, dark. Rising and glowing, man comes to be with morning; setting and dusking, he ceases to be with evening.

*Beowulf* celebrates morn and even by their light. Morn-light opens the day either to the morning-cry (*morgenswég*) of lament—"They raised up lament in a great morn-cry"—or to the mead of joy—"A man will be able to go back, to mead bravely, when the morn-light (*morgen-léoht*) over the sons of men of another day, sunclad in radiance, shines from the south." Even-light hides, just as men retire for rest—"After even-light (*aéfen-léoht*), in the firmament of heaven, goes to hide . . ." Morn opens life in light, even closes it in darkness.

After *Beowulf*, morn and even take on progressive verb forms in -ing: morning (1250) and evening (1000). Getting its job done, morn is morning in morning; and even is evening in evening. They referred to early morn in its progress of morning—a verbal noun—and early even in its progress of evening. The sun always moves, but it is moving most dramatically in these two transitions.

Morn morns first at the "guessing break of day." At twilight, the tween light, sun's rays reflect after sunset (1412) or before sunrise (1440). After day breaks, the sun rises and the "valley's hid in gold" in luminous dawn. Aurora (1483, Latin *aurum*, gold) refers to the golden goddess of dawn. "Rosy-fingered dawn," rising from the bed of Tithonus, could only be "hid in gold." In contrast, morn, cognate with murk, refers to the penumbra before the rising of the sun. Morn and aurora represent the first and last steps in the progress of the sun.

On the other hand, dawning (1297) is much older than dawn (1599), unlike morning and evening that are younger than morn and even. The archaic dawning serves John Clare's rhyming with morning. Whatever their relative age, evening, morning and dawning represent day and night in their becoming. When the sun rises, day is breaking and dawning, morn is morning—all dynamic action in Clare's "pleasant time of morning." Eve, an evening best known in All Hallows Eve/Halloween, Christmas Eve, and New Year's Eve, anticipates a saint's day. Evensong celebrates the later part of the day; as matins, the early part, when men or birds sing praises to their creator.

Less common words for evening such as *crepusculum*, dusk and gloaming anticipate the dark of night. *Crepusculum,* a little more common in its adjective crepuscular, refers to the murky time of evening or dawn. We can use this adjective in a metaphor: "The law is a crepuscular labyrinth" (1860). Dusk (1000), first a word of dark color and cognate with the second syllable of ob-fuscate, describes the darker stage of twilight (1622). Gloaming (1000), cognate with glow, but not with gloom, also refers to the darkening of twilight: "The sun was out of sight / And darker gloaming brought the night" (Burns, 1786). Anyone roaming with Harry Lauder in the gloaming had better watch his step.

If we look for drama in our lives, it should dawn on us to appreciate morning and evening that measure the cosmic drama of our days. In this drama of light and dark, we can also discern the light and dark of life. Twilight, for example, like faith, mingles dark with light. John Clare's aubade praises the dawning light of life.

## Words

We enjoy a walk in the morning and evening, because their light shines subtly. Words of these tween times mingle subtle shades of meaning.

### PIE root *mer*, sparkle

German: *Morgen*, morn
English: morn (*Beowulf*), morning (1250)

### PIE root *ap*, away

Greek: *opse*, late in the day; and *epi*, on, after
    English: opsimath, a late learner
German: *Abend*, evening
    English: even (*Beowulf*), evening (1000), eve (1250)

### PIE root *ma*, good, timely, early

Latin: *Matuta*, the Roman goddess of the dawn; *manes*, spirits of the dead

Italian: *mattina*; Spanish: *mañana*; French: *matin*
English: matins, service of morning worship

### PIE root *alb*, white

Latin: *alba*, white
Italian and French: *alba*; French: *aube*, dawn
English:
aubade, poem celebrating dawn
album, book of white pages; albino, a person of white skin
Albion, England, in reference to the white cliffs of Dover

### PIE root *aues*, bright, dawn, east

Greek and Latin: *aura*, fresh air in the morning
Latin: *Aurora*, goddess of the dawn in the east
Russian:
у́тро (ootrah), morning
завтра (zaftra), tomorrow (за+у́тро, literally, to+morrow)
(Tomorrow is 'to the morrow' of the next day (*cf.* German *Morgen*
or French *demain*).
Whatever tomorrow brings happens on the morrow.)

### PIE root *uesper*, evening, west toward the setting sun

Greek: *hesperus*, evening star; and Latin: *vesper*, evening star
Russian: вечер (vecher), evening; вечерня (vechernya), evensong

# 37. Directions on the Compass

## Literal and Spiritual Directions

The orientation of Solomon's Temple and Christian churches to the sun rising in the east orients us to origins. In language, origin and orient originate from Latin, but the directions on the compass—north, south, east and west—originate from German. These directions encompass the circle on the horizon, which we mark both as literal directions on land or sea and as spiritual directions in myth and religion.

Get to the first order of business—primordial worshippers knew where to look for the origin of life. They naturally addressed God facing east toward the rising sun. Eos, Greek goddess of dawn, ranked high as the sister of Helios and Selene, sun and moon. Aurora, Latin goddess of dawn, derives her name from the same root as Eos; and *aurum*, gold, shines brightly in the rosy fingers of both goddesses. Also far-distant on the horizon, the fabled land of gold, *El Dorado*, took a name from its king, "the golden one." In academic tradition, Orient finds its place on a literal, not a spiritual, map. In the Orient, we find lands of the rising sun. Japan and China set up their own order: East of China, the Land of the Setting Sun, Japan boasts of being the Land of the Rising Sun, which has emblazoned its flag since A.D. 700.

Close to home in the Germanic tradition, Teutons also looked toward the sun rising in the spring equinox, naming it after *Eastre*, their goddess of dawn. This goddess had such ancient authority that German Christians took Easter as the name of their holy season of resurrection. The Venerable Bede, in the early eighth century, emphasized the contrast by describing Christians "calling the joys of their new solemnity by the accustomed name of an ancient observation" (*consueto antiquæ observationis vocabulo gaudia novae solemnitatis vocantes*). His mention of *Eostur-monath* as the holy time of Christ's resurrection marks an extraordinary cultural connection. In Romance languages, by contrast, Easter has taken the traditional name of the Hebrew Paschal, Passover, season (Italian *Pasqua*, French *Pâques*, Spanish *Pascua de Resurrección*). We are so accustomed to speaking of Easter that we do not appreciate its extraordinary—and boldly Germanic—mixing of pagan with Judaeo-Christian festival in pagan garb.

North and south take us to directions on a map. Facing east toward the sun, north is to the left and south to the right. Normandy is north in France; Norfolk, north of Suffolk; the North Sea, north of the South Sea (Dutch *Zuider Zee*); and Norway, in the north. Latin *septentrionalis* (*septem*, seven; *trionem*, plow ox), north, refers to the seven stars of the seven plow oxen of the great Bear. Septentrional (1391) designates north in astronomy, but it has not displaced Germanic north.

By its etymology, north faces left; but the etymology of south from its facing right is doubtful. South has derived its name from sun. Latin *auster*, south wind, names Australia, the southern continent. Austria, by contrast, from *Marchia austriaca*, the eastern borderland of Charlemagne's empire, is a Latin translation of German Österreich, eastern kingdom. Latin *meridionalis* (*medius*, middle + *dies*, day), south, designates both time and direction: A.M., *ante meridiem*, before midday; and P.M., *post meridiem*, after midday. The sun reaches its meridian on an imaginary line in the south.

West, the complement of east, reorients us to myth and religion. From the root *ue*, west describes where the sun goes down. Eos, the dawn in the east, gave birth to her son, *Hesperus*, the evening star in the west—*vesper* in Latin. Because the maternal morning star, chases her child, the evening star, endlessly across the sky in intracosmic competition, Aurora and Vesper represent two teams chasing each other in earthly intramurals. In religious tradition, after their expulsion from the Garden, our first parents went East of Eden, where they might find redemption. Christ faced west to die, but He rises in the east to live. On maps, occident (Latin *occidere*, to fall), where the sun falls below the horizon, complements orient, where it rises.

Sun worshippers orient themselves toward the East and South. Sailors orient themselves by Sirius, the bright star in the North. Cynosure (Greek *kynos oura*, tail of the dog) describes the tail of this bear/dog star, by which they navigate. On land, we use cynosure to describe a person in possession of so many virtues that he becomes the cynosure of all eyes. Metaphorically, we navigate by this star.

A few classical concepts—orient and occident, meridian and septentrional—orient our sense of direction on a map. North, south, east and west rise from the earth as autochthons of the Germanic tradition. They—especially east and west—direct us to points on an ancient compass, which also oriented our ancestors to navigate their spiritual world.

## Words

#### Four Directions on the Compass

1. **PIE root *aues*, bright, dawn, east**
   Latin: *aurora*, dawn from the east; and *aurum (Au* in chemistry), gold
   German: *Ost* and *Ostern*, east and Easter
      English: east (890) and Easter (890)
      Italian and French: *est*; Spanish: *este*
   Latin *auster*, south wind, somehow related to, and confused with,
      PIE *aues*
   *Cf.* PIE root *heri*, to rise, flow, exist
   Latin: *orior oriri*, to rise
      English: orient (1386), rising, in reference to the sun; origin (1387)
   Latin: *ordiri*—frequentative of *oriri*—to begin
      English: order (1225), how things begin; primordial (1398), of first order

2. **PIE root *uesper*, evening, west toward the setting sun**
   Latin: *vesper*, evening star
   German: *westen*
      English: west (944); French: *ouest*; Italian: *ovest*; Spanish: *oeste*

3. **PIE root *ner*, below, to the left of the rising sun**
   German: *Norden*
     English: north (900); Italian and French: *nord*; Spanish: *norte*
4. **PIE root *sauel*, sun**
   Greek: *helios*, sun
     English: heliotrope, a flower turning to the sun
   Latin: *sol*, sun
     English: solar
   (Latin words derived from Greek words beginning with 'h' add 's': Greek *hex*/Latin *sex*, Greek *hepta*/Latin *septem*, Greek *hemi*/Latin *semi*.)
   German: *Süden*, south
     English: south (900); Italian and French: *Sud*; Spanish: *sur*

### Directions on the Compass in Russian

1. **PIE root *keuero*, north wind**
   Latin: *caurus*, northwest wind
   English: shower, originally, a cold rain
   Russian: север (sever), north
     *Cf.* Russian ropa (gora), mountain, cognate with Boreas, the north wind; and *aurora borealis*, northern dawn.
2. **PIE root *hewg*, light**
   Greek: *auge*, dawn, bright light of sun
   Latin: *augeo augere*, to increase
   Russian: юг (yug), south
3. **No PIE root identified**
   Russian: восток (vostok), east
     English: Vladi-vostok, power in the east
4. **No PIE root identified**
   Russian: запад (zapad), west
     English: zapad, Russian war games on the border of the west

# 38. Time

### Sons of Father Time

"Time, like an ever-rolling stream," Isaac Watts has observed, "bears all its sons away." Before they "fly forgotten, as a dream," their Father Time time rolls them along in his aeons and ages. In the world and on their own, these sons of time divide, and measure their father, so that they may be on time for trains, in season for opportunities or in their own age for longevity. The world is too much with them, according to Wordsworth, until they pass away like wraiths into their father's eternally-rolling stream.

In the beginning, the primeval Greek *aeon* encompasses time's ever-rolling stream as a vital force; but this immortal eternity does not serve men's mundane affairs efficiently, and their mortality forces them to divide it. They can't wait eons for things to happen! In a large time frame, an historian has said that the Christian era was "the last great aeon of God's dealing with man" (1879). English words derived from *aevum*, the Latin translation of *aion*, describe historical periods: historians call men living in prehistory as primaeval, of the first age, and those between antiquity and the early modern era as mediaeval, the middle age. Down to size for humanity, it describes longaevity in human life. More down to size, English age, derived from Latin through French, first referred to the length of a man's life or the time in which he lives: at my age, I am of an age to appreciate the age in which I age. In Greek, through Latin and French, men have brought *aion*, *aevum* and the more flexible age to describe time continuing for a relatively long time.

As a cognate of aeon, age indicates that the world divides its eternity according to the needs of its age. World, the age of man, refers to the time of human existence: brought into the world at birth, we embrace or renounce its pleasures and leave it at death for a world which some hold by faith to be better. World (832) referred at first to the temporal, and fifty years later (888), to the third planet from the sun.

The world exists for men, who spend their time so recklessly that we say that they are killing it. Mundane, a synonym of worldly, came to its present meaning by a path opposite to that of worldly. Latin *mundus* translates Greek *cosmos*, the universe well ordered. Mundane, killing time in "mundane vanities," passed from cosmic to worldly; but world that is man's world and then the third planet from the sun passed from worldly to cosmic.

Epoch marks a fixed, significant, point of time: the epoch of Christ's birth, Charlemagne's coronation, Andrew Jackson's presidency; or in modern technology, the invention of the printing press or the steam engine. Since these single events significantly affect those succeeding them, epoch has also defined a period of time. In this evolution, it parallels era (1615), at first a Latin word for copper or brass counters (Latin *aes aeris*), used in calculation. Epochs and eras also mark stages: the era of the French Revolution succeeded to the Napoleonic era.

Epoch and era describe times in the life of the world. Latin *saeculum*, generation, and its derivative, French *siècle*, describes a lifetime, usually 100 years. In this sense, the English adjective secular might be a synonym of epochal, but its meaning took another path. Ecclesiastics contrasted the secular with the religious, contrasting monks, living in God's time, with laymen living in man's time. Secular has come to represent a world without religion. "A secular kingdom," Tennyson lamented, "is but a body lacking a soul" (1875). Worldly, secular, mundane and temporal, all roughly synonymous, juxtapose human time with God's. Ask an objective sage: Is mundane, secular existence just killing time? How extramundane should the sons of Father Time get?

Time, from the Indo-European root *di-*, to divide, divies up worldly age. Cognate with time, tide refers to time both as suffix in Christmastide or eventide and the tide with which boats sail. Tidy refers to that which happens in good time: a tidy fortune or more loosely, a pretty, tidy girl. Add to these words the tidings that announce news of the time: our friend's sailing tidily with the tide at eventide betides us good tidings. Time and tide define points in eternity's stream.

We also deal with time, not individually, but sequentially. Latin *vicis*, interchange, represents sequential turns of time. In English, a vice president becomes president "by turn," vice versa, "with the turn having been turned." Mortals must all endure life's vicissitudes, uncertain 'turns' in time. From this root, English derives week, a common sequence of time. The season of sowing—redundant since season descends from the Latin *sationem*, sowing—marks the essential sequence of time in the agrarian world. It makes farmers cosmic in observing stars to sow crops. Season can also mark any appropriate time: "'tis the season to be jolly."

Let's review man's places in his father's ever-rolling stream:

> eon, eternity and age keep its stream unbroken;
> epoch, era and time divide it;
> vicissitude, week and season, follow its sequential flow.

Words for time define the ages of man's world, seasons of his year and units in his schedule. When Wordsworth descries that "the world is too much with us," he refers to mundane "getting and spending." Even when it is not too much with us, man watches its times, seasons and vicissitudes. How so e're we divide it, our mortality flows in its "ever-rolling stream."

## Words

We divide the vital flow of time into aeons of the cosmos, ages or epochs of our history, longevity of our eld, seasons of our planting, and divisions or intervals of our daily schedules—from eternity down to the last minute. Each one of these concepts elaborates its PIE root.

1. **PIE root *aiu*, vital force, long time**
   Proto-Germanic English: ever (1000), contracted to e'er, at any time
   Latin: *aetas aetatis*, age
   Italian: *eta*; Spanish: *edad*; French: *âge*
   English: age (1330)
   Latin: *aeviternitas/aeternitas*
   English: eternity (1374)
   Latin: *aevum*, age
   English: long*aevity*/longevity (1615), prim*aeval* (1653), medi*aeval* (1827)
   Greek: *aeon/aion*
   Greek English: aeon/eon (1647)—It took ages to get from ever to eon!
2. **PIE root *wic*, to contain, separate, overcome**
   Latin: *vinco vincere vici victus*, to conquer (*cf.* Caesar's *Veni vidi vici*)
   English: victor, invincible
   Russian: век (vek), age, lifetime
   PIE roots *aiu* and *wic* both provide roots that refer to force and to time.
3. **PIE root *seg*, to hold**
   Greek: *epochos*—*epi* + *ochos*—pause, check
   French: *époque* and English: epoch
   German: *Sieg*, victory
4. **PIE root *al*, to nourish, grow old**
   Latin: *alo alere*, to nourish
   English: alimentary and alimony
   German: *Älte*, age
   English:
   eld and elder
   world (832)—*wer*, man + eld, age—age of man
   world (888), planet
5. **PIE root *se*, to sow**
   Latin: *satio sationis*, sowing
   French: *saison* and English: season (1300)
   Latin: *saeculum*, generation, lifetime, usually 100 years
   French: *siècle*, century
   Latinate English: secular (1290)
6. **PIE root *temp*, to stretch**
   Latin: *tempus temporis*, time
   English: temporal (1340)
7. **PIE root *di*, to divide**
   German: *Zeit*, time

English:
> tide (700), time in Christmastide and eventide or when boats sail
> time (893); tidings (1069), news of the time
> tidy (1250), happening in good time

Two PIE roots *weik* and *wert*, curving or twisting, provide roots for time words:

8. **PIE root *weik*, to curve, bend**
   German: *Woche*, week, a sequence of time
   > English: week (950)
   
   Latin: *vicis*, turn, succession
   > French: *fois*; Spanish: *vez*
   
   Latin: *vice*, by turn, as in *vice versa*, "with the turn having been turned"
   > English: vice president (1574), president "by turn"

9. **PIE root *wert*, to twist**
   Latin: *verto vertere* and *versus*, to turn
   English: to divert/diversion, to convert/conversion
   German: *Wurst*, sausage
   Russian: время (vrema), time

### Of uncertain origin

Latin: *mundus*, the translation of the Greek *cosmos*,
> English: mundane (1475)

## 39. Night and Day / Day and Night

### Dark Nights and Radiant Days

As a boy, I did not think that proper observance of the holidays allowed opening presents on Christmas Eve or breaking Lent on Easter Eve, but I saw no special significance in trick or treating on All Hallows' Eve, Halloween, the beginning of All Hallows' Day. (A notable exception, New Year's Eve, had special significance for its midnight festivities.) A product of a secular culture which started its day at midnight, I did not know that Jews and Christians originally celebrated holy days from sunset to sunset. Although Aurora in the morning and Vesper in the evening pursue each other in infinite balance, our ancient ancestors weighed days and nights unequally. As a boy of the day, I had inherited atavistic nyctophobia.

The split of day from night has its parallel in that of the masculine from the feminine gender of their nouns. The goddess night shared similar form and feminine gender in Indo-European languages. She brought evil into the world. Her bird, the *striga* or owl, one named for screeching, the other for hooting, preyed on children as a witch or vampire. In nightmares (1290), literally, mares (German *mahr*, incubus) of the night, she flew about as a night hag (1660) suffocating men by sitting on their chests.

Night fills midnight, the witching (1387) hour, the central hour of her twelve, with "loathsome" spectacles. Hamlet, for example, before a nighttime visit to his mother, anticipates speaking to her with "daggers" about her complicity in the king's murder. He imagines this confrontation with a dark backdrop of evil: "'Tis now the very witching time of night, when churchyards yawn and Hell itself breaths out contagions to this world." Even an urbane definition of noctivagous, wandering by night, disparages women: "Beasts of prey, burglars, and ladies of fashion are the only three kinds of noctivagous *mammalia*" (1843). Night perennially fills men with fear and loathing.

In English, night (825) predates day (950), just as matriarchy predates patriarchy. The ancient historian Tacitus in his account of the Germans bears witness to their ancient custom of computing time by nights instead of days: *Non dierum numerum, ut nos, sed noctium computant* ("They do not count the number of days, as we do, but of nights"). Fortnight (1000), literally, fourteen nights, and the archaic sennight (1000), literally, seven nights, measures time by nights. Overturning all this nocturnality, the Graeco-Roman tradition has passed on a culture favoring day over night.

Day represents the radiant and divine sky. Though in a feminine declension, *dies* is usually masculine in Latin. Cognate with *deus*, god, it supplied the root of many names of divinity: Dionysus, Diana, Divona, and Tiu, the Teutonic god of war celebrated on Tuesday, literally, Tiu's day. Unlike night, the root of day refers to the brilliance of his eye, the sun. His gods inhabit the sky: Dyaus and Zeus (genitive, *Dios*), gods of sky in Sanskrit and Greek.

Words derived from the Latin *dies* encompass all that happens in a day: diet measures a day's consumption of food (1225), a day's travel (1290), a day's work (1494) or a day's meeting (1568). Similarly, a journey, derived from French *jour*, is a day's travel (1250), because men could not travel very far in the old days. Journeymen (1463) do a day's work for a day's wages. Diaries (1030) and journals (1540) record a day's activity—often on a journey! Men do the world's work in the day.

Greek had a word for the twenty-four hour cycle alone: *hemera*, day, has given English ephemeral (1576) referring to that which lives only "on a day" (eph- from Greek *epi*, on), be it fever, fame or a fly. Extended in its reference to a diurnal cycle of twenty-four hours, day is further extended to refer to an epoch: ephemeral pleasure has its day in youth. We measure our lives in days.

Day outshines night. "And the evening and the morning were the first day" (*Genesis* 1.5)—the prototypal day started with night only because God had not yet created light. "And God saw the light, that it was good"— few of us would disagree.

## Words

We understand night as dark, but day as radiant divinity may surprise us. The two form a pair, contrasting in gender, myth, and function.

### PIE root *nekut*, night

Greek: *nyx* (feminine gender), night
    English: nyctophobia, fear of night
Latin: *nox noctis*, night
    Italian: *notte*; Spanish: *noche*; French: *nuit*
    English:
        night (825), nocturnal (1385)
        noctuolent (1753), smelling stronger at night, of geraniums
German: *nacht*
Russian: ночь (noch')

### PIE root *dyews*, heaven, sky

Latin: *dies* (masculine gender), day; *diurnus*, diurnal; *deus*, god
    Italian: *giorno*; Spanish: *dia*
    French: *jour (cf. de-usque* to *jusque* for Latin 'd' to French 'j')
    English: journal, a daily report
Russian: день (den'), day

### Proto-Germanic root *dagas*, day

German: *Tag*; and English: day

# 40. Hours, Minutes and Seconds

## Long Hours and Minute Seconds

Geologists may find some use for eons, but work-a-day man fits hours right into his schedule. He finds them so useful that his busy days never seem to have enough of them. We may have heard this same lament from the Roman poet Martial (IV.8), who fit his activities into twelve daylight hours from six AM to six PM. Only with greater precision in telling time could men of later ages measure their hours in minutes and seconds. Martial enjoyed hours without worrying about minutes and seconds.

From Martial's description of his day in pagan antiquity, we can glean two explanations of activities characteristic of a particular hour. The sixth hour he describes as "rest for the weary" (*sexta quies lassis*). From *sexta*, Spanish derives *siesta*, the midday nap, Martial, by the way, was born in Spain. The ninth and tenth hour he devotes to the main meal of the day. From the ninth hour, *hora nona*, English has derived the word noon, really the sixth hour and not the ninth. Hunger offers a plausible explanation for eating sooner rather than later. Hunger and fatigue claimed their hour.

Hours were as pretty as they were practical. Like the sundial, the three classical goddesses known as *Horae* counted sunny times, since they presided over Spring, Summer, and Fall. In these seasons of flowering, growth, and harvest, this gentle triad assumed the garb of seasonal colors. Though the high-born daughters of Zeus, they particularly appealed to farmers, who cherished their cult down on the good earth. What more practical divinity might grace man's mundane time than the hours that made his fields bloom in season?

The ancient agrarian culture of Italy chose these divinities to mark the progress of its day. These graceful divinities had a place in its secular and religious life; but, like the word mind, their entrance into common use in mediaeval England had to wait on their religious duty. Mind, you may remember, first minded the commemoration of the dead before it conceived thought. In addition, before hour became common, it also had a rival in the native Germanic word for hour, stound. The word hour itself, though coming directly from pagan antiquity, had the extra duty from Christian antiquity of representing specific hours for prayer. Prime in the cloister still refers to prayers at six AM, the first hour of the day; and compline, *hora completa*, completes the day of prayer in the twelfth hour. A prayer book, called a book of hours, survives as beautiful witness to their place in religion. Like mind, hours served in the cloister before they went out into secular life.

A few words show how we count hours. Romance languages have used Latin *hora* as a root word for a timepiece. Horologe, literally, counting hours, remains a scholarly usage in English. Chaucer first used it in reference to a rooster, the village horologe of first light, which the Romans called *gallicinium*, cockcrow. Watches as horologes took their name from the person who stood watch. Once our ancestors had mechanical watches, they did not need flatfooted ones to tell them the watches o'clock.

In addition to relying on roosters, and human or manmade watches, we can also tell time by dials and bells. Dial (1430), of a day, meant sundial, sun of a day, because it told the sunny hours 'of a day.' An hourglass told them by sifting the sands of time. A bell also told them, since clock anglicized French *cloche*, meaning bell. (Clock and cloak are doublets, because a man looks like a *cloche* when he wears a cloak.) In churches, bells toll hours for prayers; and on boats, for watches. We do not have to be mariners or monks to tell time by listening to the number of times the clock strikes.

The first horologe with a mainspring counted only hours with its hour hand. The Roman numerals on its dial paid tribute to the twelve sunny hours of ancient Rome, and the sundial (1599) that mapped them. Counting minutes, much less seconds, challenged both imagination and precise thinking. Harried King Henry imagines a carefree shepherd in the pastoral carving a dial with minutes: "To carve out dials quaintly point by point, thereby to see the minutes how they run" (*3 Henry VI* 2.5.24). "A homely swain" in the pastoral, the king muses, may "see the minutes how they run," but a king enjoys no luxury of minutes too minute for Majesty.

Hours descended from the gates of the immortals; mortals gave birth to minutes and seconds. Though dissimilar words, they originated in sequentially similar phrases: *pars minuta prima* and *pars minuta secunda*. From other noun phrases, we usually retain the adjective because it defines the noun.[10] The "first minute part" and the "second minute part" make the pair, from which English has turned the adjectives minute and second into nouns. *Minuta* in the first phrase, defining a characteristic of the "first minute part," gives us the noun minute. A minute part ended up as a minute—in other words, the adjective minute and the noun minute have similar spelling but dissimilar pronunciation. *Secunda* in the second phrase, defining a characteristic of the "second minute part," gives us the noun second. The adjective second has the same pronunciation as its noun. Goddesses gave us hours, which man divided into two sets of twelve. Next, mathematicians divided them into minutes and seconds.

Thinking about the eleventh hour gives us a chill, because it refers to the final hour before the end of daylight. Who knows?—it may be our last and perhaps we should take action before it passes. We know that we all inevitably come to our final one. Minutes and seconds intensify hours. We may assure others that we will be ready in a minute, though we hope not to be held exactly to the count. Seconds play an even more minute part, when we require precise measurement of time. In any race against time, they can mean the difference between success and failure.

Seconds and minutes add up to the hours of our lives. King Henry imagines the equanimity of the "homely swain" having the power "to

Hours, Minutes and Seconds • 145

divide the times" that make life happy: "Ah, what a life were this! how sweet! how lovely!" A happy hour in our lives allows us to "divide the times," and enjoy seeing the minutes "how they run" to make the hour and day "full complete." Make the most of a minute and the day will take care of itself.

## Words

Time immemorial has given us hours, but a precise science of time has divided them into minutes and seconds.

Latin:
    *hora*, hour, season, Spring
    *Horae*, three daughters of Zeus, presiding over Spring, Summer and Fall
    *prima hora*, first hour, prime (960), first hour of prayer; (1290), six AM
    *horologium*, device for telling the hour
        Italian: *ora* and *orologio*, hour and telling it
        French: *heure* and *horloge*; English: horologe (1381)
        Spanish: *ora* and *reloj*
    German: *Uhr*, timepiece
    English: hour (1225), one of seven in prayer; (1250), one of twenty-four in a day

### PIE root *kes*, to scratch, cut, make go

Russian: час (chas), hour; часы (chasi), watch

### PIE root *steh*, to stand

German: *Stunde*, hour; English: stound (1000), hour

### PIE root *mei*, little, less

Latin: *pars minuta prima*, first minute part
    Italian and Spanish: *minuto*; French: *minute*
    English:
        minute (1377), noun, sixtieth part of an hour
        minute (1626), adjective, very small
    Russian: минут (minut)
Latin: *pars minuta secunda*, second minute part
    English: second (1588)
    Russian: секунда (sekunda)

## 41. Days of the Week

At the foundation of what would become a Tower of Babel, Babylonians named the days of the week after the sun, its planets and the moon. Following these names, they took a trip through the universe each week. In succeeding ages, Roman, Germanic and Slavic people in Jewish, Christian or modern secular cultures have either forgotten or ignored the significance of this foundation, as they claimed or renamed days on their own trip through time. Piling-up in English, these seven days raise a seven-storey Tower of Babel. Every week, we travel through it as a convenience, but the stories about its storeys, can confuse us as we untangle them.

Babylonians established the weekly sequence of seven days of twenty-four hours each, first placing the earth at the center of the universe, and then counting from Saturn, the farthest from earth, to the moon, the closest:

Saturn   Jupiter   Mars   Sun   Venus   Mercury   Moon

Three or four times in the cycle of 24 hours, each one of these celestial bodies prevails when it comes first in its sequence of seven bodies, but it only gives its name to a day when it comes first in that day's sequence of 24 hours. The first hour (hora-) is significant. When it begins a human life, it has such significance that a horoscope focuses (-scope) on it. Babylonians named each day eponymously after the planet that prevailed in that day's first hour.

In Babylonia, Saturn prevailed in the first hour of the first day, Latin *Saturni dies*, day of Saturn, Saturday (900). Of course, he prevailed a long time ago; and other gods have weighed in since then. Yahweh, particularly, after creating the world, rested on this day; and Jews, consequently, called it the sabbath, because it means "He rested" in Hebrew (*cf.* Italian *Sabato*, French *Samedi*, Spanish *sabado*, German *Samstag* and Russian суббота [subbota]). Thus, two cultures have claimed the same day as either the beginning or the ending of their week. Sabbath's claiming to be the last day conflicting with Saturn's day to be first contributes the first story to the babble.

Saturn prevails without significance in the 8th, 15th and 22nd hours of the first day, but he prevails with eponymous significance in the 1st hour. At the 25th hour, the first hour of the second day, the Sun prevails as the 1st eponymous hour of Sunday. Russian names Sunday "the rising of Christ," Вос-кресенье (Vos-kresen'ye), to commemorate Christ's rising from the dead on that day. Celebrating this resurrection, Romance languages have claimed Sunday as the day of Christian worship, Latin

*Domenica dies*, Lord's day (*cf.* Italian *Domenica*, French *Dimanche*, and Spanish *Domingo*).

English has retained a Germanic, pagan association in the name Sunday (700; *cf.* German *Sonntag*), but it has also associated the sun with God, whose son's birth the Unconquered Sun celebrates on December 25. In English, Christians make Sunday their Lord's Day, even though they do not name it for this function. They may even mistakenly call this day their Sabbath, but God did not rest this day—He rose.

The first hour of the 3rd cycle of 24 hours comes around to the Moon that prevails eponymously in the 49th hour, the 1st hour of the 3rd day. The moon names Moonday/Monday (1000; *cf.* German *Montag*), Latin *Lunae dies*, day of the moon (*cf.* Italian *Lunedi*, French *Lundi*, and Spanish *Lunes*). We pass from Sunday to Moonday (aka Monday) without realizing our turn from sun to moon, even though we may, frivolously, moon on Moonday for the loss of Sunday.

After 72 hours of the first three days, Mars prevails eponymously in the first hour of the fourth day, the 73rd hour—Latin *Martis dies* (*cf.* Italian *Martedi*, French *Mardi*, and Spanish *Martes*). Interpreting this Romance tradition, English has drawn its name for Tuesday from the Germanic tradition. As a parallel to Mars, it chose Thor's younger brother Tew to name Tuesday (1050; *cf.* German *Dienstag*). This German interpretation of Romance names has been called *interpretatio Germana*.

After 96 hours, Mercury prevails eponymously in the first hour of the fifth day—the 97th hour—Latin *Mercurii dies* (*cf.* Italian *Mercoledi*, French *Mercredi*, and Spanish *Miercoles*). In English, the chief god of the Germanic pantheon, Wodin/Odin names Wednesday (950). His parallel in the Roman pantheon is Jupiter, but Julius Caesar in his *Commentaries on the Gallic Wars* attributes that dignity to Mercury—*Deorum maxime Mercurium colunt*, "Of the gods, especially, they worship Mercury." Mercury's day, therefore, becomes Wodin's day, Wednesday.

More Babylonian babble arises from this crossing of gods in naming Thursday, the day of Jupiter, who prevails eponymously in the 121st hour, the first hour of the sixth day, Latin *Jovis dies* (*cf.* Italian *Giovedi*, French *Jeudi*, and Spanish *Jueves*). parallel to Jove as the god of thunder, Thor names Thursday (901; *cf.* German *Donnerstag*), Thor's day, even though Thor resembles Mercury. The Roman pantheon, obviously, did not square with the German one. In this confusion, therefore, Mercury's day in Romance became Wodin's day; and Jove's day, Thor's day.

Venus prevails eponymously in the 145th hour, the first hour of the seventh day, Latin *Veneris dies* (*cf.* Italian *Venerdi*, French *vendredi*, and Spanish *Viernes*). Odin's wife Freya, because she resembles Venus, names

Friday (1000; *cf.* German *Freitag*). After the seventh day, Saturn's day starts a new week.

Some cultures have tried to bring order from this chaos. Modern Italians, for example, ironically attuned to the secular, begin their week with Monday, the first day of the workweek; and Germans, with practical good sense, call Wednesday *Mittwoch*, mid-week. Russian makes a secular definition of its Sabbath by calling it a day of no work and Monday, the day after the day of no work. After Sunday and Monday, Russian simplifies the names of the days by calling Tuesday through Friday the second through the fifth days.

In the modern, industrial world, the weekend of the workweek (Italian and French *weekend*, and Russian уик-энд [uik-end]) puts the final storey on the Tower. Calling the last two days of the workweek the weekend makes business sense, but cultural and religious nonsense, because it misplaces Saturn's day both in its claim to be the first day, and also in its claim to be the sabbath, the last day of the Jewish week. It also leaves Sunday as the last day when it is really the first.

What confusion!—English speakers nowhere hear the babble of their cultural heritages with more confusing clarity than in the days of the week. Graeco-Roman, Judaeo-Christian, Nordic-Germanic and religious or secular worlds have claimed their place in the week at the expense of good order. English reassembles this Babylonian tower and passes through its week, with each day claiming its hour in the sun.

## Words

Getting through the week for work and leisure makes up such a microcosm of life that its complicated cultural framework in English points out just how many cultures in the past have left their mark on its days.

### PIE root *septm*, seven

Latin: *septem*; French: *sept*; Italian: *sette*; Spanish: *siete*; Russian: семь (sem)
Latin: *septimana*, week; Italian: *settimana*; French: *semaine*; Spanish: *semana*

### PIE root *weik*, to curve, bend

Latin: *vicis*, turn, succession
    English:
        *vice versa* and vice president
        vicissitudes (1570), uncertain 'turns' in time
        vicarious (1637), taking a turn, empathetic
German: *Woche*, week, a sequence of days, instead of a set number like 7

**Russian days of the week**

Sunday—PIE root *deh*, to do, put, place
>не-деля (ne-delja), literally, no doing; day of rest, Sunday or week
>Вос-кресенье (Vos-kresen'ye), rising of Christ

Monday—по-не-дель-ник (po-ne-del'nik), Monday (по [after] неделя [no doing])

Tuesday—вто́рник (vtornik), literally, second day (*cf.* German *wieder*, again)

Wednesday—среда (sreda), literally, middle day (*cf.* German *Mittwoch*)

Thursday—Четверг (Chetverg), literally, fourth day (*cf.* Greek *tetra*, four)

Friday—пятница (pyatnitsa), fifth day (*cf.* Greek *pente*, five)

Sabbath, Saturday—суббота (subbota), sabbath (*cf.* Greek *sábbata*)

# 42. The Months

## Dramatic Months

In January and February, I look forward to March and April when I can enjoy the open air without layers. Mild weather begins a year that I like to call my own. (Some consider the Spring Equinox around March 21st as its official beginning.) The ancient Romans would agree, but for a different reason. In their first calendar year, they named March, the first month, after Mars, the god of war, because they took special interest in the martial exercises beginning in March: *Mars Latio venerandus erat, quia praesidet armis*, the Roman poet Ovid observed, "Latium had a duty to worship Mars, because he presides over battles." Traditionally, March has marked "the time when kings go forth to battle." Because the Romans also felt a special kinship with Mars as the father of their founder, Romulus, the first month of their year commemorated both their war-like character and their descent.

In their first calculations, the Romans did not name months for the time between December and March, because the dead of winter did not deserve a name. When we are suffering from January drears, how often might we agree! On the other hand, Roman naming or not naming the first half of the year tells stories that reflect our perennial experience of passing from the dead of winter to the full bloom of June.

As Monday follows Sunday, when the moon-goddess Diana follows her brother the sun-god Apollo, April follows March, when Aphrodite follows Mars. Venus conjoined with Mars brings concord from discord. Ovid praises Aphrodite/Venus bringing martial Mars of March to peace and fruition in April: *et formosa Venus formoso tempore digna est, / utque solet, Marti continuata suo est*. "And beautiful Venus has deserved a beautiful season; and, as she is accustomed, she has been joined to Mars." In April, the wet chill of March springs to budding conception.

After the first two months when Mars, god of war in March, comes to fruition by Aphrodite, goddess of love in April, the two goddesses of May and June foster the growth. Maia, the most beautiful of the Pleiades, the mother of Mercury by an adulterous Jove, and the eponymous goddess of May, deserves her name from the greater, major, growth in her month. Goddesses like *Maia* and *Magna Mater*, The Great Mother, by their nature and in Nature, grow great and greater in fecundity. Naturally, the merry month of May has always received the greatest praise: "Hail bounteous May," exclaimed John Milton, "that dost inspire Mirth and youth and warm desire" (1630).

Mankind finds joy in May, and fulfillment in June. Unlike Maia, Juno, the legitimate spouse of Jove, oversees marriage and joins things in her month—*his nomen iunctis Iunius . . . habet*, "June has it name because it has joined things." June brides had the divine sanction of Juno *Pro-nuba*, patroness of nubiles and nuptials, long before graduation from school made June marriages convenient.

After the intensity of the first four months, the final six settled into a numbered order, but the first two, *Quintilis* and *Sextilis*, the Fifth and the Sixth, were changed to honor Julius Caesar, the eponymous creator of the Julian calendar, and his nephew Octavian, who became the Emperor Augustus. This replacement with July and August, explains September, October, *et seq.*, as the seventh, eighth, and following months.

Roman culture traces its beginnings to its first two kings, Romulus and Numa. Romulus, as the child of Mars, established its warlike character and Numa, its religion and law. After Romulus put Mars in March, Numa found something to do and therefore, something to name, in the two months before March. January takes its name from Janus, the god of doorways and beginnings. Although we may enjoy considering the spring equinox as the beginning of the new year, Janus, the god of doors and beginnings, opens the door to New Year's Day on January 1st, and bids us enter. In February, the "Roman Fathers declared purifications of Februus": *Februa Romani dixere piamina patres*. Purification seems more appropriate at the end of the old year than at the beginning of the new. Either may be the case, since February comes before the beginning of the archaic Roman year of Romulus and at the beginning of the new year of Numa.

Native Germanic religion named the days, but Roman culture named the months, because the days were so common that they developed within native traditions; but the months, abstract enough that they developed in a classical tradition. The two exceptions, Yule and Easter, pagan seasons of the Winter Solstice and the Spring Equinox, prove the rule. Yule, cognate of jolly, celebrates the season of festivity around the Winter Solstice. Easter, named after the Teutonic goddess of Spring, celebrates the season of Jesus' crucifixion and resurrection. These native pagan months, Yuletide and Eastertide name the two holy seasons of Christianity. When early Christians appropriated paganism for their own purposes, they called it taking gold out of Egypt (*Exodus* 12.35). They mined this gold from deep roots.

Ovid has offered a special resource for the etymologies of the months in his poem on the Roman calendar, *Fasti*, but he stops at June. By then, Mother Nature, having made her best efforts, mellows to harvest in the months that follow. The first six months set up archetypes of entering to purifying, concord to discord, and joy to enjoyment. Similarly, the church calendar celebrates the drama of birth, death and resurrection from Advent to Pentecost, from December to June, and leaves the rest to ordinary time. These dramas, having fostered us in season, sustain us through the rest of the year.

## Words

Starting in July and August, the months pass perfunctorily, named either for two Roman emperors or for a sequence of numbers, from September to December. January to June, on the other hand, stages a drama evocative of Euripides. Gods and goddesses vie for power in a cosmic drama that we experience as Winter warms to Spring.

### PIE root *ei*, to go

Latin: *eo ire*, to go
*Ianus*, the Roman god of beginnings; and *ianua*, door
*mensis ianuarius*, the month of Janus
    Italian: *gennaio*; French: *janvier*; Spanish: *enero*
    English: janitor, door keeper; January (1000), door to the year

### PIE root *dheu*, smoke, dust

Latin: *mensis februarius*, month of purification; *Februus*, god of purification
    Italian: *febbraio*; Spanish: *febrero*; French: *février*
    English: February (1000)

### No known PIE root

Latin: *mensis martius*, the month of Mars, god of war
    Italian and Spanish: *marzo*; French: *mars*
    English: March (1050); martial (1374), relating to Mars

### PIE root *ap/apo*, to extend

Latin: *mensis Aprilis*, month of Aphrodite, after Apru, Etruscan Aphrodite
    Italian: *aprile*; French: *avril*; Spanish: *abril*
    English: April (1140)

### PIE root *meg*, great

Latin: *mensis maius*, month of *Maia*
    Italian: *maggio*; French: *mai*; Spanish: *mayo*
    English: May (1050)

### PIE root *ieu*, youth

Latin: *mensis junius*, month of Juno; *junius*, as in junior
    Italian: *giugno*; French: *juin*; Spanish: *junio*
    English: June (1050)

# Five Senses and Their Organs between Sense and Nonsense

....

## 43. Sense and the Sensational

When my mother felt that my conduct had reached a nadir for a sentient and sensible two-footed beast, ripe in his five years of life, she observed that I did not have the sense I was born with. At other times, she also revived another old idiom by asking what possessed me to indulge in such naughtiness. Her first sentiment, however, with its focus on self-possession, did not let me claim that the devil made me do it. Common sense made good sense. Sentient and sensible mark common denominators of human reason, since they start with the five senses that motivate conduct, rational or irrational.

At first, English contented itself with its home-grown Germanic verb to feel (1000), and only felt a need to adopt the classical verb to sense six hundred years later. Much sooner, however, scholarship felt a need to adopt the noun sentence in three academic faculties: first in law, then in rhetoric and finally in grammar. First, sentence, meant a judgement in a law court (1290): sentences of judges sentence the accused. As expressions of official concurrence of will, the nouns assent and consent followed sentence ten years later (1300). Thus, the judge declaring legal sentences, to which laymen assent or consent, dons a mantle of dignity, even though he may be expressing no more than feelings.

In classical rhetoric, a sentence (1380) meant an aphorism. Authors like Sallust or Seneca delighted in the pointed style of aphoristic statement that is particularly at home in classical brevity. For example, *In maxima fortuna minima licentia est*, "In the greatest fortune is the least freedom," rings maximally in minimal concision. Sententious people exude aphoristic wisdom from their very being. Shakespeare's Polonius, given to the utterance of pithy aphorisms, embodies the sententious style, which, in excess, seems pompous and pedantic. Pity preceptors, however perceptively, preceptively preachy! Sagacity oft made opacity—*nota bene* the gnomic aorist. *Verbum sap.*—a word to the wise is, sadly, not always sufficient.

In their sentences, judges and philosophers expressed versions of truth, but grammar made the final contribution. Grammar describes a sentence as a syntactical unit of subject, verb, object (Blank blanks blank.). Whether of a judge from his seat or of a sage from his soap box, sentences should observe correct syntax. How many times have we been told to write in full sentences. But . . . stop! Hold on! Wait a minute! We read sentences, we hear 'em—even full ones, fragmented, if not fragments.

Sentences express discerning intellect, but senses start by just feeling. Sensate (1500) refers simply to a man's most basic ability to feel, so basic that its antonym insensate (1519), takes a stone as its example. A human heart may also be as cold as a stone: "No stone is more insensate than a sinful heart" (1612).

Sentiment, on the other hand, reflects the passage of sense from physical feeling in the fourteenth century (1374) to "refined, tender emotion" (1768) in the eighteenth. By the seventeenth century, its definition as "a feeling that involves an intellectual element" (1652) marked a turning point in its four hundred year history. The eighteenth century defined sentiment sentimentally (1784): "every thought prompted by a passion." Prompting of passion so weakened sentiment and her sister sensibility, equally frail from similar promptings, that Jane Austin based her first novel on the contrast between sense and sensibility. Sentiment and sensibility were too sensitive to be sensible.

In this volatile and emotional family, one or two members have gone haywire. Sensual, one of the black sheep, became lewd (1477), very soon after it first meant "pertaining to the senses" (1450). Its sensuality made John Milton feel so uncomfortable that he coined sensuous (1641) to represent senses in balance. "The idealist," Emerson observed much later, "does not deny the sensuous fact, but he will not see that alone" (1842). In such company, sensible (1374) had a hard time establishing its good name. With its first meaning "endowed with good sense" in 1584, and Shakespeare speaks of a "good sensible fellow;" but, by 1755, Dr. Johnson was condescending to it as only appropriate "in low conversation."

A man feeling re-sentment re-gresses into a tangled skein of mind and emotion. He first felt pained or regretful (1605) and soon, injured (1628). Dr. Johnson defined this nasty tangle: "Resentment is a union of sorrow with malignity; a combination of a passion which all endeavor to avoid with a passion all concur to detest." In the maelstrom of the senses, English had good reason to define their variety, but the good sense to preserve some sense of their integrity.

Feelings have always cried out for expression. If you prick them, do they not ouch? The thirteenth century started judiciously by using sentences to express judicial feeling; each successive century widened the spectrum of senses until the nineteenth century embraced them. Sensational literature (1863) has appealed to the senses so appealingly—or is it appallingly?—that "What a sensation!" constitutes high praise. Our senses have always cut with many edges of feeling, emotion, and mind. Since we have not always been sensible of them or sensible about them, we had better give our five senses and their particular organs a closer look.

## Words

Sense runs the gamut between our diverse senses like sight and insight, or touching and touching sensitivity. PIE roots for the senses introduce a variety of words that describe its mental or physical organs and evidence.

### PIE root *sen*, to notice

Latin: *sentio sentire* and *sensus*, to feel; and *sententia*, feeling
English:
>sentence (1290), judgement in a court of law; (1380), aphorism
>to sentence (1400), to pass judgement
>sententious (1440), full of meaning; (1508), full of aphorism
>to sense (1598), and sentimental (1749)

### PIE root *pal*, to touch ('p' in *palpare* interchanging with 'f' in *fühlen*)

German: *fühlen*, to feel
>Germanic English: to feel (1000), and feeling (1175)

Latin: *palpo palpare*, to touch
>Romance English: palpable (1384), able to be touched

### PIE root *skewh*, to feel

Latin: *caveo cavere*, to be aware; *Caveat emptor*, Let the buyer beware!
Russian: чуять (cujat), to sense, smell; по-чуять (po-čújat'), to smell

# 44. Eye

Some things never change. Fourteen hundred years separate Sextus Propertius in 25B.C. from Geoffrey Chaucer in A.D. 1380, but they shared a similar experience of rapture in love:

>*Cynthia prima suis // miserum me cepit ocellis,*
>*nullis intact (um) ante cupidinibus*

>Cynthia first, with her own, // me helpless seized, with her eyes,
>Untouched previously, by no desires

The literal English translation of the Latin word order points out the emphasis in Propertius' line on "her own ... eyes" robbing him of innocence previously untouched by fascination. Chaucer gives a little more credit to beauty than to fascination:

>Your yen two wol slee me sodenly;
>I may the beautee of hem not sustene.

Your two eyes will slay me suddenly;
I may the beauty of them not sustain.

The similarity in the two poets' descriptions of love may interest us, but it can not surprise us. *Semper ubique et ab omnibus*, at all times, in all places and by all people—mankind has always known eyes as both rapturing and rapt. In such universals, we enjoy good and ancient company.

Consider man well. His hand does the work of the heart; but his eyes communicate its love or hate. *Coeurs méchants*, wicked hearts, curmudgeons in English, do not extend a hand in cordial greeting, but their wicked eyes look daggers sooner than their hearts withhold their hands or their tongues hiss execrations. Happily, kind eyes communicate love as readily: "So sweet a kiss the golden sun gives not," says one of Shakespeare's lovers, "as thy sweet eye beams" (Shakespeare, *LLL*). "The ocular dialect," according to Emerson, "needs no dictionary."

"Eye beams" radiate sun beams beaming in eyes beamish with love, as the precious eye of the sky turns "meager cloddy earth to glittering gold" (Shakespeare, *King John* 3.1). In architecture, the *oculus* of a dome, its open center, admits sunlight. In mineralogy, an *oculus mundi*, a rare opal, admits sunlight by absorbing water. Actually, the eye does not, like the sun, generate light; the eye reflects it. The biblical metaphor—"The eye is the lamp of the body"—is not, therefore, strictly correct, even though its conclusion seems valid: "So, if your eye is healthy, your whole body will be full of light" (*Matthew* 6.22).

The eye does reflects a healthy mind and body. As sound echoes, Socrates tells Phaedrus, beauty flows back to beauty through the eyes.[11] Without a Platonic flight, we have ocular proof of Socrates' statement by looking into the pupil of the eye. We see there a tiny reflection of ourselves, a *pupilla*, a little puppet, from which the pupil of the eye and a pupil in a school derive their names. In the Bible, the Hebrew equivalent has been loosely translated "apple of the eye"—"Keep me as the apple of the eye, hide me under the shadow of thy wings" (*Psalm* 17.8). In this sense, God's eye reflects and holds—cherishes, we hope, under his wings—man's image.

To stop an evil eye from invidious possession, an apotropaic, literally, turns aside the evil. The most common amulet in Mediterranean culture, the *hamsa*, represents a hand with an eye in the middle. Similar to the hope of *Psalm* 17.8, the *hamsa* represents "the strong hand" of God mentioned in the Ten Commandments. Its eye represents the apple of God's eye in his strong hand protecting mankind. Powerful magic: God's eye and hand united!

From the power of God's eye to the bathos of infatuation, some men just ogle. Not an evil eye, but an impertinent one, ogling, eying amorously, gives a pastime to "a certain sect of professed enemies to the repose of the fair sex" (*The Tatler*, #145[1709]). A slang word in origin, it represents an extended, languorous glance, usually too innocent for evil minds but too long for good sense. Eyes of the fair sex radiate charm, while others can only ogle in reply, making eyes without charm.

We can appreciate the appeal of ancient company in the wide spectrum between seeing all in God's all-seeing eye to seeing nothing in turning a blind eye. Confined within the limitations of our own eyes, however, we can never get it all right in the eyes of all the world. Lowering our sights even more, especially when our own or other eyes have held us rapt, seeing with eyes beaming or menacing shares simple being. Up to our eyes in so many a sight, let's hope that we can keep them on prizes, a little higher than fleeting desires.

## Words

One PIE root accounts for Greek, Romance and Germanic words for eye. English derives words from all three branches.

### PIE root *hoku* or *hek*, vision

1. Greek: *ops*, eye or face; and *ophthalmos*, eye
    English:
        optical, relating to sight; and ophthalmologist, eye doctor
        antelope—Greek *anthos*, flower + *ope*, eye—flower eye
2. Latin: *oculus*, eye
    Italian: *occhio*; Spanish: *ojo*; French: *oeil*
    Latinate English: ocular (1575) and oculist
3. German: *Auge*, eye
    Germanic English:
        eye (700)
        to ogle (1682), to cast amorous glances

The Slavic root for eye focuses on its orb:

### PIE root *gel*, round, spherical, stone

English: clot, clod
Russian: глаз (glaz), eye

### Of obscure origin

Latin:
    *fascino fascinare*, to fascinate
    *fascinum*, phallus-shaped amulet

Italian: *affascinare*; Spanish: *fascinar*; French: *fasciner*
German: *faszinieren*

**Of obscure origin**

Russian: завораживать (zavorazhivat'), to cast a spell

## 45. Sight and Insight

Words derived from the Indo-European *ueid* point to sight as a metaphor for knowledge, but the most ancient words for knowledge derived from this root seem to prefer knowledge as their meaning. To see means to know. *Veda*, sacred knowledge in Sanskrit, provides names for the holy books of Hinduism (Rig-Veda, etc.). Also acknowledging divine inspiration, the Celts, closer to the earth than their southern neighbors, revered the druid, dru-vid by the root, the man who knew (-id) the nature of the sacred oak (*drus* in Greek).

Seeing is knowing in the material world, but as a man pushes his sight to insight, he sees beyond the visible. Divinity inspired the Vedas and druidic lore. Closer to the modern world, the adjective clairvoyant, started out, simply and literally, as clear seeing (1671), but the clairvoyant eventually saw the eternal in the temporal (1883). Even when it does not aspire to either divinity or eternity, sight seeking insight looks beyond the concrete to the abstract.

The Greeks, especially Plato, celebrated sight as insight without entirely surrendering to divinity or losing sight of sight. With the Greek verb *idein*, to see, and its noun *idea*, Plato expounded idea (1430) as a mental vision of an archetypal form. Its adjective, ideal, gives a clue to the pristine purity of the Platonic idea, which brings a little bit of heaven down to earth. Lincoln, for example, cherished Jefferson's idea of all men being created equal as an ideal. Idealists (1701) idolize ideas. A few centuries later, idea lost its aura of eternity and meant any conception of the mind (1617). Many people have idolized ideas that would not please idealists. Ideas keep slipping into ideals or, at least, firmly held abstractions, perhaps because people are too sclerotic to rethink them.

The Latin *video/visus*, has provided English with many of its obvious words for sight: vision, visual, visible. In English, however, vision denoted mystical insight of the seer (1290) two hundred years before it referred to physical sight (1491). Vision can also give advice: the passive of *videre*, to be seen or to seem, gave French *ce m'est a vis* (*cf.* Latin *Haec mihi est visum*, It has seemed to me.). From this phrase, French derived *avis*, advice, that which has been seen to be right, which meant opinion (1297), before it meant counsel (1393).

Foresight casts its sight forward. Since God, in His omniscience, possesses it perfectly, *providere*, to foresee, first referred to His providence (1350). In its contraction, prudent (1382) men are "sagacious in adapting means to ends." They insure present means succeeding to future ends. Its Latinate doublet, provident (1429), preserves the original sense of foresight by looking directly to the future: rely as we may on God's providence, we should be provident enough in this world to provide (1407) for a rainy day. Provident Savings Bank is there to help. We act on good advice to have clear vision in this world and provide for the future.

Greek idea and Latin vision attest to the ancient concept of the mind's eye. Wit, a word first used in *Beowulf*, derives from the Germanic branch of the *ueid* root. Although to be out of one's wits refers to the five senses in general, wit represented the mind's eye. It later came to mean liveliness of intelligence and expression (1579), especially in "wittycisms" (1677), a word coined by the witty John Dryden. Augmented by the suffix -ness wit becomes wit-ness (950), knowledge and the person giving evidence in court. Those endowed with wit are wise, also a word in *Beowulf*. The Germanic wiseman was the wizard (1440), and the Russian wise woman, ведьма (ved'ma), a witch. Wit as knowledge became a manner of action and the root of the suffix -wise in other-wise, like-wise, etc. Right-wise contracted to righteous (825).

Idea and vision relate seeing to knowing. Seeing, however, so obviously implies knowing that ancient words like Veda, druid and wit do not demonstrate their obvious relationship to sight. The German wizard, the Celtic druid and the Russian ведьма (ved'ma) lived by their wits without refining their occult craft by Platonic ideals or mystic visions.

## Words

What we see is what we know. From sight to insight takes us from the eye to the mind, just as vision in the present takes us to provision for the future; and a concrete idea may take us to an abstract ideal.

### PIE root *ueid/vid* to see
Greek:
    *idein*, to see, an infinitive of *horao*, I see (*cf.* pan-orama, seeing all)
    *idea*, idea
        English: idea

German: *ich weis*, I know (*cf. ich sehe*, I see)
> English: wit, wise, wisdom, and wizard—sight is insight

Russian:
> идея (ideya), idea
> идеальный (ideal'nyy), ideal; and идеалист (ideal'ist), idealist

Latin: *video videre* and *visus*, to see; *pro-video*, I foresee
> French: *je vois*; Spanish: *yo veo*
>> English: envious
>
> Latinate English:
>> invidious, a doublet of envious
>> vision, and provision, and provident

Russian:
> видеть (vee-deet'), to see; ведать (vedat), to know
> видение (videniye), vision; про-видение (pro-videniye), providence
> не-веста (ne-vesta), bride, literally not known, unknown to in-laws
>> (*cf.* Spanish *novio/novia* the new man/woman)
>
> ведьма (ved'ma), witch, literally, she who knows

### PIE root *ghlendh*, to shine

English: glint
Russian: зрения (zreniya), view; взгляд (vzglyad), sight

## 46. Imaginative Sight

Sight makes us think, but consider it well—it breaks free in flights of fancy. Let's consider a few more of its flights that expand the template of vision. Imagine the eyes of the mind contemplating the present, reflecting on the past and speculating about the future; and, also, contemplating, in past and present, how differently people see in their reflections and speculations.

In our flights, we face a challenge when we break free in thinking about words. Can't one word have just one meaning?, our simple minds ask as words unfold complex layers of meaning. It seems not, not at least, to minds that think twice and even thrice. At its root, for example, thought (839) is not what we think. Thought is what we see: to think (888), from Middle English *thenken*, to seem, survives in 'methinks,' "it seems to me." One layer uncovers another. Thoughtful thought encourages right conduct, because thinkers thank (800). Thinking is thanking—the two verbs are cognate. Thinking, therefore, both observes and appreciates. Its root tells us not necessarily what we do but what we should do. Methinks we profit by considering more thought-layered words of sight.

As we indulge our fancy about the possibilities, let Shakespeare tell the short-lived fancy of eyes in love:

Tell me where is fancy bred.
Or in the heart or in the head?
How begot, how nourishèd?
It is engendered in the eyes,
With gazing fed, and fancy dies
In the cradle where it lies (*The Merchant of Venice* III, 2).

Nourishèd by draughts from classical founts, our fancy may not be perishèd, as quickly as Cupid's. Shakespeare's founts can pour out more of their nourishment. Let the bard start a little down to earth, where the imaginative contrasts to the substantive (1386). He observes that it "bodies forth" images: "The lunatic, the lover, and the poet / are of imagination all compact.... And as imagination bodies forth / the forms of things unknown, the poet's pen / turns them to shapes and gives to airy nothing / a local habitation and a name" (*Midsummer Night's Dream* V, 1). He attributes imagination to the lunatic first and lets the lover and the poet follow. In the same passage, he reserves fantasies for "seething brains": "Lovers and madmen have such seething brains, / such shaping fantasies, that apprehend / more than cool reason ever comprehends." Imagination (1340) supplies an image; but flights of fancy soar beyond it. The chronology of the meanings of fantasy in English has left a number of layers: it first meant phantom (1325), then delusion (1340), preference (1374), and finally (1589), the flight of fancy of "the soul's swift Pegasus" (1602), in time for Shakespeare to draw out from his well.

The verb to fancy (1545), a contraction of fantasy, first meant to prefer: "I never yet beheld that special face, / Which I could fancy more than any other" (Shakespeare, *Taming of the Shrew*, II, 1). 'A young man's fancy' has preferences in love, and 'fancy free' enjoys freedom from them. From its first association with phantom, 'to fancy,' by its nature, fancied the fantastic: "If all our search has reached no farther than simile," John Locke cautioned, "we rather fancy than know." Imagination bodies forth images; fancy bodies them forth capriciously.

Just as imagine and fancy represent ancient art and philosophy, consider (1385) and contemplate (1592) represent an ancient religious rite in which the augur scanned the heavens to discover the will of the gods. From Latin *sidus/sideris*, star, to con-sider originally 'brought the stars together' for astrological consideration. King Lear calls for consideration in weighing the worth of man: "Is man no more than this? Consider him well" (Shakespeare, *King Lear*, II, 4). Ancient con-templation scanned the heavens from the temple, a sacred space for augury. In English, however, contemplation is abstract: on earth, we contemplate some intimation of heaven: "When holy and devout religious men are at their beads, / 'tis much to draw them thence; / so sweet is zealous contemplation" (Shakespeare, *Richard III*, III, 7). Contemplation (1340) meditates (1580); consideration (1572) takes on matters of worldly weight.

By itself, sight needs emphasis and direction. The con- prefix of consider and con-template emphasizes it; the re- prefix directs it: re-flect (1412) bends the eye back into time or into ourselves. To reflect, first similar in meaning to in-flect and de-flect, by 1605, came to refer to bending eyes or thoughts in backward glance: we reflect upon our past with contemplative thought. In the first act of *Julius Caesar*, reflection reveals "by some other things":

Cassius: Tell me, good Brutus, can you see your face?
Brutus: No, Cassius, for the eye sees not itself
But by reflection, by some other things.

Sight, Cassius continues, reflects both what others see of Brutus' worthiness and what Brutus himself sees of his own "hidden worthiness." It emanates from within by the eyes of a man's own heart and from without by the eyes of others.

To re-gard (1430), looks back in respect. Compounding 'to guard' and reflecting its watchful care, regard demonstrates personal concern. By the last act of *Julius Caesar* (V, 3), for example, Romans have reflected on Cassius' "worthiness" and now regard him with respect. One man expresses his "regard" for Cassius by joining him in suicide: "And see how I regarded Caius Cassius. —By your leave, gods, this is a Roman's part . . . (stabs himself with Cassius' sword and dies)."

Intuition (1497) demonstrates watchful thought. We pay a tutor tuition for tutelage, when he watches over children. Intuition understands what a person has felt without reasoned consideration; by intuition, Caesar learns much from Cassius' "lean and hungry look." To speculate (1599) started as serious consideration but now represents uncertain, hypothetical thought, "idle speculation," in Shakespeare's phrase (*Henry V*, IV, 2).

Consider how differently different eyes of the mind see. Creative minds imagine and fancy; the learned consider; the devout contemplate; the thoughtful reflect; the appreciative regard; the acquisitive speculate; the thoughtful and perceptive conjecture intuitively. We can appreciate these different ways of seeing, because we have experienced our lives through all of them.

## Words

What we see is what we know, and what we think is what we see; but imagination and fancy take us beyond mere knowledge. With careful consideration and deep contemplation, we should reflect on fancy born in the heart or in the head.

### PIE root *tong*, to seem, think

German: *denken* and *danken*, to think (888) and to thank (800)

### PIE root *im*, copy

Latin: *imitare*, to copy, imitate; and *imago, imaginis*, image
English: image and imagination
Russian: имитировать (imitirovat'), to imitate

### Proto-Slavic root *obrazъ*, image

Polish: *obraz*, picture, image
Russian:
>образ (obraz), form, icon
>со-образить (so-obrazit'), to understand, literally, to co-image
>во-ображать (vah-ahbrahzhat'), to imagine, fancy, dream
>изо-бражать (iz-obrazhat), to depict, portray, describe, image

### PIE root *bha*, to shine

Greek:
>*phainein*, to appear *phainomenon*, a thing appearing, phenomenon
>*phantasma*, appearance

English: epiphany, and theophany, and phantasm, and fantasy, and fancy
Russian:
>фантазия (fantaziya), fantasy; фантом (fantom), phantom
>Теофания (teofania), theophany
>>*cf.* Бого-явление (Bogo-yavleniye), theophany; Бог (Bog), god
>>являть (yavlyat), to show—PIE root *au*, hear, perceive

### PIE root *sueid*, shine

Latin: *sidus sideris*, star; and *considerare*, to look at thoughtfully
English: sidereal and to consider (1385)

### PIE root *temp*, to stretch, extend

Latin:
>*templum*, place marked out by Roman augurs for observation of the sky
>*contemplo contemplare*, to contemplate (1592)

### PIE root *med*, and *me*, measure

Latin: *meditari*, to meditate; and *modicus*, measured, proper
English: to meditate (1580), to muse, to reflect on thoughtfully
Russian:
> мерить (merit), to measure; and из-мерять (izmeryat'), to measure
> медитировать (meditirovat'), to meditate
> смотреть (smotret'), to look
> о-смотр (o-smotr), inspection; о-сматривать (o-smatrivat'), to inspect

### PIE root *teu*, to consider, regard

Latin: *tueor tueri* and *in-tueri*, to watch and to watch over
> English: tutor, tuition, intuition
Russian: интуиция (intuitsiya), intuition

### PIE root *spek*, to see, regard

Latin: *species*, sight; *speculum*, mirror
> English:
>> specious, appearing good, but not necessarily good (*cf.* plausible)
>> conspicuous, easily seen

### PIE root *plek*, to bend, fold, twist

Latin: *flecto flectere*, to bend; *flexus*, having been bent
> Italian: *fiasco*, flask
> Romance English:
>> to flex, and to reflect, inflect or plait
>> flask, a bottle plaited around, as a bottle of Chianti

### PIE root *gher*, to scrape, smear, tinge

English: grey
Russian:
> зреть (zret), to ripen; зрение (zrenije), sight
> зеркало (zerkalo), mirror, a calque of French *miroir*
> со-зерцать (sozertsat'), to behold, contemplate, meditate

In many languages, words for ghosts refer to their being seen:

French: *spectre*, Spanish: *espectro*
Polish: *widmo*; Russian: при-видение (privideniye), spectre

## 47. Ear and 'Earing

Our brains have sight, and then insight, as a consequence. They also function to hear, to listen, and to speak—with hearing, listening, and speaking, preferably, also in consequential order. Two ears mediated by one mouth operate from the same brain, but we all worry about the nature and consequences of their mutuality. In communication, this mutuality becomes more worrisome, because one man's mouth speaking only communicates when another man's ears listen. He hears himself speaking, but does anyone else hear him? If someone does hear, does he listen? If he both hears and listens, does he acquiesce and, if necessary, obey? We all have these worries about the sequence of communication—hearing, listening, acquiescing, and obeying. With good reason, a teacher urges, 'Those who have ears, let them hear.' Our most ancient ancestors, in creating their words for hearing, heard these worries and answered them. From the stories that these words tell, we hear tell some answers.

Now—this is intense—so listen up! The verb hear (825) intensified in hearken (1000); and the verb list (897) intensified in listen (950). Listen intensified list in about fifty years, since list was not demonstrating the strength to survive on its own. It faded into poetry—"List, list," cried the poet, when he heard some halloo, "I hear some far off hallow break the silent air" (Milton, *Comus*). Hearken (1000) and its later form hark (1175) have also become quaintly or grandly poetic—"Hark! The herald angels sing," and "Hark, hark! the lark at heaven's gate." With list, hark, and harken out of common use, English does the best it can with hearing and listening. Hearken to this fond prayer!—may our friends listen when they hear us speaking! We can manage sight and insight on our own; but in communicating them, hearing and listening need help.

First of all, hearing and listening derived strength from their roots. The word loud gives us a clue. In nature, loud describes stormy winds and waves. In human culture, loud does not sound as naturally. A cognate of listen, it may suggest that we listen to loud voices—an obvious, but dangerously facile, assumption. A cognate of Latin *inclutus*, famous, and Russian *slava*, fame, it gives us another clue. Loud has its root in the listening that inspired the muse of history, Clio, to claim and proclaim fame. "The loud etherial trumpet," Milton proclaimed, "from on high 'gan blow." Sopho-cles, famed for philo-sophy, plumbed the depths with his decibels. On the other hand, of course, a loud-mouth may win fame by sounding off in his loud clothing.

The word aesthetic gives us another clue. As a cognate of ear and hear, it shares with them common roots in perception. Senses meld in synesthesia. When I assure my friend that I hear his request for news, I, like God hearing our prayers, do more than listen. When I promise that he will hear from me soon, I will probably be doing more than speaking. I may write a letter for him to read. "I heard no letter from my master," laments Pisanio in Shakespeare's *Cymbeline*, as he observes that Fortune brings in boats that are not steered. When Adam "hearkened unto the voice" of his wife, and "ate of the tree" (*Genesis* 3.17), he did more than listen and much more than he should have. Hearing and listening gain strength by melding with other senses and following up with action.

Hearing and listening have drawn strength from their roots in fame and perception. In addition, they have, like ambitious homeowners, also gained new strength by building wings, so to speak, onto their words. List, for example, passed on its meaning to listen, before it passed out of common use. With the prefix *ob-*, Latin built up its verb *audire* to compound *oboedire*, to listen to, which, through French, gave English the verb obey. (In German, *hören*, to hear, compounded to *zuhören*, to listen). Obeying evolves from a sequence of hearing, listening, and acquiescing.

Obeying can also continue to define its acquiescence as submissive, since obedience and obeisance are doublets: A "young merchant," in an audience before a sultan in *Arabian Nights,* "made his obeisance, by throwing himself with face to the ground" (1850)—obeisance being "a bodily act or gesture expressive of submission or respect (almost always, a bending or prostration of the body)." By bending, obeisance demonstrates obedience. By prostrating, obeisance dramatizes it. Even though this kowtowing does not suit democratic manners, wouldn't we all enjoy such a reverential audience!

With *clutare/cultare*, to hear by oneself, as a suffix to the root of *auris* or *audire*, ear or to hear, Latin built the verb *auscultare*, to listen. From this verb, English has derived auscultation (1634), careful listening, now especially by physicians with a stethoscope. Auscultation, unfortunately, has become old-fashioned: "He who can listen with real attention to every thing that is said to him," said one appreciative speaker, "has the great gift of auscultation" (1836). Greek compounded another intensive, *akroaomai*, to prick up one's ears. Also an old-fashioned, but attractive, concept, acroasis (1655) anticipates sharp, intent students, all ears to their professor. By the nature of their calling, physicians and students listen carefully.

"A man who speaks with reserve, and listens with applause" (1781) should have the best chance of being heard, because his listening comes through loud and clear. In the mutual respect between ears and mouth—words spoken and words heard—good listening, one of man's most underrated skills, best prepares the listener to speak, even if we hear from him by letter. We operate best when common sense brings all our senses together.

## Words

Four PIE roots provide English with its words for hearing. English verbs to listen and to hear are derived from the first two, *klew* and *aus*. These two PIE roots combine to make a third family of words in Romance. The root *aus*, in another compound, makes a fourth family in Greek.

1. **PIE root *klew*, to hear and the fame of hearing**
   Latin:
   *clueo cluere*, to hear oneself called in some way, to be famous
   *inclutus*, heard of, famous
   English:
   to list (897), and its intensive, to listen (950)
   loud (897), that which is heard
   Russian:
   слышать (slyshat'), to hear, hearken; слава (slava), fame
   слушать (slusat), to hear, understand;
   слушат-ься (slushat'sya), to listen to, obey (reflexive of слушать)

2. **PIE root *aus*, to hear, perceive**
   Greek:
   *aisthanomai*, I perceive
      English: aesthetic
   *ous otos*, ear
      English: otitis, inflammation of the ear
   Russian: *ухо* (ukho), ear
   Latin: *audio audire*, to hear
      English: audition, auditorium
   Latin: *oboedire*, to obey—*ob+audire*, to listen to. In obstruct, ob- means 'against,' but in obsequious, it means 'in accordance with.'
      Latinate English: obedient (1225)
   Romance:
      Italian: *obbedire*; Spanish: *obedecer*
      French: *obéir* and *obéissance*
         English:
            to obey (1290)
            obedience (1225) and its doublet obeisance (1374)

Latin: *auris* and its diminutive *auricula*, ear
   Latinate English: aural, of the ear
   Italian: *orecchio*; Spanish: *oreja*; and French: *oreille*
German:
   *Ohr*, ear; *hören*, to hear; and *zuhören*, to listen to
   *horchen*, to hark, to listen closely
English: ear (825); to hear (825); to hearken/harken (1000), intensive of 'to hear,' to listen to; (1533), to search or wait for; to hark (1175)

3. **PIE root *aus*, hear + *klew*, to hear**
   Latin: *ausculto auscultare*, to listen (*auris*, ear+*clutare*, to hear by oneself)
      Latinate English: auscultation (1634), careful listening, with stethoscopes
   Italian: *ascoltare*, to hear; Spanish: *escuchar*
   Old French: *escouter*; Modern French: *écouter*
      English: scout (1553), one sent out to report what he hears

4. **PIE root *aus*, to hear, perceive + *ak*, sharp**
   Greek:
      *akouo*, I hear
         English: acoustic
      *akroaomai*, to prick up one's ears; and *acroasis*, lecture
         English: acroasis (1655)

# 48. Nose and Smell

### Common Sense to Scent

It should be as obvious as the nose on your face that, compared with the senses of sight and hearing, scent (1375) has less significance. We value it, but we value hearing more, and sight most. By sight and insight, particularly, *homo sapiens* has risen far above lower mammals like hounds, which he has valued for their special ability to follow a scent. Let's track down its traces in language. Our fellow mammals like hounds and hares demonstrate its importance. If, like them, we follow our noses, maybe we can see—oh no! I mean sniff out—why scent had enough significance to make it a doublet of sense. For the moment, let's set rational sense aside, and let scent make sense.

Back to basics in the beginning, Germanic smell (1175) predated Latinate scent (1375) by two-hundred years. Smell started its career describing the full spectrum of olfactory sensation from sweets to stinks; but, as centuries passed, it inhaled more stinks than sweets: "He who hath a quick smell is troubled with more stinks than he is refreshed with sweet odors" (1612). Modern industrial effluvia have "troubled" the hyperosmic with ever greater discomfort!

Did our ancestors distinguish between smells or scents? By 1500, scent referred to flowers and spices, to which smell, exceptionally, made "rare" reference. In using smell four times more than scent to describe his paradise lost, John Milton provides quite a few exceptions to this rarity. Starting with "smell" in the Arbor of Eden—"In this pleasant soil . . . he caused to grow / All trees of noblest kind for sight, smell, taste"—Milton prefers the "smell of grain" and "of field and grove" to the more exotic scent in "the season prime for sweetest scents and airs" or in "the scent / Of that alluring fruit." He did not live, as we do, in the shadow of the Victorians, who felt uncomfortable in referring to smells that more commonly "troubled" them with stink than "refreshed" them with fragrance.

We hesitate in choosing either smell or scent to describe garlands, but we feel confident that garlands are fragrant and gore reeks. Fragrant (1520) entered English in the Renaissance, with a classical pedigree. The Roman poet Catullus had described a friend fragrant with perfumes for a banquet—*sertis ac Syrio fragrans olivo*, "fragrant with garlands and Syrian olive." In Eden, the Serpent first spies Eve, "veiled in a cloud of fragrance"— she blooms with a fragrance all her own! Reek, on the other hand, first issued from smoke or sweat. In his poem about paradise lost, Milton uses the word only once: when Adam wakes up in his bed of flowery herbs, he was bathed in sweat, "which with his beams the sun / soon dried, and on the reeking moisture fed." Altars reek of smoke and gore. Even reek has its exception. Shakespeare surprises us by describing his mistress as reeking: "In some perfumes is there more delight than in the breath that from my mistress reeks?" "Reeks" wafts the sweet fragrance of his mistress' exhalation.

By whatever means we trace the olfactory sense—by scent, smell, fragrance or reek—our noses bring us down to earth. The common sense of *Homo sapiens* puts him on a path up to angelic understanding; but the sense common to *Homo animalis* gets him down to foxy wiles. Distinctly of the earth, ancient Romans had a word for these wiles. Martial describes a critic, endowed with satiric wit, as *nasutus*, derived from *nasus*, nose, the organ especially expressive for a man with his nose in the air:

*Nasutus nimium cupis videri.*
*Nasutum volo, nolo polyposum (Epigrams 12.37).*

You desire to seem very snooty:
I want a man to be snooty; I do not want him to be snootily hyperosmic.

The Romans valued satire as their own uniquely earthy expression. In a literary critic, the snooty, satirical wit, to which Martial refers, obviously offends him in its excess. Getting down to earth should not necessarily get nasty and, simultaneously, nastily snooty.

Metaphors for the olfactory sense do not always and inevitably describe foxy wiles. Flair in English describes an instinctual bent. As a cognate of fragrant (1520) and flagrant (1450), flair (1340) predates them in melding glow, spark, and scent. When we observe youth with a flair, we are getting a whiff of instinctual talent, which we hope to nurture from spark to flame.

Outside literary salons and schools, a man's instinctual talent may follow its nose in the market place, and act by instinct. Canny men can smell out a bargain or a secret. Nosing about, they may seem to be spying impertinently into someone else's business. We can sniff out their impertinence: "Praises in an enemy smells of craft," observed John Milton in 1649. Martial was right in criticizing the craft of a grotesquely large nose. A wickedly crafty deed can send its reek to heaven: "Oh my offense is rank," laments King Claudius, "it smells to heaven."

Imagine the synesthesia of nature's senses, as Milton describes it in Paradise:

> The birds their quire apply; airs, vernal airs,
> Breathing the smell of field and grove, attune
> The trembling leaves, while universal Pan,
> Knit with the graces and the Hours in dance,

The "quire" of birdsong and "trembling leaves" "attune" with "vernal airs" of "field and grove." Does it matter whether Pan, "with the graces and the Hours" smells the "vernal airs" or hears them? With hearing together with listening, and with sight together with insight, we dance best when common sense brings all our senses together. Our noses sniff out a golden mean, when scent also makes sense. The anosmic suffer from losing a part of their humanity. Flair can aspire to higher knowledge or to street smarts. Man has valued hounds because they can follow a scent in pursuit of their prey, but man's scent joins with all his senses to make the best sense.

## Words

After the one PIE root for nose, six PIE roots describe smell.

### PIE root *nas*, nose

Latin: *nasus*; *nasutus*, having a nose, satirical, witty
    Italian: *naso* and *annusare*; Spanish: *nariz*; French: *nez*
German: *Nase*; English: nose (897); Russian: нос (nos), nose

1. **PIE root *smeugh*, smoke**
   German: *Schmauch* and *smauchen*, smoke and to smoke
   English: smell (1175, as noun or verb, exhaling or inhaling), smoke, to smolder.
2. **PIE root *pneu*, breath**
   Greek: *pneuma*, vital spirit
   English: pneumatic, apnea
   Russian: нюхать (nyukhat'), to smell; вонять (vonyat'), to stink
3. **PIE root *bhrag*, to smell**
   Latin: *fragro fragrare/flagro flagrare*, to exhale a pleasant odor
   English:
   fragrant (1520) and flagrant (1450), both referring to pleasant odor
   flair (1340), smell; (1881), instinctive talent
4. **PIE root *hed* and *odo*, to smell**
   Greek: *odme/osme*, smell
   English:
   -osmia, sense of smell; anosmia, no sense of smell
   hyp-osmia, low sense of smell
   hyper-osmia, excessively sensitive sense of smell
   Latin: *olo olere*, to smell, to smell of (from *odor*, but made to resemble *oleum*, oil)
   Spanish: *oler*, to smell
   English: olfactory (1658), concerned with smelling
5. **PIE root *reug*, to vomit, belch**
   German: *riechen*, to smell; and *rauchen*, to smoke
   English:
   to reek (1000), to smell of smoke, sweat or blood
   to eruct, eructation
   Russian: рыгать (rygat), to burp, retch
6. **PIE root *pu*, decay, rot**
   Latin: *puteo putere*, to rot, stink, be putrid
   English: putrid

# 49. Hand

### Handy in Managing and Handsome in Manoeuvring

Let's imagine human culture back to its roots. Plumbing these depths, we can understand that culture could never have come to birth or grown to maturity without human hands. They have managed and maintained it, while also reaching out to pledge faith. They have manipulated it with self-interest, while also, reaching beyond themselves with good manners to act handsomely. Hands have so thoroughly managed life in the wilds and in the fields that they have also represented the mandate of the law by which they demand and command the lives commended to them. 'By hand' has always meant power, skill and care.

Hands manage the beasts of the field and the farm. Out in the wilds of remote Germanic antiquity, hand and hunt shared the same root, because hands seized prey by the hunt. Back home in the stable, to manage, derived from Italian *maneggiare*, first meant to handle horses. Their place in the culture before the automotive era makes it easy to understand why management started with horses. Management also took care of dogs: mastiff, derived from the Latin *mansuetus*, accustomed to the hand, served as a watch dog. Nothing bespoke care as much as training by hand.

On the farm, human hands make fields green by manuring, i.e., working by hand, and, in one part of the labor, applying manure, i.e., dung or compost. Metaphorically, teachers manure, cultivate, the minds of the young. Thoreau mixes the literal and metaphorical in speaking of his bean field: "I will not plant beans and corn with so much industry another summer, but such seeds, if the seed is not lost, as sincerity, truth, simplicity, faith, innocence, and the like, and see if they will not grow in this soil, even with less toil and manurance, and sustain me." Perhaps Thoreau chose the old-fashioned word manurance to evoke a prototypal parallel between cultivating fields and cultivating minds: "Who knows but if men constructed their dwellings with their own hands," he muses, ". . . the poetic faculty would be universally developed, as birds universally sing when they are so engaged?" Cultivating seeds of character bears fruit

Training and cultivating by hand claim special distinction, along with making by hand, manufacture. Ironically, manufacture usually refers to machine-made and not handmade goods. Did the industrialist of the nineteenth century who recommended that "the most perfect manufacture is that which dispenses entirely with manual labor" (1835) recognize the contradiction in his use of manufacture? His judgment signaled the end of the era of handicraft from the workshop.

For the oversight of his managing, manuring and manufacturing, man has received mandates about governing his animals, fields and crafts as part of his household. In Latin, *manus* represents *patria potestas*, paternal power, of the head of the household over his wife, children and slaves. We associate emancipation with Lincoln's Emancipation Proclamation, but by its original meaning, emancipation takes (-cipation) a person out of (e-) the hand (-man-) of his parent or master. More specifically related to slavery, manumission sends (-mission) a slave from the hand (manu-) of his master.

Law could mandate or demand power. A mandate (1552) gives (-date) power (man-) from a higher to a lower authority. The doublets command (1300) and commend (1325) intensify mandate. Commanding also gives an order from a higher to a lower authority: the general commands his lieutenants. Commending gives a trust from a lower to a higher authority: we commend souls to the care of God. Recommending (1386) also entrusts someone to another's care. To demand (1292), the oldest of these words, first had the same meaning as it has today, but demanding first acted legally rather than peremptorily. Without peremptory demands, let me recommend for your consideration the following categories: arrogance demands, authority commands, and humility commends.

The power of man's hand has expressed itself in manners and appearance. Derived from French *manière*, manner (1225) was a man's customary way of managing things. With this original meaning, Hamlet describes himself as "to the manner born," accustomed to the native manner of doing things. Later (1340) manners came to be rules of behavior. In a similar transition from the pragmatic to the social, the native English word handsome (1435) first meant manageable, then ready at hand (1530), skilled (1547), gracious in conduct (1621), gallant in military exploits (1665), and cutting a fine figure (1590). Handsome always connotes something impressive, whether a handsome contribution to charity or treating another handsomely, i.e., magnanimously. This monumentality colors handsome as it describes men, although our ancestors could distinguish between a pretty woman and a handsome one. How handsomely this native word has advanced beyond its Romance cousin, manageable!

Hands should also reach out in good faith. Early Anglo-Saxon leaders had names that anticipated this duty: Edmund protected wealth; Raymond, counsel; and Sigmund, victory. By their hands, Shakespeare's characters demonstrate the allegiance of their hearts. In *The Tempest*, Ferdinand falls in love with Miranda at first sight. Having offered his hand to her, she gives hers with a pledge: "And mine with my heart in it." Miranda's hand represents her heart.

According to ancient anatomy, which was more symbolic than scientific, an artery carries blood from her heart to the ring finger of her left hand. In this literal sense, Miranda has her heart in her hand. Hand-in-hand, Ferdinand and Miranda may exchange handsels as tokens of their union. How handsomely do our hands make their managing, manuring, manufacturing, and mandating meaningful by joining others hand-in-hand.

Man's hand has manured earth and maintained mandates of heaven. Giving credit for handy manual words either to classical or to native roots, we count more English weighty words from the Romance *man-* than from the Germanic hand. On the other hand, speakers of English acknowledge themselves as God's handiwork, not His manure. Words of classical Romance culture have not always taken the upper-hand over the native Germanic. God's handiwork, man is handy and tries his hand at all things.

## Words

Romance and Germanic roots for hand introduce sources of material and culture. Managing, manuring or maneuvering, hands fill the world with their work.

ROMANCE

**PIE root *man*, hand**

Latin: *manus*, hand
    Italian and Spanish: *mano*; French: *main*
        English:
            manual (1406)
            mastiff (1330), watchdog (*mansuetus,* accustomed to the hand)
            to manipulate (1831), manipulative (1836)
    Italian: *maneggiare*, to handle (horses)
        English: to manage (1561), to train a horse

Five English words derived from *manu*, by hand, compounded with verbs:

1. Latin: *manu tenere*, to hold by hand
    French: *maintenir*
    English: to maintain (1250)
2. Latin: *manu operare*, to work by hand
    French: *manoeuvre*
    English: Doublets:
        manoeuvre/maneuver (1479; 1758, in military)
        to manure, to work a field by hand (1400),
        manure, dung (1549), cultivation (1677)
3. Latin: *manu mittere*, to send by/from the hand
    English: to manumit (1432), manumission (1432), emancipation (1625)
4. Latin: *manu scriptum*
    English: manuscript (1597), written by hand. He manuscribes manuscripts.

5. Latin: *manu facere*, to make by hand
        English: manufacture (1567 as noun,1683 as verb), make by hand

**GERMANIC**

German: *hand*
English:
   hand (825), handiwork (1000); handle (noun, 800; verb, 1000)
   handsel (1430), a gift given with a handshake, a token for good luck
   handsome (1435), manageable

**SLAVIC**

Russian: рука (ruka), hand

# 50. Touch

After a man has measured and understood his world with sight, hearing, and smell, he brings it closer with touch and taste. His life does not depend on these tactile and gustatory senses; but without them, he would enjoy life less. Let's start with touch. As we get in touch with the immediacy of this sense, we can also get a feeling for its touching our lives more than we might have anticipated. It gives us tact that attains a balance; but it also gives us task that taxes this balance. Seeing such tangible evidence of touch so taxes our understanding that we can feel its influence palpably.

First, let's touch very briefly on its earliest English verbs. In A.D. 700, one of the first, an early form of greet (700), referred to rough hands, which have now reached out in greeting. Feeling (893) followed almost two hundred years later. It has always referred to both touching and understanding. A physician, for example, touches a patient's wrist to feel his pulse, because he feels concern for his health.

The etymologies of words for the senses bear witness to their relative importance. Seeing, for example, so essentially aids human life that its verbs in Romance and in Slavic have evolved from a common PIE root: in Russian, Я вижу (YA vízhu), I see; in Romance, the Latin verb *video*, I see, dropping its internal consonant 'd' in Spanish *veo* and in French *je vois* and, but retaining it in Italian *vedo*. By contrast, the verb touch does not have a common etymology in Russian, in Romance or in English. Etymology can always surprise us. To describe eating, for example, Italian and French passed over the standard Latin verb, *edere*, to eat, that must have become too common and colorless to continue to do its job adequately. Instead, they chose the colorful Latin verb *manducare*, to chomp, for their verbs *mangiare* and *manger*. Similarly, the Latin verb *tangere*, to touch, did not pass muster for inclusion in Romance or in English. Hands do such active pushing and pulling, donning and doffing, folding and molding, that *tangere* did not describe their work with enough authentic vigor. Vulgar Latin supplied a verb more colorful than the Classical one. That verb, *toccare*, to strike, supplied both Romance and English with its verb to touch. *Toc-* imitated a sound like tick tock striking the hour. Its late entry into English in the fourteenth century displaced the native Germanic words, although the Germanic verb to feel kept its place. Even with its striking origin, to touch may strike us as colorless and—the cycle comes back to its beginning—common. Handling, grazing, rubbing, patting or stroking put new life into its activity.

To clarify touch, English uses Latinate words like tangible and palpable. Latinate formality and precision lend a hand when native words need elaboration. Palpable describes what is tangible—but with a few nuances. God instructed Moses to make darkness so thick that the Egyptians could feel it: "Stretch out thine hand toward heaven, that there may be darkness over the land of Egypt, even darkness which may be felt," To translate "darkness over the land," Saint Jerome, in his Latin translation, chose to make the darkness palpable: *tenebrae tam densae ut palpari queant*, "darkness so thick that it is able to be palpable." Strictly speaking darkness is not tangible, but Moses made darkness so deep that it seemed tangible, that is palpable. John Milton chose to make palpable darkness a paradox by calling it "darkness visible."

In Shakespeare, palpable also means tangible. Hamlet's "hit, a very palpable hit," describes a tangible wound. Since the time of Jerome and Shakespeare, however, palpable has become less tangible. Currently, as a consequence of spectators seeing tangible evidence of bloodshed, their concern would become palpable. Palpable usually describes what we can see as evidence of human feeling more than what we can touch. When the public, for example, sees the tangible bloodshed of combat, their concern becomes palpable.

With more abstraction, tact describes the right touch in dealing with people—"the faculty of saying or doing the right thing at the right time." Tact refines human understanding: "Few persons have tact enough to perceive when to be silent and when to offer counsel or condolence" (1875). Since contingent describes one event depending on another, we can call tact contingent on understanding.

Sadly, we often see tact in the dictionary more than in life. The doublets, tax and task, in particular, describe touch as tactless. Derived from the frequentative of *tangere*, taxing touches intensely or painfully. Touched by grief, for example, a man, if taxed beyond endurance, may sink to despair. Like its cognate touch, discriminating by its kindness in tact, tax also discriminates by its assessments in taxation. It makes good sense in language and in life that tax collectors balance their tax with tact.

Task (1114), as the doublet of tax, at first meant the same thing: a compulsory payment to a king. Eventually, after almost four centuries, task described difficult work. Citizens in a democracy can not complain that their taxes fatten royal coffers, but they still regard paying taxes as taxing tasks, imposed, they imagine, by unfeeling taskmasters. Taskmasters are the worst! They not only allot tasks, but they require a set amount of work in a set length of time. Their tasking taxes their laborers. Tasks are never pleasant: "Alas poor Duke, the task he undertakes is numbering sands, and drinking oceans dry" (*Richard II* 2. 2). Tasks also tax our tact.

Weigh human senses in the balance: we speak of human sight, hearing, and smell, but we dignify human touch with a definite article, 'the' human touch. Sight objectifies, but touch personalizes and feeling takes the pulse of humanity. Touch and tact, tax and task touch a wide contingent of human feeling. This dignity comes with its price; when human feelings are involved, they add up to a personal, touchy subject.

## Words

Human touch gains knowledge tangibly. **The** human touch gains it tactfully. A Germanic word gives English its word feeling. A Classical Latin word gives English tangible, tact, and even tax; a Vulgar Latin word gives English touch.

1. **PIE root *pal*, to touch**
   Greek: *psallein*, to strike the harp
   Latin: *palpo palpare*, to touch
      Classical English: psalm (825), palpable (1384), palpation (1483)
   German: *fühlen*, to feel
      Germanic English: to feel (893)
2. **PIE root *tag*, touch**
   Latin:
      *tango tangere* and *tactus*, to touch; *tactus*, touch
      *attingo attingere*, to touch on, reach a goal, attain
         English:
            tact (1651), sense of touch; (1793), feeling for what fits
            contact (1626)

contingent (1400), happening or not (1613), depending on a previous condition (1727)—noun—part of a whole
Latin: *taxo taxare* (frequentative of *tangere*), to touch sharply, estimate, reproach
English:
to tax (1290), to assess; (1672), to burden
tax (1327), compulsory contribution
tax, a doublet of task:
task (1114), fixed payment to a king; (1593), difficult work
to task (1483), to impose a tax; (1530), to impose work

3. **PIE root *teu*, knock**
Vulgar Latin: *tocco toccare*, to strike—onomatopoetic alternative to *tangere*
Italian:
*toccare*, to hit, strike, touch
*toccata*, keyboard piece designed to show off a musician's touch
English:
tocsin (1586), Strike the bell!—strike (toc-)+signal (-sin), alarm
Spanish: *tocar*, to touch, knock (on a door), ring (a doorbell)
French: *toucher*, to touch
English:
to touch (1300), to touch with the hand; (1340), to affect with emotion
touch (1340)

Two PIE roots, one pulling, the other knowing, give Russian words for touch:

1. **PIE root *trag*, to draw, drag**
Latin: *traho trahere* and *tractus*, to draw
English: to treat
Russian: трогать (trogat'), to touch

2. **PIE root *woyde*, to know**
Greek: *oida*, to know; *oiesthai*, to think; and *idein*, to see
English: idea
Russian:
ощущать (oshchushchat), to feel, perceive, be aware of
ощутимый (oshchutimyy), palpable
Russian:
осязать (osyazat'), to feel by touching
осязаемый (osyazayemyy), tangible

## 51. Tongue and Taste

### Tasty and Tasteful

Man has three outward senses, seeing, hearing, and smelling. These senses describe the function of his three organs, eye, ear, and nose. He tastes with a fourth organ, his tongue, but he more obviously speaks with his tongue. More subtle than the three other senses, taste widens to broad areas of meaning. For the sake of scientific precision, gustation, a Latinate word, describes it narrowly as tasting food; but to get a taste of its nature, we need to consider it broadly.

In speaking, first of all, tongue is a PIE cognate of language, and its first appearance in 890 referred to speech and not to taste. A man learns to speak with a civil tongue when he speaks the tongues of the world. As he speaks these languages, he may learn that Latin *lingua* means tongue; and as a linguist, he may also learn that the adjective lingual describes the vowels 'a,' 'e' and 'i', because he pronounces them with his tongue.

In tasting, before the tongue does its work, the lips do theirs in smacking. The Germanic family has used its root to represent taste, as in the German, *schmecken*. It's basic—too basic—so embarrassingly basic that our refined Victorian forebears forbid such noisy relishing of food. We all inevitably catch ourselves reverting to this primitivism, but most of us, on our own, find lip-smacking annoying without reading up on etiquette. Refined taste does not advertise its enjoyments as lip-smackin' good, at least, not among refined palates, who wish lip-smackers well and hope that they dine in private.

About lip smacking or lip-smackingly good food, taste should also go back to one wise observation from the ancients: *De gustibus non est disputandum*, "About tastes, there is no dispute." We have to admit that all classes and all ages smack of this failing. Let people have the privilege of choosing the when and why of their lip smacking, and even the privilege of choosin' to drop its 'g' if they please.

Given these ramifications of taste, it need not surprise us that it shares the same root with tact. Yes, tangible tact gave English its word for taste! Latinate tact and Romance taste are doublets. If their connection in language may at first puzzle you, consider the connection of tact with taste in humanity: good taste, like tact, has the right touch. Derived from French *tâter*, to feel, taste first meant the perception of touch at the end of the thirteenth century; fifty years later, it meant the perception of flavor; and the perception of quality, by the beginning of the fifteenth. In these 130 years, taste evolved from tact to tastebuds to budding discrimination.

182 • WORLDS IN WORDS

Imagine touch evolving to taste in our own lives: at age 10, a child does not even touch the spinach on his plate at dinner, but his parents encourage him to take just a taste. Eventually, after his parents realize that creamed spinach may be more to his taste, he starts to develop a taste for it. Finally, by the age of 30, he has such good taste in its preparation that he is even educating his parents' taste for oysters Florentine or saag paneer. The child evolves from not even touching spinach to tasting it and finally developing a real taste for it and good taste for other things. Taste and touch join in refinement.

The Romance words for taste—Italian or Spanish *gusto* and French *goût*—represent similarly broad connections. In Spanish, for example, *mucho gusto* indicates "much pleasure" in meeting an acquaintance. Life has many pleasures in addition to eating and meeting. In the appreciation of art, gusto defines some very great appeal in a painting that is calculated both to please and to surprise. In English, just as you might have been surprised by taste and tact sharing the same root, choice and gusto also share the same root. Both the Romance choice and gusto are derived from the same PIE root to choose. To the broad expanse of taste in touch and tact, we can add an equally broad expanse in choice and gusto.

Though broad in their application, let's again focus these words on the evolution of the ten-year-old's taste for spinach: at first, this choosey child does not even want to touch spinach, but he has enough tact at the dinner table to taste it. Eventually, he considers it choice and relishes it with gusto. He may eventually realize that its gustatory possibilities appeal to his *goût profond*. In this and in other areas, taste evolves in a process of growth.

Russian also represents taste and touch as evolution in a process. The two Russian verbs, пробовать (probovat') and отведать (otvedat') both mean to test and also to taste. пробовать, through German *Probe* and *probieren*, refers to the proving, which tasting starts; and отведать, to the knowledge, in which it ends. Ingesting and digesting describe the full process; tasting just starts by smacking the lips and taking a bite, but perhaps only one, especially when a person at first "proves" and finally "knows" the food to be unappetizing or maybe even inedible. These Russian verbs point out the tentative testing of tasting and taste.

We all experience the two poles of living to eat or eating to live. Some of us may enjoy living at either extreme, but most of us know, at least we hope, that opposites attract, and that we can live somewhere in the middle. Gusto and good taste originating in living to eat and expanding flamboyantly with gusto suggest a path to, through, and round about, the middle. The ideas cognate with taste—touching, choosing, and testing—take us, like the ten-year-old staring at his spinach, on this path. Tact, also, has been separated from touch, but the masterful touch can never be entirely separated from hands. Life has such flavor that we need both touching, tasting and even a little lip-smacking to live by eating appreciatively.

## Words

One PIE root supplies the word for tongue/language to the three language families:

### PIE root *dnghu*, tongue

1. Romance
    Latin and Italian: *lingua*, tongue
        Spanish: *lengua*; French: *langue*
2. Germanic
    German: *Zunge*, tongue
    English: tongue (890), organ of speech
3. Slavic
    Czech: *jazyk*; Russian: язык (yazyk), tongue

Five PIE roots supply words for taste to the three language families:

I. Germanic
  1. **PIE root *smeg*, to taste**
      German: *schmecken*, to taste; and *Geschmack*, taste
      Norwegian and Swedish: *smak*, taste
      English: to smack (1340)
II. Romance
  2. **PIE root *tag*, touch**
      Latin: *tactus*, touch
          French: *tâter*, to feel, get a feel for
          English:
              to taste, (1290), to touch; (1340), to perceive flavor
              taste, (1292), perception of touch; (1340), perception of flavor; (1420), perception of quality
  3. **PIE root *geus*, to taste, choose**
      Latin: *gusto gustare*, to taste
          Italian and Spanish: *gusto*; French: *goûter*, to taste; and *goût*, taste; *choisir*, to choose
          English:
              gust (1430), taste—*cf.* taste (1340)—(1600), individual taste
              gusto (1629)

III. Romance, Germanic, and Slavic
  4. **PIE roots *bheu*, to be + *per*, outstanding**
     Latin: *proba*, test; and *probo probare*, to try, test
     German: *Probe*, test; and *probieren*, to test, taste
     English: to prove/to pree, to taste: "The proof of the puddin' is the preen."
     Russian: проба (proba), test; and пробовать (probovat'), to test, taste
  5. **PIE root *ueid/vid*, to see**
     Latin: *video videre* and *visus*, to see
     Russian:
        от- (ot), away from + ведать (vedat'), to know, control
        отведать (otvedat'), to try, taste

# 52. Nonsense

In the seventh grade, I was amused by my teacher's definition of idiot, imbecile and moron as medical terms. Accustomed to hearing these words in a fusillade of boyish billingsgate, I found them incongruous in formal English. Like most of humanity, ignorant of words and subjective in choosing them, I had not looked with objective understanding at these or any other words. Some grown-up boys, scorning those whom they consider idiots, imbeciles or morons, may dismiss them as empty-headed, not impaired. We all suffer impairment of our five senses in different ways at different times. On the dumb sides of this single human coin of either being articulate or inarticulate, we may either be dumb-struck passingly or permanently. The best we can do is to join frail humanity in living with our own idiosyncratic degrees of impairment.

Latin *stupere*, to be benumbed or amazed, denotes insensibility. Vergil describes some of the citizens of Troy gaping in awe at the Trojan horse: *pars stupet innuptae donum exitiale Minervae*, "Others, all wonder, scan the gift of doom / by virgin Pallas given, and view with awe / that horse which loomed so large." English words derived from this root usually emphasize insensibility. Tobacco or alcohol puts us in a stupor and old age makes us stupid, but stupid first meant permanently bereft of senses.

Actively contrasting to passive stupor, stupendous describes something stupefying, and not someone stupefied: "They reached the foot of that stupendous natural barrier, the Alps" (1798). Amazement may sharpen our senses at first, but almost inevitably dulls them in the end. Too many stupendous natural phenomena can so stupefy that they stultify. Just as imbibing ends in inebriation, stupefaction ends in stultification.

Stupendous also serves as hyperbole to describe Alpine human folly. Seeking competitive edge by hyperbole, if unable to find it by reason, someone comments on his opponent's "stupendous oversights": "He is apt to attribute to his opponent stupendous oversights and elementary misunderstandings" (1914). What a stupendous joke does stupefied, stupid humanity make of life!

Numb (1440), deprived of feeling, compounded into numbskull (1724), makes numbness purely derisive in reference to "every modern numbskull, who takes hold of a subject he knows nothing about" (1807, Washington Irving). Dim (1000), the opposite of bright, only referred to unclear vision in the eighteenth century: "The understanding is dim, and cannot by its natural light discover spiritual truth" (1729). The Age of Reason clarified its opposite in numb skulls and dim bulbs.

Specific groups of people act idiotically idiosyncratic. From Greek *idios*, private person, English derives idiom, a turn of phrase private to a language; and idiosyncrasy, a blend of character private to a person. A noodle (1753), like a macaroni, described an aristocrat returning from his Grand Tour, with affected, seemingly idiotic, tastes for Italian manners and macaroni. In a later century, far worse than a penchant for pasta, a dope gets dopey on dope.

From Latin *idiota*, ignorant, common man, English adapted idiot (1300) which from its first use meant one incapable of reasonable conduct from birth. Imbecile (Latin *imbecillus*, without a staff), on the other hand, meant physically weak (1549), before it meant mentally weak (1755). Modern psychiatry has adapted this word to describe an adult with the intelligence of a 6- to 9-year-old.

Compounding Greek *moros*, dull, with *oxys*, sharp, oxymoron, sharp-dullness, refers to any contradictory phrase like cruel kindness or bitter-sweet. Oxymoron itself expresses an oxymoron. Molière created the character *Moron* as a dullard in his play, *La Princesse d'Élide*. In 1910, the American Association for the Study of the Feeble-Minded chose the word moron to designate an adult with the intelligence of an 8- to 12-year-old. Though dull in understanding, a moron has the dignity of intelligence. With more humor than respect, people may say that he is not the brightest light on the porch or the sharpest tool in the shed. Idiot, imbecile and moron describe impairment of the senses from birth to adolescence. The rest of humanity progresses from the intelligence of a 13-year-old and older—but not necessarily wiser.

Many words describe *homo insipiens* with amusing hyperbole. Fools have empty heads: from Latin *follis*, a bag filled with air like a bellows, fool (1275) describes an air-head or a bubblehead. We picture these empty heads filled with ersatz gray matter: blockhead (1549), puddinghead (1726), fathead (1842). Dumb and its family—dull (975), dotard (1386), dolt (1543), and duffer (1842)—have heads filled with dust or smoke. Dizzy (825), the oldest word in English for stupidity, only referred to vertigo 500 years after it first appeared. We recreate the image of a head filled with smoke when we speak of someone foggy north of the neck.

Some people occupy a harmless and blessed class apart: a ninny acts like a baby (Italian *ninno*, baby). A natural (1533) acts as naturally as nature has taught him. Simple (1220) first described personal simplicity without duplicity. Silly, from the German *selig*, holy, consequentially deserving of pity (1425), and therefore, helpless (1587), has traditionally described women and children. Daft (1000) and its doublet, deft (1440), originally meant appropriate; but excessively appropriate conduct, like conduct similarly holy, can seem simple-minded. Cretin (1779), the Swiss word for Christian, designated a half-witted dwarf. God loves his children, simple, silly naturals all!

"Dust thou art, and unto dust shalt thou return" (*Genesis* 3.19)—we all start as silly children and only reach an old duffer's dotage if blessed with longevity. Noodledom, passing or permanent, awaits us in our dotage. Erasmus has rightly doomed us all to folly. When I or my childhood friends teased each other as morons, we knew that the word could just as easily describe us all: "See the happy moron. / He doesn't give a damn. / I wish I were a moron. / My God! perhaps I amn!" (I claim poetic license in choosing idiotic rhyme with reason.)

## Words

When the perception of our five senses fails us, roots for words describing this impairment picture us standing still or agape, even thunder-struck, or darkened in speech and understanding. These conditions may be passing or permanent.

### PIE root, *stu*, to stand; *stup*, to wonder

Latin: *stupeo stupere*, to be benumbed, astounded, amazed
    Italian: *stupido*; French: *stupide*; Spanish: *estupido*
    English:
        stupor (1398), insensibility
        stupid (1541), slow-witted; (1611), stupefied

to stupefy (1600), to benumb or astound
stupendous (1666), causing stupor, amazing

### PIE root *stel*, to cause to stand

Latin: *stultus* and its doublet *stolidus*, stupid, foolish
Spanish and Portuguese: *estulto*
English: stolid (1600), dull, impassive; to stultify (1766), to reduce to foolishness

### PIE root *stene*, to thunder

Latin: *attono attonare*, to strike with thunder
    Italian, Spanish and Portuguese: *tonto*, silly, stupid
    Spanish: *atontado*, stunned, befuddled
    English: to astonish

### PIE root *dheu*, smoke, dust

German: *dumm*, dumb, stupid
English: dumb (1000), bereft of speech; (1531), senseless

Three PIE roots give Russian words for stupidity:

### PIE root *tolku*, talk

Latin: *(t)loquor*, I speak
    English: loquacious
Russian: бес-толковый (bes-tolkovy), speechless, muddle-headed

### PIE root *ten*, to stretch

English: tense, stretched; tendentious, stretching evidence
Russian: тупой (tupoy), blunt, dull, stupid

### No known PIE root

Greek: *throsko*, I rush; *thouros*, raging, furious
Russian: дурной (durnoy), bad, mad; and дурак (durak), fool

# Kin, Kindness and Character

. . . .

## 53. Birth in Three Steps: Conception, Bearing and Birth

### Birth in Three Steps or Less

Conception, gestation and parturition, that is, conceiving the child, bearing it and bringing it forth, take the three steps to birth. Indo-European languages have used roots for conception (*kap* and *ken*), for bearing (*bher*), and for parturition (*or* and *par*) to describe the progress.

Perhaps because the nine months of gestation have literally weighed more than conception or parturition, 'to bear' has borne a double meaning and refers by its root to gestation, but also to parturition: to say that a woman bears a child means that she has carried it and brought it into the world. A woman bears a child for the nine month period of gestation, before the child is finally born by her at birth.

The Indo-European root 'to bear,' however, refers to gestation, not to conception or to parturition. (From it, by the way, springs bairn as the word for child in *Beowulf*.) 'To be born' stands so much on its own that we need to remind ourselves that it represents the passive of 'to bear.' After our mothers bear us, we are born. We even spell the perfect form of 'to bear' meaning 'to endure' differently: our mothers have borne labor so that we may be born. The basic words of birth in English, therefore, take their origin from the idea of bearing. Birth represents all three steps.

In describing birth, the English idiom 'to be delivered' makes the mother passive, instead of active. Just as the child is born, the mother is delivered. In this sense, neither the child nor its mother is active. "Deliver us from evil": to be delivered means to be liberated, when a mother is delivered of the child. The midwife, accoucheur or obstetrician, taking the active part, delivers the woman from the foetus. Both the mother and her child need help!

Like 'to bear,' parturition emphasizes one of the three steps of birth. In Latin, *parere*, to produce offspring derives its meaning from *parare*, to gather (*cf.* to pare an apple in English) and referred originally to the 'gathering' of the male and female. Parent comes from *parere*, because both parents gather in coitus to conceive. *Parere*, therefore, like 'to bear' and 'to be born,' jumped from one step to another: its primary meaning focused on gathering, but it jumped over gestation to birth itself. Also, just as in the case of 'to bear' and 'to be born' or 'to be borne,' *parare*, to gather, and *parere*, to give birth, parted company in conjugation and in meaning.

The origin of *parere* shows the same telescoping of meaning which we have seen in the forms of 'to bear' in English. The Latin tradition in parturition focuses on the conception of 'gathering' in coitus and conception. The Indo-European 'to bear' emphasizes the nine months of gestation. Understandably, the child's conception and gestation had such importance that they represented the final result. In contrast to this telescoping of meaning in Romance languages and in English, Russian represents the three steps in three separate roots; зачатие (začátije), conception; беременность (beremennost'), gestation; and роды (rody), parturition.

A birthday marks the long-expected beginning of life, but that quickening labor of one day concludes the slow work of many.

## Words

1. CONCEPTION

### PIE root, *i*, to go

Latin: *co-itus*, going together
    French: *coit*; Spanish: *coito*; Polish: *koitus*; Russian: коитус (koitus)

### PIE root *kap*, to take, grasp

Spanish: *concepcion*; French: *conception*; and English: conception

### PIE root *ken*, new

Greek: *khainos*, fresh, new
    English:
        pleisto-cene, era of most (pleisto-) new (-cene) species
        en-caenia, festival *renewing* of joy
        re-cent, fresh
Russian: начать (nachat'), to begin; and зачатие (začátije), conception

2. BEARING

### PIE root *bher*, to bear, in four families

1. German: *gebaren*, to bear children
English: to bear, birth and berth; bairn, a male child
2. Greek: *phero*, I carry
English:
metaphor, carrying (-phor) a word beyond (meta-) literal meaning: "A mighty fortress is our God."
paraphernalia, possessions a woman brings (-phernalia) from her parents' home along (para-) to her husband's

3. Latin: *fero*, I carry
   English:
   to confer, defer, prefer, refer, transfer, *etc.*
   fertile, bearing fruit; fortune, bearing good or evil
4. Russian:
   брать (brat), to take; and со-бирать (so-birat), to gather
   беременность (beremennost'), pregnancy

## 3. BIRTH

### PIE root *par*, birth, ancestor

Latin: *pario parere* and *partus*, to give birth; *post partum*, after birth
Italian: *partorire;* and Spanish: *partear*
English:
   parent and parturition
   puer-peral fever, child bearing fever; and vivi-parous, bearing live young

### PIE root *er/or/ergh*, to move, stir, spring, raise

Latin: *origo originis*, origin
   English: orient, where the sun rises
Russian:
   род (rod), birth family; роды (rody), parturition
   родитель (roditel'), parent, father; and родина (rodina), homeland
   рож-дать (rozh-dat'), to give birth

### PIE root *mel*, soft

Latin: *mollis*, soft
   English: to mollify
Russian: младенец (mladenets), newborn, infant

### Miscellaneous

Midwife, literally, the woman with (mid-, German *mit*) women giving birth
Latin: *obstetrix*; and Italian: *ostetrica*
French: *sage-femme* and *accoucheur/accoucheuse*
   Polish: *akuszerka*; and Russian: акушерка (akusherka)

# 54. Ken within Kin

Mother Nature's Indo-European roots, *gen, nat,* and *gno,* link genes and natality to knowledge. In the present, nature bears being, and by her name, "about to be born," she will also bear it in the future. The words of this PIE family connect our great mother's chain of physical being to far-reaching familial and social links.

"In the beginning"—the Torah recounts creation. To emphasize that focus, the seventy scholars translating it from Hebrew into Greek chose *genesis* as the title for its first book. Published around 250 B.C., the book of *Genesis* recounts the birth of both the earth and Judaism. Abraham, its progenitor (1347), generated (1509) progeny (1300), engendering (1325) in generations (1300) "more descendants than can be counted."

"God divided the light from the darkness." Nature, continuing God's creation, articulates it by dividing and uniting. Getting down to elements of the elements, Darwin called this process pangenesis (1868), by which cells, later refined into genes, divide to re-create themselves. In this re-creation, nature divides her *genera* (1551) into species, and then she unites the two separate genders (1384) into one flesh. Their separate gonads and genitals unite to plant seeds in pro-creation. Pre-gnancy (1529) precedes (pre-) birth (-gnancy), which social norms divide between the genuine (1661) and the spurious. We celebrate birth on its natal (1420) day, called birthday (1000) in the native tongue.

Naming Christ's birth has demonstrated an ability to call it by a special name. In French, an everyday birthday, and even an uncommon natal day or nativity, did not dignify it enough. Dropping the 't' of natal, Noel names it uniquely. Spanish wishes a Merry Christmas with *Feliz Navidad* and a happy birthday with *Feliz Cumpleanos*; Italian, with *Buon Natale* and *Buon Compleanno*. In English also, we expect to see the average baby in a crib and the baby Jesus in the creche, an alternate form of crib, of a nativity scene. A few of us dignify our birthday by calling it our natal day. Fewer still can summon the pretense to call it our nativity!

Genius (1390) and its adjective genial (1566) make genesis affable and brilliant. In antiquity, Romans celebrated and solemnized the *lectus genialis*, the "marriage bed." Edmund Spenser alludes to its geniality: "And thou, glad Genius! in whose gentle hand the bridal bower and genial bed remain." At birth, we are endowed with a genius (1390), a spirit akin to a guardian angel, by whose benign influence we become genial. (Malign influences are possible.) Those sharing the same genius are congenial (1625), a word also referring to physical conditions present at birth, until it was replaced by congenital (1796). A place or institution can also have a genius. In 1850, John C. Calhoun, a secessionist from South Carolina, observed that the genius of the United States' Constitution opposed powerful federal government: "The genius of our constitution is opposed to the assumption of power." Blessed with an extraordinary genius, a man becomes known as the genius (1647) that has blessed him. Can a mere man be a genius? In part, yes, he can; but he remains a man in all other parts. With enough pretense, a man could declare his genius, as he celebrates his nativity.

The *gen* root with the prefix 'in-' joins the links of the in-nate (1420). Plato and many others have believed that the innate idea of God has imprinted every soul at birth. In-born (1000) at first translated Latin *indigena*, the native autochthon in a place. Original flora and fauna and aborigines are indigenous (1646). Ingenious (1483) describes a man full of *ingenium*, inborn genius; and his ingenuity (1599) creates an engine (1300), at first an engine of war but, most notably, a steam engine in the nineteenth century. Ingenuous (1598) describes a man full of inborn character in its pristine, noble simplicity. Ingenuous and ingenious complement each other, one referring to inborn character and the other to inborn talent. Innate, inborn, indigenous, ingenuous, ingenious—birth has given man many an 'in.'

The ingenious story teller can do a lot with inborn qualities that characterize goodness. He combines their innocence and charm to create the *ingenue*, the guileless newcomer to a social scene. The ingenue may be as guileless as the complexities of a story require. She is so ingenuous that she gets herself into difficulties, and not ingenious enough that she can get herself out of them—the best stuff of melodrama.

The words genuine and native/naive also describe and elaborate innate simplicity. After its first reference to legitimate birth, genuine by 1840 described the sincere and honest. By the root, the naive rely on native sense, unassisted by art or experience. The ingenuous may be considered naive and vice versa; but naïveté (1673), perhaps as a borrowing from worldly-wise French, does not ring as honorably as ingenuous. In either case, we need both to cherish, and to refine, the sense that we have been born with.

Knowledge connects all the links in the chain. With the same root for birth and knowledge in French, Paul Claudel recognized their kinship: *Tout naissance est un connaissance,* "All birth is knowledge." The German cognates *kennen,* to know, and *kind,* child, give English a pair of words which can translate the French: ken is in kin.

Children consider much about parents and grandparents beyond their ken; but they do know something, and they grow to know more; because their birth has forged links, which gradually evolve. They will revolve back and forth on these links to know themselves.

## Words

Words from cognate roots for birth and knowledge trace origin and its wisdom.

**PIE root *gen/nat*, to be born**

\* \* \*

**PIE root *gno*, to know**

**FOUR DIVISIONS**

   I. Greek
   Greek:
      *genesis*, birth, genesis

         \* \* \*

      *gignoskein*, to know
      *gnomon*, pointer on a sundial that helps to know time
      *gnosis*, knowledge, usually esoteric
   English:
      gnomon, gnostic, knowing; pro-gnosis, knowing before; dia-gnosis, knowing thoroughly; a-gnostic, not knowing
   Russian:
      гномон—derived from Greek—gnomon

         \* \* \*

      гений (geniy), genius (the person)
      гениальность (genial'nost'), genius (the talent)
   II. Romance
   Latin:
      *nascor nasci* and *natus*, to be born
      *praegnans praegnantis*, before (prae-) being born, (g)*nascens*; pregnant[12]

         \* \* \*

      *nosco noscere* and *notus*, to know
      *cog-noscere*, to know completely, recognize
   French:
      *naître*, to be born
      *naissance*, birth
      Noël, dropping the 't' of *natalis (dies)*, natal (day)

         \* \* \*

      *con-naître, to know*
      *con-naisance,* knowledge

Spanish:
> *nacer*, to be born
>
> \* \* \*
>
> *co-nocer*, to know

English:
> native (1374) and naive (1654, native without the 't'); natal and nascent
>
> \* \* \*
>
> can (verb) and canny; to note and notion

III. Germanic

German:
> *kind*, child
> *kindergarten*, a garden for children
>
> \* \* \*
>
> *kennen*, to know

English:
> to know; ken (1545), knowledge, as in the phrase, beyond my ken
> couth (1000), known; and uncouth (897), not known; awkward (1732)

IV. Slavic

Russian:
> натура (natura), nature, life, exterior
> знать (znat'), to know; and значить (znachit'), to mean, to signify
> знак (znak), sign, mark, symbol, omen

## PIE root *er/or/ergh*, to move, stir, spring, raise

(more at Birth in Three Steps)

English: orient and origin

Russian:
> род (rod), birth family; and при-рода (pri-roda), nature
> родиться (rodit'sya), to be born
> рождество (rozhdestvo), Christmas; literally, birth
> с днем рождения (s dnem rozhdeniya), Happy Birthday

# 55. Kindness and Benevolence

## The Kind Doing Kindnesses and the Benevolent Doing Benevolences

With its classical pedigree, benevolence is good, and does good self-consciously. Kindness, at home and close to its roots, is good and does good innately. Whatever their roots, both classical benevolence and native kindness show the difficulty of translating birth to being, and being to doing.

The origin of kind and benign bears witness to goodness as innate. From the PIE root *gen/nat*, to be born, the English adjective kind and the Latin adjective *benignus* ascribe goodness to birth. Kind, a very old word in English, first meant innate: in *Beowulf*, a king displays strength and boldness that is kind (*gecynde*), i.e. inborn. More than four centuries later, kind evolved to describe gentle, sympathetic goodness, at the same time that the Latinate benign (1370) entered English. Benign almost immediately mellowed to a meek and mild complement to nice weather, soil (1386) or astrology, all showing a benign face: "His affairs began to wear a more benign aspect" (Fielding, 1743). Benign old men, mellowing in their "benign and placid countenance" (1777), illustrate the old saw that "good will is no skill."

Kind, on the other hand, acted skillfully. From the beginning, kind thought expressed itself in deed. Kindness first meant benefaction—"I have received some small kindnesses from him, as money, plate, and jewels" (*Timon* III, 2)—before it meant benevolence sixty years later. Lady Macbeth fears that her husband's "milk of human kindness" may be both too naturally strong and too actively gentle to endure murder. Defining kindness as doing made moralists distinguish it from being: "Who does a kindness," observed Alexander Pope, "is not therefore kind." By the nineteenth century, kindness had become so mechanical that one moralist separated it from gift-giving: "Kindness does not consist in gifts, but in gentleness and generosity of spirit" (1873). Benign did not end in dynamic goodness; being kind lives on in its potential, but it may not always end in a kind deed—indeed, why should it?

Gentility, the third family of innate virtue, has done the least to break the chains of noble birth. It entered English with such noble lineage that it did not at first part from its French origin, gentilesse. Why should *la crème de la crème* debase its *quinta essentia* in the base alloy of the native tongue? 'What highfalutin' pretense!'—many thoughtful people might point out. Words should translate themselves into being and then into doing. Chaucer, the first author to use gentilesse, also wrote a poem to prove that gentlemen acquire it by cultivation and not by birth.

Gentleman has also remained untainted. The first edition of the OED defines him solely as a person of genteel birth and quality—like Athena, springing from his father fully grown. His heritage still contradicts the Biblical prescription that man work for a living: "Long nails define idle gentility's assured sign" (1650). This family has seemed destined for their genteel prison. By a kind providence, however, gentle has manfully saved his family from endless bows and scrapes, even though his action often characterizes the gentler sex.

After such preoccupation with birth, it is a relief to see that kindness may also spring from will, love or knowledge. Slavic kindness, especially, claims a home in love and knowledge. In Russian, kindness both loves (любезность [lyubeznost']) and knows (вежливый [vezhlivyy]).

The nature of goodness being and doing, already distinct in the words kind, benign and gentility, also marks the first use of good will and benevolence. In the Vulgate, the angelic chorus at the Nativity— . . . *pax hominibus bonae voluntatis* (*Luke* 2, 14), translated by Wyclif as "peace to men of good will" (1382)—assumes good will as a synonym of good character. The same "good will" in the King James Bible, "peace, good will toward men," wishes a person well—the first meaning of the word in English (825). At the end of the ninth century (893), good will could also refer to a condition of virtuous disposition. We see active good will in the first use of the word in English and in the King James Bible's "good will toward men." Both good will and kindness will to act.

Benevolence actively did good from its first use in Latin and in English (1384). In Latin, *volo*, I wish, the second part of bene-volence, indicated good will even without the prefix bene-. The phrase, God willing, *Deo volente*, for example, assumes the goodness of divine will. *Benevolentia*, benevolence, confirms that the will is good: "Affection in human nature, the object of which is the good of another, is benevolence or love of another" (1726). Benevolence (1425) works as charity with kindness and good will.

Benevolence, like kindness, ended as charity or even taxation that is not necessarily benevolent: the man professing that "the poor exercise our benevolence" (1876) could easily display condescending kindness that is not kind. It came to describe a tax imposed by a King on his people: "subsidy, under so preposterous a name as benevolence, is malevolence indeed" (1644). William Pitt, speaking for the American colonies referred to benevolence as injustice by another name: "The spirit which now resists your taxation in America is the same which formerly opposed loans, benevolences and ship-money in England" (1775).

Good birth or good will does not always end in good deeds.
That process can sour the milk of human kindness.

## Words

What makes people kind—birth or knowledge, love or will?
Three Romance and Germanic words for kindness choose birth.

According to these words, kin best make kindred kind.
One Romance and two Slavic roots look to will, love, or knowledge.

### PIE root *gen/nat*, to be born

Three cognate word families from this root
1. Old English: *gecynde*
    English: kind (888) and kindness (1290)
2. Latin: *benignus*
    Spanish: *benigno*
    English: benign (1370)
3. Latin: *gens gentis*, race, family, clan
    Italian: *gentilezza* and *gentile*; French: *gentilesse* and *gentil*
        English:
            gentle (1225), nobly born; (1297), nobly behaved; (1552), mild
            genteel (1599), a doublet of gentle
            gentleman (1275), a man of noble birth
            gentilesse (1340)—found in Chaucer.—good breeding
            gentility (1340), noble birth; (1588), noble manner

### PIE root *vel*, to wish

Latin:
>   *volo*, I wish
>   *benevolentia* and *benevolens*
>       Italian: *benevolenza* and *benevolo*
>       Spanish: *benevolencia* and *benévolo*
>       French: *bienveillance* and *bienveillant*
>       English: benevolence (1384) and benevolent (1482)

### PIE root *leubh*, love, desire

English: to love
German: *lieben*, to love
Polish: *lubić*, to love
Russian:
>   любить (lyubit'), to love; любезный (lyubeznyy), kind
>   любезность (lyubeznost'), kindness

### PIE root *ueid/vid*, to see, know

Latin: *video videre* and *visus*, I see
Russian:
>   ведать (vedat), to know; видеть (vee-deet'), to see
>   вежливый (vezhlivyy), polite, knowledgeable

## 56. Gentility and Civility

Any mortal kind—of any race, nation or even vocation—may become known for qualities characteristic of some of its members. For example, jaunty, a cognate of gentry, and an anglicized form of French *gentil*, denoted the free and easy manners of the gentry. It described those gentry who had the time and the spirit to have free and easy manners, sparing no expense for their fun. Poor folk did not have the time or the money to be jaunty. The gentry could not claim jaunty fellows as uniquely their own, even though etymology made a claim to fame for their gentility.

Generally, some words in English descriptive of a class make distinctions that are not consistently valid. Magisterial describes masters in a school, but not all of them deserve the title. Are professionals, those engaged in professions, always professional, that is, in possession of the highest character and morality characteristic of their calling? In terms of grammar, do the nouns master and profession deserve the best connotations of their adjectives, professional and magisterial? If we trust in professional consistently describing its noun, news media disappoint us daily. (Since we live as well as we think, speak and write, we should use adjectives sparingly in good thinking, speaking and writing.) Etymology tells many stories about historical derivations that impose limitations on meaning. Sometimes these stories also demonstrate limitations on the human spirit.

Specifically, another adjective has its root in gentry: the same free and easy spirit that made gentry jaunty also made them gentle. By condescension befitting such persons of rank in sharing the good, they might show "gentle affability" (1647) toward inferiors. In other words, the gentle gentry acted like gentlemen, but this title does not indicate an origin so superior that it could describe condescension very far down the social scale. Traditionally, it has sufficed as a title for a man without one: "Gentlemen are all those who, lawfully entitled to Armorial distinction," did not have titled nobility (1882). A gentleman had a coat of arms, with the privileges of "an officer and a gentleman." This phrase, an anachronistic cliché in the modern army, arose from its designation of a separate class serving as officers in the British army. Since a gentleman ranked below the peerage, titled noblemen probably felt less duty to act like one. Some peers of the realm inspired the phrase "drunk as a Lord" in breaking the bonds of gentlemanly restraint. Jaunty, gentle and gentleman appear fragile in morality and evanescent in history.

Breathing the free air of democracy in the eighteenth century, gentleman became "a man of Chivalrous instincts and fine feelings," preferably with, but even without, genteel birth. Byron defines an aspect of these "fine feelings": "With such true breeding of a gentleman, / You never could divine his real thought" (*Don Juan*, 1821). Well-spoken discretion, tact and kindness bring chivalry and fine feelings a little down to earth for nature's noblemen. Even today, jaunty freedom from gainful employment can claim a title of gentleman, although money means little without character or breeding. In this sense, a gentleman does not necessarily act like a gentleman, any more than a person in a profession acts like a professional.

Cities have always had an influence in civilizing citizens: at first, citizenship made a man civil (1387), even when he was waging civil war. With a little humanity, civility (1382) embodied the manners of citizens, "decently polite, up to the ordinary or minimum standard of courtesy." Courtesy, of course, embodied the polished manners of the court. Fellow citizens on the street maintain, not courtesy, but civility that may be cool, but at least not rude. This distinction assumes that the average citizen has enough breeding to be civil, but not enough to be polite, and not near enough to be courteous.

Traveling from *allées* of gentlemen and alleys of civilians out to the lanes of villagers takes us from courtesy to civility out to villainy in the country. A villain (1303) at first simply lived and worked in a villa, that is, a farmhouse. Though of base birth, he could have his uses: a "trusty villain" might lighten a man's humor with "merry jests" (Shakespeare, *Comedy of Errors* I, 2, 19). Rubes from the sticks can be amusing, but watch them carefully! Once they have finished playing the fool with their jests, they might fulfill their base birth with base breeding by ending up 'untrusty' and perfectly villainous. At least, they would appear so as melodramatic villains on stage.

Russian brings together the concept of the villain with that of the gentleman: не-годяй (ne-godyay), villain, literally, not suitable, refers to a man "not suitable" for military rank. In both England and Russia, villains supplied fodder for livestock on their fields and fodder for cannons on fields of battle.

Shakespeare's Hamlet whirls these themes to a tragic dissolution. His first two soliloquies meld and smash kin with kindness and villainy. In the first, when he wishes to state the discrepancy between his family and its values, he questions whether his kin deserve the adjective kind that describes them by its etymology. Kin should be kind, but his fratricidal kin is "more than kin and less than kind" (Act I, 1). In the drama, Hamlet's Uncle Claudius, having murdered his brother and married his brother's wife, has become Hamlet's step-father, "more than kin;" and by his fratricide, he has certainly become much "less than kind." He has dissolved the fragile bonds of family.

In his second soliloquy, sharpening his sense of his uncle's crime by his own cowardice, Hamlet joins kin to villain: "O, what a rogue and peasant slave am I! ... Am I a coward? / Who calls me villain? ... I should have fatted all the region kites / With this slave's offal: bloody, bawdy villain! / Remorseless, treacherous, lecherous, kindless villain! / O, vengeance!" (Act II, 2). Hamlet's dilemma has deepened: the play has two villains who have both denied their ties of kinship. His step-father, by commission, at first, "less than kind," is, after anguished rumination, "kindless," a villain of no 'kind' at all; Hamlet, by omission, a "peasant slave" without legitimate kind. What "kindless" villain murders his brother and marries his widow; and what kind of "peasant slave" does nothing about it?

Poor Hamlet! He should have returned home to enjoy jauntily genteel family life, but fratricide has burst the bonds of its gentility and even civility. "Gentle Rosencrantz" and "gentle Gildenstern" are the only two "gentlemen" in the play, but their jaunty *bonhomie* makes them laughable, soon dead, nonentities. Fratricide and incest turn values upside down, by denying all sense of kind and kindness. Villainy, breaking from the rustic village to the royal court, makes villains of kings. Civility and gentility lose their tenuous hold. Without these two virtues, kings and slaves deny kind; and without that, they plunge into an abyss.

## Words

After kindred have made people kind, court, city or village make them courteous, civil or villainous. The Romance and Germanic heritage of the PIE roots *gno* and *gen* continues to add chapters as they ramify in social history. Russian sees these qualities in knowledge or suitability, and goodness or evil.

### PIE root *gno*, to know; *gen/nat*, to be born

Latin: *gens gentis*, race, family, clan
    French: *gentil*, kind, gentle; *genereux*, generous
        Italian and Spanish: *generoso*, generous
            English:
                gentle (1225), gentleman (1225), gentry (1380)
                generous (1588), genteel (1599)
                jaunty (1662), French *gentil* anglicized
            Russian: джентльмен (dzhentl'men), gentleman

German: *kennen*, to know (cf. *kind* and *kindergarten*)
  English: to know (*Beowulf*), kin (825), kind (888), kindred (1175), ken (1545)

### PIE root *ueik*, neighborhood

Latin: *villa*, farmhouse, villa
  French, Spanish and Italian: *villa*; French: *ville*, city
  Spanish: *villano*, a villain
  Russian: вилла (villa) and виллан (vilan)

### PIE root *ghedh*, suitable, good

German: *gut*, good
  English: good and to gather
Russian: не-годяй (ne-godyay), villain, literally not suitable

### PIE root *kuei*, honor, respect, fear

Greek: *time*, honor
Latin: *timeo timere*, to fear
English: Timo-thy, literally, the honor of God
Russian: честь (chest'), honor; учтивый (uchtivyy), courteous

### PIE root *phol*, to trick, deceive

Latin: *fallo fallere* and *falsus,* to deceive
English: false
Russian: зло (zlo), evil; злодей (zlodey), villain, literally, doing evil

# 57. Generosity and Charity

## Generosity in the Club, Charity in the Neighborhood

In addition to their reputation for being jaunty and gentle, gentlemen won a name for generosity; but they were making only the first bid—a low one—for prestige. Cultivate as they might this natural and noble instinct, they could not match citizens bestowing munificence or kings distributing largess. Gentlemen, citizens, and kings have paid their club dues in proportion to their resource. Humble folk without liberal resource or membership in the same club, do not pay the same dues and have won no special word for their gifts. The humblest of them all, the widow, who gives her mite, certainly does not belong to the club, but her neighborhood offers large possibilities.

Let's get to know a few characters in generosity's neighborhood. Derived from Latin *bonitas*, goodness, bounty first described generosity as well as goodness. Its adjective bounteous referred to the goodness of nature and nature's God, "the bounteous source of all our store," in John Wesley's hymn. Synonymous with liberality, it flowed, by God's Providence, into the coffers of the nobility: "Good Lord, bless us and all thy gifts which we receive of thy large liberality" (1566). A gentleman helped God's Providence when "the royal liberality of his nature delighted in acts of bounty" (1839). He aspires to making the highest bid of "royal liberality," even when he does not have royal resource. Lord and Lady Bountiful gained fame, and won their name, by their delight in dispensing God's "store."

A free man could afford to be liberal by education in liberal arts and by his liberality. Munificence marked its high point. Derived from the Roman muni-cipal tradition, *munus*, duty and reward, describes both what he gives and what he gets in return. Munificence gives one coin with the left hand and remuneration takes that one—maybe even another— back with the right. Prominent citizens shared these duties and rewards in a com-munity and had relief from them in im-munity. They gave in the unashamedly pagan expectation of getting by giving: munificence expected remuneration. Hobbes, in his *Leviathan* (1651), observed that this form of civic generosity paved their road to power: "Riches joined with liberality is power."

Largesse, on the highest level, described the generosity of a king who had all the power to begin with and wanted to keep his noblemen just happy enough for him to retain it. Large, a generous synonym of big, suggests its largeness that might so increase that it made royal resources decrease: "Our coffers," Shakespeare's Richard II observes, "with too great a court and liberal largesse are grown somewhat light"—"somewhat light," a regal euphemism for empty. Majesty does nothing by halves. This liberality, one grateful subject observed, "knew no bottom save an empty purse" (1661). Even though a king could not expect remuneration for his liberality, largesse was imperative—at the cry "Largesse!", gold poured out in profusion to make his gentry even more jaunty and prodigal than they were before.

Though in dearth amid profusion, the widow's mite wins a unique reward. With her humble resource, she does not enter the club like a jaunty donor, but she takes her place in the neighborhood. Her neighborhood is so large that it sets a boundary to munificence. Its charity suggests that anyone can made a bid, and not be outbid, for the creative selflessness, which is the grace of charity. By creating self-worth, charity does not give selflessly, but it invalidates the mean balance sheet—mean no matter how munificent—by which remuneration rewards munificence. In this large neighborhood, we can win our reward by charity in giving—two sides of the largest coin.

## Words

Romance and Germanic words for generosity describe free men, exchanging gifts and rewards in a structured social framework. Classical Christian charity establishes an independent framework of grace.

1. **PIE root *leudh*, of the people; therefore, legal, free in contrast to slave**
   Greek: *eleutheros*, free,
   Latin: *liber*, free
      English: liberal (1387)
   German: *Leute*, people
   English: lede (dialectical), man
   Russian: люди (lyudi), people
2. **PIE root *mei/mein*, change, exchange**
   Latin:
      *muto mutare*, to change; and *mutuus*, mutual
      *munus muneris*, duty or gift, service and its reward
      *municeps*, a man taking (*-ceps*) public duty (*muni-*)
      English:
         im-munity (1382), freedom from duty
         re-munerative (1477), profitable in rewarding duty
         muni-cipal (1540), taking duty; muni-ficent (1583), doing duty
         com-munity (1561), com-mon, and com-munion, sharing duties
   German: *gemein*, common
   English:
      mean (1665), the lower level of common—small-minded, low, stingy
      Common, the mean between extremes, can be man's best or his worst.
3. **PIE root *qa*, to desire**
   Greek: *charis*, grace, charm, elegance
   Latin: *carus*, dear, costly; *caritas*, dearness, charity
      English: charity, charisma

   **PIE root not identified**
   Latin: *largus*, abundant, copious; and *largiri*, to be generous
      French: *largesse*
         English: largesse (1225)

Russian words for community and generosity have six PIE roots:
1. **PIE root *epi* and *ob*, beside, among, toward**
    English: epi-cene, epi-center and ob-ey, ob-vious—
      words indicating proximity
    Russian:
      об-щий (ob-shchiy), common; literally, what is among
      об-щество (ob-shchestvo), society
      со-об-щаться (soobscat'sya), to communicate
2. **PIE root *ual*, power**
    Latin: *valere*, to be strong
      English: valid
    Russian:
      великий (velikiy), great; and душа (dusha), soul
      велико-душный (veliko-dushnyy), magnanimous, generous
3. **PIE root *ter*, to rub, drill**
    Latin: *tero terere* and *tritus*, to rub, wear down
      English: trite and contrition or attrition
    Russian:
      тратить (tratit), to spend, to waste; торить (torit), to beat a path, rub
      тороватый (torovatyy), generous
4. **PIE root *skei*, cut, split divide**
    Greek: *skhizein*, to cut
      English: schism
    Latin: *scindo scindere* and *scissus*, to cut
      English: scissors, shears; and to rescind, to cut back
    English: to shear, to cut; and share (cut from the whole)
    Russian:
      часть (chast'), part (cut from the whole); счастье (schast'ye),
        happiness
      щедрый (shchedryy), generous, lavish, bountiful
      Generosity cuts a slice; happiness receives it.
5. **PIE root *bhleg*, to shine; and the PIE root *er/or/ergh*, to move, stir, spring**
    Latin: *flagro flagrare*, to burn
      English: flagrant, burningly obvious
    French: *blanc*, white; Spanish: *blanco*; Italian: *bianca*
    English:
      blank and to blanch
      blanket, a blank, white woolen cloth used as a bed covering
      black—Fire, shining hot white, leaves everything black. Thus, one
        PIE root encompasses the extremes of black and white.

Polish: *bialy*, white, and *brzozowy*, birch
Russian:
блистать (blistat) to shine
белый (bielyj), white; and береза (bereza), birch; благо (blaga), good
благо-родный (blago-rodnyy), generous; literally, of good birth

6. **PIE root *bhleg*, to shine; and the PIE root *tuer*, to grasp, hold**
Greek: Sirens, literally, the Binders
Russian:
творить (tvorit), to create
благо-творительность (blago-tvoritel'nost'), charity, creating good

After spending and dividing, Russian generosity looks to heart, family and deeds:
spending, тороватый (torovatyy); and dividing, щедрый (shchedryy);
big heart, велико-душный (veliko-dushnyy);
good birth, благо-родный (blago-rodnyy);
good deeds, благо-творительность (blago-tvoritel'nost').

## 58. *How* Should I Know? or How Should *I* Know?

### Plus Ultra

Seeing can be knowing, but learning also follows a process that only starts with sight. The root meanings of words describing this process give clues to its nature.

When we separate sunshine from fog, we discern.
When we take a stand and mingle, we understand.
When we get it all together, we conceive and comprehend.

Some words in classical Latin gave Romance images of the human mind at work.

Discretion, derived from Latin *cretus*, separate, first referred to judicial power to decide a punishment in the case of a non-capital offense. By judicial discretion, a judge discerns between degrees of culpability. Justly weighed in the balance, the case may be certain, but certain notions, which he only partially discerns, may not be truly certain. If successful, the judge gains a reputation for being discreet in exercising his discretion. Discrete, for a long time, spelled discreet, until the former took the meaning 'separate' and the latter referred to judicious conduct. Early in the eighteenth century, it came to mean "kind and attentive, especially toward women" (1727). All these words describe sorting out what our eyes see.

Latin *legere*, to choose, compounded with *inter*, among, described discernment. Its noun *intellectus* described the ability 'to choose between' things. (The Russian verb *chitat*, to count or to read, and its compound *po-chitat*, to honor, highlights the same weighing of evidence.) Chaucer first used 'intellect' to translate *intelletto* in Boccaccio. Although intellect, by its root, picks and chooses, the English word took the general meaning of the Latin *intellectus* as understanding. Intellect, therefore, does not have as much discernment as its root may anticipate.

Understanding, a Germanic word also built on the Indo-European root *inter*, shows another way in which the human mind works. The 'under' of understanding is closer in meaning to the Latin *inter*, among, than to the German *unter*, under. The root of this word introduces the possibility that we may learn by standing 'among' what we see rather than by choosing 'among' its details. Under the right circumstances of human mingling, understanding proceeds by 'standing in the midst,' having interest in people and seeking experience with them. (German *verstehen* has a sense similar to that of the English understanding.) It flows in the current of their lives and does not turn aside to weigh its experience in the balance.

After discriminating 'among' things by intellect and standing 'among' them by understanding, bringing them together completes the process. Just as we apprehend (1548) a thief when we get him, we comprehend meaning when we get it. Actually, to apprehend first meant "to become aware of" (1398). Apprehension catches at an idea and comprehension hauls it in, but comprehension has limits. For example, a man can apprehend God, but he can never comprehend His nature. In his tentative apprehensions, he may become apprehensive, in grasping at straws.

When the mind takes an idea together, it conceives. A conception is the 'taking together' of ideas. (We have already seen that it first described the 'taking' of seed 'together' with egg.) When it takes an idea thoroughly, it perceives. Originally, perception was an apprehension of the senses. Only later did perceptive denote high intelligence: Ruskin speaks of "spirits most perceptive of the work of God" (1860). Perception takes the first step toward conception, just as apprehension takes the first step toward comprehension. Latinate comprehension has vivid Anglo-Saxon synonyms, because getting things together is so important that once we forget the original force of these Latinate roots, we recreate their images by saying that we grasp, catch or get it. *Capiche*?

These Latinate verbs show a mind defining its work,
but these definitions may not refine pure gold.
The intellect discerns, but most people prefer 'getting it,'
because they get a firm image of comprehension from this colloquialism.
After all, whether they have discerned certainty, or gotten certain,
they may have only gotten some certain concepts,
among more concepts that they have not discerned.

## Words

If I seek to know, I should emphasize the 'how' and not the 'I'. To be a student, by the root of the word, I should be studious. To be an expert, likewise, I should have experience. Studious and experienced, I come to knowledge under the right circumstances: picking and choosing, taking a stand and mingling, dividing and gathering. Eventually, I grasp it; and, somehow maybe, I get it.

Under these circumstances, I should learn how to get understanding, but how should I know for a certainty with my limited understanding?

**KNOWING AS SEPARATING**

<u>PIE root *da*, to divide</u>

English: deal, part; and dole, small part
Russian:
> делить (delit), to divide, share
> раз-делять (raz-delyat'), to divide, separate

<u>PIE root, *ker*, to separate</u>

Latin:
> *cerno cernere* and *cretus/certus*, to separate
> *discerno discernere* and *discretus*, to discern

English:
> certain (1297), sure or surely selected, but not precisely defined,
>    first used of things; later (1362), of people
> discretion (1292) and to discern (1350);
> discreet (1340) and discrete (1398)

Russian:
> кризис (krisis), crisis
> дискриминировать (diskriminirovat'), to discriminate

## KNOWING AS ASSOCIATING

### PIE root *per*, completely; and *steh*, to stand

German: *verstehen*, to understand, to come to complete standing in a subject

### PIE root *inter*, under, among; and *steh*, to stand

Latin: *inter*, between; and *interim (*adverb), meanwhile
    English: interim (noun), the between time
German: *unter*, under, among, between
English:
    to understand (888), to stand among, to be conversant with
    (*cf.* under-, as in 'under these circumstances;' and the Greek *epistamai*,
    I understand, literally, I stand on, the root of epistemology)

### PIE root *tolku*, talk

Latin: *loqui (tloqui)*, to speak, talk
    English: loquacious and eloquent
Russian: толк (tolk), good sense; толковать (tolkovat), to interpret

## KNOWING AS TAKING, GATHERING AND GETTING TOGETHER

### PIE root *leg*, to pick, choose, read

Latin:
    *intellegere (inter-legere*, 'r' of *inter* assimilated to 'l' of *legere)*, to choose
      between, to discriminate
    *intellectus*, intellect; *eligo eligere,* and *electus*, to pick out, elect
English: intellect (1386); elect (1400), the chosen; to elect (1494), to choose
German: *lesen*, to gather, harvest, read
Russian: интеллект (intellekt), intellect
*Cf.* PIE root *kwey*, to pay
    Greek: *tisis*, payment; and Tisiphone, a Fury avenging homicide
    Russian: читать (chitat'), to count, read; число (cislo), number
    (*Cf.* Greek *tetra*, four, as in English tetragram and teflon, as the root of
    Russian четыре [chityri])

### PIE root *em*, to take, buy (We 'take' an item when we buy it.)

Latin:
    *emo emere*, to take; *exemptus*, taken out
    *Caveat emptor*, Let the buyer beware!
      English: exempt, taken out or to take out; to preempt, to take before

### PIE root *upo*, under, up from under, over; and *em*, to take, buy

Russian: иметь (imet), to have; пон-имать (pon-imat), to understand

### PIE root *ghend*, to seize, hold

Latin:
    *prehendo prehendere*, to seize, grasp
    *comprehendere*, to seize completely, comprehend
        Spanish: *comprender*; and French: *comprendre*
        English:
            to comprehend (1340)
            apprehension (1398), to apprehend (1548), apprehensive (1718)

### PIE root *kap*, to take, grasp

Latin:
    *capio capere* and *captus*, to take, seize, understand
    *concipio concipere* and *conceptus*, to take together
    *percipio percipere* and *perceptus*, to take thoroughly
        English:
            captor and captivity
            to conceive (1340), concept (1387), conception (1300), birth; (1387), idea
            to perceive (1340) and perception (1611)
            *Capiche?* (slang), Do you get it? (*cf.* Italian: *capire*)

## 59. Faith and Credit

### Fragile Faith

Having just the right amount of confidence validates our discernment, intellect, and comprehension. Not confident that I possess this right amount, I sometimes joke that I have so little confidence in my own self-knowledge that I distrust most of what I think I know about anybody else. 'God only knows'—I conclude by leaving such speculation to a higher authority. (I am in good company in my learned ignorance: Socrates knew so much that he professed to know nothing.) Confidence or diffidence matters as much as knowing or not knowing.

    Trust and truth may not seem synonymous; but, surprisingly, they have the same Indo-European root—*deru*, solid. Trust can not be solidly true, but as solid as we can hope. The Slavic root for faith is cognate with the Indo-European root for truth. Pneumatological epistemology, the seeming oxymoron of spiritual knowledge, stands at the heart of knowing.

Faith prevails as much in commercial markets as in religious meetings.
Kept, it joins man with man as much as with God.
Broken, it separates men from each other and from God.
Let Shakespeare's *Othello* tell its tragic tale of broken faith.

As a general in the Duke's army, Othello owes fealty to his lord. When he secretly marries Desdemona, a senator's daughter, he violates this trust. "The trust, the office I do hold of you, / Not only take away," he declares to the Duke, "but let your sentence / Even fall upon my life." With a penchant for melodrama, Othello puts his life on the line, but the Duke advises Desdemona's father to accept what he can not change. Embittered, Othello's new father-in-law leaves him with a poisonous parting shot:

> Look to her, Moor, if thou hast eyes to see.
> She has deceived her father, and may thee.

Ironically, what Othello has "eyes to see"—but not Desdemona—will deceive him. Diffidence plagues confidence; distrust undermines trust. Tragedy springs from broken, bitterly poisoned, faith.

Fragments of broken faith make the totality of deceit. Deceitful men especially appreciate faith, because they succeed in so far as they pretend to guard it. Confidence men betray confidence. Iago, Shakespeare's most black-hearted villain, betrays faith for revenge. Embittered by being passed over for a promotion on Othello's staff, he preys on his general's diffidence and naive sense of melodrama to deceive him into crediting his father-in-law's warning. He wickedly makes Othello believe that Desdemona is unfaithful. "Thus credulous fools are caught," he gloats in his triumph.

Credulity wanders among the ambiguities of belief. Wavering between trust and distrust, confidence and diffidence, credulity slips too easily into confidence and trust. Sensible men credit what they examine carefully, but credulous men credit it naively. These men, whose diffidence turns too easily to confidence, Iago's callous cynicism describes in one word, "fools." His perfidious craft molds credulity as its clay.

The tragedy escalates from bad to worse. Its first deceit seems innocent: Desdemona and Othello break faith for love. With malicious perfidy, Iago breaks it for hate and revenge. In a tragic pairing of deceiver and deceived, Othello is foolish in his diffident credulity, but Iago is miscreant in taking advantage of it. Each successive act of defiance and perfidy outdoes the other in wickedness. Finally, Iago, defying whatever faith there may be of man with man or of man with God, persuades Othello, defying law and justice, to murder the innocent Desdemona. Defiance and diffidence are doublets in language and in psychology: Othello's diffidence of self, allows Iago to mislead him into defiance of law.

After the tragedy, justice finally balances her scale. Lodovico, a member of Desdemona's family, would be recreant, if he did not bring Iago to justice. Iago might hope for all his fellow citizens to be recreant in allowing him to escape as a miscreant. In other words, he could go unpunished in breaking faith, as long as others faint-heartedly failed in keeping theirs.

Tragedy evolves far beyond Desdemona's first defiance and the lesson that her father wrongly derives from it. His specific warning never comes true, but its words ring like a Sibylline oracle at the beginning of an ancient tale of ill fate. (The name Desdemona means "ill-fated" in Greek.) The Sibyl, traditionally, told the truth, but veiled it in a riddle. In Othello's tale, the warning is true in its generality but wrong in its specifics. Othello should "look to" his wife carefully but not to her deceit, as her father suggests. Desdemona never betrays her faith from the plighting of her troth to her betrayal and death. Othello's diffidence and credulity do not allow him to look beyond deceit to truth. If his father-in-law had this insight into his character, he could have encouraged him to distrust himself first:

Look to yourself, Moor, if thou hast eyes to see.
When you deceive yourself, others may thee.

## Words

Faith is so practical that we learn it as the better part of learning. Financial credit and religious creed both require it. It has strength in confidence and credence, weakness in diffidence and credulity. Miscreants violate it when recreants fail to enforce it.

### PIE root *kred*, to attribute magic power to someone, to believe

Old Indian: *sraddha*, faith, ceremony of offering balls of rice to ancestors
Latin: *credo credere*, to believe; *credentia*, credence; *credulus*, credulous
    Italian: *credere, credenza, credulo*; French: *croire, croyance, credule*
    Spanish: *creer, creencia, credulo*
    English:
        creed (1000), Christian belief; (1613), any statement of belief
        credo (1175), I believe, first word of a creed; (1587), belief system
        credence (1330), letter of credence or of recommendation
        mis-creant (1330), in-fidel, un-believing; (1593), villainous
        re-creant (1330), giving up the faith, cowardly, faint-hearted

credit (1542), belief or the expectation of payment
credulous (1576), believing too easily
Russian: кредит (kredit), credit

### PIE root *bheidh*, to trust, wait

Latin:
*fides*, faith; *fido fidere*, to have faith
*bona fide*, with good faith; *perfidia*, breaking faith
*foedus foederis*, treaty, agreement
Italian: *fede*, faith; French: *foi*; Spanish: *fe*
English:
faith (1250), as in keeping faith; (1300), religious faith
confidence (1430)
diffidence (1526), distrust; (1651), self-distrust
perfidy (1592), deceitfully breaking faith
Doublets:
Romance fealty (1300) and Latinate fidelity (1494)
Romance defiance (1300) and Latinate diffidence (1526)

### PIE root *uero*, true, pledge

Latin: *vera fides*, true faith
Czech: *vira*
Russian:
вера (vera), faith; верить (verit), to believe
до-верять (do-verjat), to trust; до-верие (do-veriye), trust
до-верчивый (do-verchivyy), credulous
легко-верный (legko-vernyy), credulous (German *leicht-gläubig*)

### PIE root *dlhgos*, long

Latin: *in-dulgere*, to favor, grant
Russian: долг (dolg), debt, duty, credit

### PIE root *ken*, to begin, to be born

Russian: начать (nachat), to begin; зачет (zachet), credit

# 60. Simple States and Complex Standing

## Standing Simply and Building Simple Stands

Words usually have contexts, neighborhoods that they call home; but the verb 'to stand' has no single address. Since the name of *homo erectus* describes him standing, his being walks hand in hand with his standing up and down many streets. Standing—literally, on two feet—has helped to move him forward. When he stood up straight, he stood higher on the evolutionary chain. Taking stands—with subtle, moral ramifications—has continued to follow human progress. *Homo sapiens* now stands higher, since he has the savvy to take stands and to make them too. He first made market stands for commerce and grandstands for races. His stands arise from mostly psychological states of his being, but some are material, like the ones in the market and on the race course

In marking out psychological neighborhoods, grammarians assign a verb representing a state of being to a category that they call stative, the adjectival form of state. The verb 'to stand' can function as a stative verb. About a weak character, we could say that it stands firm as long as it stands no test. "Stands" functions first as a stative verb and then as a dynamic one. In other words, "stands" does not take an object as an intransitive verb— . . . it stands firm—and then it does take an object as a transitive verb— . . . it stands no test. Similarly, with the verb 'to feel' as stative and dynamic, we could say that humans feel well as long as they feel no pain.

'To stand' as a stative verb, a synonym of 'to be,' has deep roots in the history of language. In French, the imperfect tense of its verb 'to be,' *j'étais*, I was, and in Spanish, all tenses of its verb *estar*, to be, originated in the Latin verb *stare*, to stand. In English also, 'to stand' may indicate that something or somebody simply, or simply dramatically, is: if we are alone, we seem a little more lonely when we say that we stand alone. So also, when we stand corrected or stand in need, our being stands out.

A man so stands between angels and demons that he can't take a stand without having it measured by standards—usually high ones. Why bother to set low standards since no one can aspire to them? In the usual idiom, a man stands tall, not small. Status marks a man's standing; but when he has it, he usually stands high on some totem pole. Speak of stature and you expect to reach high for the measurement. Statues commemorate stature.

Stative verbs shade into dynamic ones, from intransitive into transitive. When we stand trial, we endure a test, and this verb 'stand' has power to take an object. It then stands to reason that the verb can take any object: some students, for example, can't stand school or anyone and anything associated with it. They stand a good chance of being happier if they find something which they can understand. (Understanding so far extends the neighborhood of its standing root that it has already deserved separate treatment.)

After these psychological considerations about mankind's states of being, stands made of timber appear as unmoving as the stand of forest timber from which they are built. A horse should be stable in his stable; but it seems unlikely that a stallion should stall in his stall. His fame has raced far beyond the root of his name! Con-stables, who originally served as the chief grooms in stables, might make him happier, before they rode off to apprehend a horse thief.

If you can stand the burden, peruse the verb 'to stand' in the OED: its many shades of meaning take up 38 columns and that is only the beginning: search out its compounds and phrases through many more columns. For the time being, peruse the list after the next essay to see a few of its compounding complications.

## Words

In Spanish, the verb 'to stand' is a verb 'to be,' because standing stands for being. In English, standing is simple when stallions stall as they stand; but it is complex as men take stands. They pay one price for not standing firm, another for standing too firm, and the ultimate price for standing at all.

**THE SIMPLE CAST OF CHARACTERS**

PIE root *steh*, to stand

STANDING AND STATES

Latin: *sto, stare*, to stand (intransitive); *sisto sistere*, to stand (transitive)
    French: *état*, state, status; and *j'étais*, I was, imperfect tense of *être*
    Spanish: *estar*, to be—*estoy*, I am
    English:
        steel (725), a metal that stands the test for strength
        to stand (888); state (1225), state of being; (1399), governmental state
        stationary (1426), adjective, standing still, first used in astronomy
        staunch (1455), standing true to one's principles
        status (1693), in medicine, a person's standing, usually high
        stationery (1727), noun, paper sold, not by itinerant peddlers, but in
            shops standing stationary near schools
    German: *stehen*, to stand (*cf. verstehen*, to understand)
Russian: стоять (stoyat'), to stand

A STAND OF MATERIAL SUBSTANCE

Latin:
    *stabilis*, stable, firm
    *stabulum*, standing place for an aviary, beehive, cottage or stable
French: *stable* (adjective), stable; *étable* (noun), stable; *étalon*, stallion

English:
> stable (1250), a stable for horses; (1290), firm
> stud, steed or stallion—horses for breeding; originally, horse stalls

Russian:
> стадо (stado), herd; originally, cattle stall; стойло (stoylo), stall
> стая (staja), flock; стабильный (stabil'nyy), stable

# 61. The Complex Cast of Characters

## Complex States and Stating Complexity

Standing tall brings a man close to angels, but standing too tall, too long, may stall his vital flow and bring him down to demons. Heraclitus contemplated a stream and saw that it, like life, never stopped flowing. Water begins life; it flows, and so should we, because stagnant water stalls it. Standing just for the sake of standing makes us stolid. Even worse, without the flow, we wither. The evolution of the Italian adjective *stanco*—from water-resistant, to firm, dry, and finally, exhausted—represents the danger of standing too long.

Compounds of the Latin verb *stare* dramatically extend its context and take us all over a man's neighborhood. Take existence—but extend it beyond mere existing to its grand potentials. When King Lear wanted to reach beyond the mundane, he invoked "the orbs from whom we do exist." In the twentieth century, the word existential gave man's independent status quite a boost. After existence, we seek substance, the oldest English compound of standing, by bare subsistence. The Apostle Paul uses the word in its Greek form—*hypostasis,* when he speaks of faith as "the substance of things hoped for, the evidence of things not seen" (*Hebrews* 11.1). Rooted in substantial essence, our hope blooms; in insubstantiality, it withers—provided, of course, that we can discriminate between true substance and its counterfeit.

If we exist and have substance, our constancy stands firm, as John Bunyan praises it in *Pilgrim's Progress (*1526): "Constancy is your virtue whereby man or woman holdeth whole and is not broken by impatiency." Persistence shares in this virtue. Insisting too much on standing unmoved, it can get us into trouble. According to the OED, man first persisted in evil, even though he may now persist in goodness. Persistence, at its worst, takes annoyingly stubborn stands. Men call it virtuous in success, but obstinate in failure.

Obstinate and restive describe stagnant minds. Obstinacy obstructs reason: the obstinate man "does not hold opinions, but they hold him" (1680). Restive men rest in their opinions through sloth or bad habits: "It is a hard although a common case," Byron observed, "to find our children running restive" (1820). Restive horses throw their riders to remain at rest: "A restive horse is rebellious, refractory, ill-broken, which only goes where it will and when it will" (1727). The obstinate act perversely as their own worst enemies; the restive weakly acquiesce to the status quo. Before becoming annoying, perverse or weak, though, they all begin by simply taking a stand. Good, bad or indifferent, they all just stand there.

A walk through the neighborhood of existential standing can be bewildering. We observe human stands as protean as the fates of the men who walk its streets. The Russian adjective старый (staryy), old, brings this variety into focus. It originally meant staunch, but by the time its derivative meant senile (старческий), it shrank in stature. Men stand firm with age, but they wither in senescence.

## Words

Standing firm, infirm or both compounds the PIE root *steh*, to stand.

FIRM
Latin:
> *substo substare*, to stand under; *obsto obstare*, to stand against
> *consto constare*, to stand firm; *resto restare*, to stand back

English:
> substance (1300), underlying essence; obstinate (1340), standing in the way
> constant (1386), standing firm; constancy (1527), firm character
> staunch (1455), standing firm on principles
> restive (1599), standing still, inclined to rest

Latin: *sisto sistere*, to stand (transitive)
> English:
>> to persist (1536), to continue, firmly or obstinately, in a state
>> to subsist (1542), to exist as a reality
>> to exist (1602), to have a place in reality

Russian:
> со-стоять (so-stoyat'), to consist
> на-стаивать (na-staivat'), to persist, insist
> противо-стоять (protivo-stoyat'), to resist
> по-стоянная (po-stoyannaya), constant

Polish: *stary*, old
Russian:
>старый (staryy), old; originally, staunch
>старческий (starcheskiy), senile; стареющий (stareyushchiy), senescent

INFIRM

Latin: *stanticare*, to make to stand
>Italian: *stanco*, exhausted; Spanish: *estanco*, water-tight
>French: *étanche*, water-tight, firm, dried, withered
>English:
>>to stanch (1400), to make blood to stand
>>stank/tank, standing water or its container

PIE root *pro*, forward

Russian:
>прямый (pryamyy), straight
>у-прямый (u-pryamyy), stubborn (*cf.* froward)
>у-прямый как осел, stubborn as an ass (*cf.* Latin *asellus*, young ass)

## 62. Headstrong Stubbornness

One of my teachers complimented his sensible student Charlie on not zigging when he was supposed to be zagging. Even if youth, in general, might have been wayward, this youth, in particular, was not froward. A misunderstood genius, on the other hand, apparently zigs and zags obstinately. Inspired and informed or misinformed and empty-headed or just hard-hearted, they can all zig when they should zag. The intractably headstrong think or act more than the froward or the wayward. If Charlie had been stubborn, he would have persisted in being either wayward or froward. Ultimately, his zigging, zagging, or simply standing stolid, might have been a matter of opinion.

The oldest English synonym for stubborn describes a strong will: willful (1200) men act as they will, not as they think. Shakespeare explains their fate: "to wilful men, the injuries that they themselves procure, must be their Schoole-Masters" (*Lear* II. iv. 305). Some people—or is it most people?—learn the hard way. The headstrong (1398) turn their willfulness to passion and violence: "To tie a headstrong girl from love, is to tie furies in fetters" (1590). Before it meant easily annoyed, testy also meant headstrong. Desire and passion, more than perversity, drive the willful, headstrong and testy.

Tenacity holds on; pertinacity persists in holding on. In antiquity, however, pertinacity rose in the ranks: Pertinax, Roman emperor for three months in 193 A.D., virtuously held on to his reforms, until the Pretorian Guard assassinated him. Pertinax perhaps suffered from virtue too pertinacious. Twelve hundred years later, English clerics called pertinacity a moral failing. They deprecated the pertinacy (*sic*, 1386) that persisted in sin. Pertinacious first described a "bad quality," but it has lost its sharp edge of immorality and now describes annoying persistence: "the pertinacious worshippers of one God" (1655). Ancient pertinacity persisted; medieval pertinacy persisted perversely; now it persists annoyingly.

Froward (1300), native Anglo-Saxon for stubborn, has survived in modern English. Just as 'to' and 'fro' complement each other, to-ward complements fro-ward (1200). Froward youth goes fro (1200) the place toward which it should go. Frowardness (1300), perversely untoward (1526), opposite the normal zig or zag, can describe naughty children: "Human life is but like a froward child, that must be played with and humored to keep it quiet till it goes to sleep" (1689). The untowardly froward, bent on wayward (1380) ways, go their own way.

The stubborn (1386), going neither froward nor wayward, go nowhere. Stubborn, cognate with stump, fits men naturally, rather than obstinately, standing doggedly determined like stumps. When, on the other hand, Chaucer's Wife of Bath's recalls her wild youth: "I was yong and ful of ragerye (wantoness),/ Stibourn and strong, and joly as a pye," stiborn/stubborn describes her wild strength. This exception to the rule of stubborn as persistently standing still proves the rule: more often than not, stubborn folk stand violently still. Stubborn, froward youth zigs in every zag but the right one.

Stubbornness demonstrates froward energy. In addition to pertinacy, clerics used stiff-necked (1526), translating the word by which the prophet in *Acts* 7. 51 describes sinners hardening their hearts to goodness—like a horse unwilling to obey the rein—with no intention to change. They also chose obdurate (1440) to describe the hardened conscience of inveterate sinners—Shakespeare used "stern, flinty, rough, and remorseless" as its synonyms. The enlightened eighteenth century used wrong-headed (1732) to describe its cherished reason gone wrong: "the pious fraud of some wrong-headed Christian" and "the furious zeal of wrong-headed bigots" affronted its lights.

In their passions, stubborn men wrench ethics awry; the intransigent, the refractory or the contumacious also thwart business or government. Intractable and intransigent sound alike and have the same meaning, but without the same root. According to their roots, we can't treat with the intractable or transact with the intransigent. We refer to those unwilling to come to the table for discussion as intractable or intransigent, but intransigence makes intractability official.

Refractory has its root in Latin *refragari*, to vote against, the opposite of *suffragari*, to vote for, at root of suffrage. The refractory, therefore, belong to the fractious, factious opposition. Before the American Revolution, England regarded her colonies as refractory—"the most refractory of the colonies were still willing to proceed by constitutional means" (1769). Even stronger, contumacy (1386) perversely disobeys authority, especially neglecting a summons to court—"contemning and obstinately resisting authority." Derived from Latin *tumere*, to swell (*cf.* tumor), contumacious (1600) brings to mind men swelling brimful with headstrong willfulness. Recalcitrant (1843) in government or in the army, they kick (Latin *calcare*) back (re-) against authority. If some one inculcated, "kicked into" their heads, good sense, these malcontents would not kick back.

Standards make people stubborn, even when they don't think they are. Moralists draw lines between right heads and wrong, pertinent and impertinent, stiff-necked and gentle. Statesmen hope intransigents come to the table; and judges, the contumacious to court. Wayward youth or stubborn age persists in either one of two directions: zigging and zagging frowardly in the wrong direction or persisting in no direction. On the other hand, the refractory or the pertinacious may not have obvious moral or political flaws. Strong heads don't inevitably strengthen the head-strong; or full wills make them willful. We admire froward obstinacy as admirable perseverance, when some particular pig-headedness mines the gold it roots for.

## Words

Very stubborn people persist in their holding, doing, pulling, and weaving.

### PIE root *ten*, to hold

Latin:
    *teneo tenere*, to hold; and *pertineo pertinere*, to pertain
    *pertinax*, firmly tenacious, persevering
        Italian and French: *tenace*; Spanish: *tenaz* and *pertinaz*
        Italian: *pertinace*
        English: tenacious (1607) and pertinacious (1625)

### PIE root *ag*, to lead, drive, do

Latin: *ago agere*, to drive, do; and *transigo transigere*, to transact
    English: to transact (1584), agent (1600), intransigent (1879)

**PIE root *trag*, to draw, drag**

Latin:
> *traho trahere* and *tractus*, to draw
> *tracto tractare*, to discuss, handle
>> English:
>>> to treat (1297, *cf.* treatise); its doublet, to tract (1523)
>>> tractable (1502) and intractable (1545)

**PIE root *teks*, to weave**

Latin: *testa*, pot—originally woven from willow twigs—head
> Italian: *testardo*, stubborn (*cf. caparbio*, stubborn, from *capo*, head)
> French: *tête*, head; *têtu* and *entêté*, stubborn
> English: testy, headstrong

# Family
. . . .

# 63. Chaste and Unchaste

## Purity

Birthdays celebrate both the quickening moment of birth and the fulfillment of our ken within kin. In the company of offspring, or just on our own, the celebrations include progenitors, who should take the most interest in our genial fate, since it fulfills their own. In an increasingly democratic world, however, our birth does not necessarily fulfill the progenitors' hopes for a blood line. Democracy profits humanity by mixing blood lines. Our ancestors celebrated their births in some type of caste system that maintained pure blood at the expense of democracy. Purity—keeping chaste, not unchaste; undefiled, not defiled, and avoiding promiscuous mixing of blood—preoccupied them and they invented words to represent and defend it.

We may boast that our gold is pure and our horses, pure-bred, but human 24 karat purity, spiritual or even physical, sets an impossible goal. In the narrowest focus of physical purity, ritual ablution makes the impure pure for only as long as it takes to perform the ritual. Otherwise, consistent purity, consisting in the impure made pure, eludes us. When Jesus blessed "the pure in heart, for they shall see God" (*Matthew* 5.8), he was suggesting the revolutionary ideal of purity existing apart from its concrete embodiment in clean hands or pure race and birth. If we marry with this spiritual, democratic preference for "the pure in heart," we undo our ancestors' secular, pagan ideal of pure blood. A few might have welcomed the seminal ideal of all men created equal, but most have done their best to prevent its dissemination.

In antiquity, our ancestors maintained purity in religion, as part of purity in blood. The adjective *castus*, chaste, described a man doing proper service to the gods and to his family cult. The Sibyl warned Aeneas that the chaste are forbidden to view the tortures of the damned: *nulli fas casto // sceleratum insistere limen*, "The chaste and holy race / Are all forbidden this polluted place" (Dryden). Chastity involved sexual purity as part, but only part, of this right relationship. In general, in the poetic spirit of Dryden, it kept far thence all souls profane.

By contrast, when chastity entered English in the first quarter of the thirteen century, it referred specifically to purity "from unlawful sexual intercourse." Its antonym, Latin *incestus*, meaning unclean, entered English as incest, "sexual relations with those with whom marriage is prohibited." Incest is negative and chaste, only positive by abstaining from the negative. Our mediaeval ancestors created this virtue that only does good by not doing bad.

Caste and chastity have both sought physical purity. Though they share the same root in language, they arise from two different worlds, one in India and the other in Europe. Taken as a noun from the Portuguese phrase *casta raça*, chaste race, caste describes an institution that Portuguese merchants observed in India. Within strict boundaries, caste sought to guarantee that its members remained chaste. In Europe, social and moral pressures imposed chastity, but they could not keep youth chaste as easily as the caste system in India. Caste building walls with stone; and chastity, with character both defined the positive through the negative.

Promiscuity has had a history similar to that of chastity. When the Roman historian Livy records an aristocrat's horror at plebeians' miscegenation, so to speak, with patricians, he describes "promiscuous marriages": "What other force would promiscuous marriages have unless that the copulation of plebeians and patricians are made common almost in the manner of wild beasts? A man so born would not know who he is, of what blood, of what sacred rites; he would be half of patricians, half of plebeians, himself not even in harmony with himself."[13]

Promiscuous only means "mixed," but mixing had serious social consequences. Breaking blood lines breaks the family cult. No matter how well-intended or moral, mixing a patrician with a commoner set the adulterated pair adrift and left their son "not even in harmony with himself." In this tradition, the OED defines promiscuous as "sexual union, as among some races of low civilization." In the modern world, "low civilization" has set up housekeeping next door and felt right at home.

The wider world of the thirteenth and fourteenth century—and all its temptations—made the negative virtue of chastity so positive that our ancestors adopted the verb to adulterate and even invented a new one, to defile, so that they might further highlight its precious negativity. In Latin, the prefix *ad-* compounded with the verb *alterare*, to alter, formed *adulterare*, to alter for the worse, to adulterate, particularly, to corrupt women. Adultery refers specifically to the violation of the marriage bed.

In the same era, to defile, to destroy sexual purity, derives its power from a Latin word for trampling under foot. English now had two words for impurity destroying marriage: adultery and defiling. With the creation of these words, the negative triumphed. Adultery purely and simply defiles. Chaste and pure redeem unchaste and impure, but these new words have no redeeming antonyms. Some people derive special joy from the negative.

By the time of the appearance, in the fifteenth century, of the Immaculate Conception of the Virgin Mary, "a maiden, pure and undefiled, by the spirit great with child," sexual morality had taken over a number of classical word roots. Since our ancestors in the thirteenth and fourteenth centuries saw that their versions of caste were not preserving chastity, they mustered defenses to insure it. Chastity has survived as a personal virtue; even though modern mores have separated it from family cult and caste.

## Words

Mixing family blood lines so horrified our ancestors that some words have described it as a crime. To prevent it, they devised caste as a social control and chastity as its virtue

### PIE root *meik*, to mix

Latin: *misceo miscere* and *mixtus*, to mix
French: *métis*, half breed; and *métissage*, miscegenation; *promiscuité*
Spanish:
>*mestengo*, mustang, horse mixed with other herds
>*mestizo*, a person of mixed ancestry
>>English:
>>>promiscuous (1603), "massed together without order"
>>>promiscuity (1865), "promiscuous sexual union, as among some races of low civilization"
>>>miscegenation, mixing (misce-) of races (-gen-)

Germanic English: among and mingle or mongrel
Russian: мешáть (mesát), to mix; мустанг, mustang; and метис (metis), halfbreed

### PIE root *pu*, to clean

Latin: *purus*, clean, chaste
English: pure (1297), unmixed; and impure (1597); to purify, to purge

### PIE root *kassw*, to cut

Latin:
>*careo carere*, to lack; and *castus*, having been separated
>*castus*, instructed in religious rite, free from impurity
>*incestus*, unclean, defiled, criminal
>*castigo castigare*, to correct, punish, instruct

Portuguese: *casta raça*, pure race
English:
>chaste/chastity (1225), pure/purity from unlawful sex
>unchaste (1382), lascivious
>incest (1225), sex with those for whom marriage is prohibited
>to chastise (1325), chasten (1526), castigate (1607)
>caste, a class division in India to maintain racial purity

**PIE root *skidtos*, thin, clear, clean**

Russian: чистый (chistyy), pure, unadulterated, chaste

**PIE root *kailo*, whole, unharmed, well**

Russian: цело-мудренный (tselo-mudrennyy), chaste (цело+мудрый, wise)

**PIE root *krewh*, blood**

Latin: *cruor*, blood
Russian:
    кровь (krov), blood + смешение (mesheniye), mixing
    кровосмешение (krovosmesheniye), incest

**PIE root *al*, other**

Latin: *altero alterare*, to alter; *adulterare*, to alter for the worse, to
    corrupt women
English:
    adultery (1366), violation of the marriage bed; adulterer (1370)
    adulteration (1506), corrupting by spurious admixture
    adulterated (1607), defiled by adultery; (1610), corrupted

**No known PIE root**

Latin: *macula*, spot
    English: immaculate (1430), without spot of sin, virgin birth

**No known PIE root**

Latin: *fullo*, fuller, person cleaning cloth by trampling on it in water
English:
    to defoul (1290), to trample under foot, deflower
    to defile (1325), to destroy ideal purity; adj. defiled
    undefiled, 1350, untainted; 1450, chaste

**No known PIE root**

Russian:
    разный (rasnyy), different + род (rod), family, clan
    разно-родный (razno-rodnyy), promiscuous

# 64. Caste Defiled

Some words serve as an explanation for a child's birth out of caste. They describe it in terms of illegitimacy, mixing up proper distinctions, or an odd place of conception.

Illegitimate (1536) means simply not legal, from *lex legis*, law, first denoting birth outside of wedlock. In ancient Rome, *spurius*, the legal term for illegitimate, gave English spurious (1598), which first meant illegitimate in birth and, secondarily (1615), not genuine. Latin derived *spurius* from the Etruscan word, public: a *spurius* was public. In old Russia, parents wandering (блудить [bludit]) from proper conduct had a child not conceived in marriage (ублюдок [yblyudok]). Shakespeare's Thersites, however, considers illegitimacy as more than a matter of law or custom: "I am a bastard begot, bastard instructed, bastard in mind, bastard in valor, in everything illegitimate" (*Troilus and Cressida*).

Conception as outside of the marriage bed, the *lectus genialis*, offers a clue. Bastard, derived from Latin *bastum*, packsaddle, explains the origin facetiously: one only knows that conception took place on a packsaddle, a saddle being the pillow in bedding on the road. Some also relate *bastum* to barley: by this origin, conception takes place in the barn where barley is stored. In German, *bankling*, one conceived on a bench, similarly explains paternity. From *bankling*, English derives bantling (1593), a brat (1505), whose derivation from bantling seems obvious, although not clearly established. In the same way, we call someone a son of a gun.

An odd place of birth can also connote illegitimacy: Brer Rabbit, according to Uncle Remus, was "breed and born in a briar patch." Calling a child "base born" in English designates illegitimate birth. No birth could be baser on the social scale than an illegitimate one. The English, who use French to describe what they disdain to mention in their own language, call an illegitimate birth a *faux pas*, false step, and its offspring as a *terrae filius*, son of the earth. Ironically, the woman and her autochthonous offspring would be banished from polite society for this *faux pas*. Bastard, bantling, base born and *terrae filius* indicate illegitimacy by allusion to conception outside the marriage bed or at the bottom of the social scale.

Promiscuous mixing may have some dignity. Creole, derived from Spanish *criado*, from Latin *creatus*, referred to West Indian children of white fathers who acknowledged their birth. Thus, their fathers said that they had "created" them, although not in wedlock. Since colonial possessions experienced more mixing of races than their mother countries, European languages have uniformly used the word creole: French *creole*, Spanish *criolla*, Italian *creolo*, German *Kreole*, Polish *creole*, Czech *Kreolsky*, Russian креол.

Illegitimate birth can deserve a legitimate name. In the English monarchy, illegitimate children of the king were dignified with the title Fitz, derived from *fils* in French, *filius* in Latin, both meaning son. For example, Henry Fitzroy, Duke of Richmond (1519–1536), the illegitimate son of Henry VIII by Elizabeth Blount, bore his birth in his name.

Our ancestors did not consider all birth as a miracle, a gift from God. They distinguished the legitimate from the spurious by law, place, and propriety.

**Words**

Two PIE roots define paternity in Russian according to certainty or legality.

### PIE root *bhlendh*, mix up, confuse

Czech: *bloudit*, to wander
German: *blendling*, crossbreed, mongrel
Russian:
    блуд (blut), licentiousness, fornication
    блудить (bludit), to wander, fornicate; блюдок (ublyudok), bastard

### PIE root *ken*, beginning, end

Russian:
    закон (zakon), law; and законный (zakonnyy), legitimate
    не-закон-норожденный (ne-zakon-norozhdennyy), not legitimate newborn

# 65. Marriage

## Making the Match and the Proposal

From the first proposals, marriage meant business. In Russian, father-in-law and matchmaker share the same etymology (сват [svat], matchmaker; and свекор [svekor], father-in-law). A young man's father approached the parents of the girl, who, he hoped, might continue his family as his daughter-in-law. This continuity meant so much that he could not allow his son to decide on it. After signs of approval from the future father-in-law, the families make the engagement, which in Russian, literally "declared" the couple bride and bridegroom (по-молвка [po-molvka], engagement). In Russia, also, betrothal derived its name from taking the engagement ring (обручена [obruchena], betrothed; literally, having taken a ring).

Elsewhere in Europe, a true heart confirmed its intention. Troth confirmed truth, a doublet of troth. The bride and groom plighted their troth by the pledge (Latin *vas*). In the Germanic tradition, *vas vadis* becomes wed (1122), first recorded as a nuptial pledge in 1375. To wed (1000), therefore, took a wife by pledging (*cf.* wedding in 1000); wedded has an even earlier recorded usage (800).

Wage (1138), a doublet of wed, later came to refer to paying a pledge (1338). After his marriage, a bridegroom might also work for a wage, a pledge in payment for his labor. The French doublet of wage is gage (1457). Wedding, waging and gaging all made a pledge. Since the bride contributed to her family's domestic economy, the groom's family paid a bride price (купить невесты [vykup nevesty]) to compensate her loss.

By engaging (1525), a man first made a pledge and, later, held someone's attention (1642). Although an engagement did engage the attention of the public by setting a date for marriage (1742), it primarily made a pledge (1624) or, much later, an appointed meeting (1806). Engagement and wedding refer to the same pledge and its payment, although we can make many engagements with friends without pledging matrimony! The French derivation and later date (1742) of engagement suggest that it was a refinement of the marriage ritual in the eighteenth century, but wedding and engaging meant the same thing.

Marriage meant business: the wage of the engaging only has a wider context than the wed of the wedding. As to character, the bride, called the "unknown one" in Russian (не-веста [nevesta]), had to win her new family's confidence before they were happy to know her. Spanish also reflected this adjustment in calling the bride and groom the *novio* and *novia*, the new man and the new woman. The legal formality, however, which pledged secure continuity in the family line, outweighed all this potential element of character.

## Words

In preserving caste and chastity, marriage meant serious business. Its vocabulary represented the matchmaker's importance to engaged couples, the truth of their pledge, and its economic importance to their families.

### PIE roots *dru* and *doru*, wood; hence, solid and lasting

Greek: *drus* and *dendron*, oak and tree
      Classical English: dendrology, study of trees
Germanic English: tree, a doublet of troth
Russian: дерево (derevo), tree

PIE root *plek*, to bend, fold

English:
> simplex, duplex, triplex, once, twice, thrice folded
> solar plexus, the sun-like folding of the abdominal nervous system
> to plight, to fold oneself in obligation, to pledge

PIE root *sue*, one's own

Latin: *solus*, alone
English: self and suicide; sister, one's own kindred
German: *schwiegervater*, father-in-law
Polish: *swat*, matchmaker, the father-in-law of one's son
Russian:
> свекор (svekor) father-in-law
> сват (svat), matchmaker; свадьба (swadba), wedding, matchmaking

PIE root *mom*, speech, usually indistinct

French: *mot*, word
> Germanic English: to mutter (1388); Classical English: motto (1589)
Polish: *mowic*, to speak
Russian:
> молвить (molvit), to declare
> по-молвка (po-molvka), engagement, literally, declared as bride

PIE root *vad/wed*, to pledge, bind, lead

Latin: *vas vadis*, pledge
English: to wed and wage; to gage and engage

Latin: *caupo cauponis*, innkeeper, huckster
> German: *kaufen*, to buy; Kauffman, merchant
> English:
>> cheap, market (*cf.* Cheapside in London)
>> Chapman and chap, cognate of Kauffman, a peddler
> Danish: Copenhagen, a merchant's (copen-) harbor (-hagen)
> Russian: купить (kupit), to buy; купить невесты (kupit nevesty), bride price

PIE root *mon*, man; from PIE root *men*, mind: Man has mind.

German: *Mann*; and English: man
Russian:
> муж (muzh), husband
> мужество (muzhestvo), courage (*cf.* Greek *andreia*, Latin *virtus*)
> за-мужество (sa-muzhestvo), marriage, according to a woman

**PIE root *guen*, woman, related to *gen*, bearing life**

Greek: *gyne*, woman
English: quean, woman; Zena, a given name
Russian:
> жена (zhena), wife; жених (zhenikh), bridegroom
> женитьба (zhenit'ba), marriage, from a man's perspective

**Of uncertain origin**

Russian:
> об-руч (ob-ruch), hoop; archaic: wrist, bracelet, ring; literally, around hand; *cf.* рука (ruka), hand
> об-ручена (obruchena), betrothed; literally, having taken a ring

Russian: шафер (shafir), bestman, from German Schaffer, steward

## 66. The Marriage Ceremony

Once the bride and groom plight their troth, exchange engagement rings, and his family pays the bride price, they take the next step, literally, by proceeding from her home to his. Words for marriage reflect this wedding march: the Russian word is derived from the "taking" and the Latin from the "leading." The word hymn originally meant the marriage song for the passage, which the Russian Orthodox church recreates in its procession three times around the lectern.

The groom takes his betrothed by the hand, while the bride takes her veil: Latin *nubere*, to take a veil describes the woman's wedding. Wife means "the veiled one." The veil is universal in nuptials (1555) and its meaning not nebulous: it symbolizes submission. Nuns take the veil and never set it aside when they submit in marriage to Christ. Nubile (1642) describes young women ready to take the veil. Their patroness, *Juno Pronuba*, blessed her eponymous month of June as the one most propitious for their nuptials.

In Russian Orthodoxy, the crowning of the couple has such importance that one of its words for marriage means "crowning." The priest wraps his stole around the clasped hands of the couple and leads them around the lectern three times, while the best man and maid of honor hold crowns above their heads. In the Catholic or Protestant rite, the rings crown the ring finger, traditionally thought to contain a vein from the heart. The rings, therefore, crown the hearts that have pledged their faith. Symbolically, honor and glory bless the married couple, because the adjective connubial (1656) crowns bliss.

## Words

Weaving a veil and crown for the bride, ceremonially or symbolically leading her from her old home to the groom's, binding and crowning her and the groom's right hands and ring fingers—all these rituals emphasize the sanctity of betrothal.

### PIE root *bher*, to bear

Russian: брать (brat), to take; брак (brak), marriage, literally, taking (in marriage)

*Cf.* Latin: *in matrimonium ducere*, to lead into marriage

### PIE root *weyh/uebh/veg*, to weave, move back and forth

English:
    wasp—Wasps weave.
    Webster, a weaver
Latin: *velum*, sail
    French: *voile*, veil, sail
        Russian: вуаль (vual), veil
    Spanish: *vela*, sail; and *velo*, I veil
    English: veil
    German: *Weib*, wife; literally, the veiled one
Russian:
    вить (vit´), to weave; венец (vinets), woven crown
    вести под венец (vesti pod venec), to lead to the altar; literally, to lead under the crown; под, *cf.* hypo, as in hypodermic, under skin
    венчание (venchanie), wedding; literally, crowning
Greek: *humnos*, hymn, a marriage song associated with the wedding march
    English: hymn
    Russian: гимн (gimn), hymn (cf. Гамлет for Hamlet)

### PIE root *maghos*, virgin or *mari*, marriageable

Latin: *maritus*, a man having been married
    French: *marié/mariée*, bridegroom/bride; Spanish: *marido*, husband

### PIE root *sneubh*, to marry

Greek: *nymphe*, bride, maiden
Latin: *nubeo nubere*, to be married; literally, to take the veil
    (*cf. nubes*, cloud)

English:
> nubile, of an age to be married; nuptials and connubial
> nymph, lesser goddess of nature

Russian: нимфа (nimfa), nymph

*Cf.* Greek: *epitrachelion*, literally, around the neck, stole, a vestment like a scarf
> Russian: епитрахиль (epitrachil), stole

## 67. Fathers and Patrons

### Patrons and Patronage

The ancient word father (825) first referred to fathers of offspring. It had a figurative meaning more than five hundred years later (1362). Latin *pater*, father, on the other hand, carried a social burden that made fathering offspring seem superfluous.

Romans saw fatherhood in the image of their god, Jupiter, literally *Jovis Pater* (Father Jove), the parallel of the Greek vocative, *Zeus Pater* (Father Zeus). Addressing God as Father seemed presumptuous to the Jews and subsequently, to the Christians, who made the humble admission, ". . . we are bold to say," before addressing "Our Father" The Romans taught Jews and Christians about anthropomorphic divinity.

Jews were loath to ascribe fatherhood to God, but their Greek Septuagint called Jacob's twelve sons Patriarchs, literally, family (*patria*) leaders (*arches*). Christianity, commonly in the East, but rarely in the West, took up this word as a reverential title for bishop. The Roman term had a wider application: those associated with the *patres* of the first families of Rome were *patricii*, patricians. The names Patrick and Patricia bear witness to the broad application of the term patrician in the relatively democratic canons of Roman society. In English, patrician (1631), used of the nobility in contrast to the plebeians (1586), was a broader term than patriarch. In this broad application, bourgeois democracy displays its expansive dynamic.

A *pater* in Roman society acted so dynamically that the verb *patrare* described what he did. Only English criminal records used *perpetrare*, the intensive of this verb: to perpetrate (1547) commits crimes. This one ignominious end to a father's ancient authority proves as only one exception to his rule.

Earlier, the patron (1380) acted as the protector or master of an undertaking. People shared the dignity of being a patron with the Saints. The social commentary of authors from Fielding to Dickens shows how beatifically patronage patronized (1727) in the eyes of bourgeois democracy. Johnson defined a patron as "a wretch who supports with insolence and is paid with flattery." The history of the word pattern traces this degradation. First spelled like patron (1369) until its separate spelling as pattern in 1555, pattern and patron acted synonymously as models. After a while, however, it seemed that the plebeians saw fit to imitate only their patrons' patterns for clothing and china and not their conduct. In these areas, at least, patrons might perpetrate no crimes greater than bad taste.

Patrician snobbery, on the other hand, worked to the advantage of aspiring shopkeepers who ascribed dignity to customers by saying that they patronized (1801) their shops. Jonson's *Volpone* provides a satiric link between the aristocratic and the plebeian when, as a mountebank Doctor, he addresses a crowd as "most noble gentlemen, and my worthy patrons" (1601). People love to patronize, but not to be patronized. Shopkeepers, at least, had the consolation of being paid for the indignity of their patrons' patronizing patronage.

Imagine the consternation of an Eastern patriarch visiting English society of the eighteenth century, as it worked out the patrimony (1377) of the Roman democratic concept of social fatherhood. He would have seen plebeians claiming patronage and patricians offering nothing better than china patterns. *O tempora, o mores*! Cicero had no idea how the expansive dynamic of Roman republican patronage would make his bemoaning of "times and customs" a pattern of social commentary.

## Words

Fatherhood requires a life time of responsibility.
Roots for feeding, leaning, stepping and covering describe this duty.

1. **PIE root *pater*, father, the feeder**
   Latin:
   *pater patris*, father or senator; *patria*, fatherland; *patricius*, patrician
   *patro patrare*, literally, to father a deed, achieve, execute, complete
   *perpetrare*, to perform, carry out
      French: *père*, father; and Spanish: *padre*, father
      English:
         paternal, relating to a father; patrimony, a father's estate
         to perpetrate, to carry out harmful action

Greek: *patriarkhes*, father of a family, later applied to the bishop of a church
German: *patrizisch*, patrician; and *Patriarch*, patriarch
Russian: патриарх (patriarkh), patriarch; and патриций (patritsiy), patrician

*Nota Bene*: a ramification of Grimm's law, Latin 'p' interchanges with Germanic or Slavic 'v': German *vater*, father; and Russian вотчина (votchina), patrimony.

2. PIE root *stebh*, step
   Russian:
      ступень (stupen), step
      заступник (zestupnık), one stepping (ступни) behind (-за), patron, Russian translation of Параклет (paraclete)
3. PIE root *krup*, to conceal, cover; and *kem*, to cover
   Greek: *krupto*, I hide
      English: cryptic, hidden; crypt, area of a church, hidden and reserved for burial
      Czech: *kryt*, to cover; Polish: *pokrywać*, to cover
   Russian:
      по-кров (pokrov), blanket, mantle, coat
      по-кровитель (pokrovitel'), patron, protector
      по-крывать (pokryvat'), to veil
      по-кровительствовать (Pokrovitel'stvovat), to patronize;
         *cf. protégé*
4. PIE root *klei*, slant, bed, ladder
   Greek: *climax*, ladder
   Latin: *clemens clementis*, clement, literally, inclining to a person in mercy
   English:
      client, one who inclines to another for help
      clime, an area of the inclining globe
      inclination, a leaning in a particular direction
      recline, decline, *etc.*
   German: *Klient*
      Russian:
         клиент (klient), client, from the German
         *cf.* Russian: плебей (plebey), plebeian
         буржуазный (burzhuaznyy), bourgeois
         наследие (naslediye), legacy

# 68. Father and Mother and the Fatherland/Motherland

## The Fatherland

With an extraordinary cultural continuity, Latin words for God, Emperor, and country took their roots from one word, *pater*, father. Romans worshipped God as *Jovis Pater*, the Fatherland as *patria* and the Emperor as *Pater Patriae*, Father of His Country. From land to God, the family cult ran straight through their lives. Speakers of English do not have a focus so resonating of religion, ancestors and antiquity. On the other hand, the French can enjoy a *frisson* at the word *La Patrie*.

The word land (*cf. das Land* in German) dates back to *Beowulf* and its first reference to enclosed land explains its being a doublet of lawn and lea, that is, a meadow. Romance languages supply its parallel in *terra*, which English adopts in the phrase *terra firma* (1604), by which Venetians referred to their possessions on the mainland. *Terra firma*, therefore, refers to land distinct from sea. Territory (1432) refers to land around a town. Thus, land and the derivatives of *terra* refer to specific areas.

Land gained dignity by taking on paternity in fatherland (1623, *cf. vaterland*) and domesticity in homeland (1670, *cf. heimat*). Germany so fervently adopted *vaterland* in the World Wars that English has avoided it because of its association with the Hun. Motherland (1711) usually had a more limited sense of mothering something: Egypt, motherland of superstition. Mother country refers to a country with colonies (1587); just as metropolis (1590), to a city with surrounding communities.

Both the French and the Russians personify their countries by a mother, not a father, although Latin *patria* and French *La Patrie* refer to a fatherland in the feminine gender that represents abstractions. Russian Родина-мать (*Rodina Mat)* is one word for Motherland, but another, отчизна-мать (otchizna-mat'), literally means "the fatherland mother." Latin, French or Russian—father has such a wide application that it loses its literal meaning.

Country (1275) did not fare much better than land in claiming patriotic origins. Country, originating as the adjective in the Latin phrase *terra contrata*, the land opposite (*cf.* Italian *contrada*, land), soon came to mean 'native land' (1300). Like land, country assumed dignity by compounding itself with another noun: 'native' in native country (1513). Americans have given it dignity in "My Country, 'tis of thee,/ sweet land of liberty,/ of thee I sing."

English does not use the root *patria* to refer to the fatherland, but it does incorporate patriotism into its vocabulary. First describing allegiance to one's country in 1653, patriotic came to refer to devoted civic service (1757: "patriotic service to King and country"). A patriot (1605) loves his country, in England, often in opposition to the king. An expatriate (1812) has departed (1784) or been banished—expatriated (1817)—from his country. To repatriate (1611) restores a citizen to his country. Its doublet, to repair (1320), describes an ambassador's repairing to his native land to rejoin his compatriots (1611). Immigration or emigration sounds formal, and patriot or patriotic sounds bookish, because these words did not originate in an English word for country derived from *patria*.

When Americans gave George Washington the title *Pater Patriae*, "Father of his Country," they borrowed nobility from a revered antiquity. The translation of this phrase, however, reflected only a shadow of its meaning in Latin, since neither "father" nor "country" translated it adequately.

## Words

Fatherhood has three PIE roots. Motherhood has one PIE root with four divisions.

1. **PIE root *ata*, daddy (familial and informal)**
   Latin: *atta*, father, grandfather (*cf.* Aramaic: *abba*, father)
   Russian:
   > отец (otets), father; and Отче наш (Otche nash), Our Father
   > отеч-ество (otechestvo), fatherland
   > отчизна-мать (otchizna-mat'), motherland (fatherland mother)
2. **PIE root *pater*, father**
   Latin: *pater*, father
   French:
   > père and pepe, father and grandfather (*cf.* Italian *nonno*, grandpa)
   > *la patrie* (feminine gender), fatherland
   Russian: папа, dad, papa
3. **PIE root *ded* (baby talk), old man**
   Russian:
   > дед (ded), grandfather; and дядя (djádja), uncle, fellow
   > дедушка (dedushka), grandpa (*cf.* бабушка, grandmother)

**PIE root *ma/amma*, mama, mother**

1. Greek: *metron*, womb; and *meter*, mother
   English: metropolis, mother city
2. Latin: *mater*
   French: *mère* and *mémé*, mother and grandmother

Spanish and Italian: *madre*
   English: mater and matron or matricide
3. German: *Mutter*
   Polish: *matka*, mother; Russian: матка (matka), womb; and мама (mama)
4. Latin: *amita*, aunt
   Spanish: *tia*; *Tia Maria*, made with rum and coffee beans
   Italian: *zia*; and Russian: тётя (tetja), aunt
   French/German: *tante*, from Old French *ta ante*; and English: aunt

# 69. Son and Daughter

## Offspring

Even out of the birth canal, the child still bore the mark and even the name of the womb. The Gothic word for womb gave English its noun child. In general, words for child look in their roots to birth or to suckling or babbling.

English son and Russian сын (son) share the same derivation from the Indo-European root *seu*, to bear. First seen in *Beowulf*, son, along with bairn, are the most ancient English words for offspring, but they make an odd couple, since bairn, although derived from 'to bear' and 'to be born,' finds its place only in literature; but son, though common in both spoken English and in its literature, shares no derivation with any other word in the language. Bairn has relatives but no common use; son, common use but no relatives.

The root of daughter tells a different story. Cognate with Sanscrit *duh*, milk (*cf.* English dugs, breasts, in English), daughters were the 'milkers' in their families. Russian and German associated a child (дитя [dita]) and also a daughter (*tochter* and дочь [doch']) with suckling. Suckling infants was so vital that it referred rarely in English to infants but commonly to the young of animals. Its importance is evident in the Romance heritage of Latin *filius*, son and *filia*, daughter. (With this basic background, it is ironic that filial, the only English derivative of *filius*, describes the higher relationship of offspring to parent, as in filial love or filial duty.) The Indo-European root *fe-* refers to a complex of breeding, fruition and suckling. Latin *femina*, the breeder, conceives the *fetus* that pullulates with her fecundity and felicity. Latin *felicitas*, the root of felicity, refers to the happiness of physical well-being The *fe-* root covers the full spectrum of felicitous fecundity from the fetus to the feminine.

Since the Romans considered *filius* to mean son and not suckling, they picked his defining characteristic as an inability to speak. From in-, not, and -fant, speaking, an infant does not speak. (We have already seen that this fa- root gives English many words which denote speech: convivial confabulation among affable guests usually steers clear of ineffable truths.) In English, also, babies babble, and toddlers toddle.

"Out of the mouths of babes and sucklings hast thou ordained strength" (*Psalm* 8.2)—the Psalmist took infancy as a foil to God's power. Starting as the opposite of lofty divinity, children bring their mother back to basics. They may eventually aspire to the filial duty appropriate to *homo sapiens*, savvy man, but they emerge in birth as *infans fellans*, suckling and speechless.

## Words

Roots of Son and Daughter

### SON

**PIE root *sewh*, to give birth**

Greek: *uios*, son
German: *Sohn*; Russian: сын; and English: son

### DAUGHTER

**PIE root *dhugter*, the suckler**

Greek: *thugater*, daughter; and *thele*, nipple
German: *Tochter*; English: daughter
Russian:
    дочь (doch'), daughter; and дитя (dita), child
    девушка (devushka), girl (*cf.* дедушка and бабушка)

**The cognate PIE root *dhel*, to suckle for woman;
to suck for son or daughter**

Latin: *fello fellare*, to suck; and *femina*, the woman suckling children
    French: *femme*, woman
        English: feminine (1384), fetus (1398), fecundity (1447), felicity (1386)
Latin: *filius/filia*
    French: *fils*, son; and *fille*, daughter; Italian: *figlio* and *figlia*
    Spanish: *hijo* and *hija*
        English: filial (1393)

According to these roots,
    sons, in German, are born;
    but both sons and daughters, in Romance, are suckled.

## 70. Brother and Sister

### Brotherhood Includes Sisters Too

Every brother is also a man and a son; and every sister, a woman and a daughter; but brother and sister expand the concept of gender beyond man and woman, and of clan beyond son and daughter. Nothing like siblings to complicate things! Are we not all brothers, men and women, sisters and brothers? Actually, the evolutions of these words suggest this union right from the beginning. Simple observations about the two Greek words for brother and the PIE root for sister may start to explain this complication. *Phratry* meant clansman, before it meant brother, as we understand the word. By its etymology also, *adelphos* defined brothers as born of the same womb. Its feminine form *adelpha* means sister. Brother, therefore, started life as a clansman of either gender born of the same womb. Sister, by one theory of etymology, defines her nature as being of her own clan. Defining one's own starts our outreach to humanity.

Who is my brother?—one answer started with clan, and used two distinctive English words to designate its members as brothers: "Men and brethren," John the Baptist addressed his fellow Jews, "children of the stock of Abraham, and whosoever among you feareth God, to you is the word of this salvation sent" (*Acts* 13.26). Descendants of "the stock of Abraham" united in theology and ritual. In the early Christian community, the Apostles Peter and Paul also addressed "men and brethren," when they announced their good news. In Greek, the author of the book of *Acts* used *adelphoi*, which the scholars of the *King James Bible* chose to translate as brethren, not brothers. Any band of vagabonds or thieves may call themselves brothers, but these translators used brethren, with an archaic plural morpheme similar to that of children, to dignify members of a spiritual brotherhood. Soldiers call themselves, not brethren, but brothers in arms. In the *King James Bible*, brethren imparts special distinction to the community of believers in the Apostolic Age.

English has also used a second distinctive word for brother. Friar, the only English word for brother derived from Romance, describes a member of a mendicant fraternity of monks. Even two hundred years before the Reformation, Christian humanists, rejecting Roman Catholic monasticism, and its titles, friar and fraternity, adopted brethren as a term inspired by the early Christian community described in *Acts*. Brethren of the Common Life (1384), for example, joined in a monastic order distinct from contemporary Catholic orders and established with the purpose of reforming their corruption. As an emblem of this reform, it called its members brethren in a brotherhood.

At their roots, the native, Germanic words brother and brotherhood had more pertinence to secular life than the academic Romance words friar and fraternity. Just the opposite of the chronology of friar and fraternity, their secular reference came first. In 1000, brother referred to both male and female offspring; much later—500 years later—it referred to the friars of religious orders. In 1300, brotherhood referred to a secular union, almost a century before it referred to monasticism. In or out of the church, Christian humanists of the Reformation might call their brothers brethren without an uncomfortable feeling of monastic corruption.

Brethren persisted in describing members of a spiritual community, especially in reference to those in need of charity: "Then the disciples, every man according to his ability, determined to send relief unto the brethren which dwelt in Judaea" (*Acts* 11.29). This charitable reference gradually reaches out farther. When Jesus established a brotherhood among his disciples—"All ye are brethren" (*Matthew* 23.8)—he was inviting all humanity to follow him. About sixteen hundred years later, when Shakespeare's Beatrice declares in witty hyperbole, "Adam's sons are my brothers" (*Much Ado*), her joke expands this ancient brotherhood.

The seventeenth century provides many benchmarks for the expansion of human brotherhood. In 1682, William Penn founded Philadelphia, "brotherly love" in Greek. He found this word in the Bible as one of the virtues of the early Christian community. "Let brotherly love continue" (*Hebrews* 13.1), Paul exhorts Jewish Christians in Jerusalem. The motto of William Penn's city transliterates the original Greek of this sentence into Latin letters: *Philadelphia Maneto*.[14] Since Philadelphia represents both a place and a concept, Penn's prayer for the city takes on special meaning: "Oh, <Philadelphia,> that thou mayest be kept from the evil that would overwhelm thee; that faithful to the God of the Mercies, in the life of righteousness, thou mayest be preserved to the end." God preserves brotherly love as long as He preserves Philadelphia, the City of Brotherly Love.

Brethren and friar, fraternity and sorority, Philadelphia and brotherly love—these words bear such burdens of meaning that we may view them as historical artifacts. Indeed, they do trace a path through the Chosen People and their heritage of God's Word; but they end in man's salvation, because the fatherhood of their God has grown into the brotherhood of men: "There cannot but be one fraternity in learning and illumination," observed Francis Bacon in his *Advancement of Learning* (1605), "relating to that paternity which is attributed to God." Our Father wants us all to be brothers.

## Words

Four PIE roots provide words for brother. Greek *adelphos/adelpha* referred to male and female, just as the English word brother, at first, could also mean sister—either one came from the same womb. Brotherhood started out as unity in a clan.

1. **PIE root *gelb*, womb**
    Greek: *delphis*, womb; *Delphi*, womb of the earth, birthplace of Phoebus Apollo and Phoebe Diana
    English: dolphin, a marine mammal having a womb
    Greek: *adelphos*, brother, born of the same womb; *phila-delphia*, brotherly love
    English: Philadelphia, City of Brotherly Love (*Hebrews* 13.1)
2. **PIE root *bhrater*, brother**
    Greek: *phratry*, clansman
    Latin: *frater* and *fraternitas*, brother and brotherhood/fraternity
    Italian: *fratello* and *fraternità*; French: *frère* and *fraternité*
    Latinate English:
       friar (1290), fraternal (1494)
       fraternity (1330), religious order; (1390), brotherhood

Grimm's law: 'f' and 'b' interchange:
   German: *Bruder* and *Bruderschaft*, brother and brotherhood
   Russian: брат (brat) and братство (bratstvo), brother and brotherhood
   English:
      brothership (950), translation of *Matthew* 24.12
      brother (1000), secular; (1500), religious; brethren (1175)
      brotherhood (1300), secular;(1380), religious;(1780), universal

3. **PIE root *germen*, sprout, bud**
    Spanish: *hermano* and *hermandad*, brother and brotherhood
    English: brother-german (1340), brother through both parents
4. **PIE root *sue*, one's own**
    Latin: *soror*, sister
       Italian: *sorella*; and French: *soeur*
       English: sorority (1532), women united in prayer; (1900), college club
    German: *Schwester*
       English: sister
    Russian: сестра (sestra), sister

Sister perhaps related to the reflexive pronoun:
> Latin: *sui* in *sui*cide, killing of oneself; *sui generis,* of **one's own** kind
> German: *sein,* his, its; *sich,* himself/herself, itself, themselves
> Russian: свой (svoy), my, your, his, her, **one's own**, our, their
> Derived from these roots, sister refers to a woman of *one's own* clan.

Cousin:
> Latin: *consobrinus*—from *con-sororinus*—child of mother's sister
> French: *cousin*
> Russian: двою-родная сестра (dvoyu-rodnaya sestra), cousin of two generations

# Man and His Physical Frame
....

# 71. Body

## Body, Ours, Theirs, and Its

From the bottom up, corpus incorporates and body embodies creation. Starting at the bottom, *corpusculum*, little body, first meant atom. In 1660, Robert Boyle introduced corpuscle into English as a minute body of matter; which, in the nineteenth century, described a minute body of blood. Up the ladder in corporality, leprechauns (1604; lu, small + corp, body), little people, tower above atoms but cower beneath larger humanity. At the top, heavenly bodies (1380) bring atoms together to embody creation. From atoms to the sun, "All are but parts of one stupendous whole," Alexander Pope marveled, "Whose body Nature is and God the Soul."

Let's get to man's body, the main body of this essay. Body (800) first referred to the torso without head and limbs, though it has usually referred to the whole. "With a tinge of compassion," it can refer to a poor body all on its own: how can a body get through all that life has in store for it? A poor body can be just anybody. Since the end of the thirteenth century, as a suffix, it has referred to a person: somebody (1303), nobody (1338), anybody (1490), everybody (1530). A busybody (1526), a nobody trying to be a somebody, meddles in any and everybody's business. Some poor bodies fear to be nobodies but find it hard to find their place as somebodies.

In low colloquialism, 'bod' disparages and reduces a person to corporality (1398): 'Get your bod over here.' Men may make a similarly reductive comment about women: 'She has a good bod.' On the other hand, popular culture feeds on the reductive. "The Body," in the 1940's, referred to the most attractive woman in Hollywood. Let astronomers contemplate heavenly bodies—"The Body" enjoys fame that does one poor body a lot of good and makes her a star that men contemplate right here on earth.

In its impersonal reference, body refers to "the tangible part of a person's individuality taken for the whole," as in the writ of *Habeas Corpus* that asks for the presence in court of an incarcerated "body." In literature, corpus (1727) brings together the whole of an author's opus. Corpse (1315), an anglicized pronunciation of French *corps*, describes the human body without life. From Latin *cadere*, to fall, cadaver (1398), a synonym of corpse, refers uniquely to a dead body. If police believe that a missing person has been murdered, they find the *corpus delicti*, "the body of the crime," to start the investigation. So also, if a pencil is missing and believed stolen, it also becomes the *corpus delicti*. In other words, *corpus* does not necessarily mean corpse.

Body embodies individuals in union. In a body, men may come together to address their concern. If it becomes consistently important, they may incorporate to form a corporation. Incorporation (1460), to incorporate (1460) and corporation (1611) lend Latinate and legal dignity to naming a union of parts, either municipal or commercial. Members of a corporation ate such sumptuous meals at their meetings that they could incorporate their own corporation (1753) into corpulence (1581). French has lent its dignity to a *corps d'élite*, a select body. For a particular mission, an army may distinguish a select body of soldiers as a corps (1711), possessing an *esprit de corps* appropriate to its distinction. A medical corps, for example, serves a special purpose

To emphasize the virtue of units being united, Livy and Saint Paul told the fable of the various members of a human body acting independently but detrimentally to the whole. The moral of the fable demonstrates the necessity of being "many members but one body" in the body politic or in the body of Christ. Cicero's mandate that Roman statesmen care for "the whole body of the state" (... *ut totum corpus rei publicae curent*) and not just a faction assumes its integrity. The people of a nation incorporate their body politic (1532).

Saint Paul taught the body of Christ as a mystery and a community: "Now ye are the Body of Christ and members in particular" (I *Corinthians* 12.27). In Christian theology, the importance of Christ's body, *Corpus Christi*, encouraged the use of the image of spiritual incorporation by man's union with a woman in marriage or by his union with Christ in life. Friar Laurence, for example, speaks of the incorporation of Romeo and Juliet in marriage: "You shall not stay alone / till holy church incorporate two in one" (*Romeo and Juliet* II, 6, 36).

No matter what we may know about all the incorporations of this world and beyond, we can all appreciate body when we eat food without it. Body describes the fullness of the whole, especially of wine. For example, we use small amounts of pepper and garlic to give bland food body without excessive heat, so that we may enjoy full-bodied flavors.

Corpus and body incorporate all the corporality (1400) and corporeality (1620) of our lives into a happy or an unhappy whole. Alexander Pope raises man's body to the "stupendous whole" of the body that "Nature is." The ancient fable of the body's uncooperative members also teaches that men should fit happily within the whole. Starting out as homebodies, we should grow happily into the "stupendous whole" instead of growing unhappily into silly busybodies minding everybody's business but our own.

## Words

The English word body, so basic that it has no PIE root, and the Latin *corpus* describe heavenly bodies and all that is therein. Since bodies arise from earth, the Russian тело (telo) has a tellurian root.

### No known PIE root

English: body (800) and bodice (1585)

### PIE root *krep*, body

Latin:
> *corpus corporis*, body
> *Habeas corpus*, May you have (produce) the body.
>> Italian: *corpo*; Spanish: *cuerpo*
>> French: *corps*, body or body of men; *esprit de corps*

German: *Körper*, body (*cf. Leib*, originally, life; body)
English:
> corpse and corpulent
> corset (1299) and corselet (1563), close-fitting body garments

### PIE root *telo*, soil, base, ground

Latin: *tellus*, earth
English: tellurian, of the earth
Russian: тело (telo), body

### PIE root *trou*, block, stump; *ter*, to break off

English: trench, trenchant, trunk
Russian: труп (trup), cadaver

# 72. Clothing

Everybody dresses, but we may dress up, not just like anybody, but a real somebody. Whoever we are, anybodies or somebodies, clothing both clothes our bodies and has always invested our corporality with value, just as body embodies worldly corporality. Even in the Garden of Eden, clothing invested value. Adam and Eve clothed themselves with fig leaves, but God invested them with skins. We have always invested in clothing, because it invests us.

By its root, clothes simply clothe. With similar simplicity, Russian derives its word for clothing, платье (platye), from the root to weave (плести [plesti]). Humble folk kept the clothes they were not wearing in a chest and wore them when they were washing the others. Closets only evolved when wardrobes grew. Wardrobes, as rooms, first housed armor. From the beginning, however, people dressed humbly, when they were of humble estate. The aristocracy knew better. They had been born to a tradition of magnificent display. Six hundred years after the verb clothe, invest, as a verb, referred both to clothing and to the power it symbolized. Investing came late, but it drew from ancient customs. The Romans, wrote the historian Livy in the reign of Augustus, invested tribunes "both in the jurisdiction and also in the ornaments of Consuls" (1600, Holland's Livy). Power has always dressed to assert its power.

Cloth itself required time to weave it and money to purchase it. Richly woven with gold or silver, it provided the "glorious cloth of estate" (1523), draping thrones, dignifying portraits and included in the inventory of an estate. As distinctive garb, it came to describe the clothing of a particular vocation: soldiers or sailors referred to "men of our cloth" sharing the same armed service. Eventually, it identified a clergyman as a man of the cloth (1701). Although distinctive in his dark suit or cassock, man of the cloth makes clergymen seem humble.

Richly adorning some men of the cloth, vestments, usually described as holy, referred mostly to rich, sometimes costly, garb worn in sacerdotal offices before the altar. In the secular world, officials, by investiture, received power and its paraphernalia. A vest (1613) may not seem especially luxurious, but it came to Europe from the royal pomp of the East: "Artaxerxes the Great gave Mithridates a gown or vest of gold which he wore during a royal banquet" (1665). It continued as a fashion of both men and women.

Investors traveled out to the exotic Far East in search of finery and spices. Borrowing the Italian *investire* from the very wide frame of international trade, the British East India Company invested money in such luxuries in the hope of profit. Its officers invested both themselves and their company in costly vestments.

Apparel has its part in the preparation we all make for life. Paring their leafy apparatus, Adam and Eve prepared their apparel. Also with a cognate verb and noun, they readied their raiment. From French *abiller*, to fit out, habiliment also evokes an image of preparation similar to apparel and raiment. Describing simply what one holds, habit, the Latinate equivalent of habiliment, first referred to clothing and then to the uniform garb of a religious order, although an equestrienne may still refer to her riding habit. Apparel, raiment, habiliment and habit prepare, ready and fit out clothes. In his advice to his son, Polonius uses habit and apparel in this basic sense: "Costly thy habit, rich not gaudy, . . . / for apparel oft proclaims the man." Lesser men keep their habit gaudy or their apparel neglected, but all men keep it with some preparation.

Dressing rooms have mirrors so that we, especially the ladies, can get our clothing just right as we put it on. Dressing shares its root with directing. It adds dignity to putting on clothes: We put clothes on to take out the trash; we dress for a party. It also describes formal preparation. Dressing a turkey, like paring apples, prepares it for the oven. Dressing a wound protects it from infection. Soldiers particularly get things straight: they dress ranks to straighten them. Most of all, they take pride in their regalia: "Full dress creates dignity, augments consciousness, and keeps at distance an encroacher" (1743). For them, Polonius should make a stronger statement: "Apparel"—always—"proclaims the man." In the eighteenth century, dress finally won its place by replacing gown (1375) as the popular word for clothing. Gown still claims its dignity in the pomp and circumstance of academic processions, and as, in the quaint phrase of the OED, "a dress with some pretension to elegance" for the belle of the ball.

Like dress, attire also refers to setting things in order. Synonymous with tier, meaning arrangement in a rank, a tire is a wheel, attired with iron or rubber, eventually inflated by air as a pneumatic tire. Gown stately stands on its own, but attire, more than dress, takes naturally to the adjective formal.

Clothing, investing, dressing and attiring, plain weave and exquisite gowns—clothes have set and still set many milestones on the path to power. Greedy for investment, some have robbed others so that they may be robed with a speciously best self. Robe, indeed, bears witness to such crimes, since it shares the same root with rob. Before modern manufacture, especially, clothing cost so much that thieves robbed the house first of its gold and then of its golden robes. What an historical irony that lawyers and judges derived dignity from their title, gentlemen of the robe. Herein lies a spark of insight. When we claim distinction by robing ourselves, we come close to robbing it. Investing in ourselves is wise, but investing ourselves may not be.

## Words

The word clothing itself, and a few old-fashioned words—gown, garb, and robe—stand out as a set of words of obscure origin. Otherwise, PIE roots for covering, holding, weaving, and setting straight fit out words for clothing.

### PIE root *wer* and *wes*, to cover, clothe

Germanic—English: to wear
Romance:
    French: *garnir*, to equip
        English: garnish (1418) and garment (1340)
    Latin: *vestis*, clothing
        Italian: *veste*; Spanish: *vestimenta*; French: *vêtements*
        English:
            vest (1613), vestment (1300),
            to invest, to clothe with insignia of office (1533),
            to purchase goods for profit (1613)

### PIE root *reg*, to rule, set straight

Latin: *directus* and *directiare*, adjective and verb, set in a straight line
    French: *dresser*, to prepare, dress
    English: doublets, to direct/to dress (1330), set straight; (1440), clothe

### PIE root *ghabh*, to hold

French:
    *abiller*, to fit out, make ready; *habillement*, clothing
    *déshabillé*, undressed
        Italian: *abbigliamento*
        English:
            habiliment (1491)
            to habilitate, to clothe, equip; to rehabilitate
Latin: *habitus*, condition, dress
    English: habit (1225), clothing; (1290), clothing of a religious order

### PIE root *plek*, to weave

Latin: *plectere*, to plait
Russian: плести (plesti), to weave; платье (platye), dress

### Of obscure origin

German: *Kleidung*, clothing
English: cloth (800), to clothe (950), clothes (888), clothing (1200)

### Of obscure origin

Latin: *gunna*, garment made of skin
    English: gown (1375)

**Of obscure origin**

Germanic: *rauben*, to rob
Italian: *roba*, things, clothes, food
French: *derober*, to steal
Spanish: *ropa*, clothes
English:
    robe (1275), dressing gown (1854)
    wardrobe, room or closet for clothing (1387), clothing itself (1400)

**Of obscure origin**

English: garb, grace or elegance (1591), clothing of a profession,
    costume (1622)

**Of obscure origin**

Russian: одеваться (odevat'sya), to clothe; одежда (odezhda), clothing

# 73. Heart

### The Rational Heart

The heart stands at the core of many ideals that mankind has valued—so many that it has had trouble pumping, so to speak, healthy red blood to their various arteries. Bringing all those ideals home, Lactantius, around the year 300 AD, called the heart *domicilium sapientiae*, the home of wisdom. Comprehending the expanse of that home—and especially living happily in that expanse and keeping its blood flowing—challenges even the wisdom of a heart of oak.

    Pascal made one of the most famous—and misunderstood—statements about the heart: *Le cœur a ses raisons que la raison ne connaît point*, "The heart has its reasons that reason knows not." Reason alone, he meant, should not limit heart-felt religion, but secular thought has interpreted his statement as preferring sentiment to reason. Retracing the history of the heart's ideals, we can resolve this conflict that the modern world has seen between heart and head. To the heart, antiquity attributed courage and intellect in a balance of rationality with sentimentality. The pictorial image of the heart primarily symbolized devotion since the eleventh century; and since the fifteenth century, especially but secondarily, it has symbolized the devotion of romantic love.

    Heart (825) in early English first meant feeling, understanding and thought. Only later (1000) did it refer to a vital organ, but to which organ was unclear. A compound like heartburn indicates that the heart has been identified with the stomach. When we suffer a sudden fright, we say that our heart is in our mouth in referring to a flutter in the stomach. The Greek *etor*, heart, cognate with Latin *uterus* and *venter*, gives English ventriloquist, one who speaks from his stomach. Firmly in possession of anatomical understanding, we find such misunderstanding shocking; but this misunderstanding did display a degree of understanding. Because thought occupied a core position, Greek, Latin and English gave it symbolic rather than anatomical location. We also hear physicians speaking of hearts circulating blood, and poets praising hearts full of love. Careful study of anatomy eventually distinguished between organs according to their functions.

Latin *cor*, therefore, referred to the heart as the seat of intellect. "To some," Cicero said, "the heart seems to be the *animus*" (*aliis cor ipsum animus videtur*), mind, because the Latin word for 'stupid' means 'out of heart.' Homer in the first book of the *Iliad* pictures his hero's murderous thought: when Achilles contemplates killing Agamemnon, his "heart is divided two ways" (ἦτορ διάνδιχα μερμήριξεν). Not setting his whole heart on the deed, he is acting half-heartedly, midway between the extremes of acting with a faint heart or with a heart and a half.

In English, heart can refer simply to memorization when we learn something by heart (1374). Concord, in its root, means 'hearts together,' thinking as much as feeling. Carlyle referred to writers sharing reasoned conviction with readers when he described their success: "If a book comes from the heart, it will contrive to reach other hearts" (*Heroes*, 1840).

The history of cordial confirms the heart's primarily unsentimental history. As an adjective, cordial referred at first to the heart itself (1400), and later to cordial (1471) medicines serving to hearten (1526) the heart. It came also to mean heartfelt (1477) and finally simply friendly (1795). In this reference to friendly affability, cordial is a synonym of hearty: friends greet with a cordial or a hearty handshake. Hearty, the native word, sounds appropriately down to earth. Fraternal brothers extend to each other a hearty handshake in their lodge; *literati* share a cordial handclasp in their salon.

Courage, derived from Late Latin *coraticum*, first referred to thought: Sempronius in Shakespeare's *Timon of Athens* considers doing a good deed: "I'd such a courage to do him good." From its first occurrence (825), heart has meant brave thought and action. We refer to stout hearts and hearts of oak: "Heart of oak are our ships, heart of oak are our men" (1760). We hearten the disheartened by encouraging them not to be out of heart, but to take heart, and to be of good heart. Though synonymous, hearty (1380) and courageous fit different contexts. Sailors, a hale and hearty lot, similar to land-lubbers in their lodges, address each other as "My hearties!" Their superior officers, on the other hand, praise each other's courage and hope that the *literati* back in port dignify them as captains courageous.

Although words of hearty roots mostly refer to the intellect, courage has had a wide spectrum of meaning from lust (1541) to anger (1386) with a common ground of hearty activity. When, in 1565, an Englishman observed that the Cardinals of Rome mixed "pride, avarice and lechery in the greatest courage," he was mixing bravado and spirit. Although it may have first referred to thought, courage courageously broke its bonds. The meaning of courage as bravery (1375), therefore, radiates as one facet of the gem.

Finally, taking these hearty sentiments to heart, we should not be surprised that heart also came to mean love and affection (1175). In the *Tempest*, Ferdinand loses his heart to Miranda: "The very instant that I saw you, did / My heart fly to your service." The human heart is capable of all things.

In modern cliches, we often limit the range of the heart, attributing courage to men and heart to women. Hearts adorning Valentines make an industry of sentimentality. The ancient heart and its courage, on the other hand, reveal expansive inclusivity. When Hamlet expresses wonder after he has seen his father's ghost—"Would heart of man once think of it?"—he implies that heaven alone could surpass the comprehension of man's heart.

## Words

The two PIE words for heart do not at first refer to the organ that we understand as heart. One root makes it cognate with Latin *uterus* and *venter*, stomach.

### PIE root *kerd*, heart
1. Greek: *kardia*, heart
    English: cardiac, relating to the heart
2. Romance
    Latin: *cor*
        French: *coeur*; Italian: *cuore*; Spanish: *corazon*
        English:
            cordial (1400); (1471), cordial medicines; (1795), friendly
            courage (825); (1375), bravery; (1386), anger; (1541), lust

to encourage (1490); accord (1123 as verb, 1297 as noun) concord (1300), discord (1300) and record (1225)
3. Germanic
   German: *Herz*
      English:
         heart (825), first, understanding and then (1000), the vital organ
         heartfelt (1477), friendly (1795); hearty (1380), courageous
4. Slavic
   Polish: *serce*
   Russian:
      сердце (serdtse), heart
      среда (sreda), Wednesday, heart (of the week)

### PIE root *udero*, womb, belly

1. Greek: *etor*, heart; and *megal-etor*, greathearted
2. Latin: *uterus*; *venter*, stomach
   English: ventriloquist, speaking from the stomach

## 74. Friday's Child

My mother, who mistakenly thought that I was born on a Friday, told me that my fate as Friday's child was to be "loving and giving." I considered myself lucky, since the alternatives, as Thursday's or Saturday's child, did not promise a similarly amiable fate:

Thursday's child has far to go,
Friday's child is loving and giving.
Saturday's child has to work for his living.

Thor's day's child, under the influence of the god of the cosmos, can expect a "far" journey. Saturn's day's child, born under the influence of the god of hard-working farmers, "has to work for his living." By contrast, Friday's child basks in the warmth of Freya, the goddess of love. Actually, I was born on the day of Thor. Having skipped a day to dedicate me to Freya, my mother did not know that, by being born on Thursday, in the constellation of Aries, I would have "far to go." At least, I shared her hope that friends, the cognates of Freya, might lighten the travail of my travel.

Friend means loving, because it derives from the present participle of the Old English verb *freon*, to love. A cognate of free, it also describes the loving members of a family, free unlike servants, who are slaves. Friend in *Beowulf* characterizes the loving inhabitants of home—*Heorot innan waes/fréondum afylléd*, "the interior of Heorot was filled with friends." In those parlous days, charity, by necessity, started at home and perhaps did not reach far beyond it. Related also to the root of friend and free, the Germanic *Friede*, peace, characterizes Freda, Friedrich/Frederick, Siegfried, Godfrey and Geoffrey as bringers of peace. We deprive a man of peace when we affray (1314) him (Gaulish Latin *exfridare*). The man affrayed is afraid (1330)—*cf.* say/said, pay/paid, stay/staid as parallel formations. Friends unaffrayed enjoy peace and freedom.

Lovers and friends cover a lot of territory on the map of the human heart. Samuel Johnson gave friend its classic definition—"One joined to another in mutual benevolence and intimacy"—from which others are derived. Definitions of friend in several dictionaries do not mention love, except once by exclusion: "One joined to another in intimacy and mutual benevolence, independent of sexual or family love." In English, we know that a lover loves, but we have forgotten that a friend also loves since its verb form in the Old English *freon*, to love, survives only as a relic of linguistic archaeology. The fate of 'lover' in the latter part of the twentieth century should perhaps make us grateful for the isolation of friend from its loving, but potentially lubricious, root.

Avoiding love in friendship resembles Saint Jerome's avoiding 'love' in his Latin translation of the Bible, the *Vulgate*, which uses *caritas*, charity or love, and *dilectio*, delight, many more times than *amor*. This preference for 'charity' and 'delight' has created classic phrases like "Faith, Hope and Charity" in translation of Paul's triad of virtues (1 *Corinthians* 13) and "delight in the law of the Lord." In Latin, delight was not as strong as love—*Amare vim habet maiorem; deligere est levius amare,* said an ancient grammarian, "*Amare* has greater force; *deligere* is to love more mildly." Without its cognate verb, friend, therefore, both profits and suffers from its detachment from love.

From *amare*, to love, Romance languages derive similar words for love and friendship. *Amicus*, friend, by its etymology, loves. From *amicus*, English also derives words even more abstract than friend. Take, for example, amiable and amicable. Amiable people are lovable, but lovable people are not amicable. At the conference table, heads of state settle differences amicably, but not amiably. Similarly, their amity refers to friendship of a public character—"The less we have to do with the amities or enmities of Europe," observed Thomas Jefferson, "the better." By contrast, amorous has more of the ardent love, whose potential lubricity Jerome avoided in his translation of the Bible.

Friendly and free, amiable and amorous mark landmarks on the map of the heart. In extremities on this compass, we can be friendly or afraid, loving or lubricious. As he treks over this terrain every day of the week, even a man dedicated to friends on Friday must work for his loving.

## Words

English words friend and friendly derive from the Germanic tradition. Amity and amicable derive from Romance languages, which demonstrates a remarkable similarity in their words for love and friendship. This similarity sparks a question: How similar are love and friendship?

I. Germanic
PIE root *prai*, beloved, at peace; of a clan, therefore, neither serf nor slave
German: *Freund, freundlich* and *frei*
English: friend, friendly and free

\* \* \*

Latin: *proprius*, one's own, particular, characteristic
Russian: приятель (priyatel'), friend
*cf.* PIE root *witero*, more apart
Russian: друг (drug), close friend; droog in Burgess' *A Clockwork Orange*

II. Romance
Of uncertain PIE root: perhaps *ame*, either suckling or taking hold of
Latin:
*amo amare*, to love; *amor*, love; and *amans*, lover
*amicus* and *amicitia*, friend and friendship; *amabilis*, lovable
*amicabilis* and *amatorius*, amicable and amatory/amorous
Italian:
*amare*, to love; *amore*, love; and *amante*, lover
*amico* and *amicizia*, friend and friendship
*amabile*, lovable
*amichevole* and *amoroso*, amicable and amatory/amorous
Spanish:
*amar*, to love; *amor*, love; and *amante*, lover
*amigo* and *amistad*; *amable*; *amigable* and *amoroso*
French:
*aimer, amour*, and *amoureux/amant*, to love
*ami* and *amitié*; *aimable*; *amical* and *amoureux*
English:
paramour (1300), illicit lover; amorous (1303); and amiable (1350)
amity (1450), friendship

amicable (1532); inamorato (1592), a man beloved; amatory (1599) inamorata (1651), a woman beloved

Russian: амурный (amurnyy), amorous

## 75. Head

The Germanic word head at first served solely as a synonym of skull. Seventy-five years after this first meaning, it meant head man, referring to the heady condition of being the chief. Late in the fourteenth century, five centuries after its first use, when it finally referred to mind, the head man could have been said to use his head. At that point, head men might also put their heads together. Before that point, instead of enjoying a friendly *tête-à-tête*, the testy chief and the headstrong head might have had no alternative, insofar as they relied on the meanings of the word, other than going head-to-head to see who's boss. Head and its Romance cognate chief have referred more to leadership and power than to brains.

Actual rivalry between Romance and Germanic headings might have arisen after the French of the Norman conquerors in 1066 derived from Latin *caput* more English words for its head men. Chieftain has described the heroes of Trojan, Arthurian and Scottish legend. Captain, its doublet, ranks officers in the army and navy. The change of Latin 'c' to French 'ch' has given English numerous doublets—cant/chant, capture/chase and Carmen/charm. Just as chant, chase, and charm evoke romance more than cant, capture, and Carmen, the fearless swagger of chieftains make captains seem dutiful but dull. Captains have courageously manned the helms of ships and charted the course of industry, but chieftains breathe freer air.

Chief and chef also pair as doublets. The reference to a Native American tribal leader as a chief, a romantic association similar to that of chieftain, represents a later application of the word (1587). The word chief in the phrases Commander-in-Chief and Chief Justice better represents its original reference to a leader of a group or community. Chef, a French word from the phrase *chef de cuisine*, describes the chief cook in the kitchen. Chieftain/captain and chief/chef describe head men from primeval forests and fields of battle to the daily board in the boarding house and the council board in the board room.

Both Latin *caput* and English head had a wide reference. English, for example, has fountain head (1375), headland (1155), head of a ship (1485)—thus sailors hit the head when they go to latrines—or even the head (1545) on a glass of brew. The *Caput* does not lay claim to as wide a territory as the native word head. Cape (1386) as a synonym of headland, the only Romance parallel to the preceding list, is an exception that proves the rule of the native Germanic over the Romance. Referring to a promontory of land as headland, but naming it cape—Cape May or Cape Town—English and Dutch concede to the authority of the first Spanish and Portuguese explorers, just as Anglo-Saxon head conceded to Norman French chief.

Germanic English also conceded to Romance in its use of capital (1225) and capitol (1375) as the chief city and building of a state. At first an adjective in the phrase capital city (1539), capital shed its noun a century later (1667). The *Capitolium* on the Capitoline Hill in Rome had such significance as its seat of power that republican America named its chief governmental building after it. Capital/Capitol, cape and chief provide examples of authority over the heads of the English!

Head words do not describe the tops in conduct. Although 'Capital!' compliments the best, it first defined enemies as the worst (1375) and worthy of capital punishment (1526). Heady (1382) at first meant violent or impetuous and later (1628) giddy, as when the influence of spirits goes to the head. Headstrong (1398), self-willed and stubborn, is an approximate synonym of heady. Testy was at first its exact synonym: the colloquial word in Latin for head, *testa*, literally pot or shell, became the French word *tête*, head, and gave English its root for 'testy' (1374). Just as we refer colloquially to a conceited person as a head job, we call people heady and testy who have too big a head to cooperate.

We all have heads; and, in a body, we put them together to elect a head. In their special functions, we call these heads chiefs, chefs or captains. Head has described something or someone of capital importance, but it has made little headway in romantic distinction. A head oversees other heads, because it is often over their heads to use them.

## Words

Romance derivatives from the PIE root *caput* outnumber the Germanic ones, because the Norman conquest of 1066 put the French in charge of language as well as government.

### PIE root *caput*, head
  I. Romance
    1. Latin: *caput capitis*, head; and *capitalis*
        English: capital, relating to the head, as in capital punishment
        Russian: Капитал (Kapital), capital, asset

2. Vulgar Latin *capum*: head
    Italian and Spanish: *capo*
    French: *chef*
        English: chief (1297)
            Russian: шеф (sef), from French, boss, chief
        French: *chef*, head cook
            English: chef (1842), a doublet of chief
3. Latin: *capitaneus*
    French: *capitaine*, captain
        German, Czech, and Polish: *Kapitan*, captain
        Russian: капитан (kapitan), captain
    English: chieftain (1325) and its doublet captain (1375)
4. Latin: *capitellus*, little head
    French: *cadet*, younger son
    English:
        cadet, younger son sent to the army
        caddie and cad
    Russian:
        кадет (kadet), cadet
        Кадетский корпус (Kadetskiy corpus), élite corps of a military school, founded 1731, who, as White Russians, opposed the Bolsheviks in 1917
II. Germanic:
    German: *Haupt*, archaic and poetic, head, leader
    Polish: *hetman*, from the German *Hauptmann*, captain
    English: head (825)

Other PIE words for head take their derivation from roots for skull, cup and shell.

### PIE root *galw*, bald

Latin: *calva*, skull; and *calvus*, bald
    Italian and Spanish: *calvo*; French: *chauve*
Russian: глава (glava), head, chapter

### PIE root *keup*, round, hollow

English: cup (1000)
German: *Kopf*, head
    *Cf.* English:
        nog, small cup; nog, strong ale (*cf.* egg-nog)
        noggin, head

PIE root *teks*, to weave, fabricate

Latin: *testa*, pot; *testa capitis*, shell of the head
    French: *tête* and *tête-à-tête*
    English: textile

# 76. Headgear

## Hats and Caps and Capes

Since we lose seventy percent of our body heat through our heads, we have always used hats and hoods, and caps and capes to keep us warm. Our ancestors also valued special headgear because it invested them with clerical or academic status. With such status as fashion may lend, the right hat always makes a statement. In their historical status, cap (1000) and, especially, cape (1565), looking back to the Romance root *cap*, head, carry an aura of romance. Though older and native to English, hood and hat do not have the same romantic associations. As hoods lurk about in their wicked designs, heroes in capes dash in to foil them. Similarly, the Romance chieftain evokes more romance than the Germanic leader.

Headgear is so basic that it supplies English with some of its oldest words. About 630, Isidore of Seville mentioned Latin *cappa* in his book of etymologies as a head-covering for women. Any words of the learned and venerable Isidore demand attention. Living between the classical and the medieval worlds, he often cites a Latin word that is about to enter Romance languages and English. Associating a cap with women also points to its perennially covering their heads, both for modesty and also for fashion. Did Isidore observe a parade of Easter bonnets in his cathedral in Seville? The distaff side weaves virtues from her necessities!

*Cappa* in Isidore's text anticipated both a simple covering for the head, like a skull-cap (1682), and a full covering *cap-a-pie*, head to foot, like a cape. Brief or full, cap or cape has, in the past, invested authority, especially ecclesiastical. Cope (1205), an early form and a doublet of cape, describes a cape worn specifically by the clergy. Similarly, monks claimed a cowl (961), derived from *cucullus*, a Gaulish word in Latin, as uniquely their own. A man entered a monastic order by taking the cowl.

Religious orders debated and regulated the length and shape of their cap or cape. Capuchins, for example, organized in 1528 as a sect of the Franciscans, derived their name from their sharp-pointed *capuche*, little cape, which their founder, Matteo di Bascio, attested to be the original cape of Saint Francis. Capuchins either invented the coffee drink cappuccino or someone named it after their brown *capuche*. In Spain, a *sombrero* describes both a hat and a drink, perhaps of the same color as cappuccino, made with coffee liqueur and cream. With religious intent, Pope Innocent IV gave Cardinals a red hat in 1244 to symbolize their willingness as Christians to spill their own blood for their Saviour.

Saint Martin of Tours' cape became so famous that it even inspired a special type of building, a chapel, to display it. French *chape* adds 'h' to the 'c' of cape, just as English chieftain adds an 'h' to captain. From *chape*, English derived chapel, the place in which the first chaplains preserved the *chape*, the cape, of Saint Martin. We should certainly touch our caps to men of the cloth for devising caps, capes and cowls that dignify their orders and inspire buildings to celebrate them.

Monks don cowls in the cloister; priests, copes in church; and scholars, caps and gowns in academe. Scholars cap their cap with a flat board, facetiously called a mortar board, from its resemblance to the square board on which a mason keeps the mortar for his bricks. Caps became so identified with the learned professions of academics, clergy and judges that the average chap put his thinking cap on when he tried to figure out a problem. Caps symbolized—maybe, in the popular mentality, even inspired—wisdom.

Religion has always valued rituals for the dead. Covering the head has long signified mourning, as when King David reacted to the news of the betrayal and death of his friend Ahithophel: "And David went up the ascent of the Mount of Olives, and wept as he went, and his head was covered and he walked barefoot" (II *Samuel* XV, 30). Judges in England wore black caps as symbols of their mournful duty of sentencing guilty men to death. As a fashion, widows wore black caps in mourning. An early form of the cap included a triangular cloth over the forehead, which came to be known as a widow's peak.

Inspiring respect for fashion alone, French *chapeau* became such a byword that it has passed into English to describe the finest in ladies' millinery. Even for men, chapeau-bras (1764) described a man's three-corner hat usually held under the arm as part of a full-dress uniform. Way back in the fourteenth century, Russians took шапка (shapka), derived from *chapeau*, as their standard word for hat. French fashion has certainly made its mark when an entire culture tips its шапка to it! The Italians have also made their mark on fashion: a milliner, named for his origin in Milan, made hats, especially of straw. The Italian straw hat gained such fame that it was the title of a film about a lady more fashionable than moral.

Many people outside the learned professions wore caps. English has derived chaperon (1380) from *chape*/cape, which later (1720) described the woman wearing it when she protects younger women. A woman wore a kerchief (1300; French, *couvre-chief*), literally a head-covering. A jester wears a fool's cap to mock wiser men. It describes both his cap and bells and the 13½ by 17 inch paper with a watermark of a fool's cap. Football players used to wear caps and baseball players still do, with the addition of a sun visor. American youth have adopted the baseball cap as headgear in the twentieth century, but it has always symbolized youth—"cap and feather days" once described it. The Yankee doodle dandy put a feather in his cap, which has become a byword for distinction. Whether clerical or academic, fashionable or athletic, everyone used to don a night-cap before retiring to rest. They also used to down a nightcap as well: it also describes the warming drink, usually of whiskey, consumed at bedtime.

Let's put the cap on this study. A hood evokes secrecy; a cape, romance. They keep us warm, but our ancestors appreciated them as the cap-stone of respect, vocation, and fashion.

## Words

Words for headgear in English derive from one PIE root, with two families, one Romance and one Germanic.

### PIE root *kadh*, to cover, protect

Latin: *cassis*, helmet
German: *Has*, hat
    English: hat (725), hood (700)

Latin: *cappa*, cap or hat
    Italian: *cappello*, hat
        *Cf.* Spanish *sombrero* from *sombra*, shade—Spaniards sought shade not warmth, as in umbrella (Latin *umbra*, shade) and parasol
    French: *chapeau*, hat
        Russian: шапка (shapka), hat

# 77. Mind

## Mind Speaking for Man

Imagine an indignant man fueling the fire of his anger with a self-righteous flourish: 'I'm going to give that guy a piece of my mind.' Taken literally, his words can amuse as much as he may intend them to impress.

How might he cut this piece from the whole, how large or small a piece, how thoughtful the giving? He gives a clue to how small the piece will be, if he emphasizes "that guy" instead of "my mind." By emoting more than thinking, he will probably not speak for his mind at its best. Since man and mind share the same root and should be synonymous, pity this noble endowment wasted in anger! So, mind you, now—when you mind your own business, let your mind have its say.

Let's first keep in mind that no path in the history of mind should bring that angry man to the brink of his rant: its etymology gives no clue to anger. Mind in English and *mente* in Romance, from the first, have referred to intention, thought or memory. When we keep a friend in mind, we keep her in memory, not in brain or in head. On this foundation, the family of words in the roots man-, men-, min-, mon- and mus- refer to the wider work of man's mind.

Taking up the first task in that work, to mean (888) and its cognate mind (900) share roughly the same date of origin. If a person means something, he keeps it in mind as a purpose of conduct—a primary meaning of mind. As a child, it was important whether I meant to do anything that was bad. 'I didn't mean to do it' was the first meaning of 'to mean,' as it stated intention. To mean meant to signify more than a hundred years later (1000). In other words, what I meant first meant what I meant to do, not what my words meant to mean. We preserve this meaning when we call someone with good intentions well-meaning.

So many expressions refer to the association of mind with memory that we can easily understand its abstract meaning. If I have not lost my mind (1369), many expressions come to mind (1374), which associate mind with memory or intention from time out of mind (1386), although we did not refer to people out of sight and out of mind until later (1539). In one of the earliest uses of the word, the yearly or monthly mind (900) celebrated the feast day of a saint or of the dead. "To my mind," Hamlet remembers, when he refers to his memory of his father's wassail as "a custom more honored in the breach than in the observance" (I, iv, 14).

Variations on the men- root—summon (1205), mention (1300), remember (1330) and memory (1340)—started to widen the view that the English language was taking about the processes in and out of mind. Summon, derived from the Latin root *mon-* to bring to mind, as in admonish, with the addition of *sub* (sum-), meant to admonish someone of his need to be present, usually, in a court of law. By a summons, a court calls someone to appear before the bar. To make mention of something brings it to mind. To remember predates memory, because the prefix 're-' characterized colloquial Latin in the formation of Romance words.

Beyond remembering and commemorating, mentioning and summoning, English speakers used mind more generally after 1400. Being of sound mind (1395) they could either speak their mind or keep it to themselves (1400), while they conceived a thought in their mind's eye (1412) and brought it to mind (1433). Although they might be of one mind (1496) with others and know their mind (1508), they could later be of two minds (1530) and in no position to give anyone a piece of their mind (1572). Not being of a mind (1585) to do what they first intended, they might change their mind (1591). They might easily enjoy a good mind (1674) in a particular frame of mind (1711) to have half a mind (1726) to speak candidly. Half-minded, they could easily loose their peace of mind (1743) and have to apply mind over matter (1759) so that they could make up their mind (1824). These expressions remind (1645) us of English elaborating the relationship of mind to memory, intention and soundness of mind over a period of nine hundred years, with a particular emphasis on mind in the larger sense of mental power from 1395 to 1824.[15]

As cognates, man and mind share the same family. Of sound mind, *Homo sapiens* tries to know his mind well enough that he can pass beyond half a mind or even two and make up his mind in the end. It works better whole than in pieces. Wholeheartedly, he may then take upon himself the burden of minding his business in meaning, admonishing, mentioning and summoning. He takes up the burden of history by remembering. When he gets its pieces together, man takes full possession of his mind not only as family but as a friend who speaks well for him.

## Words

Mind shares its origin with man.
In its long life, it has represented many aspects of human thought.

### PIE root *men*, mind

Greek: *mantis*, seer
Latin: *mens mentis*, mind
    Italian and Spanish: *mente*
    Romance adverbial suffix:
        Italian: *abilmente*, ably (with able mind)
        Spanish: *habilmente*, French: *habilement*
    English:
        mind (900) and man (825), because he uses his mind; mindful (1340) to muse, to ponder or dream

to amuse, to divert from musing, or to bring to musing (as a diversion)

Russian:
па-мять (pamyat)—Russian prefix *pa*, later + *men*—memory
муза (muza), muse

**PIE root *aum*, perception (related to PIE *men*)
and *hew*, to perceive**

Latin:
*aveo avere*, to desire; *avidus* and *avarus*, avid and avaricious
*audeo audere*, to dare; and *audio audire*, to hear

Russian:
ум (um), mind; and умный (umnij), intelligent
раз-ум (raz-um), reason; and раз-уметь (raz-umet'), to understand

## 78. Out of One's Mind

### Crazy Words for Crack Pots

In my tender youth, after I gave some evidence that I didn't have the sense I was born with, my mother would say that I was driving her to distraction. She did not mean that I was distracting her from work, but that I was driving her out of her mind. We have always been told to keep our wits about us and stay in our right mind, so that we may not wander about beside ourselves and out of our wits. Like giving someone a piece of our mind, these images suggest quaint pictures of misplacing our mind and forgetting where we have put it; or taking leave of our wits and sitting beside ourselves, unable to get back in. Since crazy first meant cracked, doesn't it also make sense to call crazy men cracked? Modern science has made more sophisticated definitions of mental illness than these, but our language clings to simplistic images that represent concepts of insanity as the opposite of sanity, a screw loose in the machine or a crack in the old nut.

The phenomenon of divine possession in antiquity gives a clue to the difference between ancient and modern concepts of mind. The ancients regarded the mind as a slate, inscribed with human characters, until superhuman powers, heavenly or demonic, erased it and wrote in theirs. A prophet experienced ecstasy, when he was standing outside of himself (Greek *ec*, outside + *stasis*, standing), while divinity possessed him. Mantic and vatic describe prophets, through whom divinity speaks. In

Russian, a madman goes out of his mind (с-ума-сшедший [s-uma-sshed-shiy]) or is simply without it (без-умный [bez-umnyy]). Deranged (1790) and demented (1644) describe a similar departure from rationality. Since nut has represented a man's head, off of one's nut or nuts also describes possession in modern colloquialism.

German *Wüt* represents the classical words for prophet, Greek *mantis* and Latin *vates*. *Wüt*, wood, the oldest but now archaic English word for insanity, gives an example of this possession,[16] when its god Woden, raving in battle, took possession of a warrior. We commemorate Woden on Wednesday, Woden's day. Similarly, a berserker, a Norse warrior with a bear sark, shirt, raged like a bear—actually, became a bear—in battle. Men remained men until gods possessed them. When my mother asked what possessed me to drive her to distraction, she did not really think that the devil made me do it, but her language suggested that he had.

Possession might appear more diabolical or ridiculous than divine. The moon (Latin *luna*), in this sublunary world, where witches ride and demons rule, might make men lunatic (1290) or, with humorous innuendo, loony (1872). In a modern version of berserk, an irrationally violent man goes ape. Calling him crazy as a loon or a coot expresses more poetry than possession. The loon wails eerily in the evening and the coot cavorts stupidly in breeding. In contemporary life, when the post office drives one of its workers crazy, he goes postal. In whatever age, some baleful influence possesses men.

Mad tells a similar story of an old word with simplistic interpretations. As old as wood, but still used in the modern world, mad started its history referring to extravagantly foolish behavior—mad plans in a mad world—two and a half centuries before it referred to insanity. This origin in foolishness and hapless, hopeless insanity has tinged the word, "with contempt or disgust, quite inappropriate in medical use, or in referring sympathetically to an insane person as the subject of an affliction." Mad describes extravagant behavior in language as bad as the madness it describes: a man falling so madly in love with the latest fashion craze that he madly sports it about town, acts, some may say, like a candidate for a madhouse. While it referred to insanity, a madhouse (1697) offered asylum without benefit of medical treatment. It first described a place to which a reckless man should be sent. Phrenetic, from Greek *phrenitis*, inflammation of the brain, offers an exception proving the rule that most words for madness do not refer to illness. English psycho or Russian псих (psikh) refers colloquially to psychosis. Mad's reference to sanity and insanity teaches a lesson: if we do not choose our words carefully, simplistic thought turns pathos to pathology.

What possesses us to speak so carelessly? I get mad just thinking about it! Of course, I should start by correcting my own careless word choice. The Reverend John Witherspoon, Presbyterian minister and signer of the Declaration of Independence, commented on a man's saying mad when he means angry. He called it an Americanism, but careless word choice characterizes no special nationality. Since mad arose early—and with a wide reference—it has slipped from one meaning to another.

Madness may rave and rage. A mad dog suffers from rabies, originally a Latin word describing hydrophobia. From within its PIE root, rabies describes violence. Vergil uses it to represent the Sybil possessed by Apollo: *et rabie ferā corda tument*, "and her heart swells with fierce madness."[17] Just in case madness does not sufficiently represent the possession, Vergil adds *ferā*, fierce or feral, to modify it. Her rage raves like a wild animal's.

Without a feral nature, mad arose from a PIE root for changing or maiming. Other words or phrases describe our departure from the wholeness of sanity by going off the track or departing from the norm. In Latin, *delirium*, deviation from the straight track of the plow, gives a clue to the Romans' origins as farmers. Any farmer deviating from the straight track of his plow had to be out of his mind. Delirious (1703) describes a temporary state of fevered confusion; *delirium tremens* (1813), the hallucination of alcoholism. Perhaps a farmer might seek peace and quiet in the evenings in his rocking chair; off his rocker, he would have no peace. Russian нормальный (normal'nyy), sane, and не-нормальный (ne-normal'nyy), insane, describe sanity and insanity as normal or not. Deviation from the norm describes many concepts of insanity: insane consists in not being sane; unbalanced, in not being balanced. Such standards assume that insanity steps from the straight line of sanity.

Other words for madness do not picture possession, maiming or departure from the norm, but a flaw or lack. Crazy (1617) and crazed (1592) both meant full of cracks—the glaze on a tile may become attractively crazed (1400), but a crazy (1576) ship may become disastrously unseaworthy—long before crazy referred to a deranged mind. When we call someone cracked or crack pot, we revive this image of the head as a damaged vessel. Whacked or bonked, a man becomes whacko or bonkers. We call him addled (1646), because an addled egg does not hatch. With a screw loose, his mind becomes unhinged (1732). In vivid colloquialism, we can say that someone does not play with a full deck or that he is ten cents short of a dime.

Irrational and even violent madness confuses and frightens us. It so contradicts mild and rational humanity that we at first attributed it to divine or diabolical possession. In the enlightened Renaissance, Erasmus wrote his *Praise of Folly* to prove that no man can be free of it.[18] We appreciate this theory as part of his smiling Christian humanism, but we know the pathos of a funny farm where deranged people laugh when nothing is funny. Accepting life as uniformly permeated by folly may allow our carelessly facetious language to mix contentedly flawed humanity with sadly broken lives.

## Words

In his *Praise of Folly*, *Moriae Encomium*, Erasmus praises madness as characteristic of all mankind. This work of urbane, Christian humanism turns about *Homo Sapiens* to *Homo Insipiens*. In facile colloquialism, we can also dismiss the world as going mad; but our traditional words for madness often focus on primitive concepts of the mind's possession by divinity. They also reflect its departure from a norm, or its violence, which are evidence of madness but not its causes. In the modern world, health care, aided by science, has given a madhouse the dignity of an asylum or a hospital.

### PIE root *men*, mind

Latin:
>*mens mentis*, mind; and *dementia*—out of mind—madness
>*non compos mentis*, "not in complete possession of the mind"

English: demented (1644), mad; (1858), affected with dementia

Russian:
>с-ума-сшедший (s-uma-sshedshiy)—ума, mind + сойти (seti), to go out—going out of one's mind
>без-умный (bez-umnyy)—без, without + ум (um), mind—without mind

### PIE root *uat*, to inspire

Latin: *vates*, prophet, observing omens from the Vatican Hill in Rome
>English: vatic, relating to Vatican seers; and its synonym, mantic

German: *Wüt*, one filled with divine frenzy, seer; *wütend*, crazy

English:
>wood (725)—nothing to do with trees—insane
>Woden, a god raving in battle; Wednesday, the day of Woden

PIE root *moito*, to change

Latin: *muto mutare*, to change
    Latinate English: mutable
Germanic English: mad (725), wildly foolish; (1000), insane

PIE root *rebh*, violent

Latin: *rabies*, madness
    English:
        rage (1297), violent anger; (1325), madness
        rabies (1661), hydrophobia

PIE root *gno*, to know

Latin: *norma*, carpenter's square
    English: norm, normal, abnormal
    Russian:
        нормальный (normal'nyy), sane
        не-нормальный (ne-normal'nyy), insane

PIE root *spen*, to span

Russian:
    пятá (pjatá), heel; пятить (pjatit), to move back
    спятить с ума (spyatit s uma), to go balmy

PIE root *meik*, to mix

Russian: по-мешанный (po-meshannyy), deeply mixed up, balmy


# 79. Angry Mind

What makes a man angry? 'The Devil made me do it' offers a lame explanation. Most words for anger look inside man more than outside. The word anger itself takes its root from a man's anxiety in mind or body; choler, from the bile in his spleen; animosity, from his breath, mind or spirit; but ire, from drive in the swift movement of God's creation. Pathology traces it to a constriction in the throat that makes him tense; psychology separates its rationality from irrationality that divides his soul; its irrationality may become demonic evil or even a curse. Give the

Devil his due! We can see tense faces and violence, but etymology reveals causes.

In his *Republic*, Plato defines irascibility as one of the two irrational parts of man's soul. Including pride, anger, fear, courage or passion, it is superior to concupiscence, the second part that included the appetites. Man's irascibility, therefore, held the middle ground between appetite and rationality, the third part. Many words for irascibility, entering English from the early fifteenth century until the later sixteenth century, reflect passions that make the stuff of tragic character. Shakespeare, for example, uses spleen (1300), an organ of middling influence, synonymous with irascibility, in reference to gaiety, whim, impetuosity, courage and proud, hot temper. In his drama, proud men indulge unruly spleen, deaf to peace; they also happily burst it in stitches with laughter or, in whimsy, entertain a thousand spleens leading them a thousand ways, but finally drawing within its gloomy cave.

The first Latin and English words for anger reflect this dangerously ambiguous middle ground. Wrath (900) first represented God's righteous indignation and then (950) man's violent anger. Wroth, the adjective of wrath, describes stern or truculent character in *Beowulf*. Entering English four hundred years later, ire descends from the Indo-European root for divine power, cognate with Greek *hieros*, sacred and strong, and iron, the strong metal. In poetry, ire rhymes with fire: "Burn'd Marmion's swarthy cheek like fire, / And shook his very frame for ire" (1808). Irate, indignant customers know what they are talking about when they complain to the manager. Ire and wrath stand firm, but they still need control.

The origin of animosity, on the other hand, gives anger a rational root. Latin *animus*, mind, can describe courage degenerating into arrogance or anger. With this double edge, animosity first meant bravery and then anger impelling men to action. English animus describes the feeling of anger that a man tries in vain to repress. Trying to be objective, but animated by animus, he expresses anger by action. Animus and animosity describe his mind's angry intention. Since the mind may not always rule itself, an evil demon (бес [bes]) in Russian may drive a man to fury (бешеный [beshenyy]) or sinister evil (зловещий [zloveshchiy]). Beware of righteous wrath and indignant animosity—they may be the Devil's henchmen.

Greek choler (1386) and its Latin equivalent, bile (1665), attribute irascibility to one of man's four bodily fluids, which the ancients called humors. Between the sanguine, active humor of blood (Latin *sanguis*) and the passive, phlegmatic humor of phlegm, choler/bile and black choler/bile, secreted by the spleen, held the middle ground, just as irascibility held the middle ground between rationality and appetites. Choler and bile came to mean anger in 1530 and not just a bodily humor in 1836. From *cholera*, French took *colère* as its word for anger. Following a development similar to that of spleen, animosity and wrath, choleric (1386) first described a fiery nature and then an irascible one.

Atrabilious (1651), of black bile, and melancholy (noun, 1350; adj., 1526), of black choler, also refer to the humor between blood and phlegm. Atrabilious has always meant irascible. As an adjective, melancholy first meant irascible, but, in the Elizabethan era, it became fashionably sad. Animosity, wrath and choler, unlike spleen, started in strong emotions and ended in anger. On the other hand, melancholy started in anger and ended in gloom.

Different sparks set anger aflame: rationality ignites animosity; irrationality, ire; and physicality, choler and bile. In addition, external suffering ignites passion; and grief ignites anger. Anger first described grief and, later, wrath. In its origin, passion (Latin *patior, passus*, to suffer) described the suffering of Christ (1175) and later (1374), any overpowering emotion like love or hate. Much later (1530), it described an outburst of anger. Passion reflects complex emotion, but anger, simple irascibility.

Animosity and spleen flash courageously; choler and bile flow dyspeptically. Anger suffers grief; passion just suffers. Man's irascibility folds in and folds out of complex layers. Neither good, nor evil, these layers unfold a nature compounded of angels and demons. A wise man emphasizes the importance of controlling anger; he might also emphasize the importance of identifying its sources and the ways in which they affect him with good or infect him with evil.

## Words

To the question, "Why do you become angry?", we may answer, "That's a dumb question!—annoying people keep provoking me." Our answer is self-serving, because it ignores the physical manifestations of anger, which we should control. Five sets of PIE roots describe anger, as physical constriction, driving motion, bodily humor, or bad spirit and deceit. We all know that we should control anger, and understanding its vocabulary may help.

1. **PIE root *angh*, to squeeze, constrict, pain**
   Latin: *anxius*, anxious
   English: anger (1250), pain; (1325), wrath; anguish (1220), excruciating pain; (1230), excruciating distress; anxiety (1525), uneasiness of mind

2. Three PIE roots describing motion driving to anger:
   I. **PIE root *i* or *ei*, to go**
      Latin: *eo ire*, to go; *iter itineris*, going, journey
         Spanish and Portuguese: *ir*, to go
      Russian: идти (idti), to go
   II. **PIE root *eis*, to drive in quick motion, divine power**
      Greek: *hieros*, strong, quick, lively, sacred
      Latin: *ira*, anger, ire
         Italian and Spanish: *ira*
      English: ire (1300), irascible (1398), irate (1838)
   III. **PIE root *yehr*, that which goes, year (related to the PIE root *eis*)**
      Latin: *hora*, hour; *Horae*, the Hours, goddesses of the seasons
      English: year (900)
      Russian:
         яровой (yarovoy), spring, referring to a season of the year
         ярость (yarost), fury; яростный (yarostnyy), furious (*cf.* Latin *ira*)

3. **PIE root *ghel*, to shine, green**
   Latin: *cholera*, bile
      Italian: *collera*, anger; French: *colère*, anger; Spanish: *colera*, anger
      English: choler (1386)
   Russian: зеленый (zelenyy), green; желчь (zhelch'), choler

4. Two PIE roots describe spirit in anger
   I. **PIE root *ane*, to breathe**
      Latin: *animus*, mind
         English: animosity (1432), animus (1818)
   II. **PIE root *dheu*, smoke, dust**
      Greek:
         *thumos*, spirit, spirit, anger, thyme (an incense); *cf.* Latin *fumus*, smoke
         *thuma*, sacrifice
      Latin *foedus*, foul, disgusting; and *bestia*, beast
      Russian:
         бес (bes), demon—Grimm's law: 'f' and 'b' interchange.
         бесить (besit), to infuriate; бешеный (beshenyy), furious

5. **PIE root *phol*, to trick, deceive**
   Russian: зло (zlo), evil; злость (zlost), malice, fury

# 80. Mood, Humor and Temper

## Tempering Humor and Mood

The last essay recorded mind's first appearing in English about the year 900, and taking on its modern meaning about 1400. In the intervening five hundred years, mood jumped in to fill the gap. Having appeared at about the same early date, it represented the functions of mind, until the word mind itself started to take what we now regard as its proper place. Were people more moody back in the old days? The European Renaissances from 1100 to 1500 did bring enlightenment, but *Homo sapiens* has always exercised rationality to temper his moods and his humors.

For a clue to the early meaning of mind and mood, let's look back at the Latin *animus*, mind or spirit, and its translation into Anglo-Saxon *mod*. According to the historian Bede, who lived about the year 700, God "set in the mind of a monastic brotherhood" to exhume the bones of Saint Cuthbert (*inmisit in animo fratrum . . .*) so that he, in his relics, might do as many miracles after death as he did in life. Two hundred years later, an anonymous Anglo-Saxon translator of Bede's *History*, translated *animo* as *mod* (*God onsende in thara brothra mod . . .*). A nineteen-century philologist has defined *mod*, like Latin *animus*, as "the impulse of thought and action."[19]

Like *animus*, *mod* also had magnanimous moods. In his eponymous epic, *Beowulf*, of great courage (*mod*) and wise in mind (*mode*), received his meed of praise as a brave (*modig*) warrior. The Anglo-Saxon *mod* and *modig*, meaning courage or mind, and brave, have descended into English as mood and moody. Descending, both in time and in character, *mod* started like the Latin *animus*, as in magnanimity, and descended in its modern meaning to the temporary—usually gloomy or irritable—impulse of the moment. Beowulf did not win fame just because he was moody. His *mod* animated him and supplied a word for the human spirit.

German has preserved *mod* in its word, *mut*, courage, which in its compounds represents a wide spectrum of disposition from humility (*Demut*) and heart (*Gemüt*), to grace (*Anmut*) and good nature (*Gutmüt*), gentleness (*Sanftmut*) and patience (*Langmut*), all the way to magnanimity (*Großmut*) and hybris (*Übermut*). We most likely recognize *mut* in *gemütlich* that describes the warm good cheer of German hospitality. The progeny of the Proto-Germanic root *modaz* fell to moodiness in English, but jumps from humility to hybris in German.

Humor has also defined the inner life of man. This fluid concept, as part of ancient medical theory, described the four humors—blood, phlegm, choler, and melancholy—representing the four chief fluids of the body. Their disposition or tempering achieved the proper balance in human personality. Off balance, they created the inconsistency from which humor, as we know it, springs. In *Every Man in His Humor* (1598), Ben Jonson described it as "bred by affectation and fed by folly." A moralist disparaged humors, because they often overwhelmed reason: "A wise man sheds the predominancy of all humors, for he is to live the life of reason and not of humors" (1675). The rabble happily embraced their humors. Their humor became popular; wit became literary: "Wit raises human nature above its level, humor depresses it" (1759). Humor flows naturally from within our being; wit, from our wits, with more effort. Down to earth and from the heart, humor serves as a synonym of mood, when we refer to a person in a good humor or a bad humor.

To good or bad humor and mood, we may also add good or bad temper, but temper aims at a midpoint. It refers to a balanced mood or humor. Temperature first referred to balance (1430) and later to the balance of heat and cold (1670). Temperament refers to the balance of our dispositions that make up our lives. Keeping our moods in balance always challenges even the wisest among us. We can move easily to a temperate climate, but not as easily to a temperate life. "Our minds," Dryden lamented, "are constantly wrought upon by the temperaments of our bodies." No wonder mind took over for mood! Preferring the word, however, does not make preferring mind and not moods much easier.

Taking a final look at mood, humor and temper, let's imagine their adjective forms—moody, humorous and temperamental—describing people. What sort of a friend would we prefer—a moody, a humorous or a temperamental one? Certainly a moody friend would be our last choice, but a temperamental one would not rate much higher. He may be moody parading about in a highfalutin disguise. Surely, we would prefer a humorous friend. At first, he seems like a good choice, but mind hasty decisions. Not tempered by tact, kindness or simple good sense, our friend's humor might so drive us to distraction that we would happily run back to the temperamental or the moody one. According to its original meaning, humorous refers to one humor above the others. At least, the temperamental or moody friend may listen to his other muses as much as to the laughing one.

I can't humor you. Let's mind our moods and humors and deal with them. They weave the complexion of who we are, as much as our mind. Just make sure that your mind, taking their temperature each day, tempers them between zero and boiling.

# Mood, Humor and Temper

## Words

Three PIE roots provide etymologies for mood, humor and temper:

1. **PIE root *mo/me* (?), endeavor, will, temper**
   Proto-Germanic: *modaz*, mind, zeal, courage, anger
   German:
   *Mut*, courage, mood; *Anmut*, grace, elegance
   *Demut*, humility; *Gemüt*, heart, soul, mind
   *Gleichmut*, equanimity; *Großmut*, magnanimity
   *Gutmütig*, of good nature; *Langmut*, patience
   *Sanftmut*, gentleness; *Schwermut*, melancholy
   *Übermut*, hybris; *Wehmut*, wistfulness
   English: mood, mind or heart (900), courage or pride (*Beowulf*), anger (1175)
   Russian: сметь (smet), to dare, venture

2. **PIE root *ugu*, moist**
   Latin: *umeo umere*, to be wet; *umor/humor*, humidity, liquid
   Italian: *umore*, mood, humor, temper; Spanish: *humor*, mood
   French: *humeur*, mood; and its doublet *humour*, humor
   English:
   humid (1549), humor (1340);
   humorous (1380), relating to humors; (1705), witty

3. **PIE root *temp*, to stretch, extend**
   Latin: *tempero*, I mix in due proportion, moderate
   English: temper (noun, 1387; verb, 1000)

Two Slavic roots for mood:

### PIE root *nert*, power, vital energy (1380)

Greek: *aner/andros*, man
   English: android, like a man
Russian: норов (narov), temper, disposition

### No known PIE root

Russian:
   настроить (nastroit), to build, tune, incite
   настроение (nastroyeniye), mood, sentiment, humor

## 81. Maniacs and Muses

Man's mind not only comments on his world, it reminisces memories of ancestors and divinity implanted in his soul. John Locke defined God as "the eternal infinite mind which governs all things." God's mind governs man's. Man's, ironically, even named 'money' after *Juno Moneta*, "Juno the Monitor," in whose temple it was minted. His mantra, however, transcends the monetary.

From time immemorial, memory has memorialized the dead. Appropriately, 'mind,' in its earliest use (900), translates *memoria*, in commemorating a departed soul. When memory (1340) finally entered English from French, it had a similar meaning. The phrase 'in memory' evokes eternity, and its monument (1300) first meant a sepulchre memorializing the dead. 'To mourn' (888), derived ultimately from mind, was mournfully mindful of the dead. Memory evokes care, sorrow and anxiety.

Memory carries a burden. Sometimes God's mind has revealed itself to man in frightening ways. Monster (1300) delivered a divine monition (1375), i.e. an admonition (1374) giving a premonition (1456) of the future. Since the divine mind tended the growth of every plant or animal, it intended any departure from the norm to serve as a warning. A chicken born with one head more than usual, for example, presaged some evil; a star shooting from fixed constellations presaged an event of cosmic significance, such as the death of a king. Much later, inhuman cruelty defined a monster (1556).

Man seeks the divine because it has been implanted in him. Hindus embody it in a mantra (1808). In mantic arts, like necromancy, cheiromancy, oneiromancy—the suffix -mancy defines 117 words—God's mind in man's fills him with a mania (1400). But since man's mind cannot contain a god's, mania wipes away his rationality. Maniac (1604) and paranoia (1857, from Greek *para*, "beyond" and *nous*, "mind") represent abnormal psychology in modernity. In antiquity, they represented humanity filled with divinity.

Within man's control, divinity inspires him. The nine Muses, daughters of Mnemosyne, goddess of memory, empower man by their inspiration. Often pictured in a mosaic (1400), a muse reminds her devotees, who dwell in her shrine, called a museum (1615), of the music (1250) of the spheres. For Byron, nature sounds this "echo" of the divine: "There's music in the sighing of a reed:/There's music in the gushing of a rill;/There's music in all things, if men had ears:/Their earth is but an echo of the spheres." Originally adjectives, music and mosaic sprang from the

Muses. As nouns, they described sounds or stones harmonizing a reminiscence of divinity.

Plato held that what the mantic god, the divine monitor, and the Muses do for their special devotees God has done for every soul, in which He has implanted a memory of divine ideas. The process by which man remembers his divine nature is *anamnesis*, translated into English as reminiscence (1589). Reminiscence retrieves forgotten ideas.

Mourning in black, reminiscing in gold,
contemplating in mantras, frenzying in manias,
admonished by monsters, inspired by music,
man's mind is sought and seeks.

## Words

One PIE root lays a foundation for man's mind inspired and taught by God.

**PIE root *men*, to be mad, to love, think, remember, show, warn, and foretell**

Greek:
    *mimnesko*, I remember
    *mathos*, learning, Aeschylus' *pathei mathos*, "wisdom through suffering"
    *mantis*, seer; *maenas maenados*, orgiastic worshipper of Dionysus
    *mousa*, muse, goddess inspiring the thought of a poet

English:
    manic, maniac; and -mania, as in kleptomania
    mantic, the mantic arts, the arts of prophecy
    -mancy, as hydromancy, pyromancy, etc.
    praying mantis, insect with hands, forelegs, seemingly in prayer
    muse, goddess inspiring the mind of a poet
    museum, home of the muses; mosaic, work of the muses
    mathematics, originally, knowledge, now precise knowledge
    polymath, knowing many things
    mentor, wise adviser of Odysseus, often Athena in disguise
    mnemonic, memory device
    a-mnesia, without memory
    a-mnesty, without memory (of wrongdoing), truce

Russian:
    мания (maniya), mania; маньяк (man'yak), maniac
    муза (muza), museмузей (muzej), from French *musée*, museum

пá-мять (pámjat´), memory—prefix па- similar to the re- in remember
памятник (pamit), monument, memorial, tombstone

## 82. Bravery

### Bravery in Marble and in Flesh

English words for bravery describe a manly, courageous heart in terms of down to earth qualities. The facets of this description have appeared through the centuries. From the classical world, English inherited virtue and fortitude in the thirteenth and fourteenth centuries. The fifteenth and sixteenth centuries ascribed bravery to a visceral or ethnic origin, and even to the clothing or valor of a grandee. Gutsy words describe bravery starting in the nineteen century.

In antiquity, *virtus*, virtue, started with virility, which Julius Caesar claimed as the "singular," "pristine" quality of Roman soldiers. Cicero civilized this military prowess: "*virtus* must be especially sought," and "*virtus* of the mind should be preferred to *virtus* of the body" (*virtus sit expetenda maxime . . . animi virtus corporis virtuti anteponatur*). Following Cicero's advice, English preferred virtue, first in the thirteenth century (1225), as moral excellence and secondarily as bravery in the fourteenth (1350). As the vernacular junior, English confirmed its learned senior's pairing of physical courage with moral character, but a warrior of any calling recognizes these as two sides of the same coin: "In virtue there is hope," Tacitus observed, *Spes in virtute*. (Greek *andreia*, bravery, from the root *andros*, man, also describes bravery, which Andrew, André and even Andrea, possess eponymously.) With this enlightened wind filling its sails, virtue sailed off to abstraction as the chaste virtue of a woman, the practical, particular virtues of vacuum cleaners, or a musician's *virtu*.

Caesar, in a rare use of fortitude in his *Commentaries*, mentions the boast of the Gauls about their "glory of war and fortitude" (*gloria belli atque fortitudinis*). Almost fifteen hundred years later, fortitude had gone off to abstraction to take its place as the third of the four cardinal virtues and the gift of the Holy Spirit. Chaucer mentions it in *The Parson's Tale*: "There is a vertu that is called fortitudo or strength," the Parson preaches, "through which a man despiseth anoyouse thinges. This vertu is so myghty and so vigerous that it dar withstonde myghtily and wisely kepen hymself fro perils that been wikked, and wrastle agayn the assautes of the devel" (1387). Like virtue, fortitude also continued the classical tradition of bravery. Unlike virtue, however, it has remained firm in its courageous endurance of pain and adversity.

Virtue and fortitude, properly, standing on the shoulders of giants, have ascended a pedestal—two statues of an antique monument. Bravery, naturally, marched off to find gritty new life on its own native soil.

With no classical connection to bravery, valor (1330) predated its adjective valiant (1390), and referred at first to the noble value of the grandee, just as Latin *valor* meant value. It did not describe bravery until late in the sixteenth century (1581): "In the days of chivalry, the soul of valor animated every thought" (1782). This valor motivated valiant lords of the realm leading stout-hearted knights and warriors into battle. Its Latinate word root and mediaeval origin pairs Prince Valiant with King Arthur.

To describe bravery, the sixteenth century, starting with the stomach, but ending with gallant clothing, looked beyond Caesar, Cicero and Prince Valiant. Unlike the word heart, stomach (1374) had a long history as bodily organ before it meant pride (1513) and courage (1532). When Shakespeare in *Henry VIII* (1613) speaks of "a man of unbounded stomacke, ever ranking himself with Princes," he alludes to pride aspiring to noble courage. Mettle, a doublet of metal, referred to the ardent spirit of a horse or a man (1581). Spirit, though an old word in English (1250), referred to courage late in the sixteenth century (1596). Brave (1581), as courageous, from Italian *bravo* and Latin *barbarus*, barbarian, associates a man with bravado (1599), and eventually with the wild courage of a savage. Gallant (1596), derived from Spanish *vestido di gala*, ceremonial robe, gala transliterating the Arabic word for a robe adorning a guest. Gallants dressed as well as they acted. At the end of the sixteenth century, gallant braves showed their mettle by fighting with spirited bravado.

From the end of the eighteenth century through the early twentieth, bravery turned from the outside to guts and spark within. Spunk (1537) sparks courage (1773) with more spark than strength. Pluck, chicken guts plucked, got down to the intestinal fortitude of a boxer. In America, spectators at a boxing match drank a hard cider called gumption, a Scottish word originally meaning common sense. Gumption gave bravos extra doses of bravado. Nerve (1538), first sinew, eventually meant courage (1809) and audacity (1887). Gut, an ancient word in English (1000), described a rower at Cambridge University putting "his guts into" the race (1893). Pluck, nerve and guts reside in the strength of the body; spunk and gumption, in the glint of the eye.

In the history of bravery, the thirteenth and fourteenth century laid its classical foundation, the sixteenth added the social panache of a gallant's bravado, and the nineteenth looked to its spark and guts.

## Words

Bravery originates in manhood,
which may either speak like a barbarian or wear gallant clothing;
but it stands firm, with whatever dress or speech.

### PIE root *baba*, baby talk

Latin:
> *barbarus*, barbarian, people speaking in what sounded like babbling bar-bar
> *pravus*, de-praved; and *bravus*, villain
>> Italian: *bravo*, brave
>> English: brave (1485), bravado (1599)

### PIE root *uiro*, man

Latin: *vir*, man; and *virtus*—the quality of a man—virtue, bravery
> Italian: *virtu*, excellence; and *virtuoso*, a man demonstrating excellence
> English: virtue (1225), and virile (1490)

### PIE root *ual*, power, strength

Latin:
> *valeo valere*, to be strong; and *valor*, value
> *ad valorem*, according to value
>> English: valid (1330), valiant (1390), and pre-valent, con-valescence

### PIE root *bherergh*, high, strong, secure

Latin: *fortis*, brave; *fortitudo*, bravery, fortitude

### PIE root *mon*, man; from PIE root *men*, mind: Man has mind.

Latin: *masculus*, masculine
> Spanish: *macho*
German: *Mann*
> English: man (825), manly (1225), manliness (1375)
Russian: муж (muzh), husband; мужество (muzhestvo), courage

### PIE root *ker/sker*, to cut

Russian: храбрость (khrabrost'), bravery

## 83. The Virtue of Goodness

From two good ol' families of English words, virtuous and good have formed a classic union. Virtue came to this union high-born with classic pedigree; good flowed into it from deep within its native blood line. Both have make good, because the virtue of the word good is that it covers a wide range of what is fitting; and the good of the word virtue is that it covers a wide range of what is powerful. They both have histories as good as any of our morality. Virtue has ranged so widely that it started as the strength of a man and ended as the weakness of a woman, but good has grown too independently to be stereotyped. It's too good a word for our language to lose.

The diversity of good arises from its PIE root, a cognate of gather, meaning to join or unite—"We gather together to ask the Lord's blessing." We can observe the split between the moral and the non-moral uses of the word in the difference between the adjective and its substantive: in *Beowulf*, the adjective good describes that which does what it should do: a good fire keeps us warm, a ticket is good for a certain period of time. Good is good at describing what fits: a good herb heals wounds; a good debt can be paid; and any ship is a good ship, as any lady, for that matter. Even a burglar can be good at what he does, even though he does not work for the good of his berg. The substantive use of the adjective, the good, saved good, for its own good, from fitting too easily, in too many places. The good and goodness (888) referred to moral conduct as early as *Beowulf*. God's goodness (1000), the *summum bonum*, left no doubt about the morality of the word. For goodness' sake, let's not forget that God is good.

Without prescriptive morality, man's good gropes its way along a tortuous path. With reference to man, good first referred to the well born (1154). Even today, we all know people too good for the likes of us (971). Good did not refer to virtuous conduct until late in the fourteenth century: "The hand that hath made you fair hath made you good (Shakespeare, *I Henry* 3, 2, 102). The moral course of good, however, does not chart a predictable moral course. Goodfellow (1386) described a boon companion, displaying good cheer, but not necessarily goodness. God was the highest good, but men were good at so many things that human goodness had its own appropriate lambency. Goodness gracious, I've a good mind to tell what a good time we've all had in our lives with all the degrees of goodness! The good book just starts to tell the story.

Virtue tells a similar story on a limited scale. The narrowness of virtue arises from its derivation from Latin *virtus*, the quality of a man that referred to a full gamut of human potential, selfish and unselfish. A loan word from Latin, virtue entered English in the thirteenth century, with the same moral and amoral sides of its power from the beginning, but with a narrower application than that of good. As appropriate to its cognate vim and vigour, virtue referred to particular power. The humanistic tradition of classical ethics set its range of meaning, first in reference to a particular moral excellence of man and, particularly, to his observance of moral law. Although virtue might describe the power of God (1250), it could also describe the warlike prowess of man (1350) or the particular power of stones, herbs or wine. The faculty of an academic institution awards diploma's by virtue of the power vested in it. One can also speak of the virtue of one system in contrast to that of another. On the other hand, academic and antique virtue has sailed off to virtuosity.

Virtue has boasted a virtuous pedigree.
Goodness has grown in native soil,
and it has thrived beyond the piety of its classical synonym.
Goodness seeks God more genuinely than virtue;
and we should think better of forgetting it.

## Words

### PIE root, *ghedh*, join, fit

English:
> to gather
> good (*Beowulf*) and goodness (888)
> garboard, the board on the bottom of a boat joining the keel:
>> "The garboard is generally of American elm; it is best that planking above be of American elm or oak to within a foot of the water-line" (Kemp, *Manual of Yacht and Boat Sailing*).

German: *gut*, good
Russian: годный (godnyi), fit, suitable; and год (god), year

### PIE root, *bhad*, good

English:
> better, best,
> boot, not a shoe, but advantage or profit:
>> A bootless journey does not reach its goal.
> to boot, to improve, to remedy

### PIE root, *deu/duonus*, to work well, win respect

Greek: *dunamai*, I am able
    English: dynamo, dynamic and dynamite

\* \* \*

Latin: *bonus*, good; and *bellus*, beautiful
    Italian: *buono*; and *bella/bellissima,* beautiful
    French:
        *bon,* good
        *beau* (masc.)/*belle* (fem.) beautiful—A belle of a ball has a beau.
    Spanish: *bueno,* good; and *bonito,* beautiful
    English: bonus, money given to a good worker; bonny, as in bonny lassie

### PIE root *ker/sker*, to cut

Russian: храбрость (khrabrost'), bravery, and хорошо (khorosho), good health

# Physical, Psychological and Social Good
. . . .

# 84. Holistic Health

## Holistic Health

When advocates for integrated exercise, diet and lifestyle recommend holistic health, the root of their phrase derives from wholeness. The Proto-Indo-European root of the Germanic word healthy and its Romance cognate, salutary, refers to wholeness. At its root, health is holistic.

We all want to be whole, but wholeness requires that we do a whole lot more than we may want. The first English words referring to holistic health referred to it as salfivic (1591): in plain Germanic English, healing and saving first healed and saved souls, not bodies. Mind and hour, you may remember, also minded saints and set hours for prayer, before they minded men and set hours for business. Healing (825) made the soul whole 175 years before it made whole the body (1000): "The Lord healeth the broken in heart and bindeth up their wounds" (*Psalm* 147. 3).

Similarly, but with fewer years separating their spiritual and physical applications, saving souls (1225) predated saving lives (1250) by only twenty-five years. French *sauver*, to save, entered English later but more fully evolved than the native Germanic heal. As a parallel, vivacious (1645) also entered English later but more fully evolved than lively (1000). The Romance tradition, classical or biblical, has consistently arisen from deeper traditions of authors and authority than the native Germanic. Salutary (1490) and, of course, salvation (1225), in their first meanings, also referred to saving souls. Salutary now refers to a healthy lifestyle, but salvation has survived to represent the ultimate health of the soul, that is, its eternity. About the spirit, holistic health has drawn words from the Romance religious tradition. In that tradition, when someone asks, 'Are you saved?,' he most likely means, 'Do you have salvation?'

The unity of body with soul, however, makes even mortal men whole. Beowulf returns from battle whole, *hal* in Old English: *lindgestealla, lifigende cwom, / heaðolaces hal* ("battle-brother, back from the fray / alive, whole"). Only toward the end of the ninth century, after *Beowulf*, did whole mean entire, and eventually almost entirely material as in wholesale (1417). Hale and hail complement whole as doublets. Hale and hearty compliment health in the elderly. Being hale constitutes health. Halesome and its doublet wholesome described food that made men whole, hale and healthy. The Russian Saint Olga was as hale as she was holy. She and her Scandinavian relative Helga are wholesome girls. Health boasts wholeness in body and in soul.

Because health empowers life, benevolent greeting wishes for it. "Hail be thou!" (1205) must have been much older than its first date in the OED: to hail meaning to greet occurred five years earlier (1200). "Hail, fellow, well met," so emphasized the hearty good will of the meeting that it now stands as a noun phrase for a man very eager, probably too eager, to make friends. From worldly salutation to a heavenly one, Hail! both begins and serves as the title of the classic prayer, *Ave, Maria!*. Hail Mary! preserves the antique Hail! to translate its invocation. Like the archaic adjective 'quick' in the phrase, "the quick and the dead," Hail! gives special dignity to Mary's invocation. Hello Mary! would not properly dignify "Holy Mary, the Mother of God."

Hello shares no common origin with Hail!. It evolved either from halloo used in hunting or from some form of Latin *illac*, by that way, in Spanish or French *hola*, Whoa there!: "If I fly, Marcius, / Halloo me like a hare," says a Shakespearean character, who asks his friend to prevent him from hightailing from battle like a scared rabbit.

Wholesome cordials also empower raising our glasses with hale and hearty good wishes. Shakespearean characters call their toast a health: "Come, love and health to all," Macbeth says with a benevolence belied by his crime. Much earlier, men of old England said *Wes hal*, Be hale!, when they raised their glasses. *Wes hal!* has become Wassail!, at first the salutation and later the drink (1300), especially spiced wine at Christmas. In a wicked perversion of a wish for good health, Lady Macbeth speaks of deceiving Duncan with "wine and wassail." The Italians raise their glass with *Salute!*; the Spanish, with *Salud!*; and with *Salut!*, the French. In Ireland, *Sláinte* (slawncha), refers both to salvation and health. How appropriate that, in raising their glasses, the Irish join benevolence with faith.

From ancient to early modern times, Roman culture contributed to the vocabulary of health. Latin *salvia*, the herb sage, by its name, made men healthy: *Cur moriatur homo, cui salvia crescit in horto?* ("Why would a man perish, for whom sage in his garden doth flourish?") Folk medicine relied so much on herbs that salve (700), "a salutary and saving ointment," dates back as one of the oldest words in English—with healing also for the spirit: "the comfortable salve of God's word" (1563). Much later, salubrious (1547) described medicines, seventy years before it referred to climate (1615).

Latin, *salve*, Be hale!, commonly hailed a friend; and *Salve, Regina* hailed Mary, Queen of Heaven. Salute (1380) and salutation (1382), though now formal, military words for greeting, at first wished a person good health. A salvo (1591), a volley of fire, conveys a salute. 'Greetings and salutations!' addresses a person and wishes him well.

Just as the Romance salutary and salubrious have gilded the lusty German cornflower of *Gesundheit*, holistic has also modified it redundantly. In any tradition, health is whole. In greeting and toasting his friends, man has whole-heartedly wished them whole, and he has extended that wish into eternity. Wholeness arises from his deepest hope for well-being.

## Words

Four PIE roots for health focus on its power and wholeness.
With these roots, we also make healthy greetings and toasts.

1. **PIE root *solh*, whole, complete**
   Latin: *salus salutis*, health; *salubris*, healthy; *salvo salvare*, to save; *salvia*, sage
      French: *sauver*, to save
      English:
         salve (700), to save (1225); salutary (1490); salubrious (1547)
         Salut! / Salud!, a toast from French and Spanish
   Greek: *holos*, whole
      English: holistic and holocaust
2. **PIE root *ual*, power, strength**
   Latin:
   *valeo valere*, to be strong; *valetudo valetudinis*, health
   *Vale*!, Be strong! Farewell!
      English:
         valid, valedictory
         valetudinarian (1703), one constantly concerned with
            his ailments
3. **PIE root *kailo*, whole, unharmed, well**
   German: *Heil*, health
   English:
      whole (888), entire
      hale (1000) and its doublet hail (1205), health (1000), healthy (1552)
      halesome (1200) or wholesome (1200) conducive to wholeness
      Wassail!(1205), Be hale!, a toast from Danish
   Russian:
      целый (tselyy), whole (*cf.* ц in цар (tsar); цензура (tsenzura),
         censure; or in цвет (tsvet), color, which often represents a PIE kv)
4. **PIE roots *dru* and *doru*, wood; hence, solid and lasting**
   Russian:
      здоровье (zdorov'ye), health; Здравствуйте (Zdravstvuyte), Hello!
      здравый (zdravyy), robust (cf. Latin *robur*, oak)

## 85. Sound Sanity and Sanitation

When Juvenal, a Roman satirist of the first century A.D., listed blessings for which a man should pray, he ended his first line with a phrase that has become a shibboleth of physical education:

Oran/dum est ut / sit // mens / san (a) in / corpore / sano.[20]
Prayer must be made that there be // a sound mind in a sound body.

Juvenal exhorted his reader to pray for a sound mind in a sound body, without suggesting, as do modern advocates of physical education, that a sound mind arises from a sound body. When John Locke quotes this phrase in his *Thoughts on Education*, he also does not suggest that mind should depend on body, but that together they fully describe a man's "happy state"—"A sound mind in a sound body, is a short, but full description of a happy state in this World: he that has these two, has little more to wish for; and he that wants either of them, will be little the better for anything else." The insane man may have a sound body, but since *sanus*, soundly and wholly healthy applied to both, gives a "full description" of happiness, he can not sanely boast of happiness. Juvenal's choice of *sanus* as the adjective for their physical and mental health also anticipates a full and happy chapter in the progress of modern hygiene.

Sane has had a slight variation from its usual description of soundness of mind. Chaucer brought mind together with soul when he mentioned Saint Jerome 'saning' his body by fasts and his soul by prayers. Fifty years later, the noun sanity (1432) referred to soundness of body, and three centuries later, its adjective sane (1694) described it. Aside from occasional references to soundness of body, sane has mostly referred to soundness of mind.

Shakespeare first used sanity to mean soundness of mind. Hamlet has determined to act the part of a madman so that he may avenge his father's murder. Polonius, a foil to this trick, contrasts sanity and reason with Hamlet's "madness." He sees "method" in it, but he still thinks that "Reason and Sanitie" could not have "delivered" the pregnant, happy word choice that Hamlet's madness just "hits on": "How pregnant sometimes his replies are. A happiness, that often madness hits on, which Reason and Sanitie could not so prosperously be delivered of" (*Hamlet* II. 2). Polonius corroborates reason by sanity when he weighs them in the balance with madness. He uses natural pregnancy and delivery to describe unnatural birth. Hamlet knows better than Polonius: he uses reason to make his sanity seem mad.

The OED explains sanity's reference to mental health by citing the authority of the Latin pair *sanus/insanus*, in which *insanus* almost always referred to mental disorder. In English similarly, insane (1560) and insanity (1590), in their reference to mental disorder, entered English earlier than sane (1721) and sanity (1602), in their reference to mental order. By the early eighteenth century (1721), therefore, following the lead of its antonym, sane meant "sound, whole in his senses," in recording physicians' first thoughts about mental health. Sane and sanity, in their reference to mental health, have arisen in the early modern world.

More than four hundred years before the Romance sane (1694), the native Germanic sound (1200) at first meant free from disease, but it has flourished beyond the classical references of sane and sanity. Without the authority of classical authors like Juvenal, sound has expanded from mental or physical health to a broad field. In addition to being of sound mind or body, we can also enjoy sound sleep or sound economy. Soundly germinating in native soil, therefore, sound has grown beyond its physical and psychological roots.

English commonly has pairs of Germanic and Romance synonyms, like sound and sane. We have already seen, in the case of other pairs of synonyms like Romance saving and Germanic healing or of Romance vivacious and Germanic lively, that the Romance words have arisen fully developed from deeper traditions of authors and authority than the native Germanic words. This authority makes sane resonant in its descent from the classical tradition but it also limits its application. It is understandable, with this background, that we translate the Romance words *sana* or *sano* in the phrase *mens sana in corpora sano* by the Germanic adjectives healthy or sound. Surely, we are not so insane as to think that we can replace the good native words healthy or sound by a word of narrow application from the classical tradition! Let us embrace the sanity of living on our native soil, and leave such quixotic pursuit to linguists.

Just as sane served eighteenth century physicians distinguishing sanity of mind from that of the body, the *sanus* root provided the nineteenth century with words for its new concept of hygiene. Hygiene, by the way, entered English in the late sixteenth century (1597). Hygienic (1833) made its entry at about the same time as the sanitary arts. Sanitary (1842) arose specifically in the context of unhealthy, i.e. dirty, conditions of the lower classes and of an army on campaign. Since cleanliness was next to godliness, the great unwashed, citizens or soldiers, needed baths perhaps as much as evangelism. Responsible government in the nineteenth century learned that it owed sanitation (1848) as a municipal service to its citizens and as a federal service to its soldiers. *Sanus* helped to define this cleanliness as part of health.

*Sanus* from Juvenal's classic line has advanced beyond modifying mind and body. Sanitary now refers to cleanliness promoting health; and sanity, exclusively, to the health of the mind. In both cases, refinements of modern hygiene have expanded the soundness of *sanus*. Sanity and sanitation have cleansed the streets and dark corners of urban life. They bear witness to its complexity and diversity, but their blending does not ring with the fundamental simplicity of *mens sana in corpore sano*.

## Words

"Cleanliness is next to godliness," not found in the Bible, but a middle-class piety of nineteenth century urban hygiene, connects sanity in 1432 with sanitation in 1842. Their root *sano*, along with *swento*, traces a history of sound minds and bodies

### PIE root *swento*, healthy

German: *Gesundheit*, health; also, an interjection after a sneeze
English: sound (1200), healthy

### PIE root *sano*, whole, healthy

Latin: *sanus*, sound, healthy
    Italian and Spanish: *sano*
        Italian: *sanare* and Spanish: *sanar*, to cure
        French: *santé*
    English:
        sane (1694), of body; (1721), of mind; insane (1560), of mind
        sanity (1432), of body; (*Hamlet*,1602), of mind; insanity (1590),
            of mind
        to sane (1386), sanitation (1842), sanitarium (1851)

Russian words for sanity or insanity focus on the mind or spirit.

### PIE root *men*, mind

Russian:
    в своем уме (v svoyem ume), of sound mind, sane
    без-умец (bez-umets), without mind, insane

### PIE root *dheu*, smoke, dust

Russian:
    дух (dux), spirit, ghost

душа (dusha), soul; душеный (dushevolny), sane, soulful, sincere
душевно-больной (dushevno-bol'noy), insane, of weak mind

### Of uncertain origin
Russian:
рассудочный (razumnyy), reasonable
без-рассудный (bez-rassudnyy), not reasonable

## 86. Happiness

### Happiness, Content with Good Things Happening

*Ode on Solitude*, Alexander Pope

Happy the man, whose wish and care
    A few paternal acres bound,
Content to breathe his native air,
        In his own ground.

Whose herds with milk, whose fields with bread,
    Whose flocks supply him with attire,
Whose trees in summer yield him shade,
        In winter fire.

Blest, who can unconcernedly find
    Hours, days, and years slide soft away,
In health of body, peace of mind,
        Quiet by day,

Sound sleep by night; study and ease,
    Together mixed; sweet recreation;
And innocence, which most does please,
        With meditation.

"Happy the man…"—when Alexander Pope wrote this beatitude at age 12, he was announcing his career as a classical poet. Since he wrote the poem in lyric stanzas, he was also acknowledging the Latin poet Horace as his model. Horace inspired a moral ethic, in addition to a lyric form. This Roman poet loved to picture himself in the countryside "content," to use Pope's word, to breathe "native"—Italian—"air" and to enjoy simple pleasures of the pastoral. To write this earnest piece of his *juvenilia*, the young Pope had probably been more well read than well bred in this ethic. He could not have proven its worth in long years, but he had set its Horatian definition in their foundation. The attributes of his beatitude—"Happy... Content... Blest...."—describe it; and the Indo-European roots at the foundation of these words give some clues to its nature.

Happiness starts with hap, that is, chance, good or bad. When hap happens perhaps, mayhap, these happenings make us happy. Making good things happen should certainly make us happy. But, happy or not, we have gotten our cut: the Russian noun счастье (schast'ye), happiness, and its root noun часть (chast'), cut, suggests that our slice of the pie makes us happy.

When luck comes our way, we must seize it by the forelock—Be quick! It moves fast and it's bald behind—but luck and lock, by their common root, bend in various directions, as the cookie crumbles or the ball bounces. "Come what may," we say of luck, but, mayhap, we can take charge and make good hap happen. The Russian noun фарт (fart), luck, cognate with the German verb *fahren*, to ride, suggests that we may be in the driver's seat: its cognate, the verb везти (vesti), to have luck, also means to drive. *Fata nolentem trahunt, volentem ducunt*, the Stoic philosopher Seneca has said, "Fates drag an unwilling person; they lead a willing one." If we stay in the driver's seat long enough, we may zig instead of zag.

After correcting the zig, we may, perhaps, direct the zag to a straight path. The root of the Latin adjective *bonus*, good, suggests that we are good when we do good. After all, we get a bonus for doing good work. Goodness has its rewards, the best of which are not just money in the bank. Another derivative of the root further suggests that good works make us blessed: the *Beatitudes* state, among other things, that we are blessed by making peace. The root of the Russian благо-словенный (blago-slovennyy), blessed, suggests that we shine in our good deeds.

Although goodness has its rewards, the best of which are not material, it must originate in some material increase. Its spiritual radiance starts with an actual spark. Pope describes the materiality of his man's happy life: "herds with milk... fields with bread, flocks... with attire... trees... yield him... fire" Within elemental earth, from which we receive our slice of luck, fertility allows life by giving the means of its increase. The fertile increase of herds, fields, flocks and trees makes the happy man's life possible. The names Felicia and Letitia reflect the two roots of felicity and laetation, the latter a word for fertilizer. The hap of a Frenchman's happiness, the *heur* of his *bonheur*, rooted in *augurium*, the promise of increase, embodies the fertile foundation of his good life.

Romance languages show us a key to happiness. In French, *content*, means happy. If we say in English that we are content with our lot in life, we may not be smiling broadly—or smiling at all. Only by saying that we are perfectly content, do we indicate happiness. Happiness may start with a material spark, but it can not end in the merely material. The happy man must be content—perfectly content—with his cut of the pie. When the adverb 'perfectly' completes the happiness of the adjective 'content,' the contentment possesses the Horatian equanimity of the happy life. "Innocence" makes our sleep "sound."

## Words

What makes us happy? Is it all just luck or should we count our blessings? Or should we work to win them, and then cling to what we have? Five categories of words describing happiness start to answer these questions.

### 1. HAPPY HAP AND ITS TURNS

#### PIE root *kob*, to suit, fit

English:
> hap (1205), chance, good or bad; to happen (1375), to occur by hap
> happy (1375), lucky because good things happen
> per-haps (1528), literally, through haps; by chance

#### PIE root *leug*, to bend, turn

German:
> *gluck*, luck—by a good turn, bending in your direction.
> *locke*, lock of hair—bending in any direction.

English: luck and lock (of hair)

#### PIE root *uegh/weg*, to bring, to move

Latin: *veho vehere*, and *vectura*, to carry
> French: *voiture*, vehicle
> Romance English: vehicle

German: *Fahrt*, ride; and *fahren*, to ride
> Germanic English: wagon

Russian:
> фарт (fart), luck
> везти (vesti), to drive, have luck; везучий (vezuchiy), lucky

### 2. GETTING YOUR CUT

#### PIE root *skei*, to cut; and *kwezd*, piece

Latin: *scindo scindere*, and *scissus*, to cut
> Romance English: to rescind, to cut back; and scissors

Germanic English:
>    to shear, to cut; and shears
>    share—cognate of часть (chast')—piece cut from the whole

Russian:
>    часть (chast'), part cut from the whole;
>    счастье (schast'ye), happiness

## 3. BLESSINGS EARNED

### PIE root *deu*, work well, win respect

Latin: *beatus*, blessed
>    Italian: *beato*
>    English: blessed (1175), and beatitude

### PIE root, *bhel*, to shine, blaze

Latin: *flagro flagrare*, to burn
>    English: flagrant, burningly obvious

Russian:
>    благо (blago), good, blessing, weal
>    благо-словенный (blago-slovennyy), blessed

## 4. FERTILITY

### PIE root *dhel*, suckling, nourishing, happy

Latin: *felix*, fruitful, originally, in reference to fruit trees
>    Italian: *felice*, happy; Spanish: *feliz*,
>    English: felicitous (1789); felicity (1385); Felix, Felicia, and Felicity

### PIE root *prai*, beloved, free

English: free and friend
German:
>    *frei* and *Freiheit*, free and freedom
>    *Frieden*, peace; *zufrieden*, satisfied, content

### PIE root *aug*, to increase

Latin:
>    *augur*, a diviner foretelling the augury
>    *augurium*, augury, prophecy of increase;
>    augmentation, increase of the undertaking

*Augustus*, title of the augur, august in augmenting
    Italian: *Tanti auguri!*, Best wishes! (literally, Such great auguries!)
    French:
        *heur*, chance, fortune (from Latin *augurium*)
        *heureux*—literally, full of good augury—happy
        *bon-heur*, good augury, happiness
        *mal-heur*, bad augury, unhappiness

## PIE root *da*, to give

Latin: *do dare* and *dono donare* to give
    Italian: *dare*, to give; Spanish and Portuguese: *dar*; French: *donner*
    English: to donate and donor
Russian:
    дать (dat), to give
    у-дачный (u-dachnyy)—у- showing complete action—successful

## Of uncertain origin

Latin: *laetus*, originally, fertile in reference to crops, livestock or words; happy
    Italian: *lieto*, happy
    English:
        Letitia, a woman's name, happiness
        laetation (1164), fertilizing; to laetify, to fertilize

### 5. CONTENT

#### PIE root *ten*, to hold

Latin: *teneo tenere*, to hold; *contentus*, content
    Italian and Spanish: *contento*, content, happy; French: *content*
    English:
        tenacious, holding on, persistent
        content (1400), satisfied with what has been given

#### PIE root *vel*, to will

German: *wollen*, to will
Russian: до-вольный (do-volnyy), satisfied

### GOOD LUCK!

French: *Bon chance!*; Spanish: *Buena suerte!*
German: *Viel Gluck!*; Russian: удачи! (udachi)

## 87. Holidays

### Keeping the Feast

In Alexander Pope's Horatian ethic of the happy life, virtue walks hand-in-hand with happiness. Men can be perfectly content with their hap and their virtue in pursuing it, but they can hope for festivity as a periodic renewal. The ancients can also teach us an ethic for keeping our feasts, but their lesson may seem more solemn than festive. Actually, it shares equal parts of solemnity and festivity, but in a way that we may not expect. A nice combination of the two made their lives whole.

The caricature of ancient Romans that pictures them living their lives in perpetual feasts has as much truth as exaggeration. They had so many potential holy days at leisure for feasts that they defined time for work as days not at leisure: Latin *otium* describes leisure, as in the English adjective otiose, done at leisure; and its word *neg-otium*, not leisure, describes business, as in the English noun negotiation. Leisure for divine worship was the rule; business for worldly gain, the exception. Ancient piety regarded this priority to the gods' business as smart business. A word of early Christianity, liturgy, literally, "the people's work" praising God on holy days, anticipated the people's success doing business on work days. In a secular version of this priority, people serve business by taking time off today so that they return to do better business tomorrow.

We can observe this priority in the roots of words in Russian for festivity. The noun празд-ник (prazd-nik), holiday, has the same root as the adjective празд-ный (prazd-nyy), idle. Further, because Sunday requires leisure for worship; Russians call Monday the day "after no work," по-не-дельник, po (after) + ne (no) + dělja (work). Just as we ascend to the all-powerful sun on Sunday; and on Moonday, that is, Monday, we descend to our world of shadows, Russian emphasizes sabbatical leisure in naming the following day for its absence.

Our ancestors defined their lives by the divine, both in its presence and in its absence. Shakespeare, for example, first used the pair of words, vulnerable (1601) and invulnerable (1595), in both cases, to refer to a divine gift. Macbeth arrogantly boasts that he is fortune's favorite: "Let fall thy blade on vulnerable crests; / I bear a charmed life" (*Macbeth* V, 8). In battle, he boasts, "let" wounds be a mortal's lot; a 'charm' shields him. Another Shakespearean warrior, King Philip, also describes invulnerability as a divine gift: "Our cannons' malice vainly shall be spent / Against the invulnerable clouds of heaven" (*King John* II, 1, 252). Being wounded is the mortal rule; not being wounded, the immortal exception; but the one shares in the other. Achilles, for example, was invulnerable in all but his heel. A divine charm both made him invulnerable and left him vulnerable. Shakespeare's two warriors attributed invulnerability to divine favor and vulnerability to its absence, just as the Romans considered leisure as time for religion and business as its absence. In both cases, piety defined life, with secularity an exception.

In acknowledging the sublunary shadowland subordinate to solar radiance, our ancestors put holiness in the foundation of their lives. Divinity created the seasons of the world and humanity praised it in its due season. They called holy days solemn, without at first making solemn serious. Solemn, by its root, refers to days coming every year. We are reminded of this yearly return, when New Year's Day rolls around every January 1st, and we have a holiday. In our secular world, we decide how we make that holiday holy. Solemn has come to mean serious, because we had an obligation to celebrate when worship constituted solemn duty. To celebrate, also by its root, means to congregate for the purpose of praising a god. Celebrating a solemnity, therefore, observes a holy day in the season to congregate for the purpose of praising the divine. Congregating for praise cultivates the community that cultivates divinity.

Holy days also required festivity, but festivity did not make merry any more than solemnity meant austerity. Ancient festivity required meat from animal sacrifice, anathematized as an offering on the altar for a god; and, by his gracious concession, blessed as a feast on the festal board for his worshippers. Feasting creates community between humanity and divinity. Keeping faith with divinity strengthens the heart, and keeping the feast with believers nurtures and warms it.

The heritage of foundational divinity offers modern man subtle challenges; but his popular culture so embraces secularism as sophisticated and rational that it can not appreciate their worth. Condescending secularists call piety medieval; but—to take a simple vestige of solemnity—not saying grace before a meal limits and isolates its festivity. The history of the Russian word толока (toloka) represents this limitation. It refers to communal work and the feast that follows it, but the etymology of the word refers to a sacrifice to a god and the feast that follows it. This ritual of the brotherhood of man has continued into the secular world; but it has abandoned the fatherhood of God that makes it whole. Modern man suffers from isolation through many causes, but the separation of human festivity from divine solemnity has isolated him the most.

## Words

Holidays have holy origins. Praising gods and keeping the feast made them holy.

### PIE root *solo*, whole

Latin: *solemnis—solus* + *annus*, that which happens every year
    English:
        solemn, of religious obligation in yearly calendars (1325),
        of serious oaths or religious obligation (1315),
        gloomy (1601), as in Hamlet's "suites of solemn black"

### PIE root *dhes*, holy

Greek: *theos*, god
Latin:
    *ferire*, to wound,
    *festum / feria*, in paganism, a holy day for animal sacrifice and
        feasting; in Christianity, a holy day, other than the Sabbath
            Italian: *fiesta*; French: *fête*
            English:
                feast (1200), festival (1483), festive (1651), festoon (1686);
                fair (1292), from *feri,* gathering of buyers and sellers,
                      often secular, but, in origin, religious

### PIE root *qel*, to speed, crowd

Latin:
    *celebritas*, multitude, celebration, honor
    *celebro celebrare*, to frequent, praise, celebrate

### PIE root *telek*, to pound, break; sacrifice in the IE language Tocharian

Russian: толокно (tolokno), oatmeal, in origin, grinding grain as a communal task; but, usually, assistance to a farmer during harvest, or a feast after communal work

### No certain PIE root

Russian:
    празд-ный (prazd-nyy), idle
    празд-ник (prazd-nik), holiday
        *cf.* понедель-ник (ponedel-nik), Monday, по-не-дельник: по (after)
        + неделя, (nedělja), Sunday, no working, the day after Sunday, не
        (ne) + делая (délaja), not doing work

# 88. Parties

### Faring Well at the Board

The classic happy life has set down an ethical foundation of equanimity and moderation. How did our ancestors fare at their tables and their parties in this happy state of mind? We can not know for sure. *Quot homines, tot cenae*—there are as many meals as there are men. Even Horace recommended tipping the balance of moderation on occasion—*Nunc est bibendum*, "Now is the time for drinking"—but some words associated with them indicate a simplicity of which Horace would approve. The happy life at the table has handed down words that point to an elemental simplicity in the enjoyment of food.

Take the word party itself: does it indicate a social party, a political party or the party of the first part? 'Let's have a party!' has become a cliché, but we forget the original context that tells its story: in the various partings of life, a man may organize a hunting party. If some of his party get lost, he sends out a search party to find them. When the lost are found and returned home safely, he organizes a "party of pleasure" to celebrate the successful event of their adventure. His parties have had different purposes. The hunting party and the search party had specific goals, but the party of pleasure simply breathed a sigh of relief. Perhaps it could be called a party of reunion, reuniting the hunters to celebrate their adventure. Many parties of pleasure, as gatherings of old friends, serve that purpose—'Thank God, we've made it through!'

Tea parties, garden parties, cocktail parties—this antique list can also include beer, pizzas and pajamas. As each generation defines its pleasure, it comes up with different phrases; but a party, whenever one throws it or whatever one calls it, does not deserve the name without a little—no, a lot—to eat and drink. In fact, the classic party of them all is the dinner party, at which food counts for more than any activity. The best rule for the host: serve more food than guests can possibly eat. They love the groaning board, and the host who keeps a good table. Table itself has come to represent the food he puts before his guests (1400). To say that one is addicted to the pleasures of the table evokes the image of the last of the big spenders like Diamond Jim Brady, those who especially enjoyed these pleasures and definitely tipped the balance of Horatian moderation.

Table (1377), a Romance word, and board (1200), its Germanic synonym, both represent food. Though the Germanic board may groan under the weight of vittles, it does not bespeak the good life as those happy souls around the sunny Mediterranean have enjoyed it. In traditional stereotypes, serious Germans eat to live; carefree Italians live to eat. In neighborhoods of northern European stock, bed and board (1386) stand for two necessities of life. In its day, a boarding house served meals, but its board did not groan; because the land lady was not preparing food for guests and the boarders ate so quickly that they cleared the board before it could feel any strain. Boarding houses recall the day when food preparation required more work than an unmarried person could manage. Fast food and the microwave, among many conveniences, have made such residences obsolete. "Oh, how the boarders yell, when they hear the dinner bell," echoes no more down our alleys.

The Mediterranean tradition has provided the boarders with words for meals beyond their daily routine. The table and the board are basic; the bench and the basket, just as basic, but they came to describe something special. *Banca*, bench or table in Italian, provided a flat surface, a bank, for financiers, who when they ate might also use that flat surface for a banquet. In origin, banquet, board, and table have the same meaning, but a banquet in English casts its ray of Italian sunshine on Germanic frugality. Sumptuous usually describes it. With a bit of French, a simple dinner party can turn into a *soirée*. Off on a day trip in the country, picnickers carried a rush basket, *juncata* in Latin, from which they called their trip a junket. In their basket, they might also have made a pudding which they also called junket. The junket basket represented the trip and some of its food.

Russian also gets down to the basics of hospitality: за-столье (za-stolye), tableful; and пир (pir), fire, both mean feast. These two words describe a feast in terms of two elements that reach to its heart—a tableful of friends beside a hearth makes any meal festive. They add up to уют (uyut), cosiness, literally, roof, under which the tableful by the hearth warms the heart.

Depending on their bill of fare, boarders or banqueters fared well or ill at their board. 'Fare' traveled far before it ended up on the menu. Originally, a wayfarer fared through his journey; but not much later, he more generally fared through life. Before entrepreneurs like Thomas Cook offered some comforts along the way, travel meant travail. A wayfarer's well-wishers rightly considered his wel-fare, when they wished him a fond 'Fare-well!' He paid for his fare to travel and for his fare to eat. How he fared on his journey depended on whether he might fare well at the boards of his hosts. After some good meals, to the question, "How have you fared, my friend?", he might answer, "Deliciously, thank you."

If his answer was "deliciously," his chefs had probably added salt judiciously. Salt gives salami, salad, sauce, and sausage both their names and their flavor. A good chef keeps it as a staple in his kitchen. He adds salt in equal proportion with sugar as a sweetener. If he is a Russian chef, he has has a word for this balance. In Russian, sweet [сладкий (sladkiy)] means salty—what's more, its words for banquet [на-слаждение (na-slazhdeniye)] and pleasure [слаждение (slazhdeniye)] also mean salty. A balance of flavors makes a good party.

In their contentment, our ancestors happily made much of little. They might have ended in excess, but they started with a wooden slab, a fire, a friendly tableful, and a basket to hold their pudding. When their board groaned with a sumptuous repast, they called it a banquet. More often they seem to have fared through life on fare that made parties of pleasure without a French or an Italian flair.

## Words

What makes a party happy?
The gathering, the time, the scene, and the fare?
We like to think that we party in our own particular way,
but the words that we use reveal some basics.

### GATHERING

**PIE root *per*, to divide, either in parting or in partition**

English:
> party, a division of a whole (1290)
> a division of a whole for a social purpose, "party of pleasure" (1716)

### TIME

**PIE root *uesper*, evening, west toward the setting sun**

Greek: *hesperus*, evening star; and Latin: *vesper*, evening star
> English: vespers, evening worship
> Russian:
>> вечер (vecher), evening; вечеринка (vecherinka), evening party
>> вчера (vcheerah), yesterday

### THE SCENE

**PIE root *sta*, to stand, as in station, stake and standard**

English: stool
Polish: *stolek*, stool; and *stol*, table

Russian:
>    стул (stul), stool and стол (stol), table, board, cuisine, office
>    за-столье (za-stolye), literally, tableful; feast at a common table

### PIE root *peuor*, fire

English: pyre, a fire; funeral pyre, pyromaniac
Russian:
>    пир (pir), feast, literally, a fire around which the feast is held
>    пир-овать (pirovat), to feast; пир-шество (pirshestvo), feast
>    пир-ожки (pierogi), pierogi, literally, party food

*Cf. Fogo de Chão*, fire on the earth, the barbecue pit of Brazilian gauchos

### PIE root *bheg*, break, river bank, bench

Italian: *banca*, bench, table
>    English: bank (1050), bench; and banquet (1483)
>    Russian: банка (banka), bench; and банкет (banket), banquet

### No known PIE root

Latin: *juncata*, junket (1382), a basket make of rushes
English:
>    junket, a pudding (1460), a picnic (1530) in a rush basket;
>        a pleasure trip
>    junk, old rope made of rushes
Russian:
>    уют (uyut), cosiness, comfort; literally, roof
>    Food, on a table, under a roof, warms the soul.

THE FARE

### PIE root *per*, to part, either for parting or partition

Greek: *poros*, journey through
Latin: *per*, through; *portus*, port; *porto portare*, to carry
English:
>    to fare (971), to journey; to fare (1000), to get on well or ill
>    Farewell!(1377), good wishes to a person setting out on a journey
>    fare (1205), food; to fare (1393), to be fed

### PIE root *sel*, salt

English: saline, salary (literally, salt money), salami, salad, sauce, sausage
Russian:
>    соль (sol'), salt, and солод (solod), malt

сладкий (sladkiy) and солóдкий (solódkij), sweet
слаждение (slazhdeniye), pleasure
на-слаждение (na-slazhdeniye), banquet, pleasure

## 89. Work

God has built the world and our ancestors have focussed their worlds within it. The words for it show us the fruits of their labors in such variety that it has crowned the same root with a *magnum opus* and manure

First of all, long after God had finished His own "work of creating" (*Genesis* 2.3), and had put Adam in the Garden of Eden "to work it," postlapsarian man continued to work the earth. "Those who work their land," *Proverbs* reminds us, "will have abundant food." Let's work out this concept: the verb to work took an object as a transitive verb before it worked as an intransitive verb without one. In other words, men worked the earth or a trade; they did not just work—products meant more than process.

Man did divinely ordained fieldwork for food, and then divine liturgy, literally, the work of the people, for his debt of praise to his creator. After also doing homework and finally housework, he wrought, by his handiwork, wickerwork (1719), ironwork (1451), clockwork (1628)—you name it, all the world's works. From a Germanic root and, therefore, less obviously derived from work, bulwark (1418), a work of boles, that is, tree trunks, had its doublet in boulevard (1772), since roadwork ran on boles-work. Workers built the town, and then they built and manned its workhouses (1100), to which towns eventually sent so many of their indolent poor that workshops (1562) took their place as more worthy of hard work. In the old days, people worked hands on.

As industry expanded, wright, one of the oldest English words, named many a worker. What a world have these wrights wrought! Plowwrights, wheelwrights, cartwrights, millwrights, shipwrights and many other wrights kept the world moving. Less obviously, wainwrights wrought wains, a doublet of wagons. Distinguish between the two homophones of playwright: he does not write plays, he wrights them. Playwrights, we hope, both wright and write plays right. So many wrights have been wrighting that some like cartwright and wainwright have become family names.

Greek has also pitched in to lend a hand. Its work, *ergon*, gave English a root as energetic as it is abstract. Energy in Aristotle's *Rhetoric* (III, 11, 2) describes the optimum condition of one "in work." By synergy, energy increases works "with work." The Greeks can also get down to earth: George works the earth—*ge*, earth, as in geography and geometry. Reaching up to heaven, a thaumaturge works wonders; and the Platonic demiurge, literally, does people work (*demos*, people), but He actually creates them.

Still on earth, organon described both a reed instrument and an organ of the body. A bagpipe, whose sack resembles a bodily organ, provided the image of the reed or pipe organ, for which Bach composed music. What a full-throated fulfillment to such a squeaky beginning! In an organism, organs work in synergy. Greek philosophers envisioned synergy of the demiurge with organisms, the world's most impressively comprehensive work! At first humbly related to this synergy but derived from French and not obviously related to *ergon*, surgeon described a man working with his hands (Greek *cheir*, hand). Chiefly concerned with mind-work, old-fashioned medicine left hand-work to barbers. Modern surgeons take up where the demiurge left off to keep a man's synergy energetic.

Latin *opus*, and more ambitiously, *magnum opus*, introduce the work of high culture. Any man can operate, but *opus* identifies his work as art—Beethoven, Opus 29. From Latin *opificium/officium*, doing work, English has derived office and officious. Office describing worship, as in priestly offices, points to the earliest practice of man's work praising God's. Too full of his offices, a man becomes officious. God willing, his work yields abundance: intensifying Latin *opus*, *co-ops* comes together as *copia*, and copious or cornucopia in English. *Opes* means resources, with an abundance of which, man enjoys opulence. We all hope that opulence will crown our work and leave us sitting pretty, but it's hard to get away from it—Latin *omnis*, all, originally referred to all the work.

Softening the 'p' of *opus* to 'v,' French *oeuvre* has also raised work to high purpose. English oeuvre describes a work of literature. With enough hard work, we write our *chef d'oeuvre*, the chief piece of work, a masterpiece. Back down to earth for bodily sustenance, we serve hors d'oeuvres (*hors*, outside of) before a meal, literally, "outside of the work." *Oeuvre*, shrinking to the suffix -ure, has come into English in manure and inure. Farmers work manure into the soil "by hand" (*manu*, as in manufacture). Necessity, in-uring them to the work-a-day world, puts them "in-work."

As inured as we become to work, words of work show us the wondrous world that its wrights wright. Imitating God's work has inspired many a *magnum opus*. When the end crowns the work—*Finis coronat opus*—optimists look for opulence flowing from its copious cornucopia. Urbane skeptics like Voltaire have questioned this optimism. Focussing on a candid young man traveling through this crazy, sublunary world, he wrote an amusing story to make pessimists of us all. 'Tis true 'tis pity, and pity 'tis

'tis true that our inspired *chefs d'oeuvre* may end up crazily *hors d'oeuvre*; but—let's crown this work with more matter than art—whatever optimism or pessimism we consider true, *vocat officium*, duty calls us to keep at it.

## Words

Man's work first worked the earth, and then sought wealth by various means. Its words have taken various meanings. Greek *ergon* and Latin *opus*, its two classical roots, complement the native Germanic word work.

1. **PIE root *uerg*, work**
    Greek: *ergon*, deed
        English:
            en-ergy (1581), literally, in work
            syn-ergy (1660), literally, with work
        French:
            *chir-urgion*, surgeon—literally, hand work
                English: surgeon (1338), originally chirurgeon
            *lit-urgie*, liturgy—literally, people work
                English: liturgy
    German: *wirken*, to work
        English: to work (888); wright (695), a worker, also a family name

2. **PIE root *op*, work—religious or agricultural; finally, God willing!, abundance**
    Greek: *ompnia*, of corn, an epithet of Demeter, goddess of agriculture
    Latin:
        *opus operis*, work
        *officium*, originally *opi-ficium*, doing work, religious duty, duty
        *copia*, originally *co-opis*, abundant supply
        *cornucopia*, originally *cornu copiae*, horn of plenty
            (from the harvest)
        *optimus*, originally the wealthiest man, the best man
        *omnis*, originally, all work and resource, all
        *opes*, resources, wealth; and *opulentus*, full of resources, wealthy
            French:
                *oeuvre*, work (of art); *manoeuvre*, maneuver
                *hors d'oeuvre*, literally, outside of the work;
                    (1714), out of the ordinary;
                    (1742), a course served before a meal
                *chef d'oeuvre*, literally, chief of the work; masterpiece

Spanish: *obra*
Latinate English:
  copious (1387); opulent (1601); to operate (1606)
  opus (1704), a work of literature or music
  optimum (1879), the best
Romance English:
  to manure, to work (soil) by hand
  to maneuver (man-euver), doublet of manure
  to inure (in-ure), to work one into something

3. **PIE root *orbh*, deprived of parents or freedom and subjected to forced labor**
English: orphan
German: *Arbeit*, work
Russian: работа (rabota), work; рабыня (rabynya), slave

# 90. Hard Work

What a Drag!

Inspired artists have done hard work, and solid citizens have found it fulfilling, but many call work drudgery without inspiration or fulfillment to enlighten its load. "The toil of man is irksome to him," observed Oliver Goldsmith, "and he earns his subsistence with pain" (1774). Those more focused on pain than gain consider working irking; irking even when it is effectively working. Drudgery, toil, and labor describe tasks that can tax more than they return.

Drudgery draws the sharpest image of exhausting work. Derived either from Middle English *dreogan*, to work or *drugge*, to drag, a drudge (1494), synonymous with slave in the earliest sources, merely trudges. Dr. Johnson called a lexicographer a "a harmless drudge, that busies himself in tracing the original, and detailing the signification of words" (1755). A drudge drudges, just as a servant serves, with their work imposed for someone else's benefit. Maid (1390; *cf.* maid servant) also designates not only generic work, but even the gender appropriated for it. Maid, a shortened form of German *mädchen*, had the fate of domestic drudgery. What labor, other than that of birth, could this young woman have done?

Drudgery, at least, got its work done. Toil turmoiled and struggled. In such a mill, it started out confused and bound for trouble. It turmoiled men in toils of war; but eventually, when the dust cleared, it simply worked hard: "On the steeper slopes especially the toil was great" (1860). According to its etymology looking back to *tudicula*, a machine for crushing olives, toil pounds toilers to pulp.

Working and working and working, toil redounds in rhyme to moil: "For worldly wealth, men can toil and moil all the week long" (1654). Men toil in turmoil; mired in mud, they moil: "They saw him daily moiling and delving in the common path like a beetle" (1849). Literal moiling wallows in mud: "I must moil on in this damn'd dirty road, and such pay will make the journey easy" (1687). (Municipal improvement always paves dirt roads.) Metaphorical moiling wallows, mired or swamped in toil. Slogging and slaving complement it. Slog, a variant of slug, hits hard. In cricket, batsmen slog; in baseball, they slug. A man slogs cattle around a farm; on his own, he slogs over a difficult course.

As a doublet of till, without bloodshed in war, toil describes unrelenting work in the field: "To till it is a toil" (1589). Toil gets down to the good earth in describing the work of farmers. When Jesus asks his disciples to "consider the lilies of the field, how they grow; they toil not, neither do they spin" (*Matthew* 6. 28), he refers, by exception, to toiling in fields. Farmers best exemplify this fulfillment in the garden: "Let not Ambition mock their useful toil," Thomas Gray reminds us.

Like till and toil, labor works the earth. We expect it in the phrase hard labor, since its etymology from the Latin verb *labi*, to slip, describes tottering and falling under its burden. Its past tense form *lapsus* gives English lapse and collapse. In English, labor describes hard physical work, especially on farms or in mines. The labor of childbirth appeared much later (1595). Under such heavy and hard burdens, a man or woman may lapse and finally collapse.

By any name, toil, drudgery and labor so oppress us that we recreate the vivid images of their etymologies: redundantly, we call drudgery a drag; toil really beats us up; we slog through work as though moiling through a swamp; and we stagger under the burden of labor.

More than toil and much more than drudgery, labor has dignity: *Laborare est orare*, "To labor is to pray," the motto of the Benedictines, sets up labor on God's good earth as man's prayer and service to his creator. "Come, labor on," the hymn calls us, "Who dares stand idle on the harvest plain, while all around us waves the golden grain?" Adding to its dignity and fulfillment, Adam Smith has defined labor in his *Wealth of Nations* as the backbone of their productivity: "The annual labor of every nation is the fund which originally supplies it with all the necessaries and conveniences of life" (1776). In a special, American application, Abraham Lincoln praised labor as the foundation of capital.

"What does the worker gain from his toil?"—a livelihood, and we also hope, satisfaction. We may embrace it as our both our fate and our fulfillment: "The best and sweetest far, are toil-created gains" (1748). On Labor Day, we can all celebrate.

## Words

Hard work exhausts us, because it drains our strength.
Drudge, toil, and labor, by their roots, vividly picture the drain'n strain.

### PIE root *au*, to draw

Latin: *haurio haurire* and *haustus*, to draw, drain
    English: to exhaust, to draw out, drain

### PIE root *tud*, to beat, strike, push

Latin: *tundo tundere* and *tusus*, to hammer, beat
    English:
        obtuse (1570); contusion (1879)
        toil (1292), dispute or turmoil; (1594), hard work
        to toil (1292), to dispute; (1394), to labor arduously

### PIE root *trewd*, to push

Latin: *trudo trudere* and *trusus*, to push
English: intrude/intrusion, protrude/protrusion; abstruse
Russian: труд (trud), labor; трудиться (trudit'sya), to work, toil

### PIE root *mel*, to melt, soften

Latin: *mollis*, soft
    English:
        to mollify (1412)
        to moil (1548), to toil, often in mud; (1566), to wallow in mire

### PIE root *menk*, to knead

Latin: *macerare*, to macerate, soften, weaken, torment
English: to make
Russian: мучиться (muchit'sya), to agonize, to suffer pain

### PIE root *leb*, loose, hanging

Latin:
    *labor labi lapsus*, to slip, fall
    *labor*, hard work—so hard that a man slips under its burden

*lapsus linguae*, a slip of the tongue
*laboro laborare*, to labor
  English:
    labor (1300), hard word; to labor (1350), to till, cultivate
    lapse (1526 as noun, 1641 as verb)

PIE root *dheragh*, to draw

English: to draw; to drag; draught/draft; dray; drudge

## 91. Leisure

After work, leisure gives free play for activity or inactivity. It tests our mettle as we make it idle or productive. Do we just sit and stare or get up and get started? As we beguile, pass, while, wile, and fritter away time or—heaven forbid!—even kill it, leisure defines and measures the progress of civilization as much as—and certainly in our own lives—even more than work.

As doublets, Romance leisure (1303) and Latinate license (1362) both allowed freedom to do something. Like pairs of Romance and Latinate doublets, legal and loyal, for example, leisure refers to commonality and license, to municipality. Later (1350), leisure meant license to have free time—to do something or nothing. Free of occupation, the fortunate few could call themselves 'at leisure' by 1340. In this sense, leisure, as a synonym of vacation (1386), referred to a period of leisure in law courts or schools (1456). By the fourteenth century, therefore, leisure and vacation established time for activity other than work.

By the sixteenth century, licentious (1535) referred to poets or painters using artistic license in words or images. Should a translator of the Bible, for example, be literal or licentious (1785)? At almost the same time (1555) of its first use, licentious referred to lasciviously, lewdly and lustfully libertine morality. Without a plan, leisure wanders into the devil's workshop; with its plan disciplined and directed, it creates its own workshop: "It is because he had imagination and leisures of the spirit," Emerson said of Edmund Bacon, "that he is impressive to men" (1856).

Leisure has created so many challenges that the original Latin word for it has not survived in good repute. *Otium*, leisure, has ended its life in otiose, idle wasting of time. Only in Spanish has its Romance derivative *ocio*, survived as leisure and not idleness—the folks on the Iberian peninsula have preserved its idyllic dream. Even the ancient Romans suspected it. Their phrase *otium cum dignitate*, peace with dignity, indicates the Roman Stoics' need to justify leisure.

A vacation need not be vacuously otiose. Recreation (1390) re-creates the body by food and, later (1400), by amusements or comforts. Recreation recreates creation: we share creation with our Creator as we recreate ourselves on vacations. Back in the day, for example, the nobility took to the chase. In our memory, big shots took to the road or to the air. *Quot homines, tot studia*—there are as many men as hobbies.

Not all recreation recreates creatively: the couch potato did not put down roots only in the twentieth century: *sic tamen absumo decipioque diem*, "Thus do I use up and beguile the day," said Ovid of his time in exile on the Black Sea. Latin *decipere diem*, to beguile the day, probably provides the basis for to beguile meaning to divert or to amuse and at the same time (1225) to deceive. We beguile time, when we chase ennui: "By sports like these were all their cares beguiled" (1764). We also beguile time by pastimes (1490).

Although we could beguile time in leisure, recreation, and pastime before 1500, we found more leisure after 1600 to while and even to wile it away. As a compound of to muse, first meaning to gape, to amuse meant first (1430) to distract or to cheat. Eventually, to amuse in 1631 and amusement in 1698, referred to ludicrous or trifling objects of diversion, which Pope defined with a sneer: "Amusement is the happiness of those that cannot think" (1720). Imagine Pope looking down on the great unwashed gaping in amusement.

Forty years later (1762), Boswell took comfort in amusement: "It was fine after the fatigues of the journey, to find myself in a theatre, my body warm and my mind elegantly amused." The OED, mediating between these two poles, defines amusement as "the pleasant excitement of the risible faculty by anything droll or grotesque." Now that we have parks, industries and even cities devoted to amusement, how can we deny its validity, and, of course, its profit?

Entertainment gives us a means of amusement. To entertain (1481) first maintained business, as it entertains thoughts of accomplishment. Soon (1491), entertaining maintained guests. Gracious entertainment did not content itself with bed and board. Entertaining guests extended to amusing them by 1626. Whiling (1635) away time spent it in some pleasant, but trivial, diversion. The eighteenth century had its commentary on this idleness: whiling away time so much resembled beguiling it that some authors dropped the 'h': "Happy industry that wiles the toils of labor with a song" (1817). By 1728, idlers were even frittering away and killing time.

Since modern man has more time at leisure, he makes so much of it that he has to be reminded that it first mandated action; that its amusement idled away time, and that its entertainment fell to the duty of his host. The entertainment industry suggests more than parlor games after dinner. We should all hope that our leisure can give us diversion without perversion.

## Work

Roots for leisure indicate freedom to choose and free time to exercise the choice. A man's license for leisure does not need to end in otiose vacancy.

### No PIE root

Latin: *licentia*, freedom, license, boldness; *licet*, it is permitted
    French: *loisir*, leisure
    English:
        leisure (1303)
        license (1362), permission; and licentious (1535), full of permission

### PIE root *hew*, away

Latin: *otium*, leisure, free time, idlenes
    Italian: *ozio*, idleness; Spanish: *ocio*, leisure; French: *oisiveté*, idleness
    English: otiose (1844), having no practical result, nugatory

### PIE root *eu*, to be empty

Latin: *vaco vacare*, to be empty; *vacatio*, freedom from military service
    Italian: *vacanza*, vacation; French: *vacances*; Spanish: *vacaciones*
    English: vacation (1386)
Russian: праздный (prazdnyy), idle

# 92. Play, Game, and Sport

## Play and its Complications

Leisure furnishes us with opportunities to work up a sweat. With their wide play, games may disport us, back and forth, from lazy vocation to hard-working avocation. By playing games, we have either more or less than a rollicking frolic. "Work and play," observed Mark Twain, "are words used to describe the same thing under differing conditions." By games, we either put game on the table for our livelihood or fritter it away at the gaming table.

    English embraced play (725) and game (725) very early in its life. In their etymologies, play implies exercise; and game, companionship. With ply and plight as cognates, play plies briskly in exercise. It can describe sword play—a gladiator plies his sword—or the swift, elusive play of light and shade. Child's play gives free play to movement; word play gives it to words. Game, related to Gothic *gamana*, people together, suggests team spirit. Games exercise our bodies, by giving play to a number of us in a body. As the parable of Livy and Saint Paul has reminded us, there is no 'I' in a body of men.

Specific activities characterized plays and games. Hunters catch game (1290) birds and animals. In gambling, a variant form of gaming, gamblers shared dice and cards at gaming tables. True to its origin in community, game does not always involve physical activity. Play, true also to its origin in brisk exercise, referred to drama by 893. In a playhouse (1000), drama finds a home; on a playground (1794), play plays many roles. It serves as both noun and verb; but game, as a noun only, describes a board game. Play plays more than game.

Sport (1440), a form of disport (1303) dis-ports us from business. Similarly, a-vocations call us away and di-versions turn us aside. We call an avid hunter a sportsman (1706), even though hunting game occupies its own niche. In the day when landed gentry enjoyed horses in the sport of kings, sportive referred to a person having wit as golden as the content of his purse. "I am not in a sportive mood now" (1590), sets the scene for the sport of Shakespeare's *Comedy of Errors*. Although sport also referred to hunting or horses, its late entry into the arena allowed it to specialize: from the sixteenth to the nineteenth centuries, sports referred to athletic events that celebrated holidays. These sports work harder than play. Children play games; athletes do sports. Manly sports disdain child's play.

Play struts off to playhouses, skips off to playgrounds or jogs off to playing fields. On playing fields, sports find their proper arenas. They have come to refer to athletic games like soccer and football. Even though few people have either the athletic talent or the moneyed leisure to succeed in sports, many hope to be a sport. In fact, being a sport usually involves just looking and playing the part—a favorite diversion for some, since it diverts them from reality. A sporty (1896) young sport (1901) suggests a young clubman, informally dressed in sports clothes, without much to do, but with money to do it.

Parents or teachers—or, in the extreme, municipal authorities—read the riot act, when play gets wild, and playboys too boisterously and carelessly romp (1709) and rollick (1826). Ramps, vulgar and bold women, gave their name to romps. Romps and rollicks escape to an escapade (1653): "A young nobleman commits an escapade—the name given to the offenses of persons of quality" (1827). Escapades break out like wild fire. In the backwoods of Kentucky, rowdies first fought "for the mere love of fighting" (1824). They "romp about rudely" (1854). Enough of these rowdy escapades! Good sports take time out. They complement healthy 'sporting in sport with decorous deporting in deportment.

We have given man's games enough free play. Let's set a limit to our etymological play by concluding with an apt rephrasing of Alexander Pope's poem on the happy life:

> Happy the man, whose sport and game
>     A few common sense limits bound,
> Content to divert his native frame,
>     But keep life sound.

## Words

Play has a PIE root, but game stays within the limits of its Germanic family. Latin roots *ludere*, to play, and *iocare*, to joke, fill the area in Romance occupied in English by play and game. In English, these roots fill an area of meaning represented by jocular and ludicrous. On the whole, words for play and games do not spring from broad PIE roots.

### PIE root *plek*, to bend, fold

Latin: *plicare*, to fold, bend
    English: to complicate, to fold together
Germanic English: play (725), bending the limbs in exercise

### PIE root *per*, to carry

Latin: *portare*, to carry; *disportare*, to carry aside
    English:
        to disport (1374), to divert (from sadness), to play
        sport (noun, 1440), short form of disport; (1593), athletic sport;
            (1861), gambler; (1897), young clubman
        to deport, to conduct oneself; deportment, proper conduct
Russian: спорт (sport), athletic activity

### PIE root *iek*, to speak, pray

Latin: *jocus*, joke
    Italian: *giocare*, to play; French: *jouer*, to play; Spanish: *jugar*, to play

### PIE root *aig*, goat; and Greek *aissein*, to move violently

Greek: *aegis*, storm, goat skin shield for defense
Russian: игра (igra), game

## 93. 'Let's Have Some Fun'

### Diversion

In our pursuit of happiness so far, what prospect do we have that pious festivity or festive parties, creatively hard-working work or even play can hope for some fun? Ethics and piety have built their foundations on no-nonsense virtues; but exclude fun as we may, humanity possesses sense and nonsense in equal parts. The Eucharist in the early church, for example, celebrated its solemn mystery; but Saint Augustine observed that his mother Monica took as much joy from the spirits on the Holy Table as in the Holy Spirit of the Table. She experienced liturgy and festivity as two equal parts of one experience. Human spirits profit from diversion, when they enjoy it with equanimity.

Not virtuously dutiful all the time, most of us seek our cakes and ale just for the fun of it. To fun (1685) means to fool. When your friend is funning you, he is fooling you, but his fooling may give you the fun (1727)—leading you off course and bringing you back to yourself. We call our usual forms of fun diversions, "so to elude the length of time." Diversions save us from the people we should not want to be, bored and boring, sad and radiating gloom. A number of roots focus on the diverting. Unlike ethical commitments or religious feasts, diversions divert us from duty. In Russian, забыть (zabit), to forget, gives забава (zebava), diversion, its root. Likewise, we dream in musing; and a-musing dreams divert us from thought to musing—the a- of amusing means 'to.' We forget ourselves in our diversions. Killjoys grumble that a man murders the future by killing time; Horace's happy man knows that his diversion gives it life.

After play, game, and sport had been playing the field before 1500, newly minted words for play accentuated its playfulness. In the sixteenth century, children started to gambol (1513), caper (1588), and frolick (1598) in their play. On lithe Italian *gambas*, legs, a gambol leaps about in dance. Children and animals gambol in play: "The urchins gamboled round the grave-stones on the Sabbath" (1841). A goat, Latin *caper*, capers when he dances or jumps about in frolic. With less emphasis on joyful movement than gambol, but more on joy itself, frolic, cognate with frog, leaps joyfully: "Winter is the great season for jaunting and dancing (called frolicking) in America" (1829). Around the village green, children gambol; 'round the Maypole, they frolic. Gamboling or frolicking energetically, they caper. Capers often get out of hand. Today, a caper can lead to anything from a prank, to a drinking spree or a robbery.

"True lovers," Shakespeare observes, "run into strange capers." They also run into trouble by making life too lively. Sports, beware! Below capering, even closer to the earth, hopping frogs frig: "O! how they do frig it, / Jump it and jig it" (D'Urfey, *Pills to Purge Melancholy*). Capering like a kid or frigging like a clown makes sports the sport of mockery. 'Be a sport!' should observe the limits of good sportsmanship.

Fun assumes the free and easy, unconstrained motion that defines jaunty, as it boasts of its roots in the genteel, devil-may-care sport. The Russian word for jaunty бойкий (boykiy), boyish, reminds us that the gentry can afford to act like grown-up boys. Jaunty young sports aspire to gentility as well as to sportsmanship—just for the dash of it!—as they move about with a sprightly free spirit.

*Homo ludens*, sportive man, turns work to play and play to work. He gambols as a child; romps in escapades or disports in sports as a young man; and cuts capers as a spry old goat. His gamboling and gambling sound the same, even though they represent vastly different games. And yet, as vast as the difference between a child's gamboling and an old man's gambling, both escape from work to play by June frolics in January.

## Words

Fun makes us foolish; diversion turns us aside from duty;
and a caper sets us frigging a frolic—all to be jaunty.

### PIE root *uer*, to turn

Latin: *divertere*, to divert, to turn aside
    Italian: *divertirsi*, to divert oneself; French and Spanish: *diversion*
    English:
        to divert (1430), to turn away; (1660), to turn aside from work
        diversion (1600), turning aside; (1648), amusement
Russian:
    время (vrema), time; literally, turning (of the seasons)
    время-про-вождение (vremya-pro-vozhdeniye), pastime
    [водить (vodsit), to lead; and про-водить (provodit), to spend (time)]

### PIE root *selk / swelk / welk*, to drag

English: seal, an animal that drags itself
Russian:
    влечь (vlech), to draw, entice; раз-влекать (raz-vlikat), to divert
    раз-влечение (raz-vlecheniye), entertainment;
        *cf.* French *divertissement*

### PIE root *bheu*, to be

Latin: *sum esse*, to be
Russian:
    за (za), behind, beyond, on the other side of + быть (bit), to be
    забыть (zabit), to forget, neglect; забава (zebava), diversion

### PIE root *men*, mind

English:
    to muse (1340), to ponder, dream
    to amuse (1480), to divert from thought, to bring to muse
        (as a diversion)
Russian: муза (muza), muse

### PIE root *gen/nat*, to be born

Latin: *gens gentis*, race, family, clan
    French: *gentil*, kind, friendly
    English:
        gentile, genteel, gentle are doublets of jaunty
        jaunty (1674), genteel in manner; (1672), sprightly in action

### PIE root *preu*, to hop, jump for joy

German: *fröhlich*, happy
    English: frolic

### PIE root *kapr*, goat, a nimble animal

Latin: *caper*, goat
    Italian: *capriolare*, to leap like a goat; and Capri, island of
        wild goats
    French: *cabriolet*, a light, two-wheeled carriage bouncing like a goat
    English: caper (1588)—"Faith! I can cut a caper" (Shakespeare).
Russian: коза (koza), goat; and каперсы (kapersy), capers

### PIE root *bhreg*, to break

Latin: *frango frangere* and *fractus*, to break
    English: fracture
Perhaps the root of English:
    to frig (1460), to hop like a frog
        frigging, a reference to sexual intercourse
Russian: прыгать (prygat'), to jump, frolic, gambol

# 94. Joyful Fair-Going Cheer

## Jolly Good Cheer

Essays about happiness, festivity, leisure, parties and fun have have unfolded complexities that may at first confuse, because happiness and festivity do not, in their origins, make us either happy or festive; nor does fun bring us as much fun as we think it should. Etymological complexity has also required an ethic. Happiness needs work; festivity needs faith; leisure, without direction, slips into the otiose; and fun, without control, goes haywire. In their histories, words, like people, have a reach, some far, some near, but all their own. They both reveal problems and offer solutions. Let's end by celebrating our happy, festive words with jolly good cheer.

From the same root as the Spanish noun *cara*, face, cheer meant face sixty-five years before face did. Just as the word fare traveled far before it got on the bill, cheer needed some experience before it broke into a smile. With a tableful of jaunty sports around a groaning board, the question, 'How fare my friends?', has found its answer in 'deliciously.' To the next question, "What cheer?" the answer seems as obvious as the cheerful faces all round. But it was not at first obvious because cheer, at its root, did not imply cheerful. The lovesick Hermia in *Midsummer Night's Dream* is "pale of cheer," quite the opposite of cheerful. The adjective 'good' joined forces with cheer to reflect a happy face. Eventually, 'good' had cheered up cheer enough that it could separate from its noun and let it smile all by itself. By the middle of the sixteenth century, the biblical translators, who worked on an early version of King James Bible, could use the word to affirm that God loves "a cheerful giver" (1568).

Cheer has radiated a constellation of meaning. Smile has shone radiantly, but simply, as a cognate of miracle. In origin, a smile ad-mired miracles more than it laughed at a joke. When we see a baby, discovering some magic and smiling at the marvel, we see smiling in its root. Smirk was its first form. What a story it could tell of its four hundred year decline and fall into affectation and insincerity! Smirk sank to bowing and simpering in the wings; and the sunny smile took center stage. But no human expressions or the words that represent them remain free from change and deviation. The human face can reflect changes faster than the weather. The German *heiter*, cheerful, for example, shares the same Indo-European root as the Russian word for rage, ярость (yarost')—a glowing face may go to either extreme.

Smile and marvel sit in their single domain.
In all its seats, cheer has seen many kingdoms.

Grace and its cognate joy bring distant kingdoms together.
Consider some explanations for their reach.
Gratitude complements grace:
grace enters and exits graciously, asking no price;
and gratitude gratefully pays it.

Grace skips from heaven down to earth:
From above, God sends His grace,
and the Graces send theirs.
Down below, we marvel at human graces.
but some want graces from above down below.
Shakespeare's Benedick wants them all:
"Till all human graces be in one woman,
one woman shall not come in my grace."

Like Keats, we hope for joys forever—
"A thing of beauty is a joy forever;"
but, for now, we love gold joys and joyful grapes.
We take joy in the bundles of joy that recreate the world.
'Glory' came into English late,
because joy first translated God's glory.
Church bells peal Christmas joy,
but Yule bustles in to make the season jolly.

With heaven congratulating earth,
let's all rejoice beyond common mirth.

## Words

"It is a fashion to be glad," said an old sage, "joy is the grace we say to God." Cheery, joyful words take us near and far, even sending heaven's beams to earth. They inspire the bard in all of us.

### PIE root *ker*, horn, head

Latin, Greek and Spanish: *cara*, face
Latin: *cerebrum*, brain
French: *bonne chère*, good food
English: cheer (1225), face—This word evolved through 500 years:
    from face,
        to expressions on faces (1225), 'Be of good cheer,'

to the welcoming face of a host (1300),
to food and entertainment he provides (1375),
to the joy (1549) he feels,
and the encouragement he gives (1720).
Cheer has come a long way; let's give it a cheer!

### PIE root *smei*, to marvel

Latin: *mirus* and *mirabilis*, miraculous
    Spanish:
        *maravilla*, marvelous
        *cf. milagro*, miracle; religious folk charm used as a votive offering
    English: miracle and marvel
Germanic English:
    to smirk (888), to smile; smirking (1000), smiling affectedly
    to smile (1300)
Russian:
    смеяться (smeyat'sya), to laugh
    смешить (smeshit), to make someone laugh, amuse

### PIE root *kitro*, bright, clear; or *ieros*, period, year, course of the sun

German: *heiter*, cheerful
Russian: яркий (yarkiy), bright, glad; ярость (yarost'), rage

### PIE root *ga*, to rejoice, in three families:

1. Latin: *gaudeo gaudere*, to rejoice; *gaudium*, joy
    Italian: *gioia*, joy; Spanish: *gozo*, joy
    English:
        gaudy (1583), "Come, let's have one other gaudy night."
            (Shakespeare, *Antony and Cleopatra*, 3, 13)
        gaud (1430), a flashy trinket; to gaud (1532), to make merry
    French: *joie*
        English: joy (1225), enjoy (1380), rejoice (1303)
            Before English glory (1382) transliterated Latin *gloria*,
            "Joy to Father . . ." translated *Gloria Patri*.
2. A division of PIE root *ga / gar*, to praise, as in religion
    Latin: *gratia*, grace and gratitude, two sides of the same coin
        Italian: *grazioso*, gracious, pretty, charming
        French: *gracieux*, gracious, graceful, charming, elegant, slender
        Spanish: *gracioso*, gracious, amusing
        English: grace and gracious, grateful and gratitude

Latin: *gratulor gratulari*, to express joy, to give thanks
    English: to congratulate (1577), to share joy
English: bard, singer of grateful praise
Russian: жертва (zhertva), to sacrifice in gratitude, victim
3. Associated with PIE root *ga*
    Yule, the yule month, pagan festival celebrated as Christmas
        French: *joli*, pretty, smart, agreeable
        English: jolly

## PIE root *ues*, to be cheerful, feast

Latvian: *vesels*, healthy; Polish: *wesoły*, cheerful
Russian:
    веселый (veselyy), cheerful; весело (veselo), jolly, fun
    на-веселе (na-vesele), tipsy, jolly

## No certain PIE root

Latin: *alacer*, cheerful, brisk
    Spanish: *alegre*, cheerful; Italian: *allegro*, cheerful
        Russian: аллегро (allegro), Italian musical term
    English: alacrity, liveliness

# Psychological
# and Social Evil

. . . .

## 95. Evil

Saint Augustine thought that evil originated in the misuse of the good that God has created, but the etymologies of words that represent it originate more in the evidence of evil than in its causes. They represent evil as either excessive strength, weakness or excess itself. They also trace it to material and physical evidence, which we are loathe to admit, such as poverty, dirt, pain and deformity. Do good men suffering evil become bad? Not necessarily—suffering evil makes King Lear good. On the surface, if the good are good-looking, the bad are bad-looking, because they suffer from dirt, deformity, and wretchedness. To draw a lesson from this wretchedness, let's put to one side the saint's theological understanding, and get down to nasty and brutish earth.

Cognate with over, evil depicts wrongdoing as transgression passing over the good. *Yfel*, occurring once in *Beowulf*, describes Grendel's kinsmen as "evil upon the earth" (*yfel ofer eorðan*), because they blight it. Evil referred to character about a century after *Beowulf* (971). Grendel's kinsmen were over acting—actually, overeating—rather than overweening.

More common in *Beowulf*, bale and its adjective baleful represent evil actively working its worst, "destroying, blasting, injuring, paining, hurting, and tormenting." Grendel, with hateful bale (*bealoníð*), plotting bale (*bealohýdig*), causes it by slaughtering kinsmen (*morþorbealo mága*). Baleful surviving as an adjective, has left its noun to poets: Edmund Spenser laments "our feeble hearts embost with bale and bitter biting grief" (1596). Bale 'embosses' our hearts with the miseries of the world.

The adjective baleful (1000) pictures evil as a pernicious failing of the human mind, which, for example, succumbs to the baleful lust for gold. More commonly, it describes material evil: Shakespeare's Friar Lawrence refers to "baleful weeds" that will doom Romeo and Juliet; and Swift's prophet, to the "baleful dog-star" that will doom London. Baleful evil has such power that the friar can taste it and the prophet can see it streaming from heaven.

Although wicked (1275) now connotes active malice, it probably originated as a cognate of weak. This origin explains two sides of the weakness of wickedness: weakness of wretched sinners in passively succumbing to temptations, and weak strength of the Wicked One in actively provoking them. Power in deceiving, at the origin of Russian evil, злой (sloy), balances weakness in being deceived. Wickedness is weak, because it is perverse: in a world that has perversely chosen to be wicked, wicked tongues utter wicked words, and wicked men plot abominations. Bad (1297) also arose from weakness: Old English *baeddel*, hermaphrodite, did a bad job of being male. Augustine would endorse these origins of bad and wicked, because bad men do not have the strength of good men in God's creation.

Ill stumps the etymologists who can find no root for it. In modern English, ill (1200) and illness (1500) now refer to physical diseases, but they first referred to immorality. We can see this first meaning in compounds of the word: ill will, ill-tempered, and ill-mannered. Texans, the OED reports, regard an ill fellow as a man of low morals. Two and one half centuries after this first use, ill described ill health (1460). It shares this double reference to physical and moral ills with the root *mal-* from Latin and French. Malicious (1225) first referred to evil intention, but the same root formed malady and malaise (*cf.* French *mal à la tête*, headache). Evil worked actively and tangibly. Our ancestors even breathed it, when they inhaled bad air as mal-aria.

Our ancestors also attributed evil to degradation and poverty. They saw a wretch (1200) in poverty as concomitantly base and vile (1250). King Lear experiences an evolution in wretchedness, which we may take as a "physic" to such facile assumptions. He first vilifies his one sincere daughter Cordelia as ungrateful and calls her "a wretch whom Nature is ashamed / Almost t' acknowledge hers." When he suffers at the hands of his two hypocritical daughters, he starts to see human wretchedness hidden "within"—"Tremble, thou wretch that hast within these undivulged crimes." In his final degradation, he shares with all humanity the wretchedness that he has tried to condemn in a person who has too much sincerity "within" to flatter him: "Take physic, pomp. / Expose thyself to feel what wretches feel." After this descent—actually, ascent—one "gentleman" smugly pities him as a king degraded to wretch: "A sight most pitiful in the meanest wretch, / Past speaking of in a king." This "gentleman" brings the audience back to the complaisant and facile assumptions from which King Lear started his pilgrimage. Take physic, gentleman: when this regal wretch descends from his royal dignity, he ascends to human goodness.

Below kings, but in company with Lear, naughty (1377) men had naught, but they were short on cash long before they were short on morals (1529). Short on both, naughty wretches lived in physical and moral filth. Nasty (1400; *cf.* Dutch *nastig*, filthy), they were just plain filthy two hundred years before they were morally filthy (1601), and four hundred years before they were ill-tempered (1828). Naughty, nasty wretches did not have enough money to be well groomed.

Latin *vitium*, from which vicious (1340) is derived, referred to physical deformity. Did suffering vitiate King Lear's character or ennoble it? Vile was as physically repulsive (1300) as it was morally low (1290). Base and low describe social as well as moral opprobrium. Vile, vicious, and vitiate crown nasty and brutish life with evil.

"The greatest of all mysteries," said one sage "is the origin of evil." Embarrassed, however, by remaining wrapped in this mystery, we cause ourselves greater embarrassment by trivializing it with the facile assumptions of words that demonstrate how superficially we think. Crashing through mystery, this superficial mentality has defined evil by men so wretched that they cannot ascend to see themselves as little less than angels.

## Words

The three etymologies of words for evil represent it as passing over or blowing over a limit, but also deceiving. Evil has a double edge of the wretchedness that man suffers and that which he creates.

### PIE root *upo*, under or over

Greek:
    *hyper*, beyond, in hyperbole, throwing beyond
    *hypo*, under, in hypodermic, under the skin
Latin:
    *sub*, under, in subcutaneous, under the skin (*cf.* Greek hemi- and Latin semi-)
    *super*, beyond, in superlative, carried beyond
German: *übel*—going beyond—evil
English: evil (825), the -il, a diminutive form; eaves, roofing above the house

### PIE root *bew/dheu*, to smoke, blow, inflate

Latin: *furor*, fury; and *bullio bullire*, to boil
    English: ebullient (1599)
German: *böse*, evil
English: boast
Russian: буря (bura), storm

### PIE root *phol*, to make slide, trick, deceive

Latin: *fallo fallere*, to deceive
    English: fallacious, full of deceit
Russian: злой (zloy), evil

## 96. Crime and Sin

### Essential Sin and False Crime

Policemen discover somebody else's diamonds in a man's pocket. Has he committed a crime? It should be simple enough to determine, but human nature makes it complex. Incrimination winds about with bends and crooked turns. Does a man play false or just have faults? Does he blaspheme or blame? Be careful!—does he stumble as he walks or does he resolutely walk his own crooked mile? No wonder stories of crime fascinate us. They plunge us into a crisis of being, as we stumble through our own complexity.

Law first used the word crime at the end of the fourteenth century: "A crime," says Blackstone, "is an act, committed or omitted, in violation of a public law." What could be simpler? So it seems in the black and white of the law book, but from the book it goes to court, where it proceeds from crimination of the state to incrimination of the prosecutor, recrimination of the defense, and discrimination of the judge. Simplicity unfolds in one layer, but each layer of this procedure folds into complexity, unless, and sometimes even when, the accused is as guilty as sin.

Sin, by contrast, is as simple as ABC. 'A' is for Adam: "In Adam's fall, we sinned all"—Milton lays the foundation of morality and immorality. To discriminate between sin and crime: after commission or omission, crime unfolds in law courts; sin stays at home in life. Mankind is born into moral flaws that we can call sins, which may or may not violate laws. Taking up their residence in the inevitable weaknesses of human character, sins lie in wait to snare innocence.

Take, for instance, our weakness in love: *cherchez la femme*. "'Tis her crime to be loved," Joseph Addison exculpates a beauty, " 'Tis her crime to have charms." But she's so beautiful, her lover pleads, it had to be a sin—the statement has special cogency when we realize that the PIE root of sin is being. Her being incriminates his in becoming. Let's try to be discriminating: if he has stolen the diamonds for her, is she entirely without incrimination? He answers for the crime in court, but she—and all of us—share his sin in life.

In English, the word sin originated in comprehensive being, but in Romance, it just stumbled into being. Latin *peccare* first meant to stumble and its noun *peccatum* had an expressive image of a *faux pas*. The poet Horace made a plea for himself as a horse stumbling in old age: *Solue senescentem equum, ne peccet ad extremum ridendus*, "Set an old horse free, so that he may not stumble (*peccet*) in the end, an object of ridicule."

Can any one always look where he is going? The Romance word resembles the Greek word for sin, *hamartia*, missing the mark. Ain't nobody perfect.

We are easily deceived when we stumble into sin or when it sweeps us up. The doublets false and fault demonstrate these tricks. False, taken directly from Latin into English, described forgery, heresy or perjury—matters for the law. Fault, taken from Latin into Romance and then into English, described both misdeed and lack, what we do and what we do not do. If we do not appear in court, the judge renders a decision by default. We default on a loan by not paying it. *Faute de mieux*, we are left on our own resources. Bad men play false; even good men have faults.

Of course, some crooks take no misstep, miss no mark, and think, at least, that they are not deceiving themselves when they run straight to crooked ways. The PIE roots *kolp*, *skel* and *uergh*, bend, curve and twist into English culpable, *scélérat*, and wrong. Tort, the legal word for crime, twists from right, *droit* in French, a doublet of direct. Blasphemy self-consciously speaks ill of the sacred, but its doublet blame can turn the crime against the blasphemer.

Real crooks make it all seem easy. Without feeling guilt, they keep the diamonds in their pockets and play dumb. Some of us even feel incriminated at the thought of a stumble. They play false; we have faults. Let's live with sin in life, and avoid incrimination in court.

## Words

Crime derives from six PIE roots:

1. **PIE root *ker*, to separate or to cry out**
   Latin *crimen criminis*, crime (charge and verdict); *crisis*, point
       of discrimination
   English:
       crime (1384), criminal deed; (1386), criminal charge
       crimination (1583), to criminate (1645)
       to recriminate (1603), to discriminate (1628), to incriminate (1730)
   Russian: криминáл (kriminal), crime
2. **PIE root *kolp*, to bend, turn; or *qola*, strike, blow**
   Latin:
       *culpa*, fault—the culpable condition more than the culpable act
       *mea culpa*, by my fault
           Spanish and Portuguese: *culpa*, fault, guilt; Italian: *colpa*, fault,
               blame, sin

French: *coulpe*, fault
English: culpable, culprit, to exculpate
3. **PIE root *phol*, to make fall, deceive**
Latin: *fallo fallere*, I deceive; *falsus*, deceitful, mendacious
Italian: *fallo* and *faglia*, fault; French: *faute*, fault
English:
fault (1290), lack; (1377), culpability
default (1225), failure in duty; (1290), want, lack, failure to act
false—doublets of fault—(1000), fraud; (1200), contrary to truth
*faux pas*, false step; *faute de mieux*, for lack of something better
4. **PIE root *mel*, to deceive**
Greek and Latin: *blasphemo*, I speak ill of, defame
English: to blaspheme and its doublet, blame,
5. **PIE root *skel*, bending, crooked**
Latin: *scelus sceleris*, crooked deed, crime
French and English: *scélérat*, villain
6. **PIE root *bhreg*, to break**
German: *Verbrechen*, felony
English: breach

Sin derives from four PIE roots:

1. **PIE root *es*, being**
Latin: *sons sontis*, being guilty
German: *Sünde*, sin
English: sin, that which is—the condition of mankind
2. **PIE root *ped*, to walk, fall, stumble, as in *faux pas***
Latin:
*pecco peccare*, I stumble, sin; *peccavi*, I have sinned
*peccatum*, sin
Italian: *peccato*, sin; *pecca*, fault; Spanish: *pecado*, sin
French: *péché*, sin
English: peccadillo, impeccable
3. **PIE root *dhebh*, to give, receive**
Latin:
*habeo habere*, I have
*debeo debere*, I owe—contraction of *de-hibeo*, I am away
from having
*debitum*, debt
French: *avoir* and *devoir*, to have and to owe; *dette*, debt
English: habit and debit, that which is had and that which is owed
Russian: долг (dolg), debt

4. **No certain PIE root**
   Perhaps Greek:
   *chrei*, it is necessary
   *chremata*, money; literally, necessary things
       English: chrematist, a man who makes money
   *chréos*, debt
       Russian: rpex (grex), sin, *cf.* debt as sin in English

# 97. Stealing with Stealth

In public, the satirist Horace observed, a man may vociferously pray to Apollo; but in private, he may whisper a prayer to the goddess of thieves: "O Laverna, grant that I may appear holy and good, but cover my sins with night and my deceits with a cloud."[21] Without good conscience or consciousness, a man may not have much concern about appearing good. He boasts privately that he takes what he wants, when he wants it; but in the revealing light of day, he rarely lives up to his swagger. Good or bad, we all know that open criminality can not succeed for very long, unless, of course, we have won the special favor of Laverna.

Up country, criminals can pull off highway robbery, because a highway is usually deserted; but on High Street, back in town, they keep a low profile before, during, and, especially after, a heist. Lurking, stealing and absconding require clandestine plans, stealthy skulking, furtive gestures and surreptitious sneaking. Even up country, shady (1848) characters hide in the bush and shun the broad light of day.

The oldest and commonest English verb for thievery, to steal (725), combines the overt with the covert. It originates from a combination of the roots *ster* for taking, with *kel* for covering. Stealing and concealing coin two sides of the same slug. The ancient grammarian Varro confirms this crooked combination: *poetae milites latrones vocant, quod latent ad insidias faciendas*, "poets call soldiers *latrones*, because they are 'latent' for the purpose of making ambushes." In addition, the noun thief having a cognate in the Lithuanian verb to squat sharpens our picture of thieves sneaking like snakes.

Stealth, at first, described stealing, but, much later (1590), its secrecy. Macbeth, suffering from an agony of guilt, observes that a murderer "with his stealthy pace . . . / Moves like a ghost. Thou sure and firm-set earth, / Hear not my steps . . ." He pathetically asks that the earth not "hear" his steps! Stealth so obsesses that its compulsion to conceal can not stop with committing the crime: after it steals gold, it steals away into the shadows. The verb to steal, transitive and intransitive, involves both action and being. A stealthy thief steals gold because he wants it; he steals away, because he is—he may even feel—guilty. Stealth keeps its stealing a secret. An exception, stalkers stalk their prey with stealthy pace but a clear conscience, when they hunt to put meat on the table.

Stealth so obsesses stealing that lurking (1300), and skulking (1225) mask its preparation: the thief lurks or skulks in the bushes before he steals off to steal. Skulking does more sinister or fearful work than lurking does: "I must skulk," laments a man contemplating exile in a foreign land, "a dishonorable, an abandoned fugitive" (1806). After the theft, a thief absconds (1565): "The villain who had absconded for a year would not escape punishment" (1782). The thief takes three steps in his *modus operandi*: first, he lurks and skulks, then he steals and steals away; and finally, he absconds.

Covert skulking and stealth contrast with overt robbing (1225), the activity of soldiers plundering openly. Robbers stole robes so often that the two words share the same root: the image of victors despoiling the vanquished suggests the connection. Latin *latro* meant mercenary soldier as well as robber. Open robbery is an exception to the rule of stealth—we even refer to pirates as jolly rovers, maybe even with their letters of marque, roving the seven seas, bereaving ships' captains, soon bereft of cargoes and crews. The thief skulking in the night, on the other hand, colors our image of dishonesty.

The compounding of the Latin verb to steal, *surripere*, to seize from under (*sub/sur*, under), puts stealth at the base of stealing. Its adjective, surreptitious (1401), describes thievish under-handedness: a thief, for example, surreptitiously removes cash from the vault. Likewise, furtive, derived from Latin *fur*, thief, also focuses on the thief's demeanor and not his deed—the advocate of health food glances furtively over his shoulder as he eats a doughnut. Clandestine, without reference to thieves, describes that which is hidden and does not have quite as much thievish intent as furtive and surreptitious: lovers plan clandestine meetings. Good or bad, many men, diffidently fearful or fearfully meticulous, spend more time out of sight than in.

Let's set aside the sanctity of the social contract: for practical reasons, most of us should remain moral and on the straight and narrow, because few of us have so much nerve, or, concomitantly, so little conscience, that we can deal with the torture of tortuous paths. An honest man should never commit a crime, because he would not endure lurking and skulking. Guilt-ridden wretches can't even look at the sun without suffering. Only the root of the Russian вор (vor), thief, suggests that a rogue may have such an equivocating, plausible spiel that he can talk his way into deceiving and then thieving. He may even deceive himself into believing that he does not invalidate his prayer to the radiant sun god Apollo by his next one to Laverna, the shady goddess of his filthy lucre.

## Words

Stealing is easy at its roots: just take the gold, carry it away, and hide it; although, in French, flying away seems a bit too volatile.
In war, removing armor from bodies on the battlefield seems even easier, but that is the root of robbery in the spoils of war.
In hunting, also, stalking and stealth can bag a legitimate catch.

### PIE root *kel*, to cover, hide

Latin: *celo celare*, to hide (transitive)
    PIE root *kel* probably combined with the PIE root *ster*, to steal:
    English: to steal (725), the verb; and its noun, stealth (1250);
        to stalk (1000)

### PIE root *guel*, to fly

Latin: *volo volare*, to fly
    French: *voler*, to fly, steal; *voleur*, thief
    English: volatile, flighty or fickle

### PIE root *lau*, booty, gain

Latin: *lucrum*, profit; *Laverna*, the goddess of thieves
    English: lucre and lucrative
Russian:
    лов (lov), hunting, fishing, catching; улов (ulov), catch
    уловка (ulovka), trick

### Tentatively, PIE root *reup*, to break

Italian: *rubare*, to steal
Spanish: *robar*, to steal; *ropa*, clothing
English: Robbers (1175) rob (1200), by robbery (1225), robes (1275).

### PIE root *dhe*, to set down

Latin: *condo condere*, to store
    English:
        condiment (1420), food that can be stored
        to abscond (1565), to run and hide after a crime

Two Latin words for thief find their way into English and Romance:

1. **PIE root *bher*, to bear**
   Latin: *fur furis*, thief
      English: furtive
   English: to bear
   Russian: брать (brat), to take
2. **PIE root *le*, to get**
   Latin: *latro latronis*, thief, mercenary
      Italian: *ladro*, thief; Spanish: *ladrón*, thief
   Also associated with *latro*:
   PIE root *ladh*, hidden
   Latin: *lateo latere*, to hide (intransitive)
      English: latent, lying hidden

Three Slavic roots emphasize the thief's separating, seizing, and lying.

1. **PIE root *ker*, to separate**
   Latin: *cerno cernere*, and *cretus/certus*, to separate
      English: to discern
   Russian:
      украсть (ukrast'), to steal; укрытие (ukrytiye), shelter
      кремль (Kremlin), fortress separated within a town
      край (kray), side, edge
2. **PIE root *greb*, to rake, seize**
   English: to grab, to grasp or to grapple: Grapples grab grapes.
   Russian: грабить (grabit'), to rob
3. **PIE root *werh*, to speak**
   Greek: *rhetor*, a speaker
      English: rhetoric, the speaker's art
   Russian: вор (vor), a thief; врать (vrat), to lie

# 98. The Complexity of Duplicity

The Russian verb обманывать (obmanyvat'), to delude, folds into its origin the ancient well-spring of duplicity, predating even the German cognates *täuschen/tauschen* that make trading and tricking synonymous. Sanskrit *maya* describes the inevitable illusion of creation after it has been separated from its Creator. If all creation creates illusion, how easily does it delude its creatures! Apart from this delusion implicit in our world of shadows, let's make explicit the worst culprits who take advantage of its illusions.

Some duplicitous hoods do not skulk like thieves in the night. They hoodwink without wearing a hood, because they deceive simple folk in the broad light of day. Their deceit draws from deep roots, as they recreate the illusions that have always filled creation. No wonder they deceive, delude and impose in the day! Their guile beguiles in as many ways as witches bewitch.

The duplicitous double mind says one thing, but means something else.

It preys on simple, ingenuous souls, who say one thing and think that they mean it. Duplicitous words are duplex, sent by their prefixes down devious paths:

to semble (1330) and to dissemble (1513),
to simulate (1652) and to dissimulate (1533),
to tend (1350) and to pretend (1380),
to pose (1374) and to impose (1682).

Even the simple roots connote a catch, but their compounds denote duplicity.

A man sembles and simulates, **when he pretends to be** what he is not. If he envies his fellow men, he must simulate joy—as long, at least, as he wants to appear generous—when he hears of their good fortune. He dissembles and dissimulates, **when he pretends not to be** what he is. In simulating joy, this envious man dissimulates the disappointment he feels when he hears of their good fortune. He pretends to be joyful when he is not, and not to be disappointed when he is. In either case, he misrepresents reality by false pretense.

Simulation and dissimulation may work for the good, but pretending and imposing more often cross to the other side. When we tend, we stretch out in a particular direction. If we work too hard in tending, we end up feeling tense. Usually, our tendencies tend in a bad direction. According to the common use of the word, we have more bad tendencies than good ones. Its adjective tendentious shows that tendencies tend to be bad. It pairs with false, as in an account of history that is false and tendentious. To pretend only meant to claim for a relatively short time before it meant to profess falsely (1401). Does a pretender to a throne have a legitimate claim or is he imposing a fraud? To pose and to impose pose a different perspective on simulation: an impostor (1586) poses as royalty and imposes upon people by his imposture (1537). An im-postor 'puts' deceit 'on' others. Whether for a good or a bad purpose, sembling, simulating, and posing pretenders make up pretenses of being what they are not.

Verbs, like de-ceiving (1300) and se-ducing (1477), implicate duplicity only in their compounds. To deceive (*de-*, completely; and *capere*, to take) 'takes someone in'(1740). To seduce (*se-*, apart; and *ducere*, to lead) leads astray, first persuading a soldier to forsake his allegiance; and later (1560), a girl, her innocence. The simple actions of taking, leading, tending and posing become duplicitous when deceivers, seducers, pretenders and impostors implicate simplicity and honor in their deceit.

English compounds of Latin *ludere*, to mock, describe deceiving the eye of the mind or body. To delude mocks someone by false opinions. By false appearance, illusions deceive the eye that suffers hallucinations, commonly call optical illusions. Imagine a story for illusion and delusion: to deceive his gullible disciples, a charlatan makes a secret agreement by collusion with accom-plices. In colluding, he also connives (1611), literally, winking with them (Latin *connivere*). With the help of these accomplices, he so deludes his disciples that they believe the illusion of him walking on water. Bring the three levels of this mockery together: he first colludes, then he creates illusion, so that he may finally delude. Collusion, illusion, delusion, brought down to their common root, are ludicrous (1782), because their mockery deserves mockery. After this prelude, I will allude in the following and final paragraph to these three steps of deceit.

By its craft, deceit calls non-being into being. Deceivers create false impressions by illusion and delusion, simulation and dissimulation. They foist this falsity on others by deceit and imposture, in which they conspire with others by collusion and connivance. God help the deluder and the deluded—both are snared in the toils of delusion. And especially, God help us all to distinguish beacons from ghosts.

## Words

Deceit itself dates back to the sly serpent, but English words for duplicity date mostly to the fourteenth and fifteenth centuries. English was taking its time to describe this aspect of devious human conduct. Back to the beginning, German *tauschen*, to trade, with the addition of an umlaut, *täuschen*, means to trick. In antiquity, both traders and tricksters worshipped Hermes/Mercury as their patron. Both had to be mercurial, with quick feet and quick wits to succeed. Complicit in the refined complexities, first recorded toward the end of the fourteenth century, PIE roots for folding, playing, and stretching unfold some aspects of deceit.

### PIE root *leid*, to play

Latin: *ludo ludere*, to play, mock; *deludo deludere*, to delude
English:
> to delude (1450) and delusion (1420), mocking someone by
> false opinions

to collude (1525) and collusion (1397)
to allude (1533) and allusion (1548), calling attention to

## PIE root *plek*, to fold

Latin: *simplex (sim-*, one; and *plex/plicis*, fold), one-fold
English: simplex (1594) and simplicity (1374)
Russian: симплекс (simpleks), simplex

Latin: *duplex (duo*, two; and *plex/plicis*, fold), two-fold
English: duplex (1817) and duplicity (1430)
Russian: дуплекс (dupleks), duplex; and двуличность (dvulichnost'), duplicity

## PIE root *ten*, to stretch

Latin: *tendo tendere* and *tensus*, to stretch
English: to tend (1350) and pretend (1380); tendency (1628) and tendentious (1900)
Russian:
    тенденция (tendentsiya), tendency
    тенденциозный (tendentsioznyy), tendentious

## PIE root *meh*, good, timely

Sanskrit: *maya*, creating illusion
Latin:
    *manis*—archaic adjective—good; *Manes*, good spirits
    *immanis*, not good; therefore, monstrous
Russian:
    маяк (mayak), beacon or ghost; манить (manit), to beckon, attract, lure
    обманывать (obmanyvat'), to delude

# 99. Tricks

Tricks cut with a double edge of either skill, sharpened by intelligence, or duplicity, sharpened by guile. Smart can describe the middle ground between either extreme. Both have their place. Everyone at work takes pride in knowing the tricks of his trade; a magician captivates audiences with his tricks of legerdemain; and a beauty charms by mixing shy with sly. They all, however, can start more problems than they solve. Soldiers employ tricks in the chaos of battle, where they can not survive by standards of fair and unfair play. Especially in times of peace, we should take a second look at our art or craft to make sure that it does not get too artful or crafty, just as we should also take care not to let our tricks get too tricky.

Here's the crux of the moral problem: we pull tricks out of our bag to gain an advantage. Gambit first served as a ploy in a contest of strength or of wits. When an Italian wrestler tripped up an opponent with his leg, *gamba*, he called this trick a *gambetto*. In his strategy on the chess board, he also tripped up his opponent by a gambit in sacrificing a pawn to get one-up early in the game. Wrestlers or chessners employed a *gambetto* as ploys. Ploy (1722), short for employ, at first a means of employment, has only recently (1950) come to mean a tactic by which to gain an advantage. We open our game with a gambit and use our wits in devising more ploys to win.

To the tricky set of triplets, slay, sly, and sleight, we could add a fourth for distinctions with a sledge. Sly and its noun form sleight have described quick wits, quick tongues, or nimble hands in the arts. Wise men have also been sly; but not all sleights allowed them to remain wise. Milton's "sly snake" seduced Eve; and the Devil, traditionally, tempts frail souls by might or by sleight. In the chaos of battle, victory, or at least survival, requires some smart thinking. Sly soldiers, therefore, know how to do quick work in slaying their foe. The adjective has followed its tricky ways, and the noun has narrowed its focus to the legerdemain of, for example, "the sleight of casting up a number of sharp instruments into the air, and catching them alternatively in their fall" (1801). Sly wisdom has come down to juggling!

Sly soldiers have also employed feints, ruses (1410), and stratagems (1489) as strategies in battle. By a feint, warriors feign a blow to the head, for example, to make their foe raise his shield, so that they may deal a real, decisive blow to the stomach. Historians in the early Middle Ages praised heroes who distracted a warrior by a feint, and then lopped off his head for real. In their tricky relationship, the verbal doublets, feint and faint, make us wonder whether the man feinting a blow may betray a faint heart, about to faint. Is he faint of purpose and not really eager to fight? Tricks may betray weakness. Indolent good-for-nothings would fain resort to feints.

To catch a long battle line with its guard completely down, a general parries the rush of his foe by 'pouring back'(Latin *refundere/refusus*, to pour back) his battle line. In pursuit, his enemy put their shields on their backs and start the chase—but not for long, in fact, for just long enough to be shot! Abruptly halting this ruse, this feigned retreat, he quickly turns his line about so that it can fire a volley at the undefended flank of the line in pursuit. This devastating trick so typified the strategy of ancient

Parthians that historians have called it a Parthian shot. Fighting by flying inspired Shakespeare to an oxymoron: "Like the Parthian," says the wicked Iachimo in *Cymbeline*, "I shall flying fight." The general's ruse and his soldiers' rush originate as doublets from the same root. His ruse elicits their rush. In combat, strategists have used a feint or a ruse as stratagems, which first described the work of a general (Greek *strategos*, general), before it referred to a low trick. Generals employ gambits and ploys to gain an advantage against the feints and ruses which their foe may not be sly enough to employ or quick-witted enough to counter.

Not all tricks have originated in battle. Cheat (1590) arose as legal activity in government and war, but, eventually, no less duplicitous than feint and ruse. Cheat (1375), a shortened form of escheat (1290), originally described forfeits, fines, or the spoils of war that fell out (Latin *excadere*) to the king or to the state. Imagine the escheaters' temptation to cheat, as they filled the royal purse with gold! Just as brigands or publicans sinned (*cf. Matthew* 11, 19) in their duties as soldiers or tax collectors, escheaters escheated so thievishly that they became cheaters, as we know them. Thieves themselves, with a wink of grim humor, named the loot from their robbery after the legitimate cheat of victory in war. Cheating still retains its original, deceitful disguise, when thieves do not literally hold up their victims but they cheat them out of their money.

Without military stratagem or royal escheat, common cheats resort to homey tactics when, by pretending to be a long-lost cousin, they cozen (1573) their dupe. Stratagems of war and the cheats of government have some legitimate or legal origin—we call them white-collar crime. Cozening purely and simply deceives—the exception that proves the rule. One of Shakespeare's moral characters, Isabella in *Measure for Measure*, laments the proud man who "plays such fantastic tricks before high heaven / As make the angels weep." Tricksters' indignity and iniquity to God's creation brings angelic minds to tears.

"Play me no tricks!", said gentlemen in the old days, disdainful of low cunning. When we read of a rogue back to his old tricks, we recall why those gentlemen called them apish, knavish or cruel, and why we simply call them cheap.

## Words

Indo-European cultures must have valued the word trick, because Romance, Germanic and Slavic language families, have preserved their own forms of it.

**PIE root *terk*, to twist**

1. Romance
   Latin:
   > *torqueo torquere* and *tortus*, to twist
   > *tricae*, nonsense, trifles, tricks
   >> Italian: *trucco*; Spanish: *truco*
   >> French: *tour*, tour, walk about, magic trick (*cf. tour de force*)
2. Germanic
   English (1412) and German: trick
3. Slavic
   Russian: трюк (tryuk)

Other words for tricks originate in roots for fabricating, striking or bending:

**PIE root *dheigh*, to fabricate**

Latin: *fingo fingere* and *fictus*, to fabricate
> English: to feign (1300), feint (1600), faint; *cf.* fane, gladly

**PIE root *slak*, to strike**

English:
> to slay (825), sledge (1000); sly (1200) and its noun sleight (1300)
> By sleights, sly men use sledges to slay.

**PIE root *kamp*, to bend**

Italian: *gamba*, leg
> English: gambit (1656); gambrel (1547), a roof shaped like a leg
> Russian: гамбит (gambit)

# 100. Cheap Tricks

"Cheap," the last essay concluded, describes most tricks. As an exception, it mentioned tricks in war where rules of fair play do not apply. The subject of cheap tricks in this essay needs to adjust a statement from the first: cheap tricks, not just "can start," they do start more problems than they solve. Plots and intrigues fold deceit over deceit, and they unfold humiliation that cheapens humanity.

But, before we prepare for a concluding diatribe, let's look at one more distinct exception that could prove our rule that cheap tricks cheapen humanity. In the theatre, comedy delights audiences when it makes silly folk comic by bamboozling; and, especially by bamboozling the bamboozlers. Such intrigue lies deep within the soul and genius of the stage. In French, *intrigue* means plot, because, Frenchmen reason, plot can not exist without it. When a playwright makes cheap tricks appear as ridiculous as they really are, he can teach a good lesson. With a less lofty moral purpose, America's great showman, P.T. Barnum, the Prince of Humbug, also knew how to entertain by exhibiting tricks in his side-shows. In main shows or in side-shows, tricks and cheap tricks have their place.

Let's move from intellect on the stage and get back to smarts on the street. Plot and intrigue must have at least two folds to succeed. When duplicity double-deals and double-crosses, its victims do double-takes between what they think they may have and what they finally get. French and English roll up their complex folds in *complot* and plot, derived from *compeloter*, to roll into a ball. The man plotting winds the ball in composing his plot and he unwinds in imposing it. In both winding and unwinding, he hides its content and his intent. Another man implicated in this complication acts as his accomplice. In the age of reason and democracy, Dryden realized the double edge of the known and the unknown, the moral and the immoral, in plots: "Plots, true or false, are necessary things / to raise up commonwealths and ruin kings" (1681).

Derived from the same root as its cognate trick, intrigue twists through its maze, one so intricate that it usually turns with more than one twist, and probably a few more after that. Compounds of this root fold us in and out of its complications: intrigue weaves *intricate*, tangled skeins of deceit, from which its victims must *extricate* themselves. Of course, intrigue usually requires speech, which English and Russian define as special: English conspiring, breathing together in conspiracy, has a parallel in the Russian говор (gavor), murmuring, in заговор (sagavor), plot. Breathing (*spirare*) in one collusion or murmuring, говор (gavor), in the other, intriguists keep secrets in both. Plots must have enough complex and secret folds to ensnare their victims, and the more the better, especially in drama.

It doesn't take sophisticated, dramatic, many-folded complexity to take most suckers in. Just one usually does the trick. This simple duplicity takes us back to primitive man. Hunting defined his life; and in hunting, as in war, no rules apply. The Russian verb to hunt, ловить (lovit'), supplies the root of its words for sly, sleight and trick. Hunters originally snared birds by luring (1386), alluring (1401), gulling (1550), decoying (1618), and duping (1704). A bunch of feathers or carrion can lure by its lure even the sharp-eyed hawk back to the mews. Alluring brings birds to the lure. Gullible people resemble birds, like hoopoes or gulls, that are easily lured. Any humbug can gull gulls: "Nothing is so easy as to gull the people," observed Washington Irving in 1824, "if only you set up a prodigy." Catching birds does not require prodigies: decoy (Dutch *de kooi,* the cage) first described a pond surrounded by nets. A dupe (1681; Dutch *de huppe,* the hoopoe) describes a hoopoe, easily netted. Men can also be easily entangled: Sirens, derived from a word for entangling, lured men to their death, by sight and especially by song—so primitive and so real!

Some intriguists embellish humbug with razzle-dazzle to sell their bill of goods. A swindler (1782) projects so extravagantly in money matters that he becomes giddy with excitement (German *schwindeln,* to be giddy). The swindler entices (1297; Latin *intitiare,* to stir up a fire) people by dizzying hopes for profit. Entice first stirred up anger and, later (1303), temptation: Indian traders, for example, enticed native Americans with fire water.

In these intricate mazes, the hoodwinked victim, whether a credulous gull or a sceptic, resisting humbug, in the beginning, does not know up from down in the end. Baffling (1548), fobbing (1597), shamming (1681), humbugging (1751), and hoaxing (1790) add the insult of humiliation and bewilderment to the injury of deceit. Fobbing off, fooling with inferior goods or explanation, victimizes its fool, *foppi* in Old English. Shamming shames a man or makes him the victim of one pretending to be shamed.

In the same vein of a cheap trick, hoaxes victimize their dupes by hocus pocus, a sham of some sort. Scrooge calls spirits a humbug, an imposition upon his good sense, that scorns their put-on nonsense. Out in public, baffling first brought disgrace to a perjured knight and later to anyone suffering defeat. With the exception of the public embarrassment of baffling, fob off, sham, humbug and hoax entail devices that deceive. Spiritualism, for example, offered just the sort of humbug which P.T. Barnum made profitable in his side-shows and Dickens made moral in the conversion of Ebenezer Scrooge.

Shysters, intriguing the unsuspecting and swindling the innocent, should feel more shame than their gulls. They fill their flimflam, bamboozle, humbug, and razzle-dazzle with more silliness than sense. After the waters muddled by their dirty work settle, nothing remains but mortification and pollution. Naturally, these primitive impulses have perennial allure as catharsis on the stage.

## Words

Tricks twist and turn so deviously that we should look at them a little more carefully. Be careful! By its origin, the PIE root *terk,* to twist, intricates us in intrigue.

**PIE root *terk*, to twist**
1. Romance
   Latin:
   *torqueo torquere* and *tortus*, to twist
   *intrico intricare*, to plot, perplex
   Italian: *intricato*; Spanish: *intrincado*
   Italian and Spanish: *intrigo*, and *intriga*
   French or English: *intrigue*, intrigue (1612, verb; 1647, noun)
   English: intricate (1470, adjective; 1564, verb)
2. Germanic
   German: *Intrige*
3. Slavic
   Russian: интрига (intriga)

Booty can be an obvious goal of trickery. Trickery may not seem to need words for weaving, hair, and calling, but it has made use of them. Weaving has such universal importance that five Romance languages have the same word for woof.

1. **PIE root *lau*, booty**
   Latin: *lucrum*, profit
   English: lucre and lucrative
   English (Anglo-Indian, borrowed from Hindustani), loot, cognate of lucre
   Russian:
   ловить (lovit'), to catch, hunt, fish; ловкость (lovkost'), sleight
   лукавый (lukavyy), sly; уловка (ulovka), trick
2. **PIE root *trag*, to draw, drag**
   Latin: *traho trahere* and *tractus*, to draw
   Latin, Italian, Spanish, Romanian, Portuguese: *trama*, woof, weave, or plot
3. **PIE root *guou*, to call, cry out**
   Russian: говор (gavor), murmur; заговор (sagavor), plot
4. **PIE root *pilo*, hair**
   Latin: *pilus* and *capillus*, hair
   English: pile, the hair of a rug
   French:
   *pelote*, ball (made of hair); *compeloter*, to roll into a ball
   *complot*, plot, as in conspiracy (*cf. intrigue*, plot, as in story)
   English: complot (1577) and plot (1587; 1649, verb)

The first root has a Slavic but not a PIE origin; the second phrase originates in Latin.

1. Proto-Slavic: xotěti (khoteti), to want
   Czech: *chęć*, wish, and its doublet, *chuć*, lust
   Russian:
   > хотеть (khotet), to want, desire; хитрость (khitrost), ruse, stratagem
   > хитрый (khityy), trick
2. Latin: *Hoc est corpus*, This is the body (describing bread transubstantiated)
   English: hocus-pocus, nonsense or hoax
   Russian:
   > фокус покус (fokus pokus), hocus pocus
   > фокусы (fokusy), tricks

## 101. Tricky Talking

In addition to cheap tricksters' dealing in double-deals and their crossing in double-crosses, they also talk in double-talk. Talking gets a job done; talking fast gets it done fast; but fast-talking double-talk gets it done so fast that no one knows what's happened. Particularly in his words, any man can, at least, seem to be whatever he wants, but a duplicitous man steals both himself and his dupes from themselves. With a mere desire to entertain, for example, Mel Blanc made up Bugs Bunny. With a mere desire to deceive, rogues and pettifoggers make up words in bad faith.

In shifting from talking, to talking fast, and fast-talking; from words, to eloquence and grandiloquence, from bluster, to bombast, and bamboozle, we can trick others and maybe even ourselves into thinking that we are not ourselves. Self-deception plays the cruelest trick of all, although Mel Blanc never suffered the delusion of believing that he really was a tough little back-talkin' Bugs from the Bronx. On stage, men transformed by language pass beyond the comic to the burlesque. Comedy, Joseph Addison observed, "ridicules persons by drawing them in their proper characters." Burlesque, by contrast, "draws them quite unlike themselves." It either dresses "mean persons in accoutrements of heroes," or makes "great persons" act and speak "like the basest among the people" (*Spectator*, 1711). We can observe comedy on the street or even in a court of law; but we enjoy the ludicrous reversals of burlesque best when they are portrayed on the stage.

The etymology of burlesque gives a clue to its topsy-turvy. The PIE root *peuor*, fire, explains the glow in the Latin *burra*, a small cow with a nose glowing red. Because this red-nosed *burra* was also shaggy, it then referred to a shaggy garment, and finally to the rough jokes told by the rustic rube wearing it. Put these things together—shaggy cow, shaggy garment, shaggy jokes—and you can imagine burlesque in its bucolic setting. By the plural *burrae*, the Romans described the nonsense of this cow-catcher's rough jokes, the stuff of the original burlesque. According to Addison's definition of burlesque, this bucolic trickster would overturn his world by putting down "great persons," and exalting "mean persons."

By the craft of burlesque, a duplicitous villain might bamboozle (1703) with bombast, his rustic version of schooled rhetoric. This bombastic bamboozler would gull some poor fellow with unsophisticated contrivance. If he left his bucolic scene for greater freedom on the road, he turned rogue (1561; Latin *rogare*, to ask). Playing itinerant scholars, rogues 'asked' for money while bandying about a few old saws that sounded like Latin. "Jesters, rogues, and minstrels" (1570) did a song and dance appropriate to their shaggy humor. Their average shtick effused pure bull, derived from either English to bull, cheating, or French *boule*, fraud—at first, without excremental association.

Back from bulls and burlesque to civilization, duplicitous lawyers play tricks with a little more sophistication. They use Roman, not roguish, Latin, as they argue their cases. They may not engage in burlesque, but they so overreach themselves in legalese that they deceive by hyperbole. Quirks (1547) and quibbles (1629), chicanery (1613), pettifoggery (1553) and perfidy (1592) all have their origin in the language of the law. The complexity of its language has given rise to quirk and quibble. Quirk first meant a twist of any sort and later a twist of logic. Quibble derived from Latin *quibus*, by which, one word by which the pettifogger introduces a maze of fine points in law to throw dust into the eyes of the judge and jury.

Quibbles and quirks, therefore, twist and turn in deceptive reasoning, which the pettifogger employs in his chicanery. A pettifogger, derived from petty and Fugger, a family of German merchants, describes a lawyer who hustles his inferior talents in low strategy to win mediocre cases. He employs chicanery, perhaps derived from *chic*, subtle, which could describe refinements in thought. In court, tricky people are perfidious (*per*, thoroughly bad and Latin *fides*, faith), because their word has no faith.

We call roguish tricks ludicrous, and legal chicanery unethical, but poetic figures we call literature. Just as Romance derived its word to speak

(Italian, *parlare*) from the Greek form of parable, which marks speech as holy and edifying, it also derived its word to find (Italian, *trovare*; French, *trouver*) from the Greek form of trope, a figure of speech, literally, "turning" from colloquial, prosaic use. Tropes gave Troubadors treasure troves. English to contrive (1325), to plot secretly, derived some of its evil quirk from people scheming with more learning than morality. In *Hamlet*, after Polonius has discovered a method in Hamlet's madness, he devises his own contrivance: "I will contrive the means of meeting between him and my daughter." Little does he know that he is contriving his own death.

*Schema*, scheme (1553), another word for trope or figure of speech in Greek, first meant turning common speech to literary effect and, much later (1718), an underhand plot. Contrive and scheme indicate that literary language can deceive. The fast-talking reasoning of casuistry (1725) and equivocation (1380) may direct the words themselves to this deceit. Casuistry explains a case (Latin *casus*) of morality altered by circumstance. Alexander Pope first referred to it as the art of explaining away problems of conscience.

Equivocation describes, literally, the calling (-vocation) of an equal (equi-): a student equivocates, when, having done two of ten assigned problems, he "calls" his two "equal" to ten. When Macbeth starts to realize that he has been deceived by the Devil, he says that he begins "to doubt the equivocation of the fiend / that lies like truth." Both the king and the student have made lies equal to truth. Bacon calls equivocation "the great sophism of all sophisms" (1605), that evades the truth by ambiguity and subterfuge (1573).

Men almost always pull off their tricks with words. Burlesque humor on the stage and legal chicanery in court deceive, one for laughs, the other for lucre. Even when literature seeks to blend entertainment with edification and instruction, many a novice in its arts may end up scratching his head in puzzlement over its artful tropes. In the hands of rogues, they amount to no more than fast-talk. In court, men use language to tell the truth, the whole truth and nothing but the truth; and, in life, to tell the truth with just a quirk of their own contrivance. The most honest among us contrive their schemes. Language—we can't live with it and we can't live without it!

## Words

Just as bad faith perverts good faith, tricky talking perverts right talking. It does not claim any roots uniquely its own. A few PIE roots describe a context, in which it can gain power.

PIE root *peuor*, fire

Latin:
> *burra*, shaggy garment, *burrae*, trickery, nonsense
> *burrula*, little joke
>> Italian: *burla*, joke; Italian and Spanish: *burlesca*
>> French and English: burlesque
>> German and Czech: *Burleske* and *burleska*; Russian: бурлеск (burlesk)

PIE root *segh*, to hold

Greek and Latin: *schema*, form or figure
> Spanish: *esquema*
> Italian and German: *schema*; Russian: схема (skhema)
> French and English: *schème* and scheme

Cf. a PIE doublet of *segh*: PIE root *weg*, to hold, carry or transport
Greek: *ocheo*, I carry; and *okkhos*, chariot
Latin: *veho vehere*, to carry, convey; and *vehiculum*, vehicle
Russian: возить (vozit), to carry, convey; and воз (voz), cart

PIE roots *ne*, not; *gno*, to know; and *oinos*, one

Latin: *gnosco gnoscere* and *notus*, to know
English: know and gnostic
Russian:
> одно (odno), one; and знать (znat'), to know
>> не-одно-значность (ne-odno-znachnost'), "not meaning one thing," ambiguity, equivocation

## 102. The Persuasive Spiel

Parents coaxing their kids, lovers blandishing their pets, or sideshow barkers soft soaping their suckers—they all set their words in the right melody. Barkers' hyperbole, for example, may not seem immediately persuasive: 'Don't pass up this chance for the greatest show on earth;' but they harmonize it in wheedling smoothly blended with cajoling. You gotta be there to hear—and see—how well they all put it together and pull it off. Benevolent or malevolent, sincere or feigned, flattery succeeds by harmonizing and dramatizing its words with the appropriate tones, notes, and gestures.

Flatterers orchestrating their words can imagine themselves on stage. Hypocrites (1225), originally, did act on stage; and hypocrites, currently, in their own minds, at least, have never left it. At the root of their activity, hypocrites, as actors with dialogue, responded from under (Greek *hypo*, under; and *crinein*, to respond) their masks. Later, setting aside masks, as orators on the podium, they relied on theatrical skills of delivery, instead of words. Currently, without either drama or rhetoric, hypocrites simply use play acting to deceive. Traditionally, they have taken the role of persons in possession of virtue or religion, which they themselves do not possess, pretending to espouse "beliefs of a higher order" than their own. By assuming whatever role they need to play, hypocrites may also hide ulterior motives beyond simple self-promotion. Hypocritical or sincere, persuasive wiles all sound the same. This similarity creates moral dilemmas, which can baffle even the discerning.

In strict chronology, persuasion, dramatically *con amore*, first fawned (1225) and flattered (1225); then blandished (1305); and, from the sixteenth through the eighteenth century, it coaxed (1589), wheedled (1661), and adulated (1777). Throughout this process, tail-wagging, slavering, cringing canines provide the model! By their nature, happy dogs fawn before their masters with full fain joy—fain being a cognate of fawn. In their roots, adulation and wheedling start with tail-wagging. Fido fawns sincerely before his master; a man before his peers should have more dignity. Hypocrites stoop to cower and grovel, but when they "fawn like a spaniel" so that they may eventually "bite like a mastiff," they betray a predatory nature. Moral men, on the other hand, can not stand tall all the time, and their fawning like Fido does not make them predatory. They may need to flatter, originally, by either falling 'flat' in adoration or by blandishing with the 'flat' of the hand.

Men have known from ancient of days that one goddess, *blanda Venus*, blandishing Venus, turns all but the strongest into fawning, flattering Fidos. Blandish and blandishment entered English with a pedigree from ancient love poetry: *Quas mihi blanditias, quam dulcia verba parabat*, the poet Ovid marveled about his beloved Corinna, "What blandishments, how sweet the words she prepared for me!" "Nature," Joseph Addison reflected, "has given all the arts of soothing and of blandishment to the female" (1711). Like the hypocrite, however, Ovid's girlfriend can also "bite like a mastiff"—*et modo blanditias dicat, modo iurgia nectat*, "and now she speaks blandishments, and then again she contrives quarrels." Let's call Corinna a "varied and mutable" phenomenon of nature, instead of a hypocrite—*Varium et mutabile semper femina*. Did Vergil have bad grammar or good insight in using neuter adjectives, *varium et mutabile*, to modify the most feminine of all nouns?

Coaxing first made someone foolish (1586), but it also persuaded by kissing, coddling and caressing (1589). In general, flattering pets the person and his ego; but wheedling practices more guile than coaxing with its fondling blandishments. It leads sweet and simple souls into acts of "disadvantage or reproof" (1661): Satan, the Father of Lies (*John* viii, 44), wheedled Eve to eat the apple, while deluding Adam (1726).

Cajoling (1645), roughly synonymous with coaxing and wheedling, emphasizes the voice instead of the blandishments of the other words for flattery. Probably from Latin *cavus*, cave or cage, cajoling, by its root, chatters "like a jay in a cage." Chattering and joking cajolery pretends less duplicitous flattery than wheedling and less blandishment than coaxing. Friends cajole a boon companion to share in a joke; parents coax a child to take medicine; and hypocrites wheedle good men to do bad things.

The root of cajolery gives just one indication that persuasion depends on delivery as much as on words. "To deceive" in Italian (*ingannare*) and Spanish (*enganar*), from Latin *gannire*, to yelp or to chatter, describes yelping dogs or chattering women. Italians know that persuasion involves more than words: charlatan (1605), from *cialare*, to chatter, describes prattling quacks. Dutch and German also have a word for the charlatan: in Dutch, a quack is a quacksalver, a man who sells salves by prattling like a quacking duck. German, *spielen*, to play a musical instrument, described the huckster's tuneful cant. Cant (1501) contributes to this cacophony: first the wheedling talk of rogues (1640), it came to refer to the jargon of any profession. Of course, the quack trumps up his wares by airing them with the fanfare of trumpets. His spiel hits the mark best when he has greased it with blandishment. Buttering people up requires lubricious words, lubricated with harmonizing intonations.

When P.T. Barnum observed that a sucker was born every minute, he might have also given credit to his barkers, who had just the right cajolery and blandishment to bait their traps. Outside of his sideshow, men readily take the bait: "Adulation ever follows the ambitious, for such alone receive pleasure from flattery" (1766). Flatterers rehearse what ambitious men want to hear. Who knows?—these flatterers may set moral goals for their moral ambitions. We can distinguish between wheedling and coaxing in the dictionary, but we need Solomon's wisdom to distinguish between them in practice. Deeper than what happens in practice, coaxing succeeds in life, because it recalls the Edenic days when our parents cajoled us to be good.

## Words

Words may be sufficient to the wise, but few of us have the wisdom to make the most of them. We need—and we all enjoy—the music and the gestures that persuade. By its root, suasion is suave; and if thoroughly suave, with a little tail wagging, sweet talking, soft soaping, and maybe even wheedling, persuasive suasion persuades. Russian, on the other hand, draws one of its words for persuasion from the PIE root *bheidh*, faith or oath: убеждать (ubezhdat') refers to persuasion by legal coercion, just the opposite of suave persuasion.

**PIE root *ul*, tail**

Latin: *adulatio*, fawning upon, flattering
    English: adulation (1380); to adulate (1777)
German: *wedeln*, to wag the tail
    English: to wheedle (1661)

**No certain PIE root, but perhaps *mel*, soft**

Latin:
    *blandus*, smooth-tongued, flattering, fawning, charming
    *blanditia*, flattery, charm, caress
        English: to blandish (1305); mellifluous and to mollify

Russian derives its words for persuasion from five PIE roots, which portray persuasion as softening, circumventing, talking, flattering and bending.

1. **PIE root *meg*, to knead, mix, make or match**
   Latin: *macero macerare*, to soften
       English: to macerate, to soften
   Russian:
       масло (maslo), butter; and маслить (maslit'), to butter
       у-масливать (u-maslivat'), to soft soap, butter up, cajole
2. **PIE root *sed*, to sit, put down (buttocks, feet or weapons)**
   Latin: *sedeo sedere* and *sessus*, to sit
       English: sedentary and session
   Russian: сидеть (sidet'), to sit
   Latin: *cedo cedere*, to go away
       English: to cede, accede, concede, intercede, precede, recede, secede;
       *cf.* to exceed, proceed, succeed
   Russian:
       ходить (khah-deet'), to go; хаживать (khazhivat'), to visit
       об-хаживать (obkhazhivat'), circumvent, to go round, wheedle, cajole
3. **PIE root *gwou*, cow, bull; and *gowh*, to call, cry**
   Latin: *bovo bovare*, to call loudly, roar, bellow

Russian:
: говядина (govyadina), beef
: говорить (govorit'), to talk; у-говорить (u-govorit'), to coax
4. **PIE root *las*, eager, greedy, wanton; and *list*, guile**
: English: lust and its doublet list; listful, full of pleasure; listless, without pleasure
: German: *List*, cunning, craft
: Russian: лесть (lest'), cunning, flattery, adulation
5. **PIE root *skel*, bending, crooked**
: Greek: *skelos*, leg
:: English: isosceles, of equal legs; triskelion
: Latin: *scelus sceleris*, crooked deed, crime
:: French and English: *scélérat*, villain
: Russian:
:: клятву (klyatvu), an oath (made on bended knee)
:: склонить (sklonit'), to bend, persuade

# 103. Sophisticated Sleaze

Deceivers do not delude, impose and dissemble for philosophical or unselfish reasons. They employ concrete methods for tangible self-aggrandizement. Why else do they fawn or cajole but to seek applause and buyers for their meretricious glitter?

After charlatans have debased gold, they make its glitter seem pure. Ancient Greeks realized that charlatans also debased wisdom into its alloys, and they had words to describe this glitz, and the men who hawked it: sophists (1542) traded in sophism (1350) and sophistry (1340). Euripides defined sophistry in one of his plays: *to sophon d'ou sophia*, "but the wise thing is not wisdom." Sophists reason speciously, fallaciously, and deceptively. Moral men ridicule their boasting, because its blustering equivocation tells only half the truth.

Sophomore (1688), wise (sopho-)+fool (-more), appends the right moronic suffix to describe the sophist. In school, the title sophomore reminds graduating Freshmen that they must pass their apprenticeship as wise morons before they can call themselves Junior Sophs or lordly Senior Sophs. Sophomoric epitomizes the sophist's foolish wisdom, because it flaunts "high-sounding words" that make "little sense" (1859).

Sophisticated (1607), at first, also described specious reasoning that obscures the truth. By 1895, it evolved to its modern meaning of worldly-wise; and, by 1945, to describing a work of complicated or refined structure. On the other hand, we still do not expect much more from a city sophisticate than a savvy choice from a wine list. We also suspect that his sophistication may not appreciate the ingenuous gold of folk less oenophilic than he. And yet, sophistication after 1900 would enjoy its day, especially in alcoholic America.

American bourgeoisie fostered its sophisticated ideal in the city slicker or the smoothie. Ben Jonson first used slick (1350) to modify flattery in 1599; but these names allude to the city slicker's sleek appearance. F. Scott Fitzgerald describes the Roaring Twenties' version of it: "The slicker was good-looking and clean-looking; he had brains, social brains, that is, and he used all means to get ahead, be popular, and he derived his name from the fact that his hair was soaked in water or tonic, parted in the middle and slicked back." Such smooth showboating slicks up this dude for deceit. Smooth (1050) has long described the smooth tongue (1450) of sophistication. Smooth and slick dress up specious aspects of sophisticated appearance. We can't help liking smoothies—they work so hard to be liked!—even though we know they live off their slick surface.

Adjectives for deceit describe the specious nature of glitter that often turns out to be nothing more than glitz. Meretricious (1626), derived from Latin *meretrix*, prostitute, calls to mind a gaudily dressed, garishly made-up seductrix. Romance *vistoso*, by its root, also describes someone more famous for vista than for vision. The Protestant Reformation, for example, referred to "the meretricious gaudiness of the Church of Rome" (1662). (It took Protestants a long time to get over the Pope as the Anti-Christ and the Whore of Babylon.) The plausible, by its root, wins applause (1561), but it can claim specious (1565) as a synonym: "A swindler . . . , then a quack, then a smooth plausible gentleman" (Emerson, 1860). Colorable (1382) is several shades less specious than meretricious and plausible: at first meaning specious, colorable now refers to what may be as valid as color on the surface.

As often as words for the fallacious describe slick people, they also describe the shoddy wares that they hawk. Clothing gives some clues. We expect men in polyester suits to sell cheap goods, which we call tawdry (1612), sleazy (1644) and shoddy (1832). Tawdry abbreviated Saint Audrey's lace, synonymous with cheap, pretentious finery (1680) and pretentious people, attempting to appear and communicate beyond their ability (1696). Sleazy described Silesian cotton fabric of flimsy warp and woof, or equally flimsy arguments: for example, "vain and sleazy opinions about religion" (1648). Shoddy refers, more specifically, to reused woolen yarn, worthless material made to look good, and also to people who try to appear better than they are: "There are shoddy lawyers, shoddy doctors ... and, worse than all, shoddy newspapers, whose especial business it is to puff up all the shoddy in the world ... to make people believe that it is all the genuine article" (1863). Schlock (1915) and its cognate slag first described refuse, scum or dregs. In its modern meaning, it describes cheap, broken merchandise that the sleazy schlockmeister trumps up.

Deceived by the meretricious trumpery of smooth-talking slickers, gullible suckers buy their sleazy schlock. Both they and the schlockmeisters share membership in a sophisticated coterie of those who keep their fingers crossed that, by some lucky chance, they may perhaps be right, or that greater wisdom does not reveal that they are not.

## Words

Deceit is all about surface: getting and showing the right fit, but then hiding it. The first PIE root answers a grotesque question: what do a retired professor and a prostitute have in common? Let's hope that academics do not win merit by meretricious sophistry!

### PIE root *mer*, sparkle; and *smer*, part

Latin:
>*mereo merere* and *meritus*, to deserve, earn
>*meretrix meretricis*, prostitute, who has merited payment
>*emeritus*, title for a professor retired after meritorious service (1823)

English: meretricious (1626)

### PIE root *kwek*, to see; or *deik*, to show

Greek: *tekmar*, sign, token
English: token and to teach
Russian: казать (kasat'), to show; по-казной (po-kaznoy), meretricious

### PIE root *dhab*, to fashion, fit

English: deft, fitting things together, a doublet of daft
Russian:
>добрый (dobryy), good, kind
>правдо-по-добный (pravdo-po-dobnyy), specious; literally, fitting truth
>*cf.* благо-видный (blago-vidnyy), looking good

### PIE root *sem*, same

Russian: само-званец (samo-zvanets)(samó-, self + zvanets, caller), imposter

PIE root *kel*, to cover, hide

Latin: *celo celare*, to hide (transitive); *cella*, storeroom (hiding place); *clam*, secretly

Latin and English: *color*, that which covers

*Cf.* PIE root *kweytos*, bright: English white and Russian цвет (tsvet), color

## 104. Guilty Feelings

### Pricking the Conscience of the Kind

The milk of human kindness sours on our tongues when we feel guilty. By religious ritual, penitence can absolve guilt that is the consequence of sin, but a guilty conscience can bruise, bit back, and punch us out.

In their relationship with God, ancient Jews owed Him a debt for sin, just as we owe creditors money. Their neighbors in antiquity could also make amends for murder by paying a blood price. In its first meaning, Hebrew *asham*, sin, represented both the crime and the debt paid for it. In this double edge, it resembles the Greek verbs *tio*, I pay honor (to gods) and *tino*, I pay a penalty (to gods). Both the Hebrew and the Greek put us on a dilemma between good and bad, the problem and its solution.

Guilt (971), a word of unknown origin, came from nowhere, but it definitely went somewhere as the Old English translation of *debita*, debts, in the Latin Vulgate: *Forgyf us ure gyltas, swa swa we forgyfað urum gyltendum*, "Forgive us our guilts, as we also forgive our guilty." Eventually, the translators of the King James Bible chose the Latinate 'debts' in their translation. In the tenth century, guilt first referred to crime: "Among the Jews, it is a capital guilt to curse a parent"—and in the twelfth, to the responsibility for the crime: when a man curses a parent, he should feel guilt.

Our vocabulary of guilt and its expiation has evolved from Judaeo-Christian ethics. When the sinner answers the prophetic call to repent (1290)—"Repent, for the kingdom of heaven is at hand"—he takes the first step to repentance (1303) by feeling sorry for his sins. To begin with, the repentant sinner has penitence, "undergoing discipline in outward expression of repentance." He desires repentance, does penitence, and is repentant (1290) as a result.

By repentance (1303), the fourteenth century took its first step in absolving the soul from guilt. In this century, a man had the opportunity to feel contrition (1300), contrite (1340), attrition (1374), penitent (1375), conscience (1400) as regret, and, finally, absolution (1400). The fourteenth, the guiltiest of centuries!

Just as penitence inspires repentance, attrition (1374) inspires contrition (1300), although contrition predated attrition by almost seventy-five years. In the twentieth century, attrition defined a war of attrition, a phrase coined in 1914 to describe warfare in which two armies in trenches 'wear each other away.' Attrition, however, for over five hundred years, had described imperfect sorrow for sin, the first step prompting penitence, then contrition and, finally, repentance. Contrition, not just worn away, but completely crushed with sorrow for sin—"the sign of inner change of character from prior evil to succeeding good" (1858)—describes the step for which attrition prepares. Attrition and contrition provide emotional motivation for penitence and repentance. The rite of penitence (1200) requires that the sinner suffer attrition (1374) and feel penitent (1375) as a consequence. After he has done penitence and become fully aware of the burden of his sins, he feels contrite and, therefore, repentant (1290), having obeyed the call to repent. If men had felt genuine attrition by sin in the nineteenth century, they might not have suffered the cruelties of war by attrition in the twentieth.

Guilt, more than five hundred years after its first use, drifted off to abstraction in referring to emotion felt as a consequence of crime (1510). Similarly, guilty (1000) at first meaning culpable, eventually referred to an emotion almost six hundred years later (1593). Emotions, we know from experience, can get out of hand when feeling guilty even without being guilty plagues well-meaning but guilt-tormented souls: "Let guiltless souls," Shakespeare exhorts, "be freed from guiltless woe."

In guilt-ridden humanity, therefore, conscience-stricken souls do not necessarily follow the ritual path of attrition, penitence, contrition and repentance. Guilt so wounds our hearts that we have more words to describe its torment. Remorse (1374) arose in a secular context without the assurance of being shriven by penitence. 'Remorse of conscience' obsesses and mortifies. Bishop Hall puts it in an earthly eschatology: "... no Hell but remorse." Oscar Wilde omits the eschatology: "Remorse makes one walk on thorns." Less intense, compunction (1340), punches the punctilious. Compunction, formerly used in such phrases as 'tears of compunction,' has weakened in modern use to a stirring of conscience: selfish people may evade income tax without compunction.

Even less intense than remorse and compunction, to rue, from a PIE root meaning to beat, expresses regret: "I shall find sufficient cause, if not to repent, at least to rue my misconduct" (1768). Qualm, derived from a strong Anglo-Saxon root meaning to kill, now expresses less intense stirring of conscience: if selfish people should evade taxes without compunction, they would probably do so with even less of a qualm.

Without absolution, ruthless ruing culminates in remorse, mortifyingly mordant. Solvency by paying "our debts" may seem a facile solution, but it makes a beginning. Contrition then paves the way to repentance that rids minds of guilt. In this dilemma between guilt and its solution, the year 1400 gave it absolution.

## Words

Crime comes at a price, sometimes a literal one in blood money; but, more often, one that crushes our minds with regret

### PIE root *paene*, almost

Latin: *paene*, almost; *paenitet*, it causes regret—'almost' death
    English:
        penitence (1200) and its doublet, penance (1290)
        repentance (1303), penitent (1375)

### PIE root *ter*, to rub away, press, crush

Latin: *tero terere* and *tritus*, to wear away, grind, bruise
    English: contrition (1300), attrition (1374), trite (1548)

### PIE root *peug*, to strike, pierce

Latin: *pungo pungere* and *punctus*, to prick, sting, punch
    English:
        compunction (1340), punctilious (1634)
        puncture (1400, noun; 1699, verb),

### PIE root *mer*, to rub away, destroy

Latin: *remordeo remordere* and *remorsus*, to bite back, torment
    English: remorse (1374)

### PIE root *krew*, to beat, break, bruise

German: *bereuen / reuen*, to repent, regret
English:
    to rue (888), to affect with regret; (950), to regret
    ruth and ruthless, pity and without pity
Greek: *kruo*, I break

Russian:
>крушить (krushit), to destroy, shatter
>со-крушаться (sokrushat'sya), to lament, repent

**PIE root *key*, to pay, avenge**

Russian: по-каяться (po-kayat'sya), to repent
Greek:
>*tio*, I pay honor; and *tino*, I pay a penalty
>*time*, honor
>>English: Timothy, the honor of God
>
>*poine*, penalty

Latin: *poena*, punishment; *punio punire*, to punish
>English: penitent, to punish

# 105. Breaking the Law

Transgression passes over what is right to break human and divine laws, but it does not always trespass on property and jump over fences. When we literally break our neighbor's fence, we metaphorically break a law. Oathbreakers transgress only metaphorically, because they commit wrong without wringing the necks of their victims, and torts without torturing. Transgression runs a gamut: it breaks bones by throwing stones; it breaks hearts by saying unkind words, but it breaks faith by doing nothing.

In English, breaking (851) first literally broke into a house; and, later, metaphorically broke (910) an oath or a law (1000). We break the law, an image which we have derived from the Romans, who spoke of breaking a treaty or breaking faith. Breaking makes breaches, just as speaking makes speeches. Breaking laws covers such breadth that it shares territory with its cognate breaching (1000). Breaching, at first, literally broke something like a vase. Long before its verb form, however, the noun breach (1025) referred to broken laws or contracts; although, in modern English, we refer to a breach of contract and not to a breach of law.

In Latin, both verbs *frangere* and *rumpere* described breaking an oath or faith, but the violent *rumpere* had more force than the relatively subtle *frangere*. "Good faith holds life together," says Cicero, and "it is wicked and perfidious to break (*frangere*) it" (*perfidiosum et nefarium est fidem frangere quae continet vitam*, Pro Roscio 6.16); but Roman legions, Tacitus observes, "broke through (*rumpere*) reverence for their military oath" (*rupta sacramenti reverentia*, Histories, 1). The derivation of fracturing and fragmenting from *frangere* and rupturing and erupting from *rumpere* can clarify this distinction.

In English, rupture (1481), almost as early as violation, referred to breaking the law. Although we no longer rupture laws in modern English, the word may refer to a break in harmonious relations, as it first did in 1583. We can refer to WW I as a violent rupture in European hegemony. We have given rupture a wide berth, because its forceful eruption has claimed a reference to abdominal hernias since 1539. In modern Spanish, however, *romper una ley* describes breaking a law.

Infringe (1533) and infraction (1623) entered English later than breaking, but they have continued to refer to breaking the law or an oath: "Jove for your love would infringe an oath" (Shakespeare, *Love's Labor's Lost* IV, 3, 144). An exception, the Italian idiom *infrangere la legge* describes lawbreaking. Only later (1543), and rarely, did infringe refer to crushing an enemy. We do much less crushing when we infringe upon someone's rights: Thomas Jefferson, for example, writes of the act of a legislature "which may infringe upon the rights and liberties of another." Following on infringe, infraction referred only to science, but, later (1673), to breaking a law or right. The native English verb to break has retained its force in describing law breaking. Rupture, by contrast, sounds too archaic, and infringement or infraction sounds too abstract.

The classical tradition of violation made its contribution to the description of physical force from the thirteenth through the fifteen centuries, from violence (1290), and violent (1340), to violate (1432). Violence does physical violence. Macbeth justifies his murder of the guards suspected of murdering the king: "The expedition of my violent love outran the pauser, reason ... His gashed stabs looked like a breach in nature." At the end of this tragic story of violent love and ambition, "His Fiend-like Queen ... by self and violent (1340) hands, took off her life." Violation (1432), only at first, violated violently. Although the law cannot literally suffer violence, crime violates the sanctity of its body, just as rape literally violates the chastity of a woman's body. Florizel, pledging his faith to Perdita, recoils at the thought of "the violation of my faith" (Shakespeare, *The Winter's Tale* IV). In his true love, he considers man's faith as inviolate (1412) as God's covenant with man. On the other hand, with more concern for legality than for loyalty, modern French and Spanish have preserved the concept of lawbreaking as violation: *violer la loi*, and *violar la ley*.

Latinate violation and rupture still pack a punch of personal injury, but Germanic breach and Latinate infraction just pinch without much physical damage. By contrast, Germanic wrong and Latinate tort started out packing quite a punch, but their evolution has left them palely generic.

Cognate with wring (888) and worry (725), and first meaning strangle, wrong (1067) describes personal injury or infringement of right. Today, we suffer wrong or we are in the wrong—the word has stayed closer to a wrong act than a wrong done to the law. Doing wrong specifically has become wrongdoing commonly. From a classical source and with less flexibility, tort (1387) also derives from the concept of wringing in the Latin *torquere/tortus*, to wring, as in torture and extort. Since 1586, tort has described a wrongful action in the law, but not a breach of contract.

Instead of breaking laws, we may simply fail to uphold them. If we allow our bills to become past due, we become delinquent in our obligation. Latin passed on its legal term *delictum*, a failure in duty, as in the phrase *corpus delicti*, to twelve Romance, Germanic, and Slavic languages. Passing over all our duties, we may even become derelict, abandoning duty and abandoned by man—a tragic image.

Words for lawbreaking and oathbreaking go in and out of literal and metaphorical meaning. Wrongdoers no longer literally wring necks, and violators no long do violence, but they harm their victims, as they violate the laws which should protect us all.

## Words

One PIE root supplies one word in Russian for breaking the law;
two PIE roots supply English cognates, break/fracture, and violate;
one PIE root supplies the same word for crime in twelve languages,
—you can't start looking for the murderer until you've found the *corpus delicti*.

### SLAVIC

**PIE root *reue*, to break, knock down, dig up**

Latin: *ruo ruere*, to fall down
    English: ruin
Russian: рвать (rvat'), to tear; and на-рушать (na-rushat'), to break an oath

### ROMANCE AND GERMANIC

1. **PIE root *bhreg*, to break**
    Latin: *frango frangere* and *fractus*, to break
        English: infraction (1673)/infringement (1628), breaking an obligation
    German: *brechen*, to break
        English: to break (851, verb; 1300, noun), breach (1000, noun; 1547, verb)

2. **PIE root *uiro*, man and his virile vigor**
   Latin: *vis* and *vim*, force
      English: violence (1290), violent (1340), to violate (1432)

**CORPUS DELICTI**

Roman law gave the *corpus delicti* to twelve languages:

**PIE root *leikw*, to leave**

Latin:
   *delictum*, crime, a failure in duty
   *corpus delicti*, "the body of the crime," the physical proof of a crime
      Italian: *delitto*; Spanish and Portuguese: *delito*; French: *délit*
      German, Polish, and Czech: *Delikt*; Russian: деликт (delikt)
      Romanian, Dutch, and English: delict

# 106. Erring from the Straight and Narrow

The malicious man transgresses rectitude and violates sacred rights. The common man—from among the moral majority of the world's stumblebums—feels no dedication to desecration. He digresses from justice or right by wandering off or by misstepping and blundering into error.

Error and deviation depart from a norm through some mistaken notions. At leisure, in his villa among the Tuscan hills, Cicero praised the philosopher's duty to extricate the common man from the *error* of false opinions. From this Latin word, English inherited error (1300) and erring (1303) to describe this wandering from the truth: "Almighty and most merciful Father," the *Book of Common Prayer* addresses a merciful God, "we have erred, and strayed from thy ways like lost sheep." Goethe, with more than a bit of Faustian pride, imagines God recognizing this error as the striving of an ambitious man: *Es irrt der Mensch so lang er strebt* ("Man errs, so long as he strives"). Long after its metaphorical use, error could describe actual wandering—for example, the error (1594) of Odysseus after the fall of Troy. After we have strayed, we need to straighten out the error of our ways. *Errare humanum est, perseverare autem diabolicum* ("To err is human; to persevere, however, diabolical"). In his striving, Faust, oxymoronically, errs perseveringly into the diabolical.

Deviation (1603)—Latin *de via*, away from the road—entered English three hundred years after error. Like error, it first described wandering from an accepted standard or from the straight path of rectitude, but it met the scientist's need for precise measurement and the moralist's for precise conduct. The eighteenth century novelist, Samuel Richardson, set it on a course of propriety: "Worthy persons, inadvertently drawn into a deviation, will endeavor instantly to recover their lost ground." "Worthy persons," of course, correct their misconduct, but deviation's neutral description of this "lost ground" usually needs an adjective like scandalous to call the error arrant.

Sometimes, however, we can fall deeply into error. In the twentieth century, the noun deviate (1912) denoted a person of sexual perversion or social maladjustment. Aberration (1594) denotes great deviation—mental aberration or youthful aberration euphemistically describe outlandish behavior. At the other extreme, vagary, started out literally rambling off in nothing more aberrant than a daydream. We can wander between extremes in judging deviation from a norm: "Capital vices?", one sophisticate has queried, "Say, rather, fashionable errors." Amoral sophists explain away all deviation, but only the tediously punctilious erroneously condemn any evidence of it.

Delirium (1599), started out by going off the track, but ended up going haywire. A Latin word from the image of a bull going out of a furrow in plowing—*de lira*, from the furrow—it describes incoherent speech, hallucinations or even frenzied restlessness. Of course, men may sometimes enjoy being incoherent: "Opium is pleasing to the Turks on account of the pleasing delirium it produces" (1756). Without opium, modern man can enjoy being delirious with joy.

Blunder (1386), cognate with blind, stumbles blindly into error: "Bayard the blind," Chaucer's first use of the word, describes blind Bayard "that blundreth forth." "It is worse than a crime, it is a blunder" has become the final comment on bungling stupidity.

Sometimes, instead of wandering off or blundering into error, we take one misstep to put our foot in it. Horace, we have seen, used *peccatum*, cognate with *pes pedis*, foot, to describe a misstep. It takes many steps from the *faux pas* of *peccatum* to the noun sin (825), cognate with Latin *sons*, guilty—from the first misstep to final guilt! Russian adds fire to the guilt: гореть (goret'), to blaze, takes flame in грех (grekh), sin.

From *peccatum*, English derives peccadillo (1591), a venial sin, and impeccable (1531), not liable to sin—"The Pope is not only infallible, but also impeccable." Today, it means free from error: connoisseurs have impeccable taste. This tolerant Horatian and early Christian attitude toward sin, represented by *peccatum*, translates the Greek *para-ptoma*, falling by the way, in *Matthew* 6, 15. The King James Bible translates *paraptoma* as trespass, a word which aggravates the culpability of slipping or stumbling in Greek or in Latin. Later Christian ethics viewed the trespass of sin even more severely.

Can we prevent our stumbling, when we fall into a trap? Paul in *Romans* 14, 13 said that we must not put such traps in the way of our brothers. William Tyndale translated this Greek word for trap, *scandalon*, "that which one must jump or climb over" as stumbling block. Scandal (1225)—slander (1290), its doublet—describes models, whose misconduct puts stumbling blocks in the way of our good conduct.

All men sometimes stumble like stumblebums. From blundering, at one extreme, to trifling deviation, at the other, they walk a fine line between norms and exceptions, not to mention, between right and wrong. After knights errant have rescued damsels from arrant knaves, they, like Cicero's philosopher, might also display heroism in rescuing the knaves themselves from their arrant erring.

## Words

Why do men wander from the right path? Something about fords over streams, cloudy weather or the heat of their impulses throws them off.

### PIE root *ire*, to go, wander

Latin: *erro errare*, to wander; and *error*, wandering
    Italian: *errare / errore*; Spanish: *errar / error*; French: *errer / erreur*
    English:
        to err (1303) / error (1300)
        Doublets:
            errant (1340) in knight errant
            arrant (1386) in thief arrant
German: *irren*, to err

### PIE root *vag* and *wend*, to bend, curve, wander

Latin: *vagus*, wandering; and *vagor vagari*, to wander
    Italian: *vagare*, to wander; and *vagabondo*, vagabond
    Spanish: *vagar* and *vagabundo*; French: *vaguer* and *vagabond*
    German: *Vagabund*, vagabond
    English:
        vague (1425), as verb, to wander; (1548), as adjective, unclear
        vagabond (1426), vagary (1577)
German: *wandern*, to wander

### Cf. PIE root *bhred*, to wade

Russian:
>  брод (brod), ford; and бродить (brodit'), to wander
>  бродяга (brodyaga), vagabond

### PIE root *bhlend*, to mix, make cloudy

English and German: blind
English: to blunder (1386)
Russian:
>  блуд (blud), promiscuity, fornication; блуждать (bluzhdat'), to wander
>  за-блуждение (za-bluzhdeniye), error, delusion, misbelief

### PIE root *kseib/ksweyb*, to throw, swing, whip

English: to swipe
Russian: шибать (shibat), to strike, throw; о-шибка (o-shibka), error

### PIE root *gwher*, to heat

Greek: *thermos*, heat
Latin: *fornax fornacis*, furnace
English: warm
Russian:
>  гореть (goret'), to blaze, glow, burn
>  грех (grekh), sin; and грешить (greshit'), to sin
>  по-грешность (po-greshnost'), error

### PIE root *skand*, to climb, stumble

Greek: *scandalon*, stumbling block
>  Latin: *scando scandere* and *scansus*, to climb; *scalae*, steps
>>  English:
>>>  to ascend or to descend
>>>  to condescend (1340), to descend voluntarily, to yield

## 107. The Straight and Narrow

Let's straighten out all this twisting, deviating and blundering! In World War II, the popular song, "Straighten up and fly right," admonished flyboys to the straight and narrow. Long before Nat King Cole sang this admonishment of the wayward, two PIE roots, *hreg*, to straighten, and *pro*, forward, set mankind straight. The PIE roots, *streg*, rigid or *strenk*, tight, suggests that straightening may also end up straitening and leave us as straitened as we are straightened. Straightened or straitened, let's at least have some straight talk.

Twenty-five years after human rulers ruled kingdoms personally with right laws, wooden rulers ruled (1440) pages impersonally with right lines. What a difference between the two directions, one personal, the other impersonal! Men, as rulers, make laws right; yardsticks, as rulers, make lines right—one job easy, the other hard. Let's follow the straight line of this contrast. Regular (1387), derived from *regula*, conforms to a rule. At first, it referred to men under the rule of Saint Benedict, in contrast to those under secular rule. It has also described conformity to a standard: Cowper marveled at the well regulated life of the virtuous man: "How regular his meals, how sound he sleeps."

Purely mechanical, on the other hand, Latin *regio*, a line of the *regula*, consequently, described a boundary and the territory within it. In English, region (1330) also described a distinctly defined territory. When things go awry in these regions, rulers can rectify (1400) or correct (1340) deviations, but they cannot as easily correct men with mechanical precision. In spite of rulers correcting and directing on maps, their citizens may prove incorrigible instead of dirigible.

Whatever the difficulties, rules must enforce their boundaries. In Latin, *regimen* governed the *regio*. In English, regimen (1400) first regimented matters of health and, secondarily (1456), matters of government. Government enforced its regimen by a regiment, first (1390), a synonym of regimen; and, later (1579), a military unit that made incorrigibles dirigible.

Although the first English use of the adjective straight honored a nose: "her nose is straight" (1350), Isaiah's voice crying in the wilderness to make "straight in the desert a highway for our God" has honored the straight way as a highway for the godly. When the Psalmist also asked "the Lord, my God . . ." for direction: *Dirige, Domine, Deus meus, in conspectu tuo viam meam* ("Direct my way in your sight"), his first word *dirige* provided the title of the antiphon, a dirge, that seeks God's direction for the dead.

God shows men a straight path, but they regularly lose it. Dante, at the beginning of his spiritual journey, describes himself as having lost the "direct way":

*Nel mezzo del cammin di nostra vita*
*mi ritrovai per una selva oscura,*
*ché la diritta via era smarrita.*

("In the middle of the road of our life, / I found myself in a dark forest, / because the straight way had been lost.") English translates *diritta* as "straight." When we ask for directions on the street in Rome, *Sempre dritto*, "Straight ahead!," takes us directly to our destination.

Right (*Beowulf*), the oldest word in English for justice (1137), translates the German *recht*. English derived the word right from German, but English speakers derived its meaning from Roman philosophy, which defined *rectum* as right conduct: *Rectum est quod cum virtute et officio fit*, "Right is what happens with virtue and duty." By several twists and then a sharp right angle of etymological fate, rectum (1541) in English describes the "straight part" of the large intestine. What an indignity to reduce classical ethics to anatomy! Some stumblebums, however, would argue that rectitude is just a proctalgia anyway.

Closer to the German root, rightwise became righteous (825). Righteousness sounds almost as forbidding in English as its Latinate parallel, rectitude (1432), which referred to straight lines long before it referred to straight conduct (1533). English might have derived righteousness from German; but, like right, it has derived its meaning from the classical ethic of Christianity. The first use of the words demonstrates Biblical piety: righteousness, for example, translated *justitia* in the *Psalms*, *Sacrificate sacrificium justitiae*, "Offer the sacrifice of righteousness" (Psalm 4, 6). Although the twelfth century Renaissance translated *justitia* as justice, the ninth century used the native word righteousness. Though of lowly and native birth, righteous has assumed dignity as a shibboleth of piety.

Orthodox (1581) gets straight to the doctrine that makes a man righteous in religion. From right to righteous to orthodox traces the direct line of straight behavior from the moral, to the moralistic, to the strictly moralistic. Regular describes both the literal and the ethical ramifications of rectitude. Both geometric figures and conduct can be regular, but regularity in conduct often puts men in straitjackets.

## Words

The first three PIE roots describe the straight; the last two, the strait.

### STRAIGHT

1. **PIE root *hreg*, to straighten, in three families:**
   Greek: *orthos*, with the addition of the vowel 'o' to the root, straight
   English: orthodox (1581)

Latin:
> *rego regere* and *rectus*, to straighten; and *regula*, rule
> *dirigo-ere/directus*, to direct; and *corrigo-ere/correctus*, to correct
>> English:
>>> direct and dirigible; incorrect and incorrigible
>>> dirge, from Latin *Dirige*, Direct!, the first word of *Psalm* 5.9
> German: *recht*, right; *das Recht*, justice
>> English: ruler (1375), leader; ruler (1400), yardstick

2. **PIE root *pro*, forward**
   Greek: *proktos*, rectum; and Latin: *probus*, upright
   > English: Greek proctologist and Latinate probity
   
   Russian: право (pravo), right (noun); and правда (pravda), truth

3. **PIE root *streg*, rigid**
   English: straight (1300), as adverb; (1350), as adjective; and to straighten (1542)

## STRAIT

1. **PIE root *strenk*, tight, narrow**
   English: strait (1205) and to straiten (1552)

2. **PIE root *ten*, to stretch; and *tenhus*, thin**
   Latin: *tenuis*, thin
   > English: tenuous
   
   Russian:
   > тесный (tesnyy), tight, narrow
   > стесненный (stesnennyy), straitened

# 108. War and Peace

Describing the world as well paid by peace, but worsened by war, makes good moral and etymological sense. Words for war and peace in German and Russian confirm the goodness of peace and the worseness of war, but the Romance story introduces subtle distinctions in the relationship between the two.

Ancient Romans embraced peace, but they did not shy away from war, which they turned to peace by pacts. "Peace from pact"—*pax a pactione*—observes Sextus Pompeius Festus, an etymologist of the second century A.D. A product of Roman law, *pax*, by its root, binds men in an agreement. Festus further qualifies it as "a pact of conditions," *pactione condicionum*, an agreement with stipulations. Pacifism in the early twentieth century created its motto from this etymological play: *Si vis pacem, para pactum*, "If you wish peace, prepare a pact." Pacts make peace.

The roots of peace tell the story of its construction by our ancient ancestors. *Pax* and *pactum* originate in the verb *pangere* that can describe setting a boundary by driving stakes into the ground. From this root also, English derives pole and its noun doublet pale, stakes driven into the ground. Stakes mark boundaries—we go beyond the pale in passing them. Since Romans fought wars about breaking boundaries, they made peace by restoring them. Similarly, terms (1225) of peace, from Latin *terminus*, referred at first to stakes driven into the ground as physical boundaries akin to legal conditions. Peacemakers come to terms by defining place, time, and law.

In the Roman Empire, peace came with strings attached. When a Roman client nation tore them apart, Romans waged war. They anticipated war and planned for it carefully. Their aphorism—*Si vis pacem, para bellum*, "If you wish peace, prepare war"—assumes that well armed peace deters war. Romans appreciated peace as a cognate of pact, but they sharpened their swords to keep it.

The Romans' folk etymology explained *bellum* as a form of the archaic *duellum*, a duel, the derivative of *duellum*, a war fought by two—*duo*, two men such as David and Goliath. The potential similarity of Latin *bellum* with Romance *bellus*, beautiful, created an awkward confusion that, according to some etymologists, made *bellum* obsolete. *Bellum* survives in bellicose and belligerent, words borrowed from Latin in the Renaissance.

Belligerent Germans, just the opposite of peacemakers, imposed their word for war on the Romans. Spreading their Germanic *guerra*, war, through Europe, they sent Classical Latin *bellum* into exile. "The origin of the munificence" of the Germans, the Roman historian Tacitus attests, arose "through wars and robberies"—*materia munificentiae per bella et raptus*. These belli-gerents preferred *belli-cultura* to *agri-cultura*. Why work and sweat and wait for a crop to grow when you can steal one more easily and in less time?[22] In the early Middle Ages, war as a particularly German activity explains the currency of their word for it in Romance and in English. At that time, the embattled Romans took the defensive and their concept of *bellum* did not survive as the operative word. The Germans, eventually, so prevailed in war that their word *guerra* defined it. This one word, winning a war of words, epitomizes the fall of the Roman Empire and the fall of the Third Reich, as well.

German *Friede* and its cognate, *frei*, defines peace in families of free men. Thus confined within loyalty to clan, the Samaritan would not have won the epithet Good, because he would have passed by the wounded foreigner on the other side. Roman *pax* had legal limits; German *Friede*, national limits. On the other hand, the PIE root *mei*, gentle, gives the Russian word for peace, мир (mir), a gentle origin. Saint Casimir proclaims this gentleness to the world. Transcending law and nation, Russian мир (mir) makes peace pacific: like the dove after the flood, "An olive leaf he brings, pacific sign" (Milton, *Paradise Lost* 11. 860).

Under the influence of the Biblical *shalom*, peace, and the *Pax Romana*, peace came to mean tranquility. About fifty years after the first use of the word in the *Old English Chronicle* of 1154, peace of mind (1200) referred to domestic peace and quiet. Shalom originates in the root for completeness and welfare that is appropriate to Jesus' Easter greeting to the disciples, *Pax vobis*, "Peace be with you" (*John* 20.26).

Peacemaking has importance, with or without war. Not long after peace entered English, pay (1200) was its verb form derivative from French, with which the Renaissance paired its Latinate form pacify (1460). We preserve pay's original meaning of pacification when we say that someone has been well or ill paid by fair or unfair treatment. Any one who has pacified an indignant creditor can understand why pay refers to discharging a debt (1250). Later, to appease (1330) referred specifically to bringing belligerents 'to peace'(*ad-pacare*). In the high Renaissance, pacific (1548) specifically referred to working toward peace instead of war. When Magellan observed that the ocean off the coast of California appeared free of storm, he called it the Pacific.

In German, English, and Russian, war originated in roots for burdens and violence. It starts out bad, and degenerates to its cognates, worse and worst. *Pace* the last resort of the Romans' diplomacy and the Germans' sophistry, war almost always violates pacts and peace—war, worse, worst. It destroys by uprooting the pale and all in its path. Peace pays the world well by setting up pales and keeping within them. It introduced a culture of law in Rome, family in Germany and gentleness in Russia.

*Pax vobis.*
*Friede sei mit dir.*
мир с тобой (mir s toboy).

## Words

Three PIE families give Romance, Germanic and Slavic words for war and peace.

1. ROMANCE

*War*

PIE root *dau*, to burn; or *duo*, two

Latin: *duellum* and its alternate form, *bellum,* war
    English: duel (1284), bellicose (1432), and belligerent (1577)

PIE root *uers*, sweep, to stir up confusion

Latin: *verro verrere*, to sweep; *verriculum*, broom
German in Mediaeval Latin: *werra/guerra,* war
    Italian and Spanish: *guerra*; French: *guerre,* war
    English: war (1154); the comparative, worse, the superlative, worst

*Peace*

PIE root *pag*, to fix, fasten, bind

Latin:
    *pango pangere* and *pactus*, to fasten, fix, determine
    *pax pacis*, peace, treaty, compact; *paco pacare*, to pacify
    *pace*, the ablative of *pax*, "with deference," used in English
        Italian: *pace*; French: *paix*; Spanish: *paz*
        English:
            peace (1154), absence of war
            to pay (1200) and its doublet, to pacify (1460)
            pact (1429), agreement

2. GERMANIC

*War*

PIE root *gwreh*, heavy

Greek: *barus*, heavy
    English: barometer
Latin: *gravis* and its doublet, *brutus*, heavy
    English: grave and brutal
German: *Krieg*, war

*Peace*

PIE root *prihos*, beloved, of one's own clan

German: *Friede*, peace; and *frei*, free

## 3. SLAVIC

*War*

**PIE root *weyh*, to chase, pursue**

Latin: *vis*, violence
Russian: война (voyna), war; воин (voin), soldier

*Peace*

**PIE root *mei*, gentle**

Latin: *mitis*, mild, gentle
    English: to mitigate
Russian:
    мир (mir), peace and the world in which to enjoy it
    *cf.* Casimir, Proclaimer of peace; Vladimir, ruler of the world

**PIE root *kuei*, restfulness, space of time**

Latin:
    *quies*, quiet of either sleep, peace or death
    *Requiescat in pace*—"May he rest in peace (RIP)."
Russian:
    покой (pokoj), rest and the room in which to enjoy it
    ('Q' interchanges with 'p': *quies*, for example, changes to покой,
       as Latin *quinque*, five [*cf.* quintet], changes to Greek *pente*
       [*cf.* pentagon] and Russian Пять [pyat].)

# 109. Pride

### Pride in the Place or on the Face

In the first lines of his epic poem, the *Aeneid*, Vergil mentions "walls of high Rome" (*// altae / moenia / Romae*) as the final heritage of Aeneas' prowess. "High" modifies "Rome" instead of "walls," since the ideal of Rome transcends its walls. Latin *altus*, high, through its French derivative, *haut*, laid a foundation for haughty, which at first referred to high character: in the Garden of Eden, Adam was "of courage haughty and of limb / Heroic built" (*Paradise Lost IX*, 484-5). Only the Devil could disparage Adam's haughty courage. Proud men, from their edifice and its edification, look down from a high and mighty place, or they may just simply look down from raised eyebrows.

Ancient and medieval architecture rose from an eminence. In a cult of nature worship, altars on "high places" (*Numbers* 23.3) burned sacrifices to the ancient god Baal. In the cult of human greatness, haughty' might refer to the "haughty towers" (1570) that befitted the high and mighty. *Fastigium*, the highest point of an ancient building, meant both pride and pediment. On proud pediments, noble Romans displayed their escutcheons. Derived from *fastigium*, fastidious, meant proud—"Proud youth! Fastidious of the lower world" (1744)—long before it meant difficult to please. Superb also referred to fastidious buildings—"superb Troy," to whose rough-hewn virtues Renaissance Italians alluded when they raised their palazzos on cyclopean, rusticated stone. Only much later did superb mean very fine. By his name, could *Tarquinius Superbus*, Tarquin the Proud, the last Roman king, have resided anywhere else than in a superb palace? Proud Rome bespoke nobility from its heroic foundations to its haughty pediments and towers.

The democratic British, avoiding the ostentatiously fastidious pediment, reserved their escutcheons for the pediments of their fireplaces. Let the Italians look disdainfully on the polloi from their *piano nobile* above the ground floor. By one account, a Brit changed the Frenchmen's noun phrase *haut toit*, haughty roof, to the adjective phrase hoity toity to mock their highfalutin pretension; although the word first referred to giddy girls. At any rate, both Europeans and the English realized that edifices might teach edifying lessons in either noble pride on the continent or its decorous restraint in England.

Wherever they lived, *prud'hommes*, valiant men, display pride. In French, *prud*, deriving its root from Latin *pretium*, value, describes valiant manhood. French derived its word for proud from Latin *ferus*, fierce, which meant proudly high-spirited—"He is fierce and cannot brook hard language" (*2 Henry*)—before it meant wild. The English word proud, an adjective form of Latin *prodesse*, to be of use, puts utility at the root of prowess. It has meant haughty in a mostly pejorative sense from its first use—such was the Anglo-Saxons' conservative nature.

Pride does not always need to celebrate its valiant, useful deeds by lofty pediments; by a fastidious face, it might fill the need without cost. When the Israelites left Egypt with hands raised high in triumph (*Numbers* 33.3), their high-hands expressed joy. Later, high-handedness implied arrogance. A brow raised in disdain can also express superiority—*supercilium*, eyebrow in Latin, at the root of supercilious, haughtily contemptuous. Also a facial expression, but humorously colloquial, snooty describes turning up one's nose in disdain: snooty private school kids, for example, with age and wisdom, may come down to earth. The Russian word meaning pompous, на-пыщенный (napyshchennyy), is related to a verb that means to frown, which verb in English refers to turning up the nose. The Israelites did not have time to raise a lofty pediment to their triumph, but they certainly wanted to show their joy with more than a disdainful brow or a snooty toss of the head!

Nineteenth century phrenology attributed superior intelligence to a man with a high brow. High brow (1875), therefore, refers to a brow that is intellectual rather than supercilious. From *pompa*, parade in Greek, pompous refers to the conduct of a parading potentate. Some high brow, bumptious folk walk around in a parade of their own imagining. A fancy hat can some put panache in the parade. Jack Conway, an editor of *Variety* in 1924, coined 'high hat' to refer to a snob. Democracy has brought us a long way down from the lofty eminence. In America, a good strut with a high hat and a snooty look have replaced the lofty walls of nobility at least for a fancy dude on the street.

On the other hand, the haughty, the high brow, and the hoity toity should condescend, happily and without disdain, to their shared humanity. "Mind not high things," Paul urged the Romans, "but condescend to men of low estate" (*Romans* 12.16). A man condescends when, completely—that is, willingly—descending, he defers to others. Condescension has come to denote insincere, hypocritical complaisance. Paul's Roman friends prided themselves on sophistication. He was urging them to be of one mind with all their brothers, even with those not equally well versed in whatever they might have considered valuable at the time.

Democracy does not foster pride, which builds its facades literally or expressively, nobly or cheaply. In any case, it constructs its own exclusive world. An epic hero strides forth on streets of gold; a highfalutin high hat parades like a peacock down any street; a snooty little princess thinks she's too good for anyone else on her street. Pride acts democratically by condescending from its lofty self to share humanity's common lot.

## Words

High and mighty pride puts itself over, out and above, with its eyebrows raised, its nose in the air or its face in a frown.

### PIE root *hel*, to grow, nourish

Latin: *altus*, grown, high
    French: *haut*, high; *haut toit*, high roof
        English:
            haughty (1530) and hauteur
            hoity toity, English version of *haut toit*

### PIE *hypso*, high, lofty

English: hypsistarian, worshipping God as Most High
Russian: высокомерный (vysokomérije), haughty

### PIE root *bhars*, projection

Latin: *fastigium*, pediment, pride
    English:
        fastuous (1638)
        fastidious (1440), proud; (1612), difficult to please

### PIE root *uper*, over

Greek: *hybris*, hubris, pride, arrogance toward the gods
Russian: высокомерный (vysokomernyy), haughty
Latin: *superbus*, proud
    English: superb (1549), proud; (1729), very fine
Latin: *supercilium*, eyebrow
    English: supercilious (1529)

### PIE root *ghwer*, wild, fierce

Latin: *ferus*
    French: *fier*, proud
    English: fierce (1290), high-spirited and proud

### PIE root *per*, forward, in front of

Latin: *prodesse*, to be of use
    French: *prud homme*, brave man
    English: proud (1050), haughty; prowess (1290)

### PIE root *(s)na*, flow

English:
    sniffle or snot, referring to dripping mucus
    snout, nose of an animal; snooty, nose in the air; to snoop,
        to nose around
Greek: *pompa*, parade
    English: pomp and circumstance and pompous (1386)

### PIE *stel*, to put, stand

German: *stolz*, proud

### PIE root *dhem*, breath, smoke

English: damp, originally, a noxious vapor; dank, wet with moist vapor

Russian:
> на-дменный (na-dmenyy), inflated, arrogant, cavalier
> на-дувать (naduvat), to inflate
> вздувшийся (vzduvshiysya), swollen, proud
> вздуть (vzdut), to inflate

## PIE root *gurdo*, slow, heavy

Spanish: *gordo*, fat
Russian: гордый (gordyy), proud

# Social Frameworks
····

# 110. Protection Bringing Danger/ Danger Bringing Fear

## Sharp Edges of Fear and Danger

Literal-minded folk try to make words as simple as they hope their world could be: "The dictionary says that this word means such-and-such," they announce—the lexicographical master has spoken!—*ipse dixit*! But a word can frustrate their hope for simplicity, because it often either tells a complex story on its own or it has evolved complexly. This complexity starts with one meaning and evolves into another—and yet again, into another. Take the word 'nice'—it started out as *nescius*, a compound of *ne-*, 'not,' and *-scius*, 'knowing,' as in science. Knowing clarifies a topic; not knowing it flies off to airy possibilities: its silence may mark some one as coy; if coy, then fastidious; if fastidious, then discriminating; if discriminating, then nice to know. Nice passed from ignorant, through discriminating to nice, as we know it. Shades of humanity weave nicely in and out of its history.

The bliss of ignorance followed some of the ramifications of 'nice,' but words of fear and danger have a double edge implicit in their roots. Have you ever been in the woods and felt unreasoning fear? It can grip you without cause. The Great God Pan—or the panic that he inspires—has seized you. Impelled by unreasoning fear of danger, you instinctively take flight with fear. Greek *phobos*, in both its flight and its fear, tells this story. In Russian, the shock of battle (битва [bitva]), concomitant with fear (бояться [boyat'sya]), impels flight (бегать [begat]). In battle, fear and flight chase each other round the field.

Battles and fear go hand in hand; but may not know it. On their jobs, guards can get some reading done or get some sleep. But in how many films, do we see a watchman, usually some innocent, elderly fellow, killed by ruthless thieves? He should have had a second thought before he signed on to the potential danger. In the Bible, the classic guard is the shepherd of a flock. Since sheep, grazing on their own, fall prey to predators, usually wolves, they need a guard. His very presence may ward off the danger, but ravenous hunger can drive wolves to try their luck. In such a case, guarding is synonymous with danger—guard and danger in Russian are derived from the same root (пасти [paste], guard; and опасность [opasnost], danger). The probability of such attacks makes fear a cognate of peril.

Danger and fear do not always simply end in flight. The fugitive may also be a refugee hoping for refuge. Wayward boys might not have will-

• 383

ingly fled to the House of Refuge, a euphemism for juvenile prison, but storm-tossed sailors have gratefully entered the Harbor of Refuge.

In the Bible the good shepherd lays down his life for the sheep (*John* 10, 11). Guarding risks danger; danger inspires fear in a vicious circle. The evolution of 'nice' tells a tale of a fanciful spirit; but guarding, danger, fear and flight have always chased each other round walls of an ancient fortress.

## Words

All words tell stories, but some words, by their cognates, bring with them package deals of probabilities. By its root, for example, experience brings expertise, but with the empirical probability of peril in the process.

### PIE root *pa*, to feed, protect

Latin: *pasco pascere*, and *pastus* to feed; and *pastor*, the shepherd who feeds
Russian:
    пасти (paste), to tend, guard
    о-пасность (o-pasnost'), danger; о-пасно (o-pasno), dangerous
    без-о-пасность (bez-o-pasnost), safety, literally, without danger

### PIE root *per*, to lead across

Greek: *peira*, trial, test, experience
    English: empirical, relating to experience
Latin: *periculum*, danger
    English: peril
German: *Furcht*, fear; *Gefahr*, danger
    English:
        to fear (1000), to inspire fear; (1303), to feel fear
        afeard, made fearful—Fearful men are easily afeard.

### PIE root *bhaut*, to beat, strike, hew

Latin:
    *fatuus*, fatuous; literally, struck silly
    *refutare* and *confutare*, to restrain, check
Germanic English: to beat

### PIE root *bat*, to beat

English: to batter and battle
Polish: *boj*, battle; *bitwa*, battle; *bojaźń*, fear
Russian: бой (boy), battle; битва (bitva), battle; бояться (boyat'sya), to fear

**PIE root *bhegu,* to run**
(Grimms' law: 'p,' 'f' and 'b' interchange.)

Greek:
    Phobos, Greek god of fear, son of Mars, satellite of Mars
    *phobeo*, I put to flight, terrify; *phebeomai*, I flee
    *phobos*, panic, flight, fear

Latin:
    *fugo fugare*, to put to flight; and *fugio fugere*, to flee
    *refugium*, refuge
        English: refuge (1386)

Russian: бегать (begat), to run; бежать (bezhat'), to flee

## 111. Humble Abodes and Manorial Mansions

At home, we settle down to basics and then reach beyond them. Basically, we live there; and, beyond that, our aspirations—or maybe our pretensions—make much of it. Words for home—like abode, mansion and жилище (ziliste)—describe both staying and living; and the buildings—like timber, dome and дом—describe material and construction. These words tell stories about how we build and use our homes; and how much we make of them.

    The Germanic root for remaining, and the Russian root for living and 'one's own' describe home. To bide (1250), to remain, survives only in biding one's time, but its intensive verb, to abide (1250), to remain firm, has survived. Joining the verb with its noun, men abide in abodes (1576). In Jane Austin's *Pride and Prejudice, t*he insufferably "ever so 'umble" Mr. Collins calls his own abode humble. From this disingenuous humility to Slavic pride, a Russian lives (жить [zhit']) in his living (жилище [ziliste]) and in "one's own" (особа [osoba]) place (особняк [osobnyak]) that has come to describe a mansion. This aspiration, ingenuous or disingenuous, comes naturally, as we make our houses into homes and then into great houses. Without an association with a Mr. Collins, humble abodes can show just the opposite aspiration: they have come to have *gravitas* that dignifies modest dwellings.

    Romance words for home dignify the abodes of aristocrats and churchmen. Latin *manere*, to remain, through French, has given English words describing homes that entail landed estates. Manor refers to a landed dwelling. Consequently, we speak of a manor house, which originally joined land, the manor, with the house built on it. Mansion, first, the action of remaining, came to refer to the house in which one remains (1386), and more than a century later to the nobleman's house (1512). Turning from the nobleman to the church which he supported, manse (1490), first a synonym of mansion, later, a synonym of the archaic noun hide, referred to the land necessary for the maintenance of a cleric (1597) or simply to his residence (1531). The custom of a minister of a church residing in its manse draws from a long tradition of maintaining churches by manorial lands. The Norman French landholder's manor, mansion and manse required more land than the Anglo-Saxon yeoman's abode.

With four walls around us and a roof over us, our words for house also refer to its construction. House (1000) probably descended from the PIE root *kel*, to cover. Husks cover grain; hulls cover ships; and huts cover peasants. Derived from the same root, and first used in *Beowulf*, hall referred to a great, roofed chamber. Gradually, this large room became smaller, because it served as the entrance to other rooms; but it kept the same name, since it stayed in the same place. With greater proportions than house or abode, halls functioned as the great buildings of the Anglo Saxon tradition. The Slavic tradition has followed a similar path: хоромы (xaromi), palace, started its history describing wood or animal hides, cut to cover buildings.

The Indo-European root *dem*, to build, has given English the Germanic word timber (750), originally a house (*cf.* German *zimmer*, and *zimmermann*, a carpenter), but later just the stuff of which a house is built. From the root *dem*, Latin derived *domus*. Dome (1513) describes a house of stately proportions: "In Xanadu did Kubla Khan / A stately pleasure dome decree." The language of the law refers to a home as a domicile (1766). Since all the most ancient houses had the same shape as the vault of heaven, dome (1656) also refers to the round vault that encircles the building; and by synecdoche (the part for the whole), to the cathedral beneath it (1691; *cf.* Italian *duomo*). These words derived from *domus* represent literature ("a stately pleasure dome"), architecture (dome as vault), religion (dome as cathedral) and law (domicile). Ironically, they describe everything but a house; just as words derived from *mansio* refer to everything but a simple place to stay.

Halls and stately domes haunt wretched wealth;
simple domesticity hits home in an old song:
Mid pleasures and palaces though we may roam,
Be it ever so humble, there's no place like home.
*Home, Sweet Home* commends the blessed exception to the rule of personal and familial aspiration making much of homes.
House, abode, even hall, sturdy timbers built,
humbled in shadows of domes, manors and mansions.

## Words

The place, in which we remain and live,
may be a mansion for some and for others a humble abode.
Words for home also describe its construction and materials.

### PIE root *men*, to re-main, dwell

Latin: *maneo manere* and *mansus*, to remain
  French: *ménage*, *ménagerie* and *maison*
  English: mansion, manor, manse

### PIE root *kel*, to cover, hide; hollow

Latin: *cella*, storeroom, cell
  French: *salle*, hall, chamber, saloon
  Russian: зал (zal), hall, parlor, saloon; салон (salon), salon
German: *Halle*, hall
  English: hall
Russian: холл (kholl), hall

### PIE root *sue*, one's own

Latin:
  *suus*, one's own
  *sui generis*, literally, of its own type; unique
  *per se*, literally, through itself; in and of itself
    English: suicide, killing of one's self
Russian:
  свой (svoj), one's own
  свобода (svoboda), belonging to a tribe, state of a free man, freedom
Polish: *osoba*, person
Russian:
  особа (osoba), person, individual
  особняк (osobnyak), mansion, one's own personal place

### PIE root *skei*, to cut, split, divide and *kwezd*, piece

Greek: *skhizein*, to cut
  English:
    schism, schizoid
    Skoal!, a toast, in reference, to cups **cut** from shells
    piece, part cut from the whole
  Russian:
    Religion—схизма (schisma), schism; скол (skol), chip

Ethics—
    счастье (schast'ye), happiness
    часть (chast'), part (cut from the whole)
    щедрый (shchedryy), generous, lavish, bountiful
    Generosity cuts a slice; happiness receives it.
Building—хоромы (xaromi), palace, mansion
    Another slice, of hide or timber, roofed a house.

Latin: *scindo scindere* and *scissus*, to cut
    English: to rescind, to cut back; scissors (1384)
German: *Schere*, scissors/shears
    English: share, a part cut from the whole; to shear, to cut; shears (725)

## 112. The Resting Place

### Home

We can only start to enjoy our homes when they make us safe. The origin of paradise, therefore, from the PIE roots *dheigh*, to build, and *per*, around, should not surprise us. Adam's first home was a paradise and a garden, because it literally had a wall "built around" it. PIE vocabulary indicates that Adam's descendants also made their homes safe by means of walls. Paradise gardens come at a price and with a problem at their root.

The root of Russian город (gorod), city, indicates that Russian cities, like Paradise gardens, were girt with walls. After walls protected towns from time immemorial, Europeans in the seventeenth century particularly needed them in their colonial settlements for protection from hostile natives. The Dutch East India Company made the natives very hostile when it once committed genocide as a means of changing staff on one of its spice islands. Anticipating similar hostility, it built a wall at the northern end of its trading post on Manhattan Island, named New Amsterdam, and soon to be renamed New York. This wall gave its name to the Wall Street that ran alongside it. As an extraordinary exception to this rule of colonial cities with walls, William Penn established his city of brotherly love, Philadelphia, without them.

Within the walls, the English words city and home share the same Indo-European root. Specifically, Greek *keimai*, I lie down, shares its root with Latin *civis*, citizen. From *keimai*, the dead call a cemetery home. In German, however, the initial 'k' drops out to form *heim*, home, as in

Bohemia, "home of the Boi." A city is a home and a home, a city, but the two words, by their roots, define living space in radically different ways. Home tells the Germanic story; and city, the Roman story, about living space.

In A.D. 900, home was a hamlet, a small village; fifty years later, home could refer to an individual dwelling. German has many compounds of *heim*: *heirat*, for one, the care of the home, but also marriage. English preserves some indications of the Germans' high esteem of the family in the home: husband (1000), the man who lives in the home (*hus*, house; and *bondi*, dweller). The man dwelling on a piece of ground also tills it. Husbandry (1290), cultivating the land, requires him to husband (1440) its resources. Among all the important things that husbands had to do, their marriage came only as an afterthought (1290).

Sixty-five years before husband referred to a married man, his helpmate received the name of housewife (1225); although wife, as a married woman, had existed as far back as the time of King Alfred (888). Hussy, the companion of husband, at first a strong, thrifty country woman (1530), later, brazenly felt too fine for her homespun: "I, like a little proud hussy, looked in the glass, and thought myself a gentlewoman" (1741). Hussies had ambitions beyond home! English has also preserved the archaic word hide (848), the amount of land considered sufficient for the support of a family. Henry, Heinrich in German, rules (*-rich*) the home. Although the eighth royal Henry ended the popularity of this name in Englishmen's monarchy, home has remained firm in their language.

The Roman tradition offers an entirely different concept of home. Contrary to the Germanic root which referred to the village for only a short time before it referred to the home, Latin *civis*, citizen, referred to the legal integrity of the man who dwelled in the place. Cicero boasted that the declaration, *Civis Romanus sum*, "I am a Roman citizen," commanded respect the world over. Citizenship for the Roman constituted a legal and, therefore, a moveable condition; Romans enjoyed citizenship anywhere in their world. *Civitas*, citizenship and the place in which they enjoyed it, through French *cité*, became English city. Municipal autonomy, not homes, made a Roman city a city. The Romans had a tradition of law that made home the seat of legal right.

The Slavic, Romance, and Germanic traditions established homes as safe places of industry and legal right, but safety, industry and law may conflict. In the modern world, home as a place of work and family in the Germanic tradition may conflict with the Roman concept of home as a place of legal right. We redress wrongs arising from the imbalance between the German and the Roman concepts of home, even when we cannot redress the imbalance itself. To keep us safe, we still need walls, whether we can see them or not.

## Words

The roots of words for home as dwelling and city
emphasize its enclosure for a resting place or its door and seat.

1. **PIE root** *gher,* **to enclose**
    Latin: *hortus,* garden (enclosed within a *villa*)
        English: horticulture, culture of a garden
    German: *gurten,* to gird
    English: to gird, girt, girth, garden
    Latin: *hortus gardinus,* enclosed garden (twice enclosed!)
        French and Spanish: *jardin*; Italian: *giardino*
        German: *Kinder-garten,* a garden for children
    Polish: *ogrod,* garden; *grod,* fortress or castle
    Russian:
        огород (ogorod), garden; город (gorod), city (cf. Leningrad)
        горожанин (gorozhanin), town dweller
        на-града (nagrada), prize, reward of a town; горсть (gorst'), handful
2. **PIE root** *sed,* **to sit, dwell**
    Latin: *sedeo sedere* and *sessus,* to sit
        French: *s'asseoir,* to sit; *assis,* seated; and *siege,* seat
        Spanish: *sentarse* and *assiento*; Italian: *sedere* and *sede*
    English: seat and country seat
    Polish: *siedzieć,* to sit
    Russian:
        сидеть (sidet'); сиденье (siden'ye), seat; сад (sad), garden
        у-садь-ба (*u-sadít´*) + -ба (*-ba*), farmstead, homestead
3. **PIE root** *dhuer,* **door**
    Greek: *thura,* door
        English: thyroid, the door-like (-oid) gland
    German: *Tür*
        English: door
    Latin: *foris,* door
        English: forest and foreign
    Czech: *dvere,* door

Russian:
> дверь (dver), door; двор (dvor), court, yard, farm, homestead
> дворец (dvorets), palace; дворянин (dvoryanin), nobleman

Two roots for the temporal and the eternal resting place:

1. **PIE root *kei*, to lie, settle down**
    Latin: *civis*, citizen; and *civitas*, city; *civilis*, civil; and *civilitas*, civility
    Italian: *citta* and *cittadino, civile* and *civiltà*
    Spanish: *ciudad* and *ciudadano, civil* and *civilidad*
    French: *cité* and *citoyen, civil* and *civilité*
    English: city and citizen, civil and civility
    German: *heim*, home
    English: home and hamlet
    Greek:
    *keimai*, I lie down
    *coma*, sleep
     English: coma
      Latin: *caemeterium*, resting place, first used by Christians for necropolis
       French: *cimetiere*, cemetery; Spanish: *cementerio*;
        English: cemetery
    Russian: семья (sem'ya), family
2. **PIE root *kleh*, to put; *kla*, to spread out**
    English:
    lading, loading or the load itself; laden, loaded
    ladle, the spoon that spreads out
    Russian:
    класть (klast), to put, lay down, deposit
    кладбище (kladbishche),—taboo, placing the dead, *i.e.* cemetery

# 113. Domineering in the Domicile

## Describing the Host as Lord of Guests

Russian borrowed дон (Don) and донна (Donna) as formal titles from Spanish, but it drew on another concept for its common word denoting the lord of the house. This word, гос-подин (gos-podin), resembled the Greek, *despotes*, despot, originally *dems-potes*, literally, the powerful man of the house, a compound of *dems-*, house, and *-potes,* powerful. The second part of гос-подин, -подин, is cognate with *-potes*, also the second part of *des-potes*. (*-Potes*, is also cognate with the second root of the English compound omni-potent.) Householders have many functions, but, at their roots, the Russian and also the Latin, less obviously, chose to highlight their social function. At Russian parties, hosts can play the autocrat of the dinner table.

Both Latin and Russian took the PIE root *ghostis*, guest, to describe the lord's social function. In Russian, господин (gos-podin) describes him as having power over his guests. His lady is гос-пожа (gospoʹʒa). Latin put the two roots together as *hos-pes* (genitive, *hospitis*), which in English means host and guest.[23] After the Golden Age, Ovid explains, life became uncertain: man lives by theft; a guest is not safe from his host (or *vice versa*)—*Vivitur ex rapto: non hospes ab hospite tutus* (Ovid uses the same word for guest and host.). In entertaining, hosts did not merely make their boards festive with wine and song. Jove, the highest of all gods, guarded the guest-host relationship as a keystone in the arch of human culture.

In derivatives from the PIE root *ghostis*, Romance languages have followed the lead of their Roman parent in taking one word, *hospes*, to mean both host and guest. One word for two functions demonstrates the double-edged relation of the host with his guest. On the other hand, in the two English words, host and guest, the Germanic tradition describes this relationship with two words that do not resemble each other, even though they come from the same PIE root. The Slavic tradition has the same PIE root for guest, гость (gost), and then compounds it by power, гос-подин (gos-podin), to describe the host.

However the guest-host relationship may be described,—with one word or two, or with one or two roots in one word,—giving and receiving hospitality have been the stuff of life in classic tales. A god disguised as a lowly beggar knocks at the door, and begs hospitality. But who knows?

At the beginning, a host cracks open a keg with his guest as a friend, whose head he cracks open in hostility at the end.[24]

## Words

Romance, Germanic and Slavic words describe the mutuality of guests with hosts.

### PIE root *ghostis*, stranger, guest or host

1. One word meaning host or guest in the Romance tradition:
   Latin: *hospitis*, guest or host

Italian: *ospite*, host or guest; Spanish: *huesped*, host or guest
French:
>   *hôte*, host or guest
>   *table d'hôte*, table of the host, the *prix fixe* menu (*cf. à la carte*)

2. Two separate words for host and guest in the Germanic tradition:
English: host and guest
German: *Hostrechner*, host; *Gast*, guest
3. One word for guest and its compound for host in the Slavic tradition:
Polish: *gosc*, guest; *gos-podarz*, lord of guests, host
Russian:
>   гость (gost), guest; гос-подин (gos-podin), lord of guests, master
>   гостиница (gostinitsa), hotel
>   Государство (gosudahrstvuh), state (Tsar's household virtues)

## 114. The Hill and the Plain

In five lines of hexameter verse, the Roman poet Claudian juxtaposes the Palatine Hill with the Rostra of the Roman Forum in the classic contrast of haughty folk on the hill with humble folk subjected on the plain. (The very literal translation that follows attempts to recreate the caesuras of the Latin hexameters, with noun and adjective pairs in bold face type.) The understood noun subject of the verbs is the Palatine Hill.

*Non alium certe // decuit rectoribus orbis*
*esse larem, // nullo magis // se colle po/testas*
*aestimat et summi // sentit fastigia iuris.*
*Attolens apicem // subiectis regia rostris*
*tot circum // delubra videt //.*

—Claudian (*floruit* 395–404 A.D.)

Not **another place** certainly // seemed appropriate, for the rectors of the orb
To be a domestic **lar**. // More important on none other // hill does power
Esteem itself, and **of the highest** // does it sense the proud pediments **of its law**.
**Raising** its apex, // **the royal home** with the rostra subjected,
**So many** roundabout // does it see **shrines**.

Claudian boasted justifiably that no eminence more than the Palatine Hill might appropriately contrast lofty rulers with their subject citizens. Some of the most basic words we use for social structure and government are derived from the Capitoline and Palatine Hills and the Roman citizens in the Forum, which nestles between them.

The Capitoline Hill derived its name from the *Capitolium*, short for the temple of *Jupiter Capitolinus*, the greatest Roman temple and the Roman equivalent of the Parthenon in Athens. The Senate sometimes held its meetings there, because it was the moral and patriotic center of Rome. Appropriately, the young American Republic named its Capitol building after it. In the United States, only the federal or a state capital can have its capitol building, spelled with an 'o.'

On the Palatine Hill, at the opposite side of the valley from the Capitoline Hill, the Emperor Augustus built his home because of its association with Romulus and Remus, the founders of the city. Gradually, his family built more and more luxurious accommodations, until the Palatine, synonymous with the monarch's luxurious mansion, was the original palace. Paladins (1592), knight of the Palatine, guarded it. This royal magnificence is a far cry from the pastoral simplicity of the hill of Pales, the rustic goddess to whom the first shepherds dedicated it and with whom Augustus, as the archetypal Roman, sought to associate himself!

The cry was not so far, at least in opinion of the Emperor Augustus, *primus inter pares*, "first among his peers." In the Forum (1735), the open area (*cf.* forest and foreign) in which the citizens congregated for meetings and markets, the tribes elected tribunes who sat on tribunals to collect tribute and assign re-tribution. All these words originate in the three (tri-) original Roman tribes. The senescent, we hope not senile, senators of the tribes met in the Curia, where men came together (*co-viria*). America adopted Senate (1374) as the name of its upper representative chamber. Curia refers to a Papal or feudal court, derived from *co-hors*, a court is an enclosed area, like *hortus*, garden (*cf.* horticulture, culture of a garden). At first, the cohort of a king stayed in the court, but the association of court with Curia gave the word court its official and legal meaning.

The tribunal to one side of the Curia was decorated with the beaks (*rostra*) of conquered ships, from which the Rostra (1713) derived its name. Even from the palatial Palatine or the divine Capitoline, most wise Roman rulers knew enough to listen to the cry (1275) of citizens in the Curia or on the Rostra. Derived from *quiritare*, to cry (1225) meant to appeal as a Roman citizen for help. In English, people cried for mercy in the earliest use of the word.

Claudian realized the double edge of Vergil's *altae moenia Romae*, the walls of high Rome. Should the rulers of Rome be as haughty as their high buildings might make them? The Rostra always cries for the **high** moral aid of the Capitol against the **haughty** power of their palace.

## Words

### PIE root *pag*, to fasten; or Pales, the Italic goddess of shepherds

Latin: *Mons Palatinus* or *Palatium*, Hill of Pales, one of seven hills in Rome
    Italian: *palazzo*; French: *palais*; Spanish: *palacio*
    German: *palast*; Russian: палас (palas)
    English: palace (1290)

### PIE root *tri*, three

Latin:
    *tribus*, tribe, one of three divisions of the Roman state
    *tribunal*, raised platform for magistrates' seats, from *tribunus*, tribune
English: tribunal
Russian: трибуна (tribuna), rostrum; ростра (rostra)

# 115. Menials in the Noble's Domain

Words for home have indicated man's aspiration for domesticity and dominion; they can also tell stories about his titles and those of his servants. Derivatives of *domus* (home) and *mansionem* (mansion) describe the gentry, enjoying dominion, and their staff, laboring as menials.

*Domina*, the lady of the house, has survived in the English forms of Italian *Madonna* and French *dame* and *madame*. In church, servants of God address their heavenly lady, the Virgin Mary, as Madonna, My Lady. A man may also address the special woman in his life as My Lady. In households, dame started out as a genteel title, but has ended up as a generic one. Servants addressed their dame as *ma dame*/madame (1330) or madam (1297), My Lady. Like dame, it gradually lost distinction: "a title of honor," one man observed in 1696, but "grown a little too common of late."

Madam has gone up and down the social scale. It has become so generic that salesmen abbreviate it as ma'am in addressing female customers. Trade lowers standards, but the lowest lowers them the most, when prostitutes either claimed or were given this title. *Madame* bathes any situation in a glow, in addition to dignifying indecent houses with decency. How far a lady's domain—and how far her rising and falling—from earthy madam to heavenly Madonna and back!

By contrast with *domina*'s word family, no English derivatives of *dominus* describe the owner of a house. 'Master' and 'lord' represent this ownership; but *dominus* expanded his domain beyond domesticity. A clergyman or a man of learned profession had the dignity of the title, domine (900), the Latin vocative of *dominus*. A professor at Oxford is still called a don. The Greek East preserved its own form of *dominus* in despot (1574), originally *demspotes*, the powerful man (*potes*) of the house (*dems*). In English, it refers to a ruler, who deprives his subjects of civil rights. *Dominus* and *domina* tell stories about caste and subservience. Madam and Madonna, at least, infuse subservience with grace.

His Grace, the lord of the manor, possessed dominion (1430), which later came to refer to lands under his control (1512). His domination (1386) could make him domineering (1588). This domination often inspired fear: to daunt meant at first to conquer (1300) and only later to discourage or to inspire fear. Dominion, at its worst, daunted and domineered. On the other hand, true virtue may be challenged but never daunted.

Dungeon (1375), starting out as a French form of the Latinate dominion, ended up representing the worst that a lord's dominion might demand. It first referred to the fort within the larger fort, the tower from which the lord could view his dominion and in which he held domestic dominion. It was also called the keep, from the original meaning of 'to keep' as 'to observe'—we still 'keep someone in sight.' This dominion/dungeon, however, covered up dark secrets more than it opened up bright vistas, because it described the underground chamber of the tower fifty years before it referred to the tower itself. Dungeon has handed down the scary heritage which domineering domination has left in our language and in our minds.

Words for household servants show a slow degradation in their dignity. When Noah's curse condemned Canaan to be "a servant of servants ... unto his brethren" (*Genesis* 9. 25), servant (1225) meant slave, but the word has also described a wide category of service from the "servant of all work" in the household, to a public or civil servant, a servant of the Lord or 'Your Humble Servant' with which anyone may conclude a letter. Higher up the scale, the *major domo*, literally the greater man of the house (*major domus*) at first acted as the head of a royal household and later, facetiously, the head of a bourgeois household. Lower in domestic service, menial (1427), described a person serving in the menage (1297), the family living in the mansion. By 1840, when Dickens referred to "menial ... degrading tasks," it had come to have a pejorative meaning. Domestic (1545), at first used in reference to things native, as in domestic and foreign policy, later referred to servants (1612) and has survived in English as a more respectable word for servant than menial. A domestic has greater dignity than a menial, even though they both scrub floors.

Communism, knowing well the degradation of the English caste system, used лакей, lackey, as a word to describe a mindless toady of capitalism. Floors always need to be scrubbed, and modern democracy has made progress in improving the dignity of the charwoman. Madame now sounds quaintly antique as an honorific address, and 'Yes'm,' unfortunately servile. We can look back objectively on these relics of veneration or respect, and daunting domination and menial service. For us, madame may serve some genteel purpose, and dungeons only pose a threat in adventure films and Gothic novels.

## Words

The PIE root, *dem*, builds up quite a domain of words for homes and homeowners.

### PIE root *dem*, house, home, to build

Latin: *domus*, home; and *domus Dei*, house of God
    Italian: *duomo*, cathedral
    French: *dome*; Spanish: *domo*, dome

This PIE *dem* provides the roots for three words—

Polish and Russian: *dom* and дом (dom), house, home
German: *Zimmer*, room built of timber, which builds a house
English: timber, wood building a house, in which a *Zimmer* is built

Russian Orthodox churches have domes, but Russians call them cupolas:
    Latin: *cupola*, small cup
    French: *coupole*; Spanish: *cupula*; Russian: купол (kupol)
    German: *Kuppel*, dome/cupola; English: cupola, small dome.

Latin:
    *dominus* and *domina*, lord and lady of the house
        Classical English: don, as in Oxford don
    *mea domina*, my lady
        Spanish and Italian: *donna*; and *madonna*, my lady, the Virgin Mary
        Russian: дон (don), донна (donna), and мадонна (madonna)
        French: *dame* and *madame*
        English:
            dame (1225) and madame (1330)
            The 'm' of yes'm originated in five syllables of *mea domina*,
                shortened to three syllables in madonna,
                to two in madame,

> to one in ma'am,
>> and, finally, to one letter in yes'm
>> —a classic example of belittling a title

Latin: *dominare*, to dominate; and *domitare*, to domesticate, to tame
> French: *dominer*; Spanish: *dominar*; Italian: *dominare*
> English, to daunt, from French *dompter*

Polish: *dominować*; German: *dominieren*
Russian:
> доминировать (dominirovat), to dominate, from German
> домовладелец (domvladets), home owner
> домовой (domovoi), a protective house spirit in Slavic folklore

## 116. Master and Majesty

Before we can think that we have even started to master concepts of ownership, we should set mastery at the right hand of Roman Majesty, its royal cognate and the keystone in its arch. Germanic Lordship, in this hierarchy, has won its place, but it had humble origins in the *hlafweard*, guarding the loaf, and his lady, *hlafæta*, kneading it. From these modest beginnings, what a wonder that 'lord' rose to the Lord God Almighty, the master of our heavenly home. We should all do as well in making the best of our beginnings!

Mastery was born to a greater inheritance. It takes us from the lord's dark German wood to the bright terraces of Roman gardens. Greater than great, majesty and mastery master a broad hierarchy of duties. The first chapters of their history reveal a wide world of the few, greater than the many—more moral, more learned, more powerful.

Majesty, the abstract concept of this greater power, came from Latin *maiestas* directly into English to dignify the power of the state residing in the monarch. Majesty should have a dignity that kings may disregard: "The King came in with a skip;" said one observer of a royal audience of George III, "not a very proper pace, I think, for Majesty" (1782). As form of address, Highness (1173) and Majesty were interchangeable until James I preferred Majesty for the king, and deferred Highness to members of his royal family. His Majesty James I, doubtless, had been reading up on the pedigree of royal titles.

Master, the English form of *magister*, entitled positions of mastery below the King's Majesty. In general, it has described a person ruling other people, things or situations: a land owner, the master of his estate; a victorious general, the master of the field; even a pauper, with wistful irony, the master of his few coppers. More generally, a master, at first, ruled over slaves; then, servants. The terms are correlative: no masters without men in their service. How many dramas have arisen from the relationship between a master and his slaves or servants? "Such a master, such a servant" (1554) reflects the mirroring of one by the other, for better or for worse. Power makes men angels or wolves.

The English word master first referred to one instructing students (888). In this meaning, teacher has mostly supplanted master. In 1611, as Jesus was asleep in a boat during a storm, "Master," his disciples cried, "carest thou not that we perish?" (*Mark* 4, 38); but in 1973, "Teacher," his students cried, "don't you care if we drown?" Master as teacher, survives in headmaster, the principal teacher of an independent school, and in Master of Arts (MA, *Artium Magister*), the academic degree originally qualifying a person to teach. To become a master craftsman, for example, an apprentice carpenter, submitted his master-piece to qualify himself as a teacher of apprentices. And yet, master has been waiting in the wings to take center stage once again: we bestow the title of master teacher on a man with so much experience that he can teach teachers how to teach.

Those attaining the degree of Master of Arts took Mr. as a proclitic title. With the enclitic acronym of their Bachelor of Arts degree, a scholar might enfold himself in titles, Mr. John Smith, AB. In his home, servants might address him as Mr. Smith, and his son as Young Master Edward. The title Mr. had a currency so separate from Master that it also took Mister as a different pronunciation. Mister has become so common that we no longer think of it as a synonym of master.

In its ancient history, *magister* had a special distinction as the *Magister Equitum*, Master of the Knights. The British peerage adopted Mr. as a title below Knight. Eventually, Mr. resembled 'gentleman' as a title for a man without one. Its alternate form, mister, in the final chapter of its history, marked no degree of excellence at all. In fact, used without a name, 'Hey, Mister' implies disdain. Once Mr. and gentleman came down to earth, they became titles acceptable in a democracy. Mister, especially, so masterfully—but, respectfully—overarched the arch that it filled in for its every stone. We may find common words for humankind in human or mortal, but what other related titles—Majesty, master and mister—dignify the King and every male, from the highest to the lowest, in the realm? The flexibility of the classical concept has permitted its broad application.

Master has gone up on a pedestal, which we have mostly put up on the shelf. Old Masters dignify the walls of art museums. On the other hand, masters fit uncomfortably in democratic society. We shrink at the correlatives master and slaves. It can even give us a shiver: the master passion grasps at gold pieces in stories of evil men; masterminds, usually of the ilk of Moriarty, hatch wicked plots to destroy good men like Holmes. Even in compliments, it makes us think twice. Though Antony refers to the assassins of Caesar as "the choice and master spirits of this age" (Shakespeare, *Julius Caesar*), he prefers to share Caesar's fate rather than to join these new masters. We respect the magisterial authority of experts, but our democratic spirit suspects an assumption of their authority outside of the cloister of academe. Perhaps also, the practicality of the modern world appreciates flexible talent instead of singular ability. We can appreciate the second line of the couplet about the jack of all trades:

> Jack of all trades, master of none,
> though oftentimes better than master of one.

Master bespeaks an old world, as we live happily in the new—with a couple of exceptions that show that we can still appreciate the old days: we respect the reign of the *maestro* on the podium, because we know that he aspires to *crescendo poco a poco*; and we also understand the old-fashioned pretensions of the *maître d'* in the fashionable *restaurant*, as long as he shows us a good *table d'hôte*.

## Words

English master and majesty draw on roots that describe the greater person.

### PIE root *me*, great and greater

Latin:
> *magis* and *major*, greater
> *magister*, teacher, master; literally, a greater person
> *maiestas*, majesty; literally, being greater
> *magister equitum*, master of knights, ancient Roman office below dictator
>> *Cf.* Russian:
>>> конюшенный приказ (konyushennyy prikaz), stable order
>>> конь (kon), hornless animal, horse
>>> конюшня (konyushnya), stable
>> Italian: *maestro*
>> French:
>>> *maître*
>>> *maître d'hôtel, maître d'*, manager of hotel or dining room
>> German: *Meister*

English:
> master (888) and its alternate form, mister; majesty (1171)
> magisterial (1632), of a teacher, of superior accomplishment
> magistrate (1382), an official of the executive branch, enforcing laws

Russian: мастер (master) and магистр (magister)

Russian teaching and learning derive roots from custom and individuality, but its root for strength describes authority:

### PIE root *sue*, one's own

Hindi: swami, one's own teacher
Latin: *per se*, in itself; literally, through itself
> English:
>> sui-cide, killing of one's self
>> sister, a woman belonging to *one's own* kindred.

Russian:
> свой (svoy), my, your, his, her, one's own, our, their (referring to the subject of the sentence)
> освоить (osvoit'), to master (making material one's own)

### PIE root *euk / heuk*, to accustom oneself to, to learn

Russian: учить (uchit'), to teach; учитель (uchitel), teacher

### PIE root *val*, strong

Latin: *valeo valere*, to be strong; and *validus*, strong
> French: *valide*; Spanish: *valido*
> English: valid and invalid; prevalent and ambivalent

German: *walten*, to rule; Walter, a ruler
> English:
>> to wield, to handle a weapon or power
>> Arnold, *Aren-wald*, having an eagle's strength

Russian:
> великáн (velikan), giant
> велико-душный (veliko-dushnyy), generous, magnanimous
> дух (dux), spirit, ghost (PIE root *dheu*, smoke, dust)

\* \* \*

Polish: *wladac*, to wield, rule
Russian:
> власть (vlast), power, authority, rule; владеть (vladet), to be master
> Владивостóк (Vladivostok), master of the East
> Владúмир (Vladimir), ruler of the world (*cf.* Vlad the Impaler)

## 117. Authors and Authority

### Authors and Authority: Despotism or Republic?

In the Roman Republic, 'The Senate and the Roman People'(*SPQR, Senatus Populusque Romanus*) defined the state. The Senate had authority, that is, the ability to increase the power given to it by the people: *potestas in populo*, Cicero observed, *auctoritas in Senatu*, "power in the people, authority in the Senate," (*De Legibus* III, 12). Authority receives power from a higher source, in this case, from the citizens of a republic, and then it increases it. After the Senate increased the power of the people by passing laws, the people obeyed them. Law, created with authority and balanced with obedience, maintained harmony—a delicate balance and a precarious harmony.

In the Roman Empire, authority passed from the Senate to the emperor, but his authority derived its power from a higher source than the people. The gods invested imperial authority with divine power. They increased the emperor so that he, in turn, might increase the Empire. His Imperial Majesty ruled as the gods' vicar on earth, but his majesty might very easily become despotic.

Like master and majesty, authority and author pass directly from the pagan Roman Empire into the Christian Middle Ages. (We have already seen words like gentle, intellect, and fortitude passing into English with a full classical pedigree.) With their Republican and Imperial heritage, both concepts have their double edge of boon and bane. The bane may, at first, be more obvious. Imperial majesty and authority derive power from divinity and not from people. Throughout history, earthly authority, assuming heavenly sanction, has usually done as much harm as slave masters. It should not surprise us that authority (1230) predated author (1300). Roman authors, on the other hand, have done as much good as the school masters teaching their texts.

Authority, an English word by the thirteenth century, represented the moral and legal majesty of Saint Peter's succession and the divine right of kings. Endowed with such authority, popes and kings could rightfully enforce obedience. "A king rules by divine right," pronounces Carlyle's satiric voice in *Sartor Resartus*. "He carries in him an authority from God; or man will never give it to him;" and only "in such obedience to the Heaven-chosen" is freedom even conceivable (1831). The experience of history in centuries following the thirteenth has demonstrated that man has not found freedom in obedience to kings. Shakespeare describes the travesty of selfish pride dressed in authority: "Proud man, dressed in a little brief authority, / Plays such fantastic tricks before High heaven" that angels would either weep or, if they were human, die laughing (*Measure for Measure*). At best, imperial authority, "both disease and cure (1680)," has stifled more truth than it has revealed.

And yet, men persist in looking to authority for cures. The authoritarian (1879) invented authoritarianism—the nineteenth century put stock in many an '___ism' to solve its problems. Six and one half centuries after religious authority empowered popes and kings, secular authority might empower one mortal, whose charisma has made him just a little more than mortal. This man's authority, unfettered by priest-craft, might increase his country's power in a military despotism. Quite apart from cure, these secular authorities have infested the world with disease. In the twentieth and twenty-first centuries, their authority to destroy has surpassed that of the "heaven-chosen" in the many centuries before them.

In their histories, authority and majesty have turned the concrete to the abstract, moving from earth to heaven, but bringing heaven back to earth. Abstract faith does not blend harmoniously with concrete authority. Authors increase creation and knowledge. In the beginning, Jove was the author (1374) of creation; as parents, in turn, are the authors (1300) of the creatures of creation. These authors increase creation. Firmly down to earth, an author also increases knowledge by writing a book. Respect for the learning of classical antiquity endowed ancient authors (1380) with authority. Quoting Cicero or Aristotle increased a man's credibility. Well into the eighteen century, people respected classical authors as superior fonts of wisdom. In the twenty-first century, they still provide fresh insights into the nature of man. As a modern example of authorial authority, *auteur* describes a film director who marks his work with his own individuality.

August, as an adjective, describes authority. When the nephew and heir of Julius Caesar chose Augustus as his title, he willed to the world this dignified adjective. (He also gave his title to the month of August, but we pronounce august with emphasis on the -gusto.) An august presence promises an increase of good things. It promises as much as man can give and perhaps more: "The ancient philosophers looked upon this universe as one august temple of God" (1664). But beware!—the promise proves empty, if authority appears august only because it parades well-tailored in pomp.

Prestige provides a foil to august authority. It first meant trick or illusion, which the nineteenth century attributed to Napoleon: "the prestige with which Napoleon overawed the world is the effect of a stage trick" (1838). By a dazzling blaze of victory, he sought to increase "the charm or the prestige, as he was wont to call it, that attached to his name" (1815).

In the twenty-first century, we equate prestige with authority. Though polar opposites in origin, they resemble each other. Imagine a Roman Senator moving the people of the Republic with "grandiose language, ringing rhymes, and prestigious metaphors (1887)." Such grandiloquence veils its prestige in authority. Let's pray that people in any age have enough discernment to lift the veil.

## Words

By their etymology, author and authority increase power and knowledge. Biblical authors praise God as the Almighty Author of creation. Almighty or humble, authors have authority, because they increase creation. By its etymology, prestige seeks to deceive, but it looks like authority.

### PIE root *aug*, to increase

Latin:
> *augeo augere* and *auctus*, to increase
> *auctor*, author, the increaser; *auctoritas*, authority, increasing
>> French: *auteur* and *autorité*
>> English:
>>> authority (1230), author (1300); to augment (1400), to increase
>>> auction (1595), a sale in which prices increase
>>> august (1673), inspiring reverence
>> German: *Autorität*, authority
>> Russian:
>>> автор (avtor), author; авторитет (avtoritet), authority
>>> *Cf.* увеличивать (uvelichivat'), to augment

### PIE root *streig*, to squeeze

Latin:
> *stringo stringere* and *strictus*, to squeeze, tighten
> *prae-stringere* and *prae-strictus*, to bind, blindfold, trick
> *prestigium*, trick, illusion
>> English:
>>> strict; to constrict, restrict
>>> prestige (1756), trick; (1815), dazzling effect
>> French and German: *prestige*; Italian and Spanish: *prestigio*
>> Russian: престиж (prestizh)

## 118. Sedate Authority

Beowulf rests after a battle by sitting on a settle in the king's hall. Although the noun settle, the oldest word for seat in English, occurs in *Beowulf* simply as a place to sit, pride of place also resides in settles compounded with words of power: king's-settle, treasure-settle, high-settle. Beowulf rests on his settle, but power invests the king's. A symbol of God's power on earth, the demonic Grendel dares not approach it. Along with the words for seat, the medieval poet of *Beowulf* had inherited a long tradition of powerful seats, on which courts have session, judges preside, bishops rule a see, and lords of the manor possess land. Evil sits insidiously in the bush, but it eventually answers to goodness enthroned in its seat.

Pagan and Christian Romans passed on their tradition of judicial, royal, and ecclesiastical seats. The *Magna Carta*, drawing from Roman judicial tradition, appointed assizes to visit English counties. A Roman judge sat in a session in a county seat, and the as-sessor sat beside him to help in determining standards for taxes and measures. Without its first syllable, assize is size, a standard for measuring. When he departs from the seat of authority, he surceases. Sedentary and sedate first described judges and judicious wisdom. A sedentary court did not travel, in contrast to an ambulatory one that did. Sedate, with a dignity worthy of a judge, first described cool and judicious judgement. Judges, it seems, make wiser decisions when they sit than when they stand.

Sitting takes the weight off our feet and adds it to the thoughts in our heads. In an ancient gymnasium, philosophers philosophized on an exedra, a semicircular seat off the colonnade. Exedras have become popular garden ornaments, and, because of their semicircular shape, famous as whispering walls. You can sit and whisper on famous ones in New York's Central Park and Philadelphia's Fairmount Park. In a church, the bishop's seat represented his authority. The noun see refers uniquely to it. His seat, *cathedra*, named his church, *ecclesia cathedralis*, church of the *cathedra*, shortened to cathedral. Since the bishop of Rome spoke infallibly from this seat, speaking *ex cathedra* has come to refer to authoritative statement.

In Latin, *sedes* meant both seat and habitation. The lord of the manor resides in a country seat. To possess originally meant to sit with power over land; in other words, it meant to inhabit. Authorities reside in residences and authority resides in them. Seats of important people have had significance. Most of us simply hope that we do not lose our seats when we leave them for a few minutes in a movie theater.

Israel's Sanhedrin constituted the first ruling body described in terms of its sitting members. In the Roman Senate and the British Parliament, the two opposing parties have sat on opposite sides of the room and one who sits on another side in protest is a dis-sident. A man sitting in front of (pre-) a meeting presides as pre-sident. George Washington first presided over the Constitutional Convention in Philadelphia; and the Chief Executive of the United States of America was named president in his honor. Unlike kings, lords or bishops, Washington realized that all power ultimately resides in the people.

Although power might have resided in enthroned kings, cathedraled bishops, possessed lords of the manor, and, more recently, in presiding presidents, the average man also sits down to business. The synonyms sedulous and assiduous describe his constant, unremitting effort, with sedulous adding an extra measure of painstaking persistence.

Not every man sitting down to work does a job that is sedate. *Banca* in Italian, the bench on which moneychangers sat, has given English the word bank. Their usury in antiquity and the Middle Ages made their work scandalous. Jesus had reason to overturn their tables. The bench, on which butchers slaughtered animals, a shamble, was usually such a bloody mess that a shambles refers to any sort of mess. Bankers for the wealthy have made a shambles of finance for all but their clients.

Not every man sitting down to work does a job that is even lawful. A thief, sitting in ambush, plots insidiously; and a hostile army, sitting in front of a city, lays siege. Obsession described such a siege against (ob-) a city, a term later applied to hostile action of an evil spirit and, finally, of a fixed idea.

Seats of power symbolize legal, religious and civic authority. Sedulous and assiduous picture the common man at his best; insidious and ambush, the thief at his worst. If sedentary judges, bishops and kings labored assiduously, they were not just sittin' pretty. Their anxieties about insidious bankers and bushwhackers, or the sieges and shambles of war may so obsess them that they take sedatives to keep them sedate.

## Words

Sittin' pretty can be pretty difficult to define, but the phrase gives an impression of complacent well-being. As we sit, we can relax and take a good look.

### PIE root *sed*, to put down, sit, dwell

Latin: *sedeo sedere* and *sessus*, to sit; *sella*, seat; *sedes*, seat or habitation
    Italian: *sedia*; Spanish: *sitio*
    French: *siege*; *sied* or *se* (Old French), seat or see of a bishop

German: *Sitz*
English:
    settle (897), noun, the oldest word for seat
    seat (1200), sedulous (1540), sedentary (1598), sedate (1663)
Latin: *assideo assidere* and *assessus* to sit by
    English: assize (1164) and its doublet, size (1400); assiduous (1538)
Latin: *dissidere*, to sit apart
    English: dissident (1534)
Latin: *supersedere*, to sit above
    English: surcease (1428)
Latin: *obsidere* and *obsessus*, to sit in the way of, besiege
    English: obsession (1513)
Latin: *possidere* and *possessus*, to sit in power (*pot* + *sidere*), to inhabit
    English: to possess (1483)
Latin: *residere*
    English: residence (1380), to reside (1456)
Latin: *praesidere*, to preside
    English: president (1374), to preside (1611)
    Russian: пред-седательствовать (pred-sedátel′stvo + ovat),
        to preside
Russian:
    сидеть (sidet'), to sit; сиденье (siden'ye), seat; сад (sad), garden
    усадить, у- (*u-*) + садить (*sadít'*), to seat, set
    усадьба (*usadít'*) + -ба (*-ba*), farmstead, homestead
Polish: *siedzieć*, to sit; *usiąść*, to sit down; *siedzenie*, seat

Greek:
    *hedra* / *edra*, seat, as in Sanhedrin (*syn*, together + *hedrin*, sitting)
    *cata* / *catha*, down
    Latin:
        *cathedra*, seat
        *ecclesia cathedralis*, cathedral, church of a bishop's see/seat
        *ex cathedra*, from the seat (of authority)
            French: *chaise*, a seat
            English: cathedral (1297), exedra (1706)
        Russian: кафедральный собор (kafedral'nyy sobor), cathedral
            meeting

## PIE root *bheg*, to bend

Italian: *banco*, bench or bank
    English: bank

**PIE root *skabh*, to prop up, support**
Latin: *scamellum*, a little bench
   English: shamble

## 119. Royal Realms and Regular Rules

King (836), as a cognate with Germanic kin, associates kingship with kinship, and suggests that kings rule kin. On the other hand, a wide strain of Indo-European language invests kingship in the *rajah* of the Indians, the *rix* of the Celts, Eric the Red of the Norsemen, and *Tarquinius Rex* of the Romans. English derives king from a Germanic root, but rajahs and their riches derive from roots that suggest that they, along with others beneath them, direct men in straight paths.

Take the oldest English words of royal root: rich (900), rector (1225), reign (1272), and realm (1290). They could tell stories about the riches of their reigns and realms. Rich, not surprisingly, with its claim to royal ancestry, associated power with wealth, since the king in theory owned all the kingdom. Power or wealth—which one comes first? Fundamentally, the earth, is rich in minerals, and its soil, rich in nutrients, which secondarily, make the king and his men rich. What makes men rich?—more than the wealth hiding below, or growing above, the soil. In love, one of Shakespeare's characters considers its power rich beyond account: "Our duty is so rich, so infinite, / That we may do it still without account" (*Love's Labor's Lost*). Love offers men an embarrassment of riches.

Although rector first meant vicar, it later (1387) came to refer to the ruler of a country and, finally (1464), to the head of a university. The rector ruled his rectory (1536), just as the bishop ruled his bishop-ric. By the nineteenth century (1849), the rector's rectory had shrunk from the institution, which he had ruled, to the residence, in which he ruled. King and kingdom stand magnificently alone in English, but the tradition represented by the *reg-* root supplied both the nuts and bolts and the poetry of royalty and rule.

Latin *regnum*, royal power, became English reign and also denoted the king's royal power: Queen Victoria's reign lasted 63 years in a country so richly motivated by ambition that it made her subjects rich. Both Germanic and Romance word families share the cognates of rich and reign as important words in either culture. In German, for example, *Reich* means both reign and rich.

Realm rules as the fourth oldest royal word in English. In French, *reial reiama*, royal regimen, combined to form realm, which Milton abstracted in "realms of Night" (1667). Kingdom (1000) had the same meaning as realm by about 1250. Although reign and realm do not surpass king and kingdom in age, they communicate the majesty of their ancient antecedents. The king can king (1420) in his kingdom, but he should, more idiomatically and poetically, reign in his realm.

After rich (900), rector (1225), reign (1272), and realm (1290) had taken their thrones, directing (1374), direction (1407) and director (1477) went off to set things straight. An author first directed his book to someone as its dedicatee; soon he was directing any letter to its addressee. Directing a course or an arrangement to someone set its direction. Directors set that course and guided it. They directed its direction. They had their rule books, directories, and they sometimes became so notable that we know them still as the *Directoire* of the French Revolution.

In the fourteenth century, also, the root *reg-* split into doublets that describe the king's rule. Chaucer first used the Latinate regal and its French doublet royal in 1374: 'regal justice' in his translation of Boethius, and 'royal blood' in his romance of *Troilus*. The Latinate regal fits the law; the Romance royal, the mention of blood. Royal and regal sound more impressive than the Germanic kingly (1382), just as realm sounds more romantically regal than kingdom. What would the royal and the regal be without regalia (1540)? This neuter plural of the Latin adjective *regalis*, describes the king's privileges, chief of which are insignia like his crown and scepter. Latin words in English like regimen, rector, and regalia indicate importance of rule in law and in the church.

In English, the *reg-*, *rect-* and *regul-* roots describe rulers and their rules. As doublets of regulation (1672), ruler (1375), in his rule, rules a country, a choir, a roost or a roast. Add rails (1320) as a triplet, because they set fences or trains straight. Regents (1425) rule in the French king's minority or incapacity. In the Latin of academic titles, *magistri regentes*, masters regent (1387), superintended a university. Ruler and regent represent authority in government, church or school. History has shown that no Reich lasts forever. Regime (1792), a doublet of regimen, usually refers to the old order, the *ancien regime* of French monarchy—old regimes pass away.

Europe has had so much varied experience of rulers and their reigns that no other PIE root has doubled up in as many pairs as *reg*. Their names, doubling up in Rex and Roy, Eric and Erich, and Heinrich and Henry, indicate their variety. Their rules, doubling up in regal and royal, and regimen and regime, indicate their variety. In directing, their skills double up in direct and dress, directory and *directoire*, and address and adroit. Addressing this topic requires an adroit hand, starting from, but passing beyond, the rules of regular experience.

## Words

English derives most of its words for ruling from one PIE root, *reg*.

### PIE root *reg*, to rule

Hindi: *rajah*, king
Celtic: suffix -rix/-ric, king, in Vercingeto-rix or Eric
Latin:
> *rex regis*, king; *regnum*, reign
>> Italian: *re*, king; *regno*, reign; and *ricco*, rich
>> French: *roi*, *regne*, and *riche*; Spanish: *rey*, *regnado*, and *rico*
>
> *rego regere* and *rectus*, to rule
> *dirigo dirigere* and *directus*, to direct
>> Italian: *dirigere*, to direct; and *destro*, right
>> French: *diriger* and *droit*; Spanish: *dirigir* and *derecho*
>> English: to direct (1374); its doublets, to dress (1330) and address (1539)

German: *Reich* (noun), reign; and *reich* (adj.), rich

Slavic provides an exception to the Romance etymology of rich:

### PIE root *bhag*, share

Greek: *phagein*, to eat, receive a share
Russian: бог (bog), god; and богатый (bogatyy), rich

Other words for kings:

### Of uncertain origin

English: king (836)
German: *Konig*, king
> Russian: князь (knyaz), prince

Two Latin names that have become royal titles:
Latin: *Caesar*
> German: *Kaiser*
> Russian: цар (tsar/czar), derived from Caesar

Latin: *Carolus Magnus*, Charles the Great
> French: Charlemagne
> Russian: король (korol'), king
> Polish: *krol*, king

# *E Pluribus Unum*—
# Unity from
# Plurality

· · · ·

## 120. Dignity

Straight conduct has had such wide significance that it has created doublets like regime with regimen, and address with adroit. In addition to getting things straight, men have also wanted to fit them with standards. Orthodoxy and dogma fit in with belief; decency and decorum fit in with behavior; and decor fits in with decoration. Fitting in with standards has had such fundamental significance that Latin *decorum* and French *décor* have come entered English packed and ready to go. Regal or royal befits kings; decorum fits anyone, except Bozo the Clown.

The Indo-European root *dek*, to take, has helped to describe what standards men have been taken up because they have seemed right. From this root, English dogma (1600), the accepted opinion, transliterates the Greek word as a "formulation of doctrine, stamped with ecclesiastical authority." From the same root, Greek *doxa*, opinion or praise, enters English as ortho-dox (1611), "straight" in accepted opinion; and para-dox (1540), "contrary" to accepted opinion. Doxology sings "praise," as the creatures' fitting offering to their creator. Latin g*loria* translates this Greek word at the beginning of the Latin hymn, *Gloria in excelsis Deo*, "Glory to God in the highest."

From Latin, decorum (1568), and, from Latin through French, decor (1656), directly represent what fits together in conduct and architecture. Vitruvius, the ancient authority on Roman architecture, defined *decor*: *Decor est emendatus operis aspectus, probatis rebus compositi, cum auctoritate* ("Decor is the emended appearance of a work, having been composed by approved elements (*rebus*), with authority"). In an interpretive translation, "consistency" can translate Latin *decor*. Vitruvius goes on to explain decor as the "consistency" of the masculine Doric order with the celebration of Hercules and of the feminine Corinthian order with that of Venus. The Doric and Corinthian orders of classical architecture have the "authority" to provide this "consistency." In French, *décor* also describes decoration fitting for a stage; and, finally, the decoration fitting for a room. Decor makes things fit consistently. In interior decoration, for example, a Pennsylvania German decor fits in with folk art, but not with the NeoClassical.

Related to the decor of the stage set, decorum in drama requires that characters' actions fit the dignity of their roles. Life imitating art, decorum describes consistency in conduct. Saint Ambrose describes it as the beautiful flower blooming on the healthy plant. It acts naturally and moderately. On the other hand, for the sake of their antics, buffoons cast it aside.

• 413

In his work *On Moral Duties*, Cicero defines *decens*/decent as a concept of appropriate conduct: "What is decent is apparent. Indeed, it is decent both to use reason and speech prudently, and to do what you may do considerately; and, in everything, to see and to observe whatever may be true. And, on the other hand, it is as indecent to be tricked, to err, to slip, to be deceived, as it is to go off the track and to go out of one's mind. . . ."[25] Cicero calls decency "apparent," because it fits things together with reasonable moderation.

In English, decent (1495), therefore, describes what is morally suitable. In 1664, funeral obsequies served as a "decent solemnity" to celebrate the dignity of a personage of high rank; but even the lowest wretch would have deserved a decent burial. Decent, eventually, so fit the worth of common humanity that it lost some of its dignity: "Respectable means rich and decent means poor" (1813). In clothing, for example, decent used to mean fitting; now it's down to bare essentials. Like common, it describes the barely respectable: Can't we expect common decency in this day and age?!, asks the exasperated critic of the modern scene. Whatever the mores of the day, decency and decorum arise from natural balance.

Some fits cherish pretensions that reach beyond common decency. Dignity (1225), a cognate of decent (1495), with age, has grown more dignified than its humble relative. Like decent, dignity started out by prescribing what fits. The ghost of Hamlet's father speaks indignantly of his love that is worthy of his nuptial vow: "love . . . of that dignity . . . went hand in hand even with the vow I made to her in marriage." The king, whose love went "hand in hand" with his vow, has suffered an indignity from the "shameful lust" of his brother, an "adulterate beast." Dignity, when violated, becomes indignant (1590). Indignity (1589), a word of almost the same date as indignant also describes the moral high ground of disdain. The ghost joins anger to the disdain, which he feels at the sight of evil attacking goodness. His royal heart suffers from this great indignity. Unlike the bare decency of everyman, dignity has lost none of its dignity.

In morality, dignity maintains its own self-worth; but, in the stratified society of ancient Rome, dignity also referred to the honorable office (1290) of the incumbent dignitary (1672). From morality, but especially from this official propriety, dignity can end up very dignified. It deigns (1297) condescendingly; and, more often, disdains (1380) scornfully. The magisterial teacher, for example, deigns to answer a student's naive question, even though he feels disdain. With less dignity, dainty (1225), the doublet of dignity, came to mean delicious food: Milton's "daintiest dishes" (1627) fit in with pretty and delicate people. Dainty persons, especially, have dignity.

Different fits suit different folks: decorum suits the sober; decor, the aesthete; dignity, the worthy; dainty, the delicate; and decent, the humble. These good fits match the who with just the right where and when. Of all of them, decency has the greatest significance, because it fits everyman.

## Words

One PIE root provides Romance and English with words for dignity and decency.

### PIE root *dek*, to take
Latin:
> *deceo decere*, to be fitting
> *decens decentis*, fitting
>> Italian and Spanish: *decente*, decent
>> French and English: *décent* and decent
>
> *decor*, elegance or grace, beauty or charm
>> French and English: *décor* and decor
>
> *decorum*, propriety
>> Italian and Spanish: *decoro*, decorum
>> French: *décorum*; English: decorum
>
> *dignus*, worthy
>> Italian: *degno, degnar* and *disdegnare*, worthy, to deign and to disdain
>> French: *digne, daigner* and *dédaigner*
>> Spanish: *digno, dignar* and *desdeñar*
>> English: dignity (1225), to deign (1297) and disdain (1380)

Four PIE roots provide Russian with words for goodness that fits, goes or stands together, and that also has regard for persons.

1. **PIE root *dhab*, to fashion, fit**
   Latin: *faber*, craftsman
   > Latinate English: fabric and to fabricate
   Germanic English: the doublets deft and daft
   Russian:
   > добрый (dobryy), good, kind
   > по-добный (po-dobnyy), similar

2. **PIE root *sed*, to sit; and *sod*, to go**
   Latin: *sedeo sedere* and *sessus*, to sit; and *cedo cedere*, to go
   Russian:
   > под-ходить (pod-khodit')—literally, going close—to fit
   > под-ходящий (pod-khodyashchiy), suitable, fitting

3. **PIE root *sta*, to stand**
   Russian: при-стойный (pri-stoynyy)—literally, standing near—proper
4. **PIE root *lig*, image, likeness**
   German: *gleich*, like, similar; and *Leichnam*, corpse
   English: like; and lich gate, gate to shelter a body before burial
   Russian:
   > лицо (litso), face, person
   >
   > при-личный (pri-lichnyy), decent; perhaps literally, toward the person, respectfully *ad hominem*

## 121. God

About the senses, I have observed that we operate best when common sense brings them all together; just as decency brings together everyman's sense of appropriate conduct. I might also hope to bring together all the past 120 essays, a seemingly Herculean task, since their worlds have had all the variety of human creation. Alexander Pope may give some encouragement and direction: "All are but parts of one stupendous whole," he might say of words, "Whose body Nature is and God the Soul." God as the animating "Soul" gives hope for a decent and sensible center.

So, then, enough of this palaver about man's words and their worlds; let's get back to the centrality of God's Word: "In the beginning was the Word and the Word was with God and the Word was God" (*John* 1. 1). Greek *logos* is "the Word," God's word creating by fiat—*Fiat Lux*, "Let there be light." Logos is the Word, and its primacy proves the rule and the power of words.

All of us value—understandably, we may overvalue—our enthusiasms. In his essay on friendship, for example, Aelred of Rievaulx, so extols friendly virtues that he concludes by suggesting that God is friendship. In a different frame of mind, God may be the sublimity of words well put in a poem or dough baked flavorfully in a pizza. Having extolled the virtue of words, I may also suggest that God is word; but John, the beloved disciple, said long ago that God is THE WORD.

How can words describing God represent a fitting capstone of the pyramid of language? Words representing God describe aspects of power. Deity and day are cognate, because God shone radiantly around the Mediterranean. For the ancient Romans, *sub divo caelo*, under divine heaven, placed man under god, whose name is *Diespiter*, Father (*pater*) of Day. God did not live in heaven, he was heaven; and *deus* gave Romance its words for God—Italian *dio*, French *dieu* and Spanish *dios*.

Jews also basked under the same sun-lit sky of the Mediterranean, but they praised God as its creator. In Hebrew, Adonai, My Lord, derives its etymology from the verb "to rule." The Slavic countries called God бог (bog), Dispenser, the same meaning as its Sanscrit root *Bhaga*. In Greek, *nomos*, law, as in Deutero-nomy, Second Book of the Law, also took its origin from the verb to dispense; and nemesis, goddess of vengeance, dispensed its just deserts. God could not rule without an army: he was the Lord of the Hosts, Lord Sabaoth, from the Akkadian *sabu*, soldier.

Greeks idolized Him in marble;
Jews dared not even write or speak His name.
How ironic, therefore, that His Greek and Hebrew names are cognate:
Adonis radiated beauty; Adonai transcended it.

In invocations, the Indo-European tradition confidently and boldly addresses God as Father: Father Zeus in Greek, Father Jupiter in Latin, Abba Father in Aramaic. Successive invocations derived from the Lord's Prayer: "We are bold to say: Our Father . . ." (*Audemus dicere: Pater Noster* . . .)—Отче наш (Otche nash), Our Father, in Russian. God represent the power of universal fatherhood.

In the Germanic tradition, God/*Gott*, as an object of worship, means "the invoked being." When we invoke "Our Father," 'Good God' or 'by Jove,' we confirm the root of God's Germanic name. Greek *theos*, God, as in theology, derives from an Old Indian root that means pious, and also alludes to the cult. But cult sinks to magic, when it invokes its abracadabra. Indeed, abracadabra is another way of representing Abraxas, the supreme god of the mystic Basilidans, who sought to use God's name as a charm, a word to conjure by. When man worships shibboleths, they become false gods. Idolizing power in gods by words degenerates into superstition.

Adding the suffixes, -ty in English, -*heit* in German and -ство (-stvo) in Russian to God's name makes Him an abstraction. Divinity or deity, *Gottheit*, and божество (bozhestvo) are principles of theology. Saint Augustine coined *deitas*, deity, as a translation of Greek *theotes*, godhood. In its first use, divinity was the science of divine things, taught in divinity school. Divinity shines the light of scholarship on God. John Locke, for example, uses deity in the context of rational theology: "A rational creature . . . cannot miss the discovery of a deity."

There's a wideness in man's words that is the wideness of God's world: nature itself or its ruler, dispenser of law and life, object of piety, or just an idea. Ironically, the Word that first created the heavens or at least filled and illuminated them, may not now fill more than a word in a line of a book. God's Word has left us with our words that can lead us back to

His creation. Language, what a frail invention of our thought! We are so unable to live without it that we must do our best to live with it. With it and without it, we can seek, and be sought by, the soul from the idea on the page back to the Dispenser of All.

### Words Invoke God

#### PIE root *ghau*, to call, invoke

Greek: *kaleo*, I call; *krazo*, I scream, cry aloud
English: God, literally, the invoked being
German: *Gott*; *Gottheit*, deity
Hungarian: *koldus*, beggar, who cries out his special cant; *koldulni*, to beg
Russian:
> колдун (kɐldun), wizard, who invokes spirits;
> Hungarian beggars and Russian wizards cry out prayers.
> вы-зывать (vy-zyvat'), to call out, invoke

#### PIE root *bhag*, share

Sanscrit: *bhaga*, dispenser, gracious lord; *Bhagavad Gita*, "Singing God's Song"
> Czech: *Bohuslav*, God's glory; Polish: *Bog*
Russian:
> бог (bog), god
> богдан (bogdan), a proper name, gift of God, *cf.* Theodore/Dorothy
> богатый (bogatyy), rich
Greek: *phagein*, to eat, to receive a share
> English: esophagus; and sarcophagus, tomb, literally, the flesh-eater

# 122. One-Two-Three, I-You-He

Oneness came late into Proto-Indo-European vocabulary, because it has existed in metaphysical abstraction more than in the physical fact. In fact—as much as anything in PIE exists 'in fact'—'one,' linguists speculate, made a late appearance in PIE as a pronoun, not a number. A clue to this origin: the indefinite article 'an' and 'one' are cognate. In English, also, 'one' may function as a pronoun: e.g., one acts as one thinks she should. We also see evidence of this use in Romance: Italian *uno* and French *un* mean 'one' and 'an.'

To represent God's oneness about the year 900, Old English anness/oneness translated *unitas* in Bede's *Ecclesiastical History*. From the year 1300 and beyond, the Latinate word unity represented the concept: "Our

God is one, or rather very oneness, and mere unity" (1594). What can be more basic than one? We start our moral lives from the oneness of individual singularity. "Among all the ideas we have," John Locke observed, "there is none more simple than that of unity or one." No idea more simple, but unity among multiplicity does not easily find a home in a world of individual singularities. Tom Paine observed its importance in democracy: "'Tis not in numbers but in unity that our great strength lies" (*Common Sense*, 1776). Unities not multiplicities make individuals and nations strong.

Unity has moral ramifications: without goodness, it can accomplish little. Plato reminds us that it requires and creates goodness: good men are in union with themselves and consequently with others; but bad men, never (Jowett's Plato, 1871). In one of his *Adages*, Erasmus makes a radical statement of its nature: "One man, indeed, is no man. The meaning is that one man, deprived of all help, can accomplish nothing distinguished."[26]

Unfortunately, an army best exemplifies unity: "The army is one, and that is the oneness of unity. The soldier is one, but that is the oneness of the unit" (1851). United, soldiers win wars; divided, citizens do not foster the peace that their soldiers have won. Unitarians worship God as a theological unity, but men united should extend divine fatherhood to human brotherhood.

In moral terms, consider an explanation for the slow evolution of 'one' in PIE: 'one' only had meaning after 'two' had cut in. Why should a monad ever think of anything outside itself? Cain existed singularly without Abel; with him, he chose fratricide instead of brotherhood. Can singularity choose an alternative more perversely and tragically simple?

Two is the numerical plural of one, just as you is the moral plural of I.

Two puts one on the horns of a dilemma: either you strengthens I—bad grammar but good morality—or you weaken me—bad morality, but good grammar. Language gives evidence of the bad alternative: duel, cognate of dual, brings moral effort to a bad end. *Duellum*, the popular origin of Latin *bellum*, assumes a duel of two, one against one, either David against Goliath; or a *bellum* of more than one against more than one, David's Israelites against Goliath's Philistines.

Without a moral direction, duplex describes a double fold or a double house; duplicity, double-talk. As a philosophical tenet, dualism assumes conflict between opposites: matter with spirit, body with soul or God with Devil in Manichaean dualism. Dubious puts one on the two horns of doubt.[27] In sum, two puts one in dualism, duels, duplicity, and doubt. These etymologies cause us doubt: should I venture out for I and Thou, or remain at home for *numero uno*?

Three adds trilemma to dilemma,
but one-two-three can happily fulfill you and me in I-you-he.
The third horn brings peace to the two
I-you-he combines for good more readily than I-you.
He and she became one to procreate you and then me.
Their unity bequeaths you and me a legacy of brotherhood.
Three also supplies a he or a she for testimony about you and me.
And then law supplies an it to legislate you and me if we fail in unity.
We see our lives in these threes; and they build our lives.
Have we created divine trinities or have they created us?
Consider the months: Venus in April unites with Mars in March;
and Maia in May unites with Juno in June to bring this unity to fruition.
Trinities suggest that I-you-he does more than help to conjugate verbs.
The Dispenser of All with his Words and their spirit give us unity.

## Words

Easy as one-two-three is too easy. Turning it about,
—three (803)-two (825)-one (855)—makes better chronology and morality.

### PIE root *oino*, one

Latin: *unus*, one
      Italian: *uno*, one, an; Spanish: *uno*, one; French: *un*, one, an
English:
      one (855) / an (950)
      oneness (885) and its OE form anness (885)
      alone (1300), from OE all + ana, all one
      unity (1300) and unit (1570)
Russian: один (odin), one, an; and единство (idinstva), unity

### PIE root *duo*, two

Latin:
      *duo*, two
      *duellum*, archaic form of *bellum*, war, a duel between two nations
      *duplex*, two-folded; *dubius*, between two choices
          Italian: *due*; Spanish: *dos*; French: *deux*
English:
      two (825); duel (1284), doublet of dual (1607)
      duplicity (1430), acting in two ways, deceitful; dubious (1548)
      dilemma (Greek), two horns, *cf.* on the horns of a dilemma
Russian: два (dva), two; and двойственность (dvojstvini), duality

# NOTES
• • • •

1. Since scholars have debated the date of *Beowulf*, the *OED* cites the poem rather than its date.

2. *Nec tamen est clamor, sed parvae murmura vocis,*
   *qualia de pelagi, siquis procul audiat, undis*
   *esse solent, qualemve sonum, cum Iuppiter atras*
   *increpuit nubes, extrema tonitrua reddunt.*

   "And it is not a shout, but the murmurs of a small voice, / like murmurs from the waves of the sea, if anyone should hear them from a distance, / or like the sound, when Jupiter has struck the black clouds, / the clouds return as distant thunder" (Ovid, *Metamorphoses* 15).

3. "The first alphabetic writing in ancient Greece was a writing of proper names. . . . The writer appears to us first and foremost in the role of name-giver (*onomatothetes*). . . . As soon as writing arrived in Greece, it was put in the service of names" (*Phrasikleia, An Anthropology of Reading in Ancient Greece*, Jesper Svenbro).

4. In this book, the lists give different forms of a Latin noun or verb that have given English different words. The Latin infinitive *vivere* is the root of vivacious, and its perfect participle *victus*, the root of victuals. Without these different forms, the reader may not recognize that vivacious and victuals come from different forms of the same verb.

5. "The wind breathes" translates the Greek *pneuma . . . pnei*, and the Latin of the *Vulgate, spiritus . . . spirat.*

6. *. . . Inständig nur und stark*
   *ertönt aus dem Gehölz der Regenpfeifer,*
   *man denkt an einen Hieronymus:*
   *so ser steigt irgend Einsamkeit und Eifer*
   *aus dieser einen Stimme, die der Guß*
   *erhören wird.*

7. *Iam caelum terramque meo sine numine, venti,*
   *miscere, et tantas audetis tollere moles?*

8. "Incised by you, beeches preserve my names. Marked by your sickle, I am both read as Oenone; and as much as the trunks, so much do my names grow. Grow! and as my titles, rise up straight!"

9. Then Father Aeneas speaks as follows from the high poop deck,
   and he extends in his hand a branch of the peace-bringing olive.

10. As examples of adjectives used as nouns, Latin *caseus formaticus*, "formed cheese," must have highlighted the adjective "formed" because, from it, French derived *fromage* and Italian, *formaggio*; but Spanish retained only the noun *caseus*, from which it derived *queso*. Also, Latin *vinum aegrum*, sour wine, taken together as one word, vinegar, in English, provided the adjective "sour" from which German derived *Essig*, and Italian *aceto*.

11. οἷον πνεῦμα ἤ τις ἠχὼ ἀπὸ λείων τε καὶ στερεῶν ἁλλομένη πάλιν ὅθεν ὡρμήθη φέρεται, οὕτω τὸ τοῦ κάλλους ῥεῦμα πάλιν εἰς τὸν καλὸν διὰ τῶν ὀμμάτων ἰόν—As a breeze or some echo changes places from the smooth rocks back whence it arose, so also the stream of beauty, going into the beautiful through the eyes (255c).

12. *Cf.* the PIE root *kenk*, to gird: French: *enceinte*, literally, gird by the cincture of the foetus. No PIE root—Spanish: *embarazada*, burdened; *cf.* embarrassment of riches.

13. *Quam enim aliam vim conubia promiscua habere nisi ut ferarum prope ritu volgentur concubitus plebis patrumque? Ut qui natus sit ignoret, cuius sanguinis, quorum sacrorum sit; dimidius patrum sit, dimidius plebis, ne secum quidem ipse concors* (Livy, *History* 4.2).

14. In Greek and Latin, the future imperative *maneto*, "thou shalt remain," has a parallel in the English word memento that in Latin means "thou shalt remember." A memento commands us to remember something.

15. J. Earle, "The History of the Word 'Mind'" (*Mind*, vol. VI, 1881, 301–320) emphasizes the exclusivity of mind in reference to the commemoration of the dead and its wider use, in accordance with Latin *mens*, in the Renaissance.

16. In Shakespeare's *Midsummer Night's Dream*, when Demetrius is lost in the wood and going crazy without his beloved Hermia, he plays with two meanings of wood: "Here I am, and wood within this wood, because I cannot meet my Hermia."

17. *et rabie fera corda tument, maiorque videri / nec mortale sonans, adflata est numine quando / iam propiore dei* (Vergil, *Aeneid*, 6. 49–51), "and her heart swells with fierce madness; and she seems larger, and not sounding mortal, when she was filled with the divine power, ever closer."

18. *Atqui hoc ipsum est, inquiunt, miserum, Stultitia teneri, errare, falli, ignorare. Imo hoc est hominem esse*, "And yet, they say, this is wretched, to be held by Folly, to err, to be deceived, to be ignorant. Nay, indeed, this is to be a man" (Erasmus, *Moriae Encomium*, 32).

19. J. Earle, *Mind*, 1881, page 303.

20. The phrase, *mens/san(a) in/corpore/sano*, is the second part of a spondaic hexameter line. The spondees slow the line in an impressive cadence appropri-

ate to prayer. Spondee refers to the libations make as drink offering in Greek religion.

21. ... "*Pulchra Lauerna,*
*da mihi fallere, da iusto sanctoque uideri,*
*noctem peccatis et fraudibus obice nubem*" (Horace, *Epistulae* 16).

22. "Indeed, it seems (to them) dull and lazy to acquire by sweat what you may be able to get by blood"—*pigrum quin immo et iners videtur sudore acquirere quod possis sanguine parare* (Tacitus, *Germania* 14).

23. Host, derived from *hospitis*, like French *hôte*, drops the internal consonant p, but unlike *hôte*, it retains the s. Hotel drops the s, but hostel retains it. Hospitality retains the two syllables of its Latin root.

24. Since the guest/host relationship was uncertain, host and hostile share the same root. It may end in amity or enmity.

25. *Quid deceat apparet. Nam et ratione uti atque oratione prudenter et agere quod agas considerate omnique in re quid sit veri videre et tueri decet, contraque falli, errare, labi, decipi tam dedecet quam delirare et mente esse captum; et iusta omnia decora sunt, iniusta contra, ut turpia, sic indecora.*

26. *Vir quidem unus, nullus est. Sensus est, nihil egregium prestari posse ab uno homine, omne auxilio destituto.*

27. In Vergil *Aeneid* 1. 218 *dubius*, dubious or doubtful, assumes two alternatives: *amissos longo socios sermone requirunt, / spemque metumque inter dubii, seu vivere credant, / sive extrema pati nec iam exaudire vocatos* (... their care attends/ The doubtful fortune of their absent friends: / Alternate hopes and fears their minds possess, / Whether to deem 'em dead, or in distress).